AQUINAS & SARTRE

Stephen Wang

AQUINAS & SARTRE

ON FREEDOM, PERSONAL IDENTITY, AND THE POSSIBILITY OF HAPPINESS

The Catholic University of America Press
Washington, D.C.

The paper used in this publication meets the minimum requirements of American National Standards for Information Science—Permanence of Paper for Printed Library Materials, ANSI Z39.48-1984.
∞

LIBRARY OF CONGRESS CATALOGING-IN-PUBLICATION DATA
Wang, Stephen, 1966–
Aquinas and Sartre : on freedom, personal identity, and the possibility of happiness / Stephen Wang.
p. cm.
Includes bibliographical references and index.
ISBN 978-0-8132-1576-1 (cloth : alk. paper) 1. Thomas, Aquinas, Saint, 1225?–1274. 2. Sartre, Jean-Paul, 1905–1980. 3. Liberty. 4. Identity (Psychology) 5. Happiness. I. Title.
B765.T54W25 2009
128.092′2—dc22 2008038321

CONTENTS

PREFACE

There are some profound similarities in the thought of Thomas Aquinas and Jean-Paul Sartre. The purpose of this book is to show that these two thinkers, despite their many differences, have a common philosophical understanding of the nature of human freedom.

I am well aware that this suggestion will strike many readers as being far-fetched. There are some obvious historical and philosophical difficulties in the task of comparing Aquinas and Sartre, let alone finding any connections between them. Aquinas is the Scholastic theologian par excellence, completely immersed in the atmosphere of medieval Christendom, a man formed by his prayer and his preaching. Sartre is one of the twentieth-century's most notorious and influential iconoclasts, the great antinomian, who could write that "existentialism is nothing else but an attempt to draw the full conclusions from a consistently atheistic position."[1] Though they spent many years in the same area of Paris, their lives were separated by seven hundred years of intellectual and cultural history and by the most fundamental differences in faith.

Perhaps for these reasons there have been very few writers who have been interested in comparing the thought of Aquinas and Sartre.[2] Not even Maritain's well-known work, some of which sets out explicitly to evaluate and refute Sartre, re-

1. Jean-Paul Sartre, "Existentialism and Humanism," in *Jean-Paul Sartre: Basic Writings*, ed. Stephen Priest (London: Routledge, 2001), 45. Sartre himself softens this polemical statement in the lines that follow.

2. See, e.g., Joseph C. Mihalich, *Existentialism and Thomism* (New York: Philosophical Library, 1960); Frederick J. Crosson, "Intentionality and Atheism: Sartre and Maritain," *The Modern Schoolman* 64 (1987); Joseph J. Romano, "Between Being and Nothingness: The Relevancy of Thomistic Habit," *Thomist* 44 (1980); Gianfranco Basti, *Filosofia Dell'uomo* (Bologna: Edizioni Studio Domen-

ally does justice to Sartre's project in *Being and Nothingness.*[3] A 1996 edition of the *American Catholic Philosophical Quarterly* dedicated to Sartre succeeded in bringing him to the attention of Catholic philosophers, but it did not attempt to make many connections between Sartre and thinkers such as Aquinas who stand at the heart of the Catholic philosophical tradition.[4] My own research has convinced me not just that there are some points of contact between Aquinas and Sartre, but that their approach to a number of key philosophical issues—centered around the question of freedom—is almost identical. In my conclusion I summarize this approach, and try to present a combined Thomistic-Sartrean theory of freedom. Here in this preface I offer a summary of the summary in order to give the reader a taste of what is to come; and toward the end I make one or two introductory points about how I have structured this work.

The best way to understand their common approach is to think of what happens when we face a choice. When there are different options before me, and I have to make a decision, a number of factors will usually influence that decision. Three of the most important factors are undoubtedly who I am, where I am, and what I am seeking. In other words, my personal identity, the objective circumstances in which I find myself, and the goals I am seeking will all have some kind of influence on the choice I eventually make. They make up what we could call the "total situation" that informs my choice.

In philosophical theories about human action, it is common to assume that this total situation, once I start reflecting on it, is something stable and accessible. So when I have a choice to make, I think about what kind of

---

icano, 1995), 293–96; the brief reflections in Denis J. M. Bradley, *Aquinas on the Twofold Human Good: Reason and Human Happiness in Aquinas's Moral Science* (Washington, D.C.: The Catholic University of America Press, 1997), 532; and M. Qizilbash, "Aristotle and Sartre on the Human Condition: Lack, Responsibility and the Desire to Be God," *Angelaki* 3, no. 1 (1998): 34, endnote 13.

3. *Existence and the Existent,* for example, fails to get to the heart of Sartre's distinction between essence and existence, and is more an exposition of Maritain's Thomism than of Sartre's existentialism. Maritain wrongly insists, for example, that Sartre's vision of the human being is devoid of a place for an intelligible nature or essence. See Jacques Maritain, *Existence and the Existent,* trans. Lewis Galantiere and Gerald B. Phelan (Garden City, N.Y.: Doubleday & Company, 1956), esp. 15–16.

4. There is an essay on Sartre and Yves Simon, but most of the articles (comparing Sartre with Foucault, Ricoeur, etc.) could have appeared in any general philosophical journal. See *American Catholic Philosophical Quarterly* 70, no. 4: Jean-Paul Sartre (1996).

person I am (what would suit me, what I am interested in, what I am capable of, etc.); I think about the objective circumstances confronting me (what is going on here, what needs to be done, what the practical options available are, what the consequences of any action will be, etc.); and I think about the goals I am seeking (what my ambitions are, what my hopes are, what my fears are, what my dreams are, etc.). My understanding of this total situation will be a starting point for the process of deliberation that leads to making a choice.

Philosophical theories that are more "intellectualist" argue that my understanding of this total situation will determine which way the decision goes: my will (my orientation to a particular course of action) will always follow the direction suggested by my intellect (by my understanding of what this total situation means). Philosophical theories that are more "voluntarist" argue that my choice will not, ultimately, be determined by my understanding of this situation: my will acts independently from my intellect, and I can respond to this total situation in any way I like, even if it makes no sense of what I have come to understand. It should be obvious that intellectualist theories have a more deterministic conception of human action—there is not much room for freedom. And voluntaristic theories have plenty of room for freedom, but human action becomes irrational and capricious.

Aquinas and Sartre find a third way of understanding human action that avoids both the determinism of intellectualist theories and the irrationalism of voluntarist ones. They do this by questioning the very assumptions of these theories. They do accept the idea that certain factors have an important bearing on our decisions and that our understanding of the "total situation" will determine how we act—this is why they are not voluntarists. But they both argue that when we deliberate about a choice, these factors themselves are not fully determined. My personal identity is not static: I can question who I am, I can reinterpret the meaning of my identity, I can rethink the significance of my life. The objective circumstances confronting me in this choice are not clear-cut: there are different ways of interpreting things, different points of view, different conclusions to be drawn. And the goals I am attracted to are more ambiguous than I might have imagined: I can make new priorities among the goals I already have, I can set some of them aside for a time, I can even seek new goals that I have never considered before.

For Aquinas and Sartre, there is no single way of understanding the total situation before me. This is precisely why I face the dilemma of having to choose, because each of the options before me is attractive and makes sense on its own terms. Reason, when it confronts reality, is not led to a single conclusion about what is going on or what should be done. This is not because of any doubt about the objectivity of reality, it is because it is part of human nature to be able to interpret reality in different ways, to reinterpret the meaning of one's own existence, and to redefine the goals one is seeking. What is extraordinary about human beings is that we can change the way we look at things, change the way we look at ourselves, and change the goals we are seeking—this is what allows us to make a choice.

Freedom, on this model, is not about accepting or rejecting a predetermined understanding of what a certain situation involves, it is our ability to determine for ourselves which kind of understanding will guide our deliberations. The will neither follows the intellect (intellectualism) nor goes its own way (voluntarism)—instead it is intimately involved in the very working of intellect itself, and helps the intellect to determine which way it will see the world. Freedom is still about deciding what to do, but for Aquinas and Sartre the question of what to do depends on the deeper questions of how to see things, who to be, and what to seek. All of this, it bears repeating, is done without denying the objectivity of reality, without falling into relativism or subjectivism—since for Aquinas and Sartre it is the nature of objective reality that it can be interpreted in different ways, and it is the nature of human reason that it can consider these differences.

Reason is not fully determined. Human identity is not fixed. Happiness can take many forms. These are some of the powerful insights that Aquinas and Sartre share. Freedom is therefore not a capricious choice that turns us against our rational understanding of what is important and good. It is rather the necessity of interpreting the open-ended significance of ourselves and our circumstances. Our freedom to choose between different goals is inseparable from our freedom to interpret the world in different ways, and to choose—within certain limits—what kind of person we will become. This is why the question of freedom cannot be separated from the questions of personal identity, of the nature of human understanding, and of our longing for fulfillment in a future happiness.

Some readers may be unconvinced by these ideas. Others may be interested in the ideas themselves, but may remain unconvinced that they represent the authentic teaching of Aquinas or Sartre. My main purpose in this work is to show that Aquinas and Sartre both understand freedom in this very distinctive way, and to show that these two thinkers, who are not usually mentioned in the same breath, have so much in common. In the process I hope that some other purposes will be served: Aquinas scholars will benefit by rereading Aquinas in the light of Sartre. Sartre helps us to see that many of Aquinas's ideas about reason and personal identity are more radical than they seem at first. The link with Sartre will also help students of Aquinas to see more clearly the relevance of Aquinas's thought to modern and postmodern debates. Sartre scholars will benefit by appreciating that his key insights were already present in the philosophical tradition, even if they were underappreciated. This book does not suggest that Aquinas directly influenced Sartre (although there is a clear line from nineteenth-century Scholasticism to phenomenology), but it does argue that Aquinas's philosophical precision can help us to unlock the meaning of some of Sartre's more puzzling or exaggerated thoughts about freedom. Contemporary philosophers investigating the questions of freedom, objectivity, act theory, personal identity, human fulfillment, philosophical anthropology, etc., will benefit from a fresh presentation of the thought of two major historical figures who have contributed to these discussions. Finally, these careful readings of the texts will provide some original insights into the thought of Sartre and Aquinas that should be valuable in their own right. This book corrects some one-sided views of each thinker that have become predominant both in the popular imagination and in academic thought: Sartre is not a voluntarist (if this is taken to mean that human decisions are based on a gratuitous movement of the will unconnected with one's rational understanding of the world), and Aquinas is not a intellectualist (if this is taken to mean that one's practical decisions are based solely on the conclusions reached independently by the intellect as it interprets the world). I thus takes sides in some ongoing Sartrean and Thomistic debates, and try to contribute to these debates.

A glance at the table of contents should make it clear how the book is structured. After the historical introduction, there are four main parts, which deal with (1) the open-endedness of human identity, (2) the relationship between objectivity and subjectivity, (3) the process of making a choice, and (4) the possibility of finding fulfillment through our choices. Each part presents Sartre's understanding of a key topic and then that of

Aquinas. On the whole, the texts of one author are analyzed without much reference to the other, so that each author can be understood on his own terms, and so that the exposition is not prejudiced by the comparison that is made. The comparison itself only occurs toward the end of each part, and more particularly in part four. The similarities will stand out and speak for themselves once the ideas of Sartre and Aquinas have been properly understood and placed side by side.

Each main part begins with Sartre, for two reasons. First, he is closer to us in time. Despite the distance between English-language philosophy and continental philosophy, Sartre's ideas will be more accessible to many readers than Aquinas's. They are part of our culture—whether we like it or not. It will help to look back through this more familiar figure to a more distant one, presenting Sartre's conclusions with all their force, then showing that Aquinas reaches the same conclusions in a different philosophical language—a language that is too familiar to many Christian theologians and too alien to many secular philosophers to be appreciated properly. The second reason for starting with Sartre is that this reflects the development of my own ideas. As I began to work in this area, I found myself making connections between existentialist critiques of the view that there is a fixed human nature and the concept of character development in contemporary virtue ethics. In both philosophies, human life is open-ended, and it is up to us, within certain limits, to develop our own identity and form our own character. This led me to investigate Sartre as the key exponent of existentialism and Aquinas as a central figure in the development of virtue ethics. The focus then shifted from ethics to wider questions of philosophical anthropology.

This book concentrates on some key texts from the writings of Aquinas and Sartre. There are also references to the sometimes contradictory interpretations of each philosopher that have been offered by scholars over the years. On a few occasions, when the background is important, there are references to the biographical, historical, or philosophical context in which certain arguments were developed. I do believe, however, that each thinker, in his own texts, is developing *an argument* that can be followed on its own terms. While it would be a distortion to imply that Aquinas and Sartre are interlocutors in a timeless debate about some supposed "perennial philosophy," it is nevertheless true that each thinker offers us a view of what it is to be human, and these views can be discussed and compared despite their different contexts. It is essential to follow the line of thought that is being developed and weigh up the central insight that is being presented.

The advantage of concentrating on these key texts is that it gives a clear focus to the work, and I can analyze in detail some difficult and highly nuanced arguments. The disadvantage of this concentration is that many important topics and connections remain unexplored. I spend far too little time, for example, on Aquinas's thinking about virtue, character, friendship, right and wrong, or law; or on Sartre's thinking about bad faith, the Look, being-for-others, the body, or existential psychoanalysis. I do not move into a discussion about concrete ethics and ethical norms, but remain at the level of what could be called fundamental ethics or action theory. These lacunae threaten to distort the whole account of the human being presented here. This is the price paid for specialization, and the distortion will not be too great if one keeps this work in perspective and remembers that it forms one small part of a wider philosophical anthropology.

There is an almost exclusive concentration in this work on the individual human being, which is a serious limitation. I make only passing reference to interpersonal relationships, the family, love, society, or politics—subjects that Aquinas and Sartre deal with extensively. My only defense is to refer again to the aim of this project, which is to examine the nature of human freedom. All of our relationships, whether intimate and personal, or diffuse and political, somehow involve bonds between individual human beings, and all of them depend somehow on our free response to the relationship and our search for fulfillment in that relationship. So if we are to understand the nature of society and of human relationships, we shall have to understand what it is for the individual who is in relationship to be free and to seek happiness. The communal and the political have to have some basis in the personal.

One of the stumbling blocks to a sympathetic reading of both Aquinas and Sartre is the teleological nature of their act theory. For these thinkers, human beings are always seeking some goal or end (*telos,* in Greek), seeking fulfillment in some form, and this raises the suspicion that in these theories human action is unavoidably "selfish." It is enough to say here that a teleological theory of action leaves as much room for love, kindness, asceticism, altruism, and self-sacrifice as any other theory—but these virtues will always relate in some way to the self. In other words, in a teleological theory, the most selfless acts—if they are mine—must relate in some way to my choices, to my reasons for acting, and to my hopes for the future. These hopes may be centered purely on the good of another, or on the fulfillment of a project that will benefit me not at all, as much as on the pleasures of my own body, or on the success of my own work. Whichever end I choose, it necessarily becomes a part of my own project. I may not be doing it "for myself," but I am certainly doing it because I want to. The crude categories of "selfish" and "selfless" are not very helpful here: Aquinas and Sartre believe that we are always seeking our own good; the good is simply what we seek. The remarkable thing about human freedom, however, is that it allows us to identify the good of another (and indeed the good of absolutely anything at all) with our own good. So if I choose to give my life for my spouse, my children, my country, or even for a stranger or an enemy, then there is no contradiction between this self-sacrifice and the self-fulfillment that personal action always involves. The fact that we can seek a personal good that means something to ourselves is the very thing that allows us—if we so choose—to reach out to others and to place our good outside ourselves.

It is important to recognize that Aquinas is a theologian whose understanding of human freedom cannot be separated from his Christian faith and Sartre is a philosopher who appeals only to reason. Aquinas's whole thinking is thoroughly informed by his Christian upbringing, by the Christian culture in which he lived and worked, and by the theological formation he received. Divine revelation and Christian reflection color the whole *Summa.*[5] At the same time, however, within the theological flow of the work, Aquinas constructs a number of philosophical arguments that make sense in their own right and do not depend on theological convictions or faith.[6] Much of his analysis—of intellect and will, human action, and the desire for happiness—depends on reason and not on an appeal to revelation. The argument about happiness in the first questions of Part I-II

5. On the theological nature of the *Summa,* see, e.g., Jean-Pierre Torrell, *Saint Thomas Aquinas, Vol. 1: The Person and His Work* (Washington, D.C.: The Catholic University of America Press, 1996), 148–55; Leonard E. Boyle, "The Setting of the *Summa Theologiae* of St. Thomas—Revisited," in *The Ethics of Aquinas,* ed. Stephen J. Pope (Washington, D.C.: Georgetown University Press, 2002), 6–7; and Servais Pinckaers, *The Sources of Christian Ethics,* trans. Sr. Mary Thomas Noble (Edinburgh: T & T Clark, 1995), 21–25. See also my introduction below.

6. Fergus Kerr muses: "Perhaps we should rescue Thomas from philosophy altogether—but then, after all, he *is* a great philosopher, indeed that is one of the sources of the ambiva-

of the *Summa,* for example, is philosophical, even though the conclusion is also a theological conviction that would stand without the appeal to reason. So when Aquinas concludes that human beings cannot be perfectly happy in this life, the impasse he reaches is philosophical, just as Sartre's is. At this level, he and Sartre are doing the same kind of thinking.

The introduction that follows describes some of the historical and intellectual context in which Aquinas and Sartre were writing; it looks at the thinkers who most influenced them; and it examines some of the interpretation of their work that has since taken place. Readers who are already familiar with these areas, or who simply want to begin with the philosophical discussion itself, are advised to skip over this introduction and begin reading at chapter 1.

---

lence of his thought. He is a philosopher and he is a theologian, and we are never going to agree where to put the emphasis"; see Fergus Kerr, *After Aquinas: Versions of Thomism* (Oxford: Blackwell, 2002), 210.

ACKNOWLEDGMENTS

Many people have helped me in many different ways as I have been researching and writing this book. I would like to acknowledge some of them here and offer them my sincere thanks.

A number of people read early drafts of my work, or discussed it with me, and gave me invaluable feedback. These include Margaret Atkins, Bruce Burbidge, Martin Crowley, Kevin Flannery, Thomas Flynn, Fergus Kerr, Aidan Nichols, Amanda Perreau-Saussine, Emile Perreau-Saussine, and Ben Quash. Diana von Glahn gave a great deal of time and attention to proofreading an earlier version of the text.

I began this research at the University of Cambridge, and staff there at the Divinity Faculty, the Philosophy Faculty, the University Library, and Queens' College were unfailingly helpful. My stay at Cambridge was made possible by a three-year research grant from the Arts and Humanities Research Council.

My bishop, Cardinal Cormac Murphy-O'Connor, encouraged me to consider doing some academic research, and then gave me enough time free from pastoral responsibilities in which I could pursue it. Friends, colleagues, and those I lived with in Cambridge gave me enormous support and encouragement, and were patient and understanding with me when the pressures of study took their toll. Alban McCoy, the chaplain at the Cambridge University Catholic Chaplaincy, invited me to live at Fisher House for two years and welcomed me into the life and mission of the community there. Aidan Nichols, then the prior, invited me to live in the Dominican community at Blackfriars for the rest of my time in Cambridge. I have been finishing this book while living and working at Allen Hall, London—the seminary of the Diocese of Westminster—where the staff and students have sustained me with their kindness and good humor.

My family deserves a special mention: my parents, Man Kin and Elizabeth Wang; my brother, Chris; my sister-in-law, Kerry; my nephew, Matthew; and my sister, Mary.

Staff at the Catholic University of America Press have guided this work through the publication process with great care and courtesy. Gregory LaNave showed the initial interest in this work and sent it off to expert readers, James Kruggel gave me advice on revising it and saw it through the process of being accepted for publication, and Philip Gerard Holthaus has copyedited and proofread the final text. Three readers commissioned by the press read the whole text and made detailed suggestions about how it could be improved. One of these was Thomas Flynn; the other two were anonymous. Their incisive and generously given comments helped me to rethink and improve some key parts of the text.

Above all, I would like to acknowledge the support I received from three people. Janet Soskice guided me in this work from start to finish. She helped me to develop my initial ideas, to organize and write them up, and then to revise and improve them. Christina Howells guided my work on Sartre and helped me in my thinking about the whole project. Timothy McDermott helped me to think through my ideas about Aquinas, and talked more widely with me about Thomistic philosophy and theology. All three, with great generosity, gave me the benefit of their time, interest, expertise, and friendship. In their different ways they helped me to think more carefully, to read and write with more sensitivity, and to approach the truth with more humility and more love.

I am enormously grateful to all these people and institutions.

This book includes material reworked from the following articles: "Reason and the Limits of Existential Freedom: Why Sartre Is Not a Voluntarist" (*Philosophy Today* 50, no. 3, [2006]: 338–48); "Aquinas on Human Happiness and the Natural Desire for God" (*New Blackfriars* 88, no. 1015 [2007]: 322–34 [published by Blackwell Publishing on behalf of the Provincial Council of the English Province of the Order of Preachers]); "Incompletion, Happiness, and the Desire for God in Sartre's Being and Nothingness" (*Sartre Studies International* 12, no. 1 [2006]: 1–17); "The Ambiguity of the

Self and the Construction of Human Identity in the Early Sartre" (*American Catholic Philosophical Quarterly* 81, no. 1 [2007]: 73–88); "Subjective Objectivity in Aquinas: The Interdependence and Reflexivity of Intellect and Will" (*Acta Philosophica* I, vol. 16 [2007]: 91–108); "Motivation and the Establishment of Ends in Satre's Act Theory (*Sartre Studies International* 14, *no. 1 [2008]: 13–25);* and "The Indetermination of Reason and the Role of the Will in Aquinas's Account of Human Freedom" (*New Blackfriars* 90, no. 1025 [2009]; published by Blackwell Publishing on behalf of the Provincial Council of the English Province of the Order of Preachers). These articles are used with permission.

ABBREVIATIONS

The Bibliography contains complete details on the following publications.

BN: Jean-Paul Sartre, *Being and Nothingness: An Essay on Phenomenological Ontology*

DM or *De malo:* Thomas Aquinas, *Quaestiones disputatae de malo.* The main passage considered is question 6 of *De malo* ("Whether human beings have a free choice of their acts or whether they choose from necessity"), which is just a single article that is then divided into sections. For example, *DM* 6ad7 refers to the response to the seventh objection in question 6. The Latin text is from the Leonine edition of Aquinas's *Opera Omnia* (complete works), vol. 23. The English translation is from St. Thomas Aquinas, *On Evil,* translated by Jean Oesterle. The body of this single article is very long, and for this reason, instead of just referring in the customary manner to *DM* 6c [*corpus*/body], I also provide line numbers for each quotation in square brackets. These refer to the line numbering in the Leonine edition.

DV or *De veritate:* Thomas Aquinas, *Quaestiones disputatae de veritate.* The numbers refer to the question, then the article, then the section of the article. For example, *DV* 22:3c refers to question 22, article 3, the body *(corpus)* of the article. The Latin text is from the Leonine edition of Aquinas's *Opera Omnia* (complete works), vol. 22, parts 1–3.The English translation is from Thomas Aquinas, *The Disputed Questions on Truth,* translated by Robert W. Mulligan, James V. McGlynn, and Robert W. Schmidt.

EN: Jean-Paul Sartre, *L'être et le néant: Essai d'ontologie phénoménologique* (Paris: Gallimard, 1943) *and* Jean-Paul Sartre, *L'être et le né-*

ant: Essai d'ontologie phénoménologique, édition corrigée avec index par Arlette Elkaïm-Sartre (Paris: Gallimard, 1996).

Two page references are given for each reference to *EN,* e.g., *EN* 478/509. The first number refers to the corrected 1996 edition, from which I have quoted. The second number refers to the original 1943 edition, which is the one most often cited in secondary works.

IM: Jean-Paul Sartre, *The Psychology of the Imagination,* and Jean-Paul Sartre, *L'imaginaire*

Two page references are given for each reference to *IM,* e.g., *IM* 12 [32]. The first number refers to the English translation, the second in square brackets refers to the French original.

ST or the *Summa:* Thomas Aquinas, *Summa theologiae.* The numbers refer to the part of the Summa, then the question, then the article, then the section of the article. For example, *ST* I-II.5:2ad2 refers to Part I-II, question 5, article 2, response to second objection. The Latin text is from the Leonine edition of Aquinas's *Opera Omnia* (complete works), vols. 4–11. The English translation is from St. Thomas Aquinas, *Summa Theologica,* translated by Fathers of the English Dominican Province, 5 vols.

TE: Jean-Paul Sartre, *The Transcendence of the Ego: An Existentialist Theory of Consciousness,* and Jean-Paul Sartre, *La transcendance de l'ego: Esquisse d'une description phénoménologique*

Two page references are given for each reference to *TE,* e.g., *TE* 40 [23]. The first number refers to the English translation, the second in square brackets refers to the French original.

NOTES ABOUT THE TEXT

In order to allow the reader to refer to commonly available English editions of the main primary texts, I use the translations mentioned in the Abbreviations section. Sometimes, however, I alter a translation slightly, without comment, if I judge that it could be more suitably phrased. This is sometimes to correct mistakes, but more often to make a translation more literal so that it is easier to follow the philosophical vocabulary. In this, I have been greatly helped by the work of Jean-Pierre Boulé and Timothy O'Hagan, *A Checklist of Errors in Hazel Barnes' English Translation of Jean-Paul Sartre, L'être et le néant* (Norwich: University of East Anglia for the British Society of Phenomenology, 1987).

Translations of other non-English works are by me unless otherwise noted.

If a citation includes italicized words or phrases, then these occurred in the original texts cited, e.g., "C'est d'exister *à distance de soi* comme présence à soi." In other words, I have not added any italics to cited words or phrases for my own emphasis.

When I refer to a part or a chapter (e.g., "We saw in chapter 3 that . . .") I am referring to a chapter in this book, unless it is clear from the context that I am referring to another work.

AQUINAS & SARTRE

INTRODUCTION

Aquinas: Historical and Intellectual Background

Thomas Aquinas was born at Roccasecca, midway between Rome and Naples, probably in 1225.[1] He was an oblate at the Benedictine abbey of Monte Cassino and then a student at Naples. After becoming a Dominican friar he spent the rest of his life studying, teaching, and writing in Cologne, Paris, Rome, and other Italian locations. He died in 1274 at Fossanova, south of Rome, on his way to the Council of Lyon.

Aquinas was not teaching in a vacuum, and the questions of freedom, identity, and happiness that concern us here were already much discussed in the thirteenth century. The cluster of problems concerning human freedom and action that are debated by contemporary English-speaking philosophers under the title "freedom of the will" were discussed in the Middle Ages under the heading *liberum arbitrium,* free decision or free judgment.[2] It was a matter of debate whether the will or some other faculty was the bearer of this freedom—if it existed at all. Before

1. For biographical information, see James A. Weisheipl, *Friar Thomas D'aquino: His Life, Thought, and Works* (Washington, D.C.: The Catholic University of America Press, 1983); Simon Tugwell, "Thomas Aquinas: Introduction," in *Albert and Thomas: Selected Writings,* ed. Simon Tugwell (Mahwah, N.J.: Paulist Press, 1988); and Jean-Pierre Torrell, *Saint Thomas Aquinas, Vol. 1: The Person and His Work* (Washington, D.C.: The Catholic University of America Press, 1996). When there are discrepancies in these accounts, I follow Torrell.

2. For this account of *liberum arbitrium* in medieval thought, see J. B. Korolec, "Free Will and Free Choice," in *The Cambridge History of Later Medieval Philosophy,* ed. Norman Kretzmann, Anthony Kenny, and Jan Pinborg (Cambridge: Cambridge University Press, 1982), 630–34. The term predates medieval theology and had been used in classical literary and legal formulations to indicate the power to decide or the freedom to act; see Daniel Westberg, *Right Practical Reason: Aristotle, Action, and Prudence in Aquinas* (Oxford: Clarendon Press, 1994), 81–82. A classic and still unmatched study is Odon Lottin, "Libre arbitre et liberté depuis saint Anselme jusqu'à la fin du XIIIe siècle," in *Psychologie et morale aux XIIe et XIIIe siècles,* vol. 1, 2nd ed. (Gembloux: J. Duculot, 1957), 11–389.

the thirteenth century various aspects of human freedom had been distinguished (by Bernard of Clairvaux, John of La Rochelle, Odo Regaldus, and others). In the early part of the thirteenth century William of Auxerre argued that free decision is essentially an act of reason; Philip the Chancellor that it is principally a matter of the will (although reason and will are in substance the same faculty but two different activities); and an anonymous writer from the same period that it is a third power distinct from both. The relation of reason, will, and freedom of decision remained a major topic throughout the century. It became characteristic of Dominican writers to associate freedom closely with reason, and of Franciscans to locate it more in the will.

Happiness, *beatitudo,* was another concept with a long history.[3] There was a theological conviction, much influenced by Augustine, that true happiness is to be found only in the contemplation of God in the world to come. There can be no happiness in this world because "all men, so long as they are mortal, are also necessarily wretched."[4] For the most part, prior to the thirteenth century, the Boethian concept of happiness that grew out of this attitude was generally accepted: the fragility of earthly things admits of no perfect condition; and human happiness is to be found only in another world where multiplicity is made one and fragility is exchanged for permanence.[5] Yet Aristotelian and even some Christian conceptions of human nature also understood happiness as the perfection of human nature, in which human achievements must play some part. Is there such a thing as a purely human good that can be attained by one's own actions? What connection do our present attempts to find fulfillment have with a future fulfillment that will transform our very existence? There seemed to be a need to distinguish between different types of happiness. It was William of Auxerre (died 1231) who first made the theological distinction between *perfect happiness*, experienced by the saints in heaven, and *imperfect happiness*, which we can taste here in the present. It was against this background that Aquinas developed his own interpretation of happiness.

One of the most significant factors that influenced in a more direct way Aquinas's teaching on subjects such as human freedom was the long-

3. See Georg Wieland, "Happiness: The Perfection of Man," in *The Cambridge History of Later Medieval Philosophy,* ed. Norman Kretzmann, Anthony Kenny, and Jan Pinborg (Cambridge: Cambridge University Press, 1982), 673–79.

4. Augustine, *De civitate Dei,* IX, 15.

5. Cf. Boethius, *Consolatio* III, pr. 9 and 10.

running dispute about "Latin Averroism" or "radical" (or "heterodox") Aristotelianism.[6] These are the modern labels sometimes given to a complex of doctrines and interpretations of Aristotelian philosophy supposedly arising from the teaching of Averroes (Ibn Rushd) and accepted by certain members of the Faculty of Arts in Paris in the second half of the thirteenth century.[7] One of the leaders of the Latin Averroist group was Siger of Brabant, first mentioned in documents in 1266. There were political and territorial aspects to the dispute: members of the Faculty of Arts wanted to assert their independence from the Faculty of Theology. But the issues were substantive: the "unicity" of the intellect (whether all human beings share one intellect), the eternity of the world, the denial of free will, the restriction of the influence of divine providence. Albert the Great and Thomas Aquinas, among others, had been arguing against many of these Averroist interpretations of Aristotle throughout the 1250s and 1260s.

Aquinas's most direct involvement came in his *De unitate intellectus contra Averroistas,* which refutes the doctrine that the possible intellect is a substance separated from the body and the same for all human beings. This polemical work was written in 1270, just before the bishop of Paris, Stephen Tempier, seeing these teachings as a threat to Christian faith, condemned thirteen Averroist propositions on 10 December of that year.[8] The key issue for Aquinas is whether human beings are in control of their own acts. If there is only one intellect, then there can only be one will (because the powers of intellect and will are so closely connected), and this attack on the knowing individual is what undermines all personal moral responsibility.[9] The knowledge gained by individual human beings must be diverse and distinct, even though it may be knowledge of the same thing.[10]

6. See Jan A. Aertsen, "Aquinas's Philosophy in Its Historical Setting," in *The Cambridge Companion to Aquinas,* ed. Norman Kretzmann and Eleonore Stump (Cambridge: Cambridge University Press, 1993), 24–25; Weisheipl, *Friar Thomas D'aquino: His Life, Thought, and Works,* 272–79; Torrell, *Saint Thomas Aquinas,* 182–94; and Gregory Martin Reichberg, "Aquinas on Moral Responsibility in the Pursuit of Knowledge," in *Thomas Aquinas and His Legacy,* ed. David M. Gallagher, Studies in Philosophy and the History of Philosophy (Washington, D.C.: Catholic University of America Press, 1994), 64–69.

7. There are doubts about whether Averroes himself is the actual source for these doctrines. See Torrell, *Saint Thomas Aquinas,* 192.

8. On the condemnations of 1270 and their background, see John F. Wippel, "The Condemnations of 1270 and 1277 at Paris," *Journal of Medieval and Renaissance Studies* 7 (1977): 169–201.

9. St. Bonaventure also connects the doctrine of determinism with that of the unicity of the intellect for all human beings in a work of 1268. See Torrell, *Saint Thomas Aquinas,* 182–83.

10. Aquinas writes: "It is therefore one thing which is understood by me and by you. But

I mention this Averroist dispute just to give one example in this introduction of how Aquinas wrote in a particular context, for a particular reason. It will not be possible or necessary in this present work to go deeply into the background of every aspect of Aquinas's teachings—but at least we can remind ourselves that there is a background, often with pressing political and ecclesiastical features, as well as philosophical and theological ones.

The main writings of Aquinas considered in this work are the *Quaestiones disputatae de veritate,* the *Quaestiones disputatae de malo,* and the *Summa theologiae,* so it is worth giving some more specific background to their composition.[11] After lecturing on the Bible, the main academic task of a master of theology in Paris was to take part in disputations—some of them "private" (the master teaching his students within the confines of the school) and some of them more formal and "public." The texts of the *Quaestiones disputatae* were often written up at some remove from the original classroom discussions, but they reflect the way in which issues were clarified by the thorough consideration of conflicting points of view. *De veritate,* however, which seems to have grown out of private disputations, was adapted, written up, and distributed very soon after the discussions took place—a testimony to the vibrancy of intellectual life in Paris at the time. The disputes took place sometime in the three years of Aquinas's first teaching period as a master in Paris, from 1256 to 1259.

Question 6 of *De malo,* which concerns us most here, seems to have a history independent from the rest of the text; but its date, and its significance in an argument about the development of Aquinas's thought, remain much disputed. Torrell places it a little before or after the Avveroist condemnations of December 1270. But Kevin Flannery argues that it is a much earlier work than usually thought, from no later than 1259, and that parts of *De veritate* 24:1 are in fact based on *De malo* 6.[12]

---

it is understood by me in one way and by you in another, that is, by another intelligible species. And my act of understanding is one thing, and yours another"; Thomas Aquinas, "De Unitate Intellectus Contra Averroistas," in *Sancti Thomae De Aquino Opera Omnia,* vol. 43 (Rome: Editori di San Tonomaso, 1976), book 5, 312.

11. See Tugwell, "Thomas Aquinas: Introduction," 248–55; Leonard E. Boyle, "The Setting of the *Summa Theologiae* of St. Thomas—Revisited," in *The Ethics of Aquinas,* ed. Stephen J. Pope (Washington, D.C.: Georgetown University Press, 2002), 2–9; and Torrell, *Saint Thomas Aquinas,* 60–65, 145–55, and 202–4. I often suggest in this book that Aquinas "writes" something or other, but in fact works such as the *Summa* was *spoken* in dictation to one of Aquinas's secretaries.

12. See Torrell, *St Thomas Aquinas,* 336; and Kevin L. Flannery, *Acts Amid Precepts* (Edinburgh: T & T Clark, 2001), 247–49.

There is still disagreement about the exact times and places of composition of the various parts of the *Summa theologiae.* Of the two parts that concern us (Part 1a, the *Prima Pars*—the first part; and Part 1a2ae, the *Prima Secundae*—the first part of the second part), the *Prima Pars* was probably begun in Rome in 1265 or 1266 and completed by the time Aquinas left for Paris in late 1268 to begin his second regency there. The early sections of the *Prima Secundae* may have been taught in Rome, but they were probably not written up before Aquinas arrived in Paris. Torrell accepts R.-A. Gauthier's textual argument that the *Prima Secundae* was not written before 1271 since it draws heavily on a translation of Aristotle's *Rhetoric* that was not available to Aquinas before the end of 1270.[13]

Whatever the exact details of its provenance, the *Summa* marks a decisive shift in Aquinas's approach to teaching theology. Moving to Rome in the autumn of 1265, to the community of Santa Sabina on the Aventine Hill, he was given the task of setting up a *studium* for students from various Dominican houses around the province as they prepared for priesthood and the Dominican apostolate. He was free to devise a curriculum of his own, and free to break out of the narrow tradition of practical (moral) theology that formed the heart of clerical studies at that time. The *Summa* was designed to introduce beginners to theology in an orderly, intelligible, and interesting way. He abandoned the traditional practice of basing his own teaching on the *Sentences* of Peter Lombard, and decided to give his teaching a "dogmatic" or "systematic" theological structure. The moral or anthropological part of the whole, the *Secunda Pars,* is thus prefaced by a theological section on God, the Trinity, and Creation, and is rounded off with a third Christological section on the Son of God, the Incarnation, and the Sacraments. The study of the Christian life is given its proper theological context. Human beings are created by God, and only return to him through the grace of Christ and the sacraments.[14] The proper organization of the *Summa,* as Ignatius Eschmann has emphasized, is understood through the various prologues that punctuate the text.[15] And so at the be-

13. Torrell, *Saint Thomas Aquinas,* 145–46.

14. On the debate about the validity of applying the *exitus-reditus* scheme to the *Summa,* see ibid., 150–55. M.-D. Chenu first proposed this Neoplatonic scheme, and it has been given continued support by M.-V. Leroy. But A. Patfoort believes it is inadequate.

15. Ignatius Theodore Eschmann, *The Ethics of Saint Thomas Aquinas: Two Courses* (Toronto: Pontifical Institute of Mediaeval Studies, 1997), 10–12.

ginning of the *Prima Pars* Aquinas proposes to teach sacred doctrine by treating first, of God; second, of the rational creature's advance toward God; and third, of Christ, who as a human being, is our way to God.[16]

Aquinas: Philosophical and Theological Influences

Aquinas is often called an Aristotelian, and with much merit, but his intellectual influences extend far beyond "the Philosopher."[17] Servais-Théodore Pinckaers gives a list of the authors Aquinas cites in the *Secunda Pars*, arranged according to frequency of citations.[18] The top ten nonscriptural sources are: Augustine, 1,630; Aristotle, 1,546; Gregory the Great, 439; Pseudo Dionysius, 202; Cicero, 187; Jerome, 178; John Damascene, 168; Ambrose, 151; Isidore of Seville, 120; and Roman law, 102. The list goes on, and finishes with Ptolemy, 1. The numerous citations themselves are merely the tip of the iceberg, and the influence of works such as Aristotle's *Nicomachean Ethics* and Boethius's *De consolatione* pervades the text. There are 1,839 citations from the Old Testament and 2,003 from the New Testament. The Psalms, the Pentateuch, the Wisdom Books, the Major Prophets, and the writings of Matthew, Paul, and John predominate among the biblical citations.

The Scripture quotations are not just illustrative adornments or proof-texts, they betray the evangelical dimension of this central anthropological section of the *Summa*. The seemingly philosophical questions at the beginning of the *Prima Secundae* about the final end are shaped by considerations of the Gospel beatitudes, even though this is not immediately apparent from the text. One would need to go back to Aquinas's commentary on the Gospel of St Matthew to see how his Aristotelian philosophy of the human act is marked by his reflections on the blessedness proposed by Christ in the Gospels.

Despite much revisionist thinking in this area, one can still cautiously say that Aristotle is Aquinas's deepest philosophical influence.[19] The reception of Aristotle's works in Latin translation helped shape thirteenth-

16. *ST* I.2 Prol.

17. For the influences on Aquinas, see Boyle, "The Setting of the *Summa Theologiae* of St. Thomas—Revisited"; and Servais-Théodore Pinckaers, "The Sources of the Ethics of St. Thomas Aquinas," in *The Ethics of Aquinas*, ed. Stephen J. Pope (Washington, D.C.: Georgetown University Press, 2002).

18. Pinckaers, "The Sources of the Ethics of St. Thomas Aquinas," 17–18.

19. See the doubts summarized by Fergus Kerr, *After Aquinas: Versions of Thomism* (Oxford: Blackwell, 2002), 9–10, and the works referred to in the notes there.

century thought in Western Europe.[20] The study of Aristotle spread through the universities and was officially approved at the University of Paris when the Faculty of Arts stated that its lecture programme must include all the works of Aristotle. When Aquinas went to study liberal arts at the University of Naples in 1239 the natural philosophy of Aristotle was already studied there. He began what would be an intense dialogue with Aristotle's thought, and he would go on to adopt Aristotle's key philosophical convictions. But there are significant Platonic elements in his thought too. At the beginning of his career he uses the Neoplatonic scheme of the *exitus-reditus* (the going out and coming back) of all things to structure his commentary on the *Sentences* of Peter Lombard,[21] and he uses the Platonic notion of participation in metaphysics to describe the relationship between created being and God. Nor does Aquinas confine himself to commenting on the works of Aristotle. He writes commentaries on works such as *De trinitate* and *De hebdomadibus* by Boethius, and *De divinis nominibus* by Pseudo-Dionysius. Two minor works by Aquinas, probably from his first years in Paris, show the philosophical influence of Avicenna (Ibn Sina) and Averroes (Ibn Rushd): *De ente et essentia* is marked by the thought of Avicenna on the nature of essence, and Averroist ideas are reflected in *De principiis naturae.*[22]

One example of the continuing debate about the true extent of Aquinas's Aristotelianism can be found in the discussion of human happiness. There are no doubts about Aquinas's own views: imperfect happiness can be tasted in this life, but perfect happiness can only be found in the next life in the vision of God. The disagreement is about whether Aquinas is betraying Aristotle's thought in the *Nicomachean Ethics,* or developing what is implicit there, or fulfilling this thought in an unexpected but perfectly compatible way.[23] This connects with disputes within Aristotelian stud-

20. See Aertsen, "Aquinas's Philosophy in Its Historical Setting."

21. See Torrell, *Saint Thomas Aquinas,* 43, for the significance of this theological reorganization.

22. Ibid., 47.

23. See Denis J. M. Bradley, *Aquinas on the Twofold Human Good: Reason and Human Happiness in Aquinas's Moral Science* (Washington, D.C.: The Catholic University of America Press, 1997), esp. 379–400 and 27–68; John Bowlin, *Contingency and Fortune in Aquinas's Ethics* (Cambridge: Cambridge University Press, 1999), esp. 140–42; Anthony J. Celano, "The Concept of Worldly Beatitude in the Writings of Thomas Aquinas," *Journal of the History of Philosophy* 25 (1987); and Anthony Kenny, "Aquinas on Aristotelian Happiness," in *Aquinas's Moral Theory: Essays in Honour of Norman Kretzmann,* ed. Scott MacDonald and Eleonore Stump (Ithaca, N.Y., and London: Cornell University Press, 1998).

ies about whether Aristotle's highest form of *eudaimonia* (happiness, well-being) is an "inclusivist" end (which contains multiple goods such as moral virtue and contemplative wisdom), or an "exclusivist" or "dominant" end (which would lie in the single good of theoretical wisdom); or whether the *Nichomachean Ethics* is actually an unresolved text that contains contradictory accounts of human happiness.

I support Denis Bradley's nuanced conclusion that Aquinas's doctrine goes far beyond Aristotle's, but is not incompatible with it: "Aquinas's claim that only the beatific vision will satisfy man's desire for happiness falls entirely outside of the ken of Aristotle's philosophy," and "the Thomistic notion of 'imperfect happiness' does not rest on Aristotle's admissions about the imperfect character of human contemplative *eudaimonia*"; yet at the same time "Aquinas thinks that his own doctrine, that men naturally desire a perfect happiness, is plausible precisely on Aristotelian grounds."[24] As Anthony Kenny has written, Aquinas's distinction between imperfect happiness in the present life and the perfect happiness of divine vision "corresponds to an ambiguity in book 10 [of the *Nicomachean Ethics*] itself," where Aristotle encourages us to strive toward a contemplation that is both a fulfillment of our natural human activity and something that is constitutively beyond us.[25] This particular discussion makes us aware of the more general point, that Aquinas is an interpreter and not just a follower of Aristotle, and that Aristotle's own position on many important issues is far from clear even to scholars today.

Aquinas: Subsequent Interpretation

Aquinas's work has generated divergent responses and controversy from the very beginning. Only three years after his death, the bishop of Paris censured a list of 219 theses, some of which have been associated (rightly or wrongly) with the writings of Aquinas; and a few days later some "Aristotelian" positions associated with his name were condemned by the Faculty

24. Bradley, *Aquinas on the Twofold Human Good: Reason and Human Happiness in Aquinas's Moral Science*, 399–400.

25. Kenny, "Aquinas on Aristotelian Happiness," 24. This ambiguity is carried into Catholic moral theology in the debate about whether we can have a natural desire for a supernatural end. For the issues involved, particularly as they are stirred up by proponents of the so-called new natural law theory, see Benedict M. Ashley, "What Is the End of the Human Person? The Vision of God and Integral Human Fulfillment," in *Moral Truth and Moral Tradition: Essays in Honour of Peter Geach and Elizabeth Anscombe*, ed. Luke Gormally (Dublin: Four Courts Press, 1994).

of Theology in Oxford at the behest of Robert Kilwardby, the archbishop of Canterbury, himself a Dominican friar.[26] Philosophers and theologians have disagreed about the interpretation and significance of his work over the centuries.

A particularly rich period of interest followed the publication of Leo XIII's encyclical *Aeterni Patris* in 1879 which endorsed Aquinas's teaching for Catholic students. The end of the nineteenth century and the beginning of the twentieth century witnessed the emergence of different "Thomisms": Désiré Mercier founded his Higher Institute of Philosophy at Louvain to modernize Aquinas's philosophy in the service of the physical and social sciences; the French Dominicans at Le Saulchoir read Aquinas as a philosophical realist who would help them escape the dead ends of various modern philosophical systems; Jesuits in France and Belgium such as Pierre Rousselot and Joseph Maréchal laid the foundations for what would later be called "transcendental Thomism"; Jacques Maritain was beginning his Thomistic project by the 1920s; and Étienne Gilson's historical interest in Aquinas gave rise to "existential Thomism" after the Second World War.[27] In this later period further varieties of Thomism developed so that by the second half of the century the differences between the approaches of the various neo-Thomist schools were becoming more entrenched and even irreconcilable.[28]

What are we to make of this cacophony of Thomistic voices? Near the beginning of his book *After Aquinas: Versions of Thomism* Fergus Kerr writes:

> However celebrated his reputation as the "Angelic Doctor," as *doctor communis*, particularly since the revival of Thomism in the late nineteenth century, Thomas's theology has always been in contention. If his theology is "angelic," it is not because it floats above and beyond history; if his teaching is "common," it is not because it has always been accepted.[29]

26. For a brief account of the events, and for references to some of the secondary literature, see Torrell, *Saint Thomas Aquinas*, 298–304.

27. See Gerald A. McCool, "Is Thomas' Way of Philosophizing Still Viable Today?," *Proceedings of the American Catholic Philosophical Association* 64 (1990): 2–9.

28. For accounts of divergent twentieth-century interpretations of Aquinas, see the six essays in part 3 of Stephen J. Pope, ed., *The Ethics of Aquinas* (Washington, D.C.: Georgetown University Press, 2002), 355–455.

29. Kerr, *After Aquinas: Versions of Thomism*, 14.

Current readings of Aquinas's work "are so conflicting, and even incommensurable, that integrating them into a single interpretation seems impossible."[30] Kerr, with others such as Hans Urs von Balthasar, Henri de Lubac, and Etienne Gilson, is particularly impatient with the tendency of twentieth-century neo-Thomists to calm and domesticate Aquinas and turn him into an ally against the dark forces of modern philosophy rather than an unsettling interlocutor. But the sheer diversity of conflicting interpretations does not surprise him, and indeed for him it points to the richness and complexity of Aquinas's own thought. Kerr quotes Balthasar, who writes that Aquinas displays "an astonishing breadth, flexibility, and mutability of perspectives which allow quite automatically the aporetic element in his thinking to emerge."[31] Likewise, de Lubac writes that "the ambivalence of his thought in unstable equilibrium, ransom of its very richness [*rançon de sa richesse même*], explains how it could afterwards be interpreted in such opposed senses."[32]

Now and then in this work I enter into the fray of contemporary Thomistic interpretation and take a position. It will be important, for example, to determine whether Aquinas did or did not change his mind significantly on the question of the priority of intellect or will. Did he, to put it crudely, move from an intellectualist to a more voluntaristic position?[33] My main purpose, however, is to stay with the primary texts and to see how the arguments presented there unfold. I hope to spend more time examining Aquinas's ideas than those of his interpreters.

Sartre: Historical and Intellectual Background

Jean-Paul Sartre was born in Paris on 21 June 1905.[34] His father died the following year, and he and his mother went to live with her parents in

30. Ibid., 15–16.

31. Ibid., 15; quoting from the article by Hans Urs von Balthasar, "On the Tasks of Catholic Philosophy in Our Time," *Communio* 20 (1993).

32. Kerr, *After Aquinas: Versions of Thomism,* 15; quoting from the book by Henri De Lubac, *Surnaturel: Études historiques* (Paris: Aubier, 1946), 435–36.

33. See the section "Objectivity and the Human Subject" in chapter 4 below.

34. For biographical information on Sartre, see Annie Cohen-Solal, *Sartre: A Life* (London: Heinemann, 1987); Ronald Hayman, *Writing Against: A Biography of Sartre* (London: Weidenfeld & Nicolson, 1986); the annotated chronologies in Michel Contat and Michel Rybalka, eds., *Les Écrits de Sartre: Chronologie, Bibliographie Commentée* (Paris: Gallimard, 1970); and Kenneth Thompson and Margaret Thompson, *Sartre: Life and Works* (New York/ Bicester, U.K.: Facts on File Publications, 1984).

Meudon. They moved back to Paris, then to La Rochelle (with his new stepfather), and eventually settled in Paris in 1920. Sartre entered the prestigious École Normale Supérieure in 1924 where he settled on philosophy as his major interest. He taught philosophy in various places at *lycée* level for most of the 1930s. He was conscripted at the beginning of the war, captured, and sent to prisoner-of-war camp—from which he escaped in 1941 by posing as a civilian. He taught at another *lycée* in Paris for the next three years. The rest of his life was spent as the archetypal French intellectual: writing, editing, teaching, debating, lecturing, talking, traveling, campaigning, resisting. The royalties from his books saved him having to take a paid university teaching post, so he had an enormous amount of social and intellectual freedom. He died in 1980.

Sartre was not a religious person, although he became more open to religious questions at the end of his life. He had the distinction of having his works put on the Index of prohibited books by the Catholic Church in 1948. He was baptized a few weeks after his birth at the church of Notre-Dame de Grâce in Passy, presumably under the influence of his maternal grandmother who was Catholic. He had a nominally Catholic upbringing, and though he didn't go to mass regularly, Sartre's clearest childhood "religious" memories were of being taken to hear organ music in St. Sulpice or the cathedral of Notre-Dame. He certainly knew Catholic priests well over the years: Stalag XII D, for example, his prisoner-of-war camp at Trèves, was full of priests, and as a writer and teacher he formed a natural bond with them, joining in their Gregorian plainsong rehearsals, and teaching them the ins and outs of Heidegger's *Sein und Zeit.*

The subtitle to Sartre's great work *Being and Nothingness* is "An Essay on Phenomenological Ontology," and he stands firmly in the phenomenological tradition of philosophy. In the last years of the nineteenth century the work of Henri Bergson and Maurice Blondel anticipated certain aspects of the Husserlian outlook, so there was a kind of receptivity to German phenomenology among French thinkers. Husserl thus received a slow but favorable reception in France during the late 1920s and early 1930s, and was welcomed as someone who could develop themes present implicitly in French philosophy.[35]

35. See Christian Dupont, "Receptions of Phenomenology in French Philosophy and Religious Thought, 1889–1939" (Ph.D. dissertation, University of Notre Dame, 1997), 10–22.

It is interesting to note that Thomists were among the first intellectuals in France to engage themselves with German phenomenology.[36] The Société Thomiste held a study day at Juvisy, south of Paris, on 12 September 1930, to reflect on the philosophy of Aquinas in the light of the phenomenological movement. Jacques Maritain convened the meeting and pointed to the fact that phenomenology was close to Thomism on account of its roots in Brentano. Maritain paid careful attention to Husserl in his *The Degrees of Knowledge* (first published in French in 1932). "Strange as it seems," writes Maritain, "at the very outset of the phenomenological movement a kind of activation of post-Kantian philosophy took place by means of contact with Aristotelian and scholastic seeds, as transmitted by Brentano."[37] This is not yet an encounter between Aquinas and Sartre, but one could go so far as to say that the roots of both Aquinas's Scholasticism and Sartre's phenomenology lie in Aristotelian soil.[38]

I will go on below to discuss in more detail the direct influences that shaped Sartre's thought. In this historical section it is worth giving a little background to the composition of the text of *Being and Nothingness* itself. This massive tome was written in about two years, between the summer of 1940 and October 1942.[39] Sartre went into military service at the beginning of the war and was sent to a meteorological unit. His light duties meant that he actually had more time and space to think philosophically than he had had when he was teaching in Paris; he was freed, physically and emotionally, from past demands and routines; he was able to write; and the fact that he had no philosophy books with him meant that had to think through his own ideas for himself and rediscover the key thoughts of, for example, Heidegger and Husserl without consulting them.

Sartre worked on finishing his novel *L'Age de raison,* but was impatient to start his philosophical book about "nothingness." He began this work in the summer of 1940. It was written on the floor, since Sartre was by now held in a large unfurnished room with fourteen fellow prisoners, and in

36. See ibid., 402–37.

37. Quoted at ibid., 437.

38. For Brentano's influence on Husserl, see David Bell, *Husserl* (London and New York: Routledge, 1990), 3–28.

39. See the biographical works mentioned above, and especially Hayman, *Writing Against: A Biography of Sartre,* 148–66. We know so much about this period because of his letters to Simone de Beauvoir and his war diaries, some of which survived. Hayman's chronology, at 153–210, differs slightly from Contat and Rybalka, eds., *Les Écrits de Sartre: Chronologie, Bibliographie Commentée,* 83–87.

these conditions he had completed 76 pages by 12 August. He continued working furiously on the text once he returned to Paris. Imprisonment and then living under the Occupation gave a new edge and resonance to ideas about liberty that had largely been worked out before the war. *Being and Nothingness* was completed in October 1942 and published in the summer of 1943. It's important to note that the text was completed in a period when Allied victory in the war was far from assured. In other words, the social and political context was one of defeat and not of impending triumph. This monumental defense of freedom was written in a time when freedom seemed to be an impossible dream.

Sartre: Philosophical and Theological Influences

It would be impossible to mention all the literary and philosophical influences on the young Sartre before the time of writing *Being and Nothingness.*[40] As he prepared to sit his entrance exam for the École Normale Supérieure he was reading Henri Bergson's *Time and Free Will* and was struck by its discussion of our consciousness of duration.[41] Bergson's idea that human beings can only be understood as a flight into the future prepared him for the German phenomenology he would later encounter. At the École Normale Supérieure he struggled against the dominance of the French intellectualist school mediated by Alain (Emile-Auguste Chartier), and would later find an antidote to this in the work of Gaston Bachelard and gestaltists such as Wolfgang Köhler.[42] In his year at the French Institute in Berlin (1933–1934) he was reading Husserl, Scheler, Heidegger, and Jaspers.[43] He had some acquaintance with the work of Kierkegaard,[44] and

40. See esp. Michel Rybalka, Oreste F. Pucciani, and Susan Gruenheck, "An Interview with Jean-Paul Sartre," in *The Philosophy of Jean-Paul Sartre,* ed. Paul A. Schilpp, The Library of Living Philosophers Vol. 16 (La Salle, Ill.: Open Court, 1981); William Ralph Schroeder, *Sartre and His Predecessors: The Self and the Other* (London: Routledge & Kegan Paul, 1984); Thomas W. Busch, *The Power of Consciousness and the Force of Circumstances in Sartre's Philosophy* (Bloomington: Indiana University Press, 1990); Dupont, "Receptions of Phenomenology in French Philosophy and Religious Thought, 1889–1939," esp. 212–45; and Herbert Spiegelberg, *The Phenomenological Movement,* 3rd ed. (The Hague, The Netherlands: Martinus Nijhoff, 1982), esp. 473–501.

41. See Ronald Aronson, *Jean-Paul Sartre: Philosophy in the World* (London: Verso, 1980), 30; and Hayman, *Writing Against: A Biography of Sartre,* 186.

42. See Adrian Mirvish, "Sartre on Perception and the World," *Journal of the British Society for Phenomenology* 14 (1983), esp. 160–67, and "Sartre and the Gestaltists," *Journal of the British Society for Phenomenology* 11 (1980).

43. See Spiegelberg, *The Phenomenological Movement,* 485.

44. He later attributed his reluctance to familiarize himself with Kierkegaard's work to the

of Hegel, although it seems that he only took Hegel up in a serious way after the war.[45]

The three dominant influences on his thought are undoubtedly Descartes, Heidegger, and Husserl. Descartes was the intellectual starting point in his formal studies.[46] He corrected and built on this foundation but never abandoned it: the idea of the *cogito,* of a consciousness conscious of itself, questioning itself, and the liberty that comes with this self-questioning. Doubt, as he wrote in his essay on Cartesian freedom, is what brings about the power of escaping, disengaging oneself, and withdrawing; it is the basis of humanism. No one before Descartes, Sartre believed, had stressed this connection between negativity and free will.[47] Ronald Hayman has written that Sartre never forgave Heidegger for not taking consciousness as the starting point of philosophy: "Underneath Sartre's radicalism is a bedrock of Cartesian conservatism."[48]

Sartre had been acquainted with Heidegger's philosophy at least since his time in Berlin, but a serious study only began later in the 1930s.[49] Sartre certainly seized upon Heidegger for some of his insights, and in the heyday of postwar existentialism their names were often linked. But by the time of writing *Being and Nothingness* the differences between the two had become more apparent. Heidegger becomes a kind of foil for Sartre, who criticizes his focus on *Dasein* and his lack of attention to the constructive role of consciousness and subjectivity. Heidegger, likewise, in his *Letter on Humanism,*[50] which was in part a response to Sartre's 1945 lecture "Exis-

spelling of his name: "Before then [1939–40] I knew he existed, but he was only a name for me and, for some reason, I did not like the name. Because of the double *a,* I think . . . That kept me from reading him"; see Rybalka, Pucciani, and Gruenheck, "An Interview with Jean-Paul Sartre," 10.

45. See ibid., 9–10.

46. See Aronson, *Jean-Paul Sartre: Philosophy in the World,* 31; and Busch, *The Power of Consciousness and the Force of Circumstances in Sartre's Philosophy,* 1–2, 5–7.

47. Translated as Jean-Paul Sartre, "Cartesian Freedom," in *Literary and Philosophical Essays* (New York: Collier Books, 1962).

48. Hayman, *Writing Against: A Biography of Sartre,* 189.

49. See Spiegelberg, *The Phenomenological Movement,* 473–501; Michel Haar, "Sartre and Heidegger," in *Jean Paul Sartre: Contemporary Approaches to His Philosophy,* ed. Hugh J. Silverman and Frederick A. Elliston (Pittsburgh, Pa.: Duquesne University Press, 1980); and Francis Jeanson, *Sartre and the Problem of Morality,* trans. Robert V. Stone (Bloomington: Indiana University Press, 1980), 80–82.

50. Reprinted in English translation in Martin Heidegger, *Basic Writings* (San Francisco: HarperSanFrancisco, 1993).

tentialism Is a Humanism,"[51] is highly critical of the subjectivity that he believes has infected all modern metaphysics. Sartre's ontology of consciousness is much closer, ultimately, to Husserl than to Heidegger.

The significance of Husserl in Sartre's intellectual formation cannot be overestimated.[52] German phenomenology was in the air in France in the late 1920s and early 1930s, but Sartre does not seem to have read any of the several French introductions to the movement before the summer of 1933. Raymond Aron first introduced Sartre to Husserl in the spring of 1933, and convinced him that his philosophy would speak to Sartre's own preoccupations: overcoming the polarization between idealism and realism and affirming both the power of reason and the reality of the visible world as it appears to our senses. Sartre then read Emmanuel Lévinas's "La théorie de l'intuition dans la phénoménologie de Husserl" and was immediately won over. He went on to study Husserl's *Ideen* in Berlin that autumn.

The initial attraction to Husserl seems to have been in the area of method: here was a philosopher who allowed one to take seriously the experience of everyday life, the concrete experience of the novelist as well as the reflective experience of the philosopher. In Berlin Sartre drafted an essay that expresses his newfound Husserlian convictions: that the intentionality of consciousness is what allows philosophy to overcome the separation between subjective experience and the objective world; that both idealism and realism are bankrupt because of their common assumption that knowledge somehow involves a mental space populated by some kind of intermediary mental contents; that philosophy must start as a descriptive science of the facts of experience rather than a transcendental reflection on the conditions for the possibility of that experience.[53] There are questions about whether Sartre fully understood Husserl's project, and he certainly ended up as a critic rather than a disciple—but there are no

51. First published in French in 1946; for an English translation, see Jean-Paul Sartre, "Existentialism and Humanism," in *Jean-Paul Sartre: Basic Writings,* ed. Stephen Priest (London: Routledge, 2001).

52. See Busch, *The Power of Consciousness and the Force of Circumstances in Sartre's Philosophy,* 3–4; Dupont, "Receptions of Phenomenology in French Philosophy and Religious Thought, 1889–1939," 212–19, 35–45; and Thompson and Thompson, *Sartre: Life and Works,* 26–29.

53. Jean-Paul Sartre, "Intentionality: A Fundamental Idea of Husserl's Phenomenology," *Journal of the British Society for Phenomenology* 1, no. 2 (1970). The essay was written in the period 1933–1934 but not published until 1939.

doubts about the initial effect Husserl had on Sartre's thinking, and the continuing force he exerted on his philosophical development.

Sartre: Subsequent Interpretation

The publication of Sartre's *Being and Nothingness* stimulated many reactions.[54] From within the French phenomenological tradition, Merleau-Ponty gave one of the most considered responses, both sympathetic to the aims of Sartre's project and fiercely critical of its underlying ontology of consciousness.[55] Sartre's view of consciousness, for Merleau-Ponty, is still dualistic: its openness to the world and its distinction from it are so emphatic that it has nothing to ground it. There is not enough emphasis on the "interworld" between subject and object, where consciousness encounters a set of predetermined meanings over which it has no control. Herbert Marcuse is an example of someone who gave a more politically pointed reply to Sartre's exposition of liberty in *Being and Nothingness:* "If philosophy, by virtue of its existential-ontological concepts of man or freedom, is capable of demonstrating that the persecuted Jew and the victim of the executioner are and remain absolutely free and masters of a self-responsible choice, then these philosophical concepts have declined to the level of a mere ideology."[56] A. J. Ayer, in the English analytical tradition, at least showed some interest in what was happening across the Channel, but he was famously dismissive of Sartre's use of the term *le néant* ("nothing") to refer to an "insubstantial

54. For rich collections of essays that reveal many of the different approaches taken to Sartre over recent decades, see Hugh J. Silverman and Frederick A. Elliston, *Jean-Paul Sartre: Contemporary Approaches to His Philosophy* (Pittsburgh, Pa.: Duquesne University Press, 1980); Paul Arthur Schilpp, *The Philosophy of Jean-Paul Sartre,* The Library of Living Philosophers, Vol. 16 (La Salle, Ill.: Open Court, 1981); Robert Wilcocks, ed., *Critical Essays on Jean-Paul Sartre* (Boston: G. K. Hall, 1988); Ronald Aronson and Adrian Van den Hoven, *Sartre Alive* (Detroit, Mich.: Wayne State University Press, 1991); and Christina Howells, ed., *The Cambridge Companion to Sartre* (Cambridge: Cambridge University Press, 1992).

55. See the section "The Objective Resistance of the World" in chapter 3 below; and M. Merleau-Ponty, *Phenomenology of Perception,* trans. Colin Smith (London: Routledge & Kegan Paul, 1962), esp. part 3. The work was first published in French in 1945. On the differences between Merleau-Ponty and Sartre, see Monika Langer, "Sartre and Merleau-Ponty: A Reappraisal," in *The Philosophy of Jean Paul Sartre,* ed. Paul A. Schilpp (La Salle, Ill.: Open Court, 1981); Jeanson, *Sartre and the Problem of Morality,* 187; and Hubert L. Dreyfus and Piotr Hoffman, "Sartre's Changed Conception of Consciousness: From Lucidity to Opacity," in *The Philosophy of Jean Paul Sartre,* ed. Paul A. Schilpp (La Salle: Open Court, 1981).

56. Herbert Marcuse, "Existentialism: Remarks on Jean-Paul Sartre's 'L'être et le néant,'" *Philosophy and Phenomenological Research* 8 (1948): 322. See the section "The Persistence of Existential Freedom" in chapter 5 below.

and mysterious" substance.[57] These references just give a taste of some of the reactions roused by Sartre's work.

There are a number of critical questions that have generated much discussion in the years since 1943 and could detain us now, but I will look briefly at just two that have greater bearing on this present work: the first concerns Sartre's appropriation of Husserl; the second concerns Sartre's own philosophical development.

Did Sartre properly understand Husserl's phenomenology? Did he correct it? Did he betray it?[58] As early as 1933/1934, when Sartre drafted his *The Transcendence of the Ego,* he was distancing himself from Husserl's apparent understanding of the transcendental Ego.[59] For Sartre, the Ego in Husserl's scheme was in danger of becoming reified, and it was undermining the transparency and impersonality of consciousness that made a philosophy of intentionality possible in the first place. Sartre saw phenomenology as a way of overcoming the idealism inherent in Kant's transcendental philosophy, but he feared that Husserl was drifting into Kantianism. This is why Sartre insists in his *The Transcendence of the Ego* that there is only a *transcendent* Ego (a personal identity that is an object to our impersonal consciousness) and not a *transcendental* Ego (which would lie behind our experience and constitute our fundamental identity).

Peter Caws sympathizes with Husserl and believes that Sartre leaves no room for the "I" of consciousness: the total transparency of consciousness robs us of the possibility of individuality and of personhood.[60] Herbert Spiegelberg writes that Sartre's critique of Husserl is unconvincing and lacks an adequate grasp of the phenomenological issues involved. "By denying [consciousness] a centre and the dimension of inwardness he deprives it at the same time of its existential weight."[61] Thomas Busch,

57. A. J. Ayer, "Novelist-Philosophers: V. Jean-Paul Sartre," *Horizon* 12 (1945): 19; and Phyllis Sutton Morris, *Sartre's Concept of a Person: An Analytic Approach* (Amherst: University of Massachusetts Press, 1976), 24–25.

58. See the section "Consciousness and Intentionality" in chapter 1 below.

59. Jean-Paul Sartre, *The Transcendence of the Ego: An Existentialist Theory of Consciousness,* trans. Forrest Williams and Robert Kirkpatrick (New York: Hill & Wang, 1957). See the introductory essay by his translators, Forrest Williams and Robert Kirkpatrick.

60. Peter Caws, *Sartre, The Arguments of the Philosophers* (London, Boston, and Henley, U.K.: Routledge & Kegan Paul, 1979), 52–60.

61. Herbert Spiegelberg, "Husserl's Phenomenology and Sartre's Existentialism," in *The Context of the Phenomenological Movement* (The Hague, The Netherlands: Martinus Nijhoff, 1981), at 60.

however, argues that Sartre was an attentive observer of the Husserlian programme and was in fact playing on an ambiguity within Husserl's phenomenology.[62] James Edie believes that Sartre was actually being faithful to Husserl without realizing it: the central ideas of *The Transcendence of the Ego* are already in Husserl's *Ideas,* and Husserl was fully aware of the necessity of distinguishing between the "empirical Ego" (that gives us an identity in the world) and the "transcendental Ego" (that lies behind our intentional experience of the world and only becomes an "object" of consciousness through reflection).[63] What matters for us is Sartre's perception of this disagreement, whether real or mistaken. It forced him to bring more precision to his own understanding of intentionality and to clarify the difference between the identity that constitutes us and the identity we constitute for ourselves through our freedom. Later, by the time of *Being and Nothingness,* Sartre would develop a more sophisticated take on what the "impersonality" of consciousness did and did not mean.[64]

The other critical question worth examining briefly is that of Sartre's own philosophical development, and particularly the question of whether he later abandoned the ontology of *Being and Nothingness* that is so central to my own work. In later interviews he seems to repudiate an excessive emphasis on the scope of human freedom in his earlier work;[65] and no one disputes the fact that his later work, more concerned with politics and biography, pays closer attention to the determining forces that mold our situation and our personality. Under the influence of thinkers such as Freud, Lacan, and Marx, Sartre's notion of consciousness gave way to that of lived experience—where our identity is inseparable from the constraints and conditions of the external world. Christina Howells writes that Sartre was led "to reduce the slender autonomy of the individual subject as the transparency

62. Thomas W. Busch, "Sartre's Use of the Reduction: *Being and Nothingness* Reconsidered," in *Jean-Paul Sartre: Contemporary Approaches to His Philosophy,* ed. Hugh J. Silverman and Frederick A. Elliston (Pittsburgh, Pa.: Duquesne University Press, 1980), 28.

63. James M. Edie, "The Roots of the Existentialist Theory of Freedom in 'Ideas I,'" *Husserl Studies* 1 (1984): 245–50; and James M. Edie, "The Question of the Transcendental Ego: Sartre's Critique of Husserl," *Journal of the British Society for Phenomenology* 24 (1993): 105–15.

64. See Leo Fretz, "Individuality in Sartre's Philosophy," in *The Cambridge Companion to Sartre,* ed. Christina Howells (Cambridge: Cambridge University Press, 1992), 71–83; and Rhiannon Goldthorpe, "Sartre and the Self: Discontinuity or Continuity?," *American Catholic Philosophical Quarterly* 70, no. 4 (1996): 525–30.

65. See, e.g., Jean-Paul Sartre, "The Itinerary of a Thought," in *Between Existentialism and Marxism* (New York: Pantheon Books, 1974), 44.

and lucidity of consciousness [were] muddied by the murkier waters of the *vécu* or 'lived experience'" and in considering the growth of an individual such as Flaubert in *The Idiot of the Family* "personal characteristics that Sartre would previously have represented as part of a freely chosen project are now interpreted as ineradicable structures of the infant's facticity."[66]

Despite these significant developments, I would maintain that the two fundamental elements of facticity and freedom, which lie at the heart of *Being and Nothingness,* remain in Sartre's later works. The language has changed, and the description is more nuanced, but Sartre does not give up on his central insight that we have both to make ourselves and to recognize that we are made, to inherit an identity and go beyond it.

> In *Being and Nothingness,* what you might call "subjectivity" is not what it would be for me today: the little gap in an operation by which what has been internalized is reexternalized as an act. [. . .] The individual internalizes his social determinants: He internalizes the relations of production, the family of his childhood, the historical past, contemporary institutions, then he reexternalizes all that in acts and choices that necessarily refer us to everything that has been internalized.[67]

Howells warns us against thinking that in the later Sartre human beings are dissolved into the structures that traverse them. She quotes Sartre's own contention that human beings must maintain "the perpetually resolved and perpetually renewed contradiction between man-as-producer and man-as-product, in each individual and at the heart of each multiplicity."[68] In Sartre's later works we are conditioned all the way down, and responsibility is now more about identifying and integrating the many antecedent influences that have conditioned us than abandoning them. But the responsibility remains, and within our conditioning we are free agents, able to assume and make something of that conditioning, and not merely vehicles for inhuman forces operating through us.[69] So Sartre develops but does not repudiate his phenomenological ontology.

66. Christina Howells, "Conclusion: Sartre and the Deconstruction of the Subject," in *The Cambridge Companion to Sartre,* ed. Christina Howells (Cambridge: Cambridge University Press, 1992), 337.

67. Jean-Paul Sartre, *Situations IX* (Paris: Gallimard, 1972), 102–3.

68. Howells, "Conclusion: Sartre and the Deconstruction of the Subject," 342.

69. See David A. Jopling, "Sartre's Moral Psychology," in *The Cambridge Companion to Sartre,* ed. Christina Howells (Cambridge: Cambridge University Press, 1992), esp. 105–8 and 130.

Part One

HUMAN BEING

Chapter 1

IDENTITY AND HUMAN INCOMPLETION IN SARTRE

The Nature of Human Action

Human beings do many different things. Why, then, does someone do one thing rather than another? What explains the action? Our answers to these questions will point to a great range of "causes," "reasons," "motives," or "motivations"—in ordinary conversation we do not distinguish between these words very carefully. Often, however, a satisfying answer falls into one of two categories. A first type of answer tells us something about who the person is and what the person is like: "She treats the patient because she is a doctor"; "He runs away because he is a coward"; "They go to the cinema because they like films." These explanations refer in some way to the identity of the acting person. A second type of answer says something about the circumstances that give rise to the activity: "We feed the children because they are hungry"; "He washes the cup because it is dirty"; "I get out of bed because the office where I work opens in an hour." These explanations refer in some way to the objective demands of the situation, to whatever it is that needs moving forward or putting right, to the change that needs bringing about in the world. So we can understand why human beings act by looking to some aspect of their personal identity or to the objective demands to which they respond.

Jean-Paul Sartre, however, is unsatisfied with this kind of explanation because he thinks it is back to front. It is not true, in his view, that we act in a certain way because of our identity and the objective demands we meet. Rather, it is by acting in a certain way that we establish a particular identity and allow a certain set of demands to guide our action. Instead of saying "He runs away because he is a coward," we should say "He is a coward because he runs away." Instead of saying "I get out of bed because I have to be at the office in an hour," we should say "It is by getting out of bed that I turn the possibility of going to work into an obligation." These descriptions are counterintuitive and may seem forced; they may even strike some readers as patently false. Surely, to take one of the other examples, she is a qualified doctor, whether she treats the patient or not. Surely the cup is dirty, whether he washes it or not. I hope to clarify in this chapter what Sartre does and doesn't mean by his awkward inversion of everyday language. He wants to show that our freely chosen actions establish our identity and give force to certain demands. Our commitments allow us to become people we might not have become and illuminate a set of priorities that might have remained obscure. We are not slaves to our being but creators of our existence.

In his reflections on action Sartre goes to the very heart of what it is to be human. He shows that our free actions are not the consequence of our identity, they are its foundation, and it is our nature as human beings always to go beyond who we are toward a freely chosen self. In this chapter we will examine the ambiguity of human identity that arises because of the nature of human consciousness as being-for-itself. Then we will be in a position to understand how human beings create imaginative possibilities for themselves and choose to pursue certain of these possibilities, thus establishing their identity as persons.

Anguish, Vertigo, and the Ambiguity of Identity

It should be made clear at the outset of this chapter that Sartre is very aware of the many factors that do constitute an identity for each human being. His aim is not to deny the reality of human identity but to question whether it is enough to account for one's actions. It is worth alluding to some of these factors that make up our identity as human beings in *Being and Nothingness.*[1]

La facticité ("facticity") is the word Sartre uses to stand for the innu-

1. *BN* is subtitled "An Essay on Phenomenological Ontology." Its four parts deal with "The Problem of Nothingness" (negation, bad faith, etc.), "Being-for-Itself" (presence to self, factic-

merable facts about our life that we have not chosen.[2] These make up the contingency of our being, the sense in which our life is given, discovered, inherited, and dependent on circumstances outside our control. We are bodily creatures, in a certain time and place, with a personal history, living in certain conditions. There are many undeniable facts about our individual psychology. Sartre lists the various characteristics, habits, states, etc., that make up the psychic unity of our ego.[3] These include not only latent qualities that inform our behavior (such as industriousness, jealousy, ambition) and actual states that embody a certain behavior (such as loving or hating), but also a whole pattern of acts. Our acts manifest the unified purposes of the psyche as they are embodied in the world. Human acts take on a kind of objectivity and our purposes unfold with some continuity: boxers train, scientists do research, artists create their work, politicians campaign.

Our individual facticity is itself dependent on a particular language, a concrete community, a political structure, and on being part of the human species.[4] We are, in other words, natural and cultural beings who at no point determine the conditions and facts of our being. If we need this complex environment in order to have an identity, we also need relationships with other people in order to comprehend our own identity. It is through the mediation of others that we can apprehend ourselves. We appreciate ourselves in a new way, for example, when we are known or desired or loved. "I recognize I *am* as the other [*autrui*] sees me"[5]; "*I* see *myself* because *somebody* sees me."[6]

In these different ways Sartre reveals an immensely rich understanding of all that makes up an individual human life, and concerns himself deeply with questions of sociology, culture, language, psychology, and human relations. All of this makes up the facticity of our being, the givenness of our unique human identity. We should remember throughout this chapter that Sartre never denies that human beings have an essence: "Essence is everything about the human being which we can indicate by the words: that *is*."[7] For each human being, "certain original structures are invariable."[8]

---

ity, temporality, knowledge, etc.), "[Being] For-Others" (the look, the body, relationships, etc.), and "Having, Doing, and Being" (freedom, psychoanalysis, etc.).

2. *BN* 79–84; *EN* 115–20/122–27.

3. *BN* 162–70; *EN* 197–206/209–18.

4. *BN* 509–31; *EN* 554–76/591–615.

5. *BN* 222; *EN* 260/222.

6. *BN* 260; *EN* 299/318.

7. *BN* 35; *EN* 70/72.

8. *BN* 456; *EN* 500/532.

Rather than being antiessentialist, Sartre's philosophy could be termed a "qualified essentialism."[9] His sole qualification is that the human essence is never enough. Sartre emphasized that the totality of essence that constitutes our identity cannot adequately define a human being as human because our consciousness of this totality is an essential aspect of our being. We have a relationship with the totality, an attitude to it, a responsibility for it. It's for this reason, as we shall now see, that human identity is ambiguous, insecure, and insufficient to account for our actions.

In a section of *Being and Nothingness* concerning *angoisse* ("anguish"), Sartre gives two examples of individuals who discover that their identity is insecure. First, *the cliff walker.*[10] Someone is walking along the side of a dangerous cliff, on a narrow path, without a guardrail. He is anxious. It is not a straightforward fear that the path will give way (it looks firm enough) or that a gust of wind will knock him over (the air is calm), it is a fear that he might willingly throw himself off and jump to his death. He doesn't trust himself.

Many people have had an experience of vertigo akin to this. On the one hand, looking into the abyss, we want to live; on the other hand, we become aware of our freedom. We notice that the "desire to live" is not an unchangeable part of our psychological makeup. We observe it. The more we reflect on it, the more we realize that we are not bound by it, and we become dizzy with the possibilities that open up before us. We could be reckless and jump, for no reason at all, and this is what really terrifies us. It's a very particular example, but it illustrates the way our confidence in our identity can suddenly be undermined. In the most ordinary situations we can be struck with vertigo: we may suddenly appreciate, for example, that we can do something in a different way, that we can rethink our priorities, that we can change, that we don't have to be the person we have been. Human identity is ambiguous. Normally we enjoy the security of moving for-

9. He was afraid that a so-called Aristotelian philosophy of essence would involve the total determination of the individual, but in fact his own view is compatible with an Aristotelian theory of natural kinds. For Sartre's suspicions about Aristotelianism, see Thomas C. Anderson, "Sartre and Human Nature," *American Catholic Philosophical Quarterly* 70, no. 4 (1996). For the compatibility of Sartre and Aristotle, see M. Qizilbash, "Aristotle and Sartre on the Human Condition: Lack, Responsibility and the Desire to Be God," *Angelaki* 3, no. 1 (1998); and Frederick A. Olafson, *Principles and Persons: An Ethical Interpretation of Existentialism* (Baltimore, Md.: Johns Hopkins University Press, 1967), 87–88.

10. *BN* 30–32; *EN* 65–67/67–69.

ward steadily on the basis of who we are, but now and then we are struck by a parallel awareness that we could be someone else.

The experience of vertigo is one form of anguish: we realize that we cannot guarantee the perpetuation of the motives that have influenced us up to this point. Identity is not a straight-jacket, it does not predetermine the future. At this moment, halfway along the dangerous path, we may feel confident; but in a few steps, who knows what we might do? "If *nothing* compels me to save my life, *nothing* prevents me from precipitating myself into the abyss. The decisive conduct will emanate from a me [*un moi*] which I am not yet."[11] Normally, of course, most people finish their walk safely. Sartre wants us to realize that the decision to walk carefully is not determined by our identity; instead, it is the decision itself that determines our identity and ensures that we continue to be people who want to live. It's a subtle distinction, the importance of which will become more apparent.

The second example of anguish is *the reformed gambler.*[12] This person has sincerely decided never to gamble again. He has taken a firm resolution to quit. He considers himself to be a reformed gambler, and he relies on this identity to get him through the temptations that come his way. Yet now, as he nears the gaming table, his resolution melts away.

> What he apprehends then in anguish is precisely the total inefficacy of the past resolution. It is there, doubtless, but fixed, ineffectual, *surpassed* [dépassée] by the very fact that I am conscious *of* it. The resolution is still *me* to the extent that I realize constantly my identity with myself across the temporal flux, but it is no longer *me*—due to the fact that it has become an object *for* my consciousness. I am not subject to it, it fails in the mission which I have given to it.[13]

The identity the gambler established for himself as reformed is fragile. He wishes it constrained him and guaranteed his new way of life, but this very wish betrays his knowledge that both gambling and not gambling are equally possible for him. The present identity (as resolved and reformed) is illusory, it is really a memory of a previous identity (who he was at the time of his resolution)—it is already surpassed and it will not be effective unless it is remade once more.

11. Sartre often oscillates between the first and third person; see *BN* 32; *EN* 67/69.

12. *BN* 32–33; *EN* 67–69/69–71.

13. *BN* 33; *EN* 68/70.

The cliff walker is anguished because he can't ensure that his present resolution to live will survive all the way along the path; the gambler is anguished because his past resolution not to gamble isn't sustaining him in the present. For both characters, their very consciousness of an identity comes with a corresponding detachment as they realize that they are not bound by it. By searching for reasons, they objectify them and make them ineffective. This realization is what paralyzes Matthieu in Sartre's novel *The Age of Reason.* He wants to justify his actions and base them on good reasons, or at least on some overwhelming desire, but by interrogating these motives, by trying to establish whether they are compelling, he distances himself from them. The process of examining them shows they have no binding power over his future; the search for obligations leads him to freedom because it uncovers the fact that alternative courses of action are also viable.[14]

However strong it seems, the price of being conscious of an identity is a corresponding liberation from that identity, and an ever-present responsibility for continuing or denying that identity. We experience this responsibility through anguish. This is not just a point about the fact that our identities change for various reasons, since anguish does not come about when a past identity is forgotten and a new one adopted. Instead, anguish is a sign that human beings are separated from themselves, from the very identities that constitute who they are now. We can review the present and not just the past. We have a continual responsibility to re-create our identity through our choices.

Sartre's examples may seem extreme: we are not often paralyzed by vertigo or struggling with addiction. The reader may suspect that he is deliberately choosing to examine situations that lie outside our normal experience of deliberating and acting, moments of high drama or psychopathology. Anguish, perhaps, should be confined to the world of the novelist or the consulting rooms of the psychiatrist. There are a few brief responses to this. First, it is often only in moments of crisis or difficulty or extremity that we appreciate the fragility of our own identity. Second, such moments may not occur often in the life of any individual, but they seem to occur in some form to most human beings, and in this sense Sartre's examples have a wide applicability. Third, the heightened sensitivity we have in extraordinary situations can give us a greater appreciation for what is happening

14. Jean-Paul Sartre, *The Age of Reason* (London: Penguin Books, 2001).

in ordinary life. Sartre believes that in theory we can stop at any moment and reflect in this way. Aquinas, in a similar vein, will use murder, adultery, and shipwreck to exemplify universal aspects of the process of human deliberation. Fourth, if in the most ordinary of circumstances we were to have an experience of anguish, this experience would actually make those circumstances seem extraordinary. Anguish by definition undermines our identity and disrupts our world, so even if we chose examples that were set safely within the confines of mundane human behavior they would nevertheless prove to be unusual and disruptive. In other words, it is impossible to talk about a routine experience of anguish since anguish necessarily undercuts our routine.

There are many ways of trying to avoid the responsibility for ourselves that comes with anguish. In Sartre's scheme they all come under the heading of *la mauvaise foi* ("bad faith" or "self-deception"). For our purposes the most instructive type of bad faith is *la sincérité* ("sincerity"). This is a technical term in Sartre's vocabulary. It is the attempt to be who we are, to make our life match our identity, to conform our external actions with our supposed inner reality.[15] Sartre's first example is a little misleading: the café waiter who tries so hard to make the right gestures and voices that he seems awkward and patronizing.[16] We might say that he is simply not being a good waiter, but Sartre is interested in the way he strains too hard to match his actions with some conception of who he is. The real contradiction lies in his desire to make himself what he believes himself to be. "What *are we* then if we have the constant obligation to make ourselves what we are, if our mode of being is having the obligation to be what we are?"[17] The ideal of sincerity, to be what one is, "supposes that I am not originally what I am."[18] So as soon as we spot whatever "essential" aspect of our being it is that we want to achieve, we realize that we are neither identified with this nor bound by it. To explain or excuse our behavior with reference to "who we are" is already to put some distance between our present actions and the past "identity" that supposedly caused it. We stake a claim to a "self" *(soi)* and immediately betray our distance from it.

15. A better translation might be "genuine," which has the connotation of *matching up to what we really are*—in contemporary English the word "sincere" implies simply *wanting to tell the truth.*

16. *BN* 59–60; *EN* 94–95/98–100.

17. *BN* 59; *EN* 93–94/98.

18. *BN* 62; *EN* 97/102.

Total, constant sincerity as a constant effort to adhere to oneself [*à soi*] is by nature a constant effort to dissociate oneself from oneself [*se désolidariser de soi*]. One frees oneself from oneself by the very act by which one makes oneself an object for oneself [*On se libère de soi par l'acte même par lequel on se fait objet pour soi*]. To draw up a perpetual inventory of what one is means constantly to redeny oneself and to take refuge in a sphere where one is no longer anything but a pure, free look [*un pur et libre regard*].[19]

The list of characteristics that can form this "inventory" is wide-ranging: we try to identify not only with our public roles, but also with our attitudes, our emotions, our moral character, our sexual preferences.[20] By referring to these we can give ourselves a reason to act, but we should also acknowledge that we freely choose to refer to them and that they do not constrain us.

Through anguish the reformed gambler apprehends "the permanent rupture of determinism."[21] Anguish is thus one manifestation of freedom, which is characterized "by a constantly renewed obligation to remake the *Me* [*le* Moi] which designates the free being."[22] Sartre uses the terms *moi* ("me") and *essence* ("essence") to refer to that aspect of human identity which at each moment is inherited from the past. The *moi* has a historical content that has to be reaffirmed, adjusted, or rejected as soon as it is recognized. Essence is what we have been and what we are—it is the past as it impinges on the present and forms it. "Due to this fact it is the totality of characteristics which *explain* the act."[23] But we must keep in mind Sartre's two examples of anguish: the characteristics that are allowed to constitute the person's identity at each moment depend on which act he freely chooses and not the other way round. The gambler's resolution is important only if he is keeping it; the walker's desire to live protects him only if he preserves it at each step. For this reason Sartre writes:

The act is always beyond the essence; it is a human act only insofar as it surpasses every explanation which we can give of it, precisely because anything that one can describe in the human being by the formula "that is," by that very fact *has been*.[24]

19. *BN* 65; *EN* 100/106.
20. *BN* 55–67; *EN* 89–102/94–104.
21. *BN* 33; *EN* 68/70.
22. *BN* 35; *EN* 70/72.
23. *BN* 35; *EN* 70/72.
24. *BN* 35; *EN* 70/72.

Sartre summarizes this idea later in *Being and Nothingness* concluding with one of his most misunderstood phrases:

> By the sole fact that I am conscious of the motives which inspire my action, these motives are already transcendent objects for my consciousness; they are outside. In vain shall I seek to catch hold of them; I escape them by my very existence. I am condemned to exist forever beyond my essence, beyond the motivations and motives of my act. I am condemned to be free.[25]

The language may sound overblown (there is not much difference between saying "I am free" or "I am always free" and "I am condemned to be free"), but the truth conveyed is clear: if we are conscious of and present to any aspect of our identity, then it loses its hold over us and we have to choose how to respond to it. It's important to remember that Sartre does not deny that human beings have an essence, he simply denies that this essence can be enough to determine our choices. It is in this significant but limited sense that we are forever beyond our essence.

We should clear up some possible misunderstandings at this stage. First, Sartre never imagines that anguish is present within all our activities. He acknowledges that in most everyday situations we are acting *without* anguish; we are usually caught up in things without much reflection, taking for granted a certain identity and certain goals.[26] Even in the midst of the most spontaneous or habitual act, however, "there remains the possibility of putting this act into question."[27]

Second, there is no suggestion that our identity is cut off from a world of causes and influences. Take the café waiter: He may avoid sincerity and freely choose what to make of his life and his role. Yet his starting point is that he is a café waiter—this is the facticity of his situation, and it makes the drama of realizing what it means for him to be a waiter quite different from "the drama pure and simple" (i.e., without any facts to ground it) of pretending to be a diplomat or a sailor when he is not.[28] However we respond to the facticity of our essence, it remains present to us as a factual necessity even if we reconstruct it through our decisions about how to act.

25. *BN* 439; *EN* 484/515.

26. *BN* 35–36; *EN* 70–71/73–74. Cf. the discussion of unreflective consciousness in *TE* 48–49 [31–32], where we act in a world of objects, which have values and qualities, without any reflection on the *moi* that is acting.

27. *BN* 36; *EN* 71/74.

28. *BN* 83; *EN* 119/126.

Third, Sartre does not think that everything human beings do is within their control. He would accept that many "actions" that human beings "do" are involuntary (we hiccup, sleepwalk, blush), many are instinctive (we eat when we are hungry, we smash things in anger, we run from danger), many unfold almost unconsciously (we drive with astounding skill while on a kind of mental autopilot, we sing a song without paying it much attention), and many have unforeseen consequences. He notes, for example, that "the careless smoker who has through negligence caused the explosion of a powder magazine has not *acted*."[29] Sartre simply says that sometimes we are conscious that an action is ours, conscious that there are alternative courses of action. The fact that we can take a view on certain actions, that we can deliberate and decide between alternative possibilities, shows that in these cases we are free to determine the course of our action. Only a deliberated act such as this can be an *acte humain,* a "human act."[30]

Fourth, Sartre's argument is not undermined by someone insisting that this experience of detachment and freedom is just an illusion: "You think you are free, but really everything is determined, and even your belief in freedom is psychologically determined." Sartre's method is phenomenological. He starts with human experience and tries to clarify what is found within that experience. In this case, we do not experience a psychological belief that "we are detached and free," some stubborn conviction that would form the basis of our philosophy. Rather, we experience the detachment itself. It is not a conclusion or an implication. Anguish is the very experience of being unable to identify with our presumed identity, of being at a distance from who we are, of having to choose without adequate grounds for choosing, of having to be free. This is the starting point of Sartre's phenomenology, the original data on which his philosophy is built. It does not reveal a prejudice in favor of freedom. On the contrary, to insist that *all* human actions are determined would be to impose a prejudice on the data of experience and contradict it. This prejudice would be a form of bad faith.

Consciousness and Intentionality

Our experience of anguish and of freedom in certain situations comes about because of the nature of human experience as such. Sartre empha-

29. *BN* 433; *EN* 477/508.
30. *BN* 35; *EN* 70/72.

sizes that we experience everything as conscious beings. We are conscious of what we experience and aware of this very consciousness. We are present to ourselves, and consequently distant from ourselves, and the ambiguity we experience with respect to a given identity refers to a more fundamental ambiguity at the heart of our being. Anguish and freedom, therefore, lead us to a discussion of human consciousness.

In his understanding of human beings, Sartre's debt to Husserl is enormous.[31] Before discovering Husserl he felt that French philosophy at the time offered him two options: idealism, which placed the subject outside the natural world, and reduced that world to appearances or meanings; and realism, which reduced the human subject to the status of one natural object among others, and assumed the world was objectively determinate and intelligible even outside the context of human action and enquiry.[32] His preoccupations, as he said in a later interview, were about "how to give man both his autonomy and his reality among real objects, avoiding idealism without lapsing into a mechanistic determinism."[33] Husserl gave him a third way that would acknowledge both the radical interdependence of subject and world and the distance between them. Husserl's phenomenology allowed him to start with the basic phenomena of human experience.

Sartre explains in the introduction to *Being and Nothingness* that at the heart of all human experience there is some form of *conscience* ("consciousness"). Consciousness is always intentional, which means that it is consciousness *of* something; it always posits a transcendent object (one that is "outside" itself); it has no content (nothing "inside" it).[34]

The first procedure of a philosophy ought to be to expel things from consciousness and to re-establish its true connection with the world, to know that consciousness is a positional consciousness *of* the world. All consciousness is positional in that it transcends itself in order to reach an object, and it exhausts itself in this same positing. All that there is of *intention* in my actual consciousness is

31. For Husserl's reception in France, see Dupont, "Receptions of Phenomenology in French Philosophy and Religious Thought, 1889–1939."

32. Michael Hammond, Jane Howarth, and Russell Keat, *Understanding Phenomenology* (Oxford: Basil Blackwell, 1991), 97, give a helpful overview of the two "schools."

33. Quoted in Busch, *The Power of Consciousness and the Force of Circumstances in Sartre's Philosophy*, 3.

34. For Husserl's development of Brentano's theory of intentionality, see David Bell, *Husserl* (London and New York: Routledge, 1990), 3–28 and esp. 115.

directed toward the outside, toward the table; all my judgments or practical activities, all my present inclinations transcend themselves; they aim at the table and are absorbed in it.[35]

A first implication of intentionality is that "transcendence is the constitutive structure of consciousness; that is, that consciousness comes about *directed towards* a being distinct from itself."[36] This "ontological proof" is Sartre's rebuttal of idealism: he argues that consciousness implies and requires the apprehension of things that are not constituted solely by that very consciousness. Things are present to our consciousness and not merely represented in it. Sartre wants to go beyond Berkeley's dictum identifying the appearance of an object with its being ("*Esse est percipi,*" "To be is to be perceived") by showing that appearance to consciousness requires what is beyond consciousness.[37]

A second implication of the directedness of intentional consciousness, however, is that there is no need to suppose that consciousness is an independent substantial subject.[38] There is certainly consciousness *of* something and there is "subjectivity itself"—but no subject.[39] Subjectivity does not require the substantial being of any subject, it requires the not-being of the subject, the recognition that what is known is other than oneself. As Thomas Busch puts it: "All attempts to objectify this self create a realm of discourse which does not contain subjectivity. The epistemological starting point of Sartre's existential philosophy is the irreducible subject/object relationship."[40]

In the immediacy of experience, the one who experiences does not intrude into that experience. Hazel Barnes, adapting a phrase used by William James, suggests that for Sartre "consciousness is not an entity but a process of attention."[41] We are left simply with consciousness, which Sar-

35. *BN* xxvii–xxviii; *EN* 18/18.

36. *BN* xxxvii; *EN* 28/28.

37. Cited at *BN* xxvi; *EN* 16/16. See *BN* xxvi–xxxii; *EN* 16–23/16–23.

38. For a valuable survey of the vexing question of "the subject" in late twentieth-century thought, see Christina Howells, "Conclusion: Sartre and the Deconstruction of the Subject," in *The Cambridge Companion to Sartre,* ed. Christina Howells (Cambridge: Cambridge University Press, 1992).

39. *BN* xxxiii; *EN* 23/24.

40. Busch, *The Power of Consciousness and the Force of Circumstances in Sartre's Philosophy,* 7, commenting on *TE.*

41. Hazel E. Barnes, *An Existentialist Ethics* (New York: Alfred A. Knopf, 1967), 13.

tre calls "a nonsubstantial absolute" [*un absolu non substantial*]: "absolute" because rather than relating *to* human experience, it *is* this human experience; "nonsubstantial" because it is "total emptiness (since the entire world is outside it)."[42] If the starting point of philosophy is our conscious experience of something, then it makes no sense to speak of consciousness existing before an experience and receiving the effect subsequently "like water which one stains."[43] "Since consciousness is not *possible* before being [*avant d'être:* the temporal (not positional) sense of "before"], but since its being is the source and condition of all possibility, its existence implies its essence,"[44] that is, there is no need to postulate another kind of preconscious essence of consciousness that would be outside its present existence. Francis Jeanson nicely summarizes these two Sartrean implications about being and about subjectivity: "One can affirm only that which *is* but which the affirmant *is not.* Were there no *being* one would have nothing to affirm, and, if one were *himself* being, one would be content merely to be, without any affirmation."[45]

This conclusion about the emptiness of consciousness can seem baffling. It may help to trace the development of Sartre's thinking in his earlier work, particularly in *The Transcendence of the Ego.*[46] There are certainly significant differences between *The Transcendence of the Ego* and *Being and Nothingness.* In his earlier essay Sartre is not concerned with the reflexivity of consciousness, with human subjectivity or with personhood.[47] Yet there is a freshness and excitement about his insights into intentionality here. Sartre expresses his admiration for Husserl's phenomenological programme, which allows the intentional objects of consciousness to be studied as they are and avoids reducing questions about the world to ques-

42. *BN* xxxii; *EN* 23/23.

43. *BN* xxx; *EN* 21/21.

44. *BN* xxxi; *EN* 21/21–22.

45. Francis Jeanson, *Sartre and the Problem of Morality,* trans. Robert V. Stone (Bloomington: Indiana University Press, 1980), 157. When so many philosophies try to explain the uniqueness of human beings by *adding* vague properties onto the definition of what is it is to be human (such as "dignity" or "value" or "soul"), it is fascinating that Sartre chooses to *take away* from our nature: we are *less than* what we seem to be, and this is why we can be conscious.

46. See the excellent Translators' Introduction in Jean-Paul Sartre, *The Transcendence of the Ego: An Existentialist Theory of Consciousness,* trans. Forrest Williams and Robert Kirkpatrick (New York: Hill & Wang, 1957), 11–27.

47. For the differences, and for the development of Sartre's thinking, see Leo Fretz, "Individuality in Sartre's Philosophy," in *The Cambridge Companion to Sartre,* ed. Christina Howells (Cambridge: Cambridge University Press, 1992), esp. 67–84.

tions about the nature of thought or the thinker. Sartre believes, however, that he has a significant disagreement to make. Husserl postulates a "transcendental ego," an "I" or subject that stands behind consciousness, making it possible and unifying it. For Sartre and others this was a betrayal of intentionality. It is an unnecessary return to idealism; it renders objects and their characteristics dependent on the activity of the ego; and it calls for some third reality to mediate between ego and world.

Instead, insists Sartre, consciousness is simply the sheer activity of transcending toward objects. There are no intermediary mental entities within consciousness or between it and the world. It is, as Thomas Busch puts it, a category mistake to apply the mode of object relations and causality to a transcendental consciousness that is an act rather than an object.[48] All content is on the side of the object,[49] and even the things we know about ourselves as subjects (in general or in particular), even "the psychic and psycho-physical me [*moi psychique et psycho-psychique*]," are objects for consciousness.[50] This is why Sartre allows for a *transcendent* ego (which can be an object of our awareness) but not a *transcendental* ego (which would account for and determine the awareness itself). "The consciousness which says 'I think' is precisely not the consciousness which thinks."[51] Therefore "the transcendental field becomes impersonal; or, if you like, 'pre-personal,' *without an I* [sans Je]."[52] The unity of consciousness is given by the unity and permanence of the transcendent object, whatever it is, not by a unifying ego. A section from the conclusion of *The Transcendence of the Ego* expresses this very clearly.

48. Busch, *The Power of Consciousness and the Force of Circumstances in Sartre's Philosophy*, 9.

49. Kathleen Wider sees similarities between Sartre's and Wittgenstein's view of the self, which is a limit for the world, a formal condition for its possibility. "For Wittgenstein you can describe the world completely, give all the propositions of natural science, state all meaningful propositions, and still there is something left over—a something that is nothing and so cannot be spoken of but can be shown. What is left over is the metaphysical self." See Kathleen Wider, "A Nothing about Which Something Can Be Said: Sartre and Wittgenstein on the Self," in *Sartre Alive*, ed. Ronald Aronson and Adrian Van den Hoven (Detroit, Mich.: Wayne State University Press, 1991), 337. Wittgenstein writes: "This is the way I have travelled: Idealism singles men out from the world as unique, solipsism singles me out alone, and at last I see that I too belong with the rest of the world, and so on the one side *nothing* is left over, on the other side, as unique, *the world*. In this way idealism leads to realism if it is strictly thought out." See Ludwig Wittgenstein, *Notebooks, 1914–1916*, trans. G. E. M. Anscombe, 2nd ed. (Oxford: Basil Blackwell, 1979), 85e.

50. *TE* 36 [18].

51. *TE* 45 [28].

52. *TE* 36 [19].

The Transcendental Field, purified of all egological structure, recovers its primary transparency. In a sense, it is a *nothing,* since all physical, psycho-physical, and psychic objects, all truths, all values are outside it; since my *Me* has itself ceased to be any part of it. But this nothing is *all* since it is *consciousness of* all these objects. There is no longer an "inner life" [. . .] because there is no longer anything which is an *object* and which can at the same time partake of the intimacy of consciousness. Doubts, remorse, the so-called "mental crises of consciousness," etc.—in short, all the content of intimate diaries—become simple *representations.*[53]

Sartre's attack on the transcendental ego has elicited contradictory responses, as we have seen in the historical introduction to this present work. Some defend Husserl and say that consciousness must have at least some structures and modes of apprehension in order to shape the world of experience[54] and in order to individuate the subject who experiences this subjectivity.[55] Others argue that Sartre is actually faithful to Husserl's ideas if not to his terminology, and that he advances against Husserl what was Husserl's own position. For Husserl the transcendental "attitude" is more a reflexive awareness of our unreflective subjective experience,[56] and the consciousness that constitutes this "transcendental ego" as an object is never itself grasped, it has a kind of anonymity akin to Sartre's impersonality.[57] Herbert Spiegelberg, in his great history of phenomenology, at the same time as recording Sartre's debt to Husserl and Heidegger, judges that the most original feature of Sartre's conception of consciousness is its essential negativity.[58] It is enough for us to see its place in Sartre's own phenomenology without deciding whether he was fair to Husserl or not.

Self-Consciousness and Being-for-Itself

Together with this transparent consciousness, however, there is always some form of *self-consciousness,* and this is what concerned Sartre much

53. *TE* 93–94 [74–75].

54. Ronald Aronson, *Jean-Paul Sartre: Philosophy in the World* (London: Verso, 1980), 91–96.

55. Peter Caws, *Sartre: The Arguments of the Philosophers* (London, Boston, and Henley: Routledge & Kegan Paul, 1979), 52–60.

56. James M. Edie, "The Question of the Transcendental Ego: Sartre's Critique of Husserl," *Journal of the British Society for Phenomenology* 24 (1993).

57. James M. Edie, "The Roots of the Existentialist Theory of Freedom in 'Ideas I,'" *Husserl Studies* 1 (1984).

58. Spiegelberg, *The Phenomenological Movement,* 502–5.

more by the time he wrote *Being and Nothingness.* Although we don't need to refer to any subject when we experience things, we are nevertheless unreflectively aware of our own experiencing (which makes us self-conscious), and in addition we can be reflectively aware of a subject of the experience. These distinctions are crucial. In order to be conscious of something, there must be *consciousness of the consciousness of this thing,* otherwise there would be "a consciousness ignorant of itself, an unconscious consciousness—which is absurd."[59] In other words, in the moment of awareness, we are aware that we are aware. But this does not require an infinite regress of further consciousnesses, each one standing back from the previous conscious awareness to affirm it. Instead, there must be "an immediate, non-cognitive relation of the self to itself [*de soi à soi*]."[60] This is nonreflective (it is not the subject reflecting on his experience after the event), and nonpositional (it is not the subject making itself into the object of a new positional consciousness). It takes a kind of unformed, sideways glance at the positional consciousness and makes it possible.[61] This is a more technical account of what has already been formulated in *The Transcendence of the Ego:*

> The type of existence of consciousness is to be consciousness of itself [*conscience de soi*]. And consciousness is aware of itself *in so far as it is consciousness of a transcendent object.* All is therefore clear and lucid in consciousness: the object with its characteristic opacity is before consciousness, but consciousness is purely and simply consciousness of being consciousness of that object [*conscience d'être conscience de cet objet*]. This is the law of its existence.[62]

In *Being and Nothingness* Sartre calls this *conscience (de) soi,* "consciousness (of) self"[63]—putting the "of" in parentheses to show that this "self" is not an explicit object of knowledge, nor merely an implicit condition of consciousness, but rather the implicit consciousness that accompanies and is one with any consciousness of an object. In English one is able to use the word "self" as a prefix and say "self-consciousness" which conveniently lessens the danger of considering this "self" to be an object. It may seem that immediate self-awareness is revealed through reflection and a kind of questioning introspection. However, "it is the non-reflective consciousness

59. *BN* xxviii; *EN* 18/18.
60. *BN* xxix; *EN* 19/19.
61. *BN* xxix; *EN* 19/19.
62. *TE* 40 [23–24].
63. *BN* xxx; *EN* 20/20.

which makes the reflection possible; there is a pre-reflective *cogito* which is the condition of the Cartesian *cogito*."[64] The two are inseparable, necessarily circling round each other. "Every conscious existence exists as consciousness of existing."[65]

The immediacy of experience, therefore, exists for a witness, "although the witness for which consciousness exists is itself."[66] This is something Sartre calls *la présence à soi* ("presence to self"),[67] where the self represents "an ideal distance within the immanence of the subject in relation to itself."[68] The only alternative to this is some form of dualism. Francis Jeanson expresses the dilemma well:

> If my consciousness can grasp itself only by becoming distinct from itself, if I cannot be conscious of myself without making myself double, then there must be an irreducible duality between the "I" that I am as reflecting subject and the "me" that I also am as the unreflecting subject who acts and lives.[69]

Self-consciousness, then, accompanies consciousness. Sartre arrives at this conclusion by a process of elimination. He cannot allow that the conscious subject is simply one with its intentional object, unaware of its own awareness—this would destroy subjectivity and consciousness themselves. All versions of realism have the same effect by assuming that the subject is one object within the world of objects, and there is no way of introducing distance and difference into consciousness in a world where everything is immanent. Nor can he allow that the conscious subject is separate from its intentional object—this would isolate the subject and trap it within itself. All versions of idealism face this impossibility of bridging the gap between subject and world; they become dualistic or monistic, depending on whether they preserve the notion of world or not. So Sartre suggests a third way: there must be a difference within a unity; a distance that is empty; a self that is not itself. These are not paradoxes intended to undermine rational thinking, like the koan of a Zen master ("What is the sound of one hand clapping?")—they are attempts to describe something (consciousness) that simply cannot be described in the categories of object and identity.

64. *BN* xxix; *EN* 19/20.
65. *BN* xxx; *EN* 20/20.
66. *BN* 74; *EN* 111/117.
67. *BN* 77; *EN* 113/120.
68. *BN* 77; *EN* 113/119.
69. Jeanson, *Sartre and the Problem of Morality*, 114.

The being of consciousness as consciousness is to exist *at a distance from self* as a presence to self [à distance de soi *comme présence à soi*], and this empty distance which being carries in its being is Nothingness [*et cette distance nulle que l'être porte dans son être, c'est le Néant*].[70]

So these are the two senses in which negation exists in the heart of human beings. First, there is no subject of experience, there is just consciousness *of* something. This is open, transparent, empty. Second, even though we are conscious (of) being conscious, in an implicit way, we can never know or identify with the one who is conscious; we are immediately present to ourselves and our experience, and at the same time immediately withdrawn from them. Without reflection, our attention is directed outward, to objects, away from ourselves, with an implicit awareness of ourselves as conscious subjects; in reflection, our attention is directed to the process of attention, which thus becomes an object.

As conscious beings we are fractured, without a stable identity, distant from ourselves, and this inner negation allows us to be conscious and to act. What then remains? One could argue that in Sartre's account there is nothing left of the subject at all, there is just the world-as-experienced. We are so identified with the world that no comments or criticisms are possible. There is no human experience. *Being and Nothingness,* however, has a rich understanding of the human subject, which is constituted in the process of going beyond and reinterpreting the self to which we are present. This brings us to concept of *l'être-pour-soi,* being-for-itself.[71]

The key to Sartre's understanding is his contention that *there is an identity that is denied.*[72] This is quite different from saying that there is no human identity. We have seen how Sartre pays full attention to the numerous aspects of each human life which make up an individual identity, the extensive catalogue of answers we could give to the question "Who am I?" But he insists that no aspect of our identity can exist as ours unless we have some distance from it. Affirmation always involves taking a point of view on what is affirmed. Sartre was delighted to discover Heidegger's descrip-

70. *BN* 78; *EN* 114/120.

71. The language is Hegelian (being-for-itself, being-in-itself), but I will not go into the Hegelian background since Sartre uses these phrases for his own purposes which will become apparent from the texts I examine.

72. *BN* 178; *EN* 214/227.

tion of the human being as a "creature of distances."[73] At the same time, this "distance" must not create a separation from my identity that would turn it into someone else's. Therefore there is a negation of identity that takes place within that very identity. "An impalpable fissure has slipped into being."[74] There is never a "coincidence" between what we are and our consciousness of this.[75] "Thus in order for a *self* [*un* soi] to exist, it is necessary that the unity of this being include its own nothingness as the nihilation of what is identical [*comporte son propre néant comme néantisation de l'identique*]."[76] It shouldn't surprise us that Sartre's language is strained here: the peculiar type of reflection involved in self-consciousness cannot be described in the terms we use for things in their objectivity and self-subsistence. Just as intentionality was a way for Husserl to conceive of a quite distinct mode of being (i.e., "relation"), so Sartre needed to conceive of a distinct mode of being, not "a unity that contains a duality" but "a duality that *is* unity."[77]

No human being can exist without an identity, without a great list of experiences, characteristics, and convictions. These make up our *être-en-soi,* our "being-in-itself"—everything about us that is given.[78] At the same time, no human being can exist who is solely a given identity. Without some inner fragmentation, some presence to self, some nihilation of identity, there can be no human identity, since what makes us human is the fact that we can recognize, confirm, question, adapt, and surpass this very identity. We are *être-pour-soi,* "being-for-itself," insofar as we view and respond to the identity of our being-in-itself. Sartre highlights the dislocation implicit in any recognition of oneself.[79]

For Sartre the word *soi,* "self," is reflexive. It indicates a relation between the subject and itself, and it can be neither a "real" identity (an ob-

73. See Hayman, *Writing Against: A Biography of Sartre,* 133.

74. *BN* 77; *EN* 113/120.

75. *BN* 74; *EN* 110/116.

76. *BN* 78; *EN* 114/120.

77. *BN* 76; *EN* 112/118.

78. Strictly speaking, we never encounter pure being-in-itself, instead we meet being-in-itself in "the world" as it is understood in the light of our purposes; see chapter 3.

79. In the same period Lacan was warning of the dangers of identifying with the image we have of ourselves (because this struggle to associate with this "other" self must involve alienation). See Jacques Lacan, *Écrits: A Selection,* trans. Alan Sheridan (London: Tavistock, 1977), chapter 1, on the mirror stage. The earliest version of this essay was first given as a paper in 1936. For comments on some connections between Lacan and Sartre, see Howells, "Conclusion: Sartre and the Deconstruction of the Subject," 328–31.

jective, established, fully formed self) nor a detached, disembodied, alternative substance that takes a point of view on one's identity. The presence of the for-itself to the in-itself, to use Sartre's pregnant phrase, is "pure *denied identity* [*pure* identité niée]."[80] Another long citation summarizes these arguments:

In fact the *self* [*le* soi] cannot be apprehended as a real existent; the subject can not *be* self [*le sujet ne peut* être *soi*], for coincidence with self, as we have seen, causes the self to disappear. But neither can it *not be* self since the self is an indication of the subject itself. The self therefore represents an ideal distance within the immanence of the subject in relation to itself, a way of not being its own coincidence, of escaping identity while positing it as unity—in short, of being in a perpetually unstable equilibrium between identity as absolute cohesion without a trace of diversity and unity as a synthesis of a multiplicity. This is what we shall call *presence to self* [présence à soi]. The law of being of the *for-itself,* as the ontological foundation of consciousness, is to be itself in the form of presence to self.[81]

"Presence" here is the very thing that saves the human being from an ossified identity, and is therefore quite different from that metaphysical "presence" attacked by Derrida, a presence that he thought reduced us to being one "being" among other beings.[82] Sartre's presence to self destabilizes and decenters the subject since it places us perpetually at one remove from who we are, without creating an alternative center of stability.

One question arises: Why is Sartre's language so absolute and so negative? Is this an example of what Peter Caws has called "that peculiar taste for philosophical melodrama which has so alienated sceptical Anglo-Saxons from their excitable Continental colleagues,"[83] which incited A. J. Ayer famously to accuse Sartre of trickery and nonsense as early as 1945?[84] Would it not be possible to use more nuanced verbs to describe this distance from our identity? Instead of an identity being denied and fragmented and nihilated, why could it not be qualified or limited or put

80. *BN* 178; *EN* 214/227.

81. *BN* 76–77; *EN* 113/119.

82. See Christina Howells, *Sartre: The Necessity of Freedom* (Cambridge: Cambridge University Press, 1988), 196–98.

83. Caws, *Sartre,* 66.

84. A. J. Ayer, "Novelist-Philosophers: V. Jean-Paul Sartre," *Horizon* 12 (1945).

in context or transcended or even completed or perfected? One answer is that Sartre would indeed approve of these terms, and uses similar ones. His negation is nuanced. Sartre has a fondness for the verb *dépasser,* "to surpass": we have seen how one's identity as a reformed gambler, one's past resolution, is "*surpassed* by the very fact that I am conscious *of* it."[85] This word is the French equivalent of Hegel's *aufheben,* which carries the threefold connotation of transcending, negating, and preserving.[86] Even if Sartre gives the word connotations of his own, and avoids a Hegelian philosophy of recuperation,[87] his choice of language shows that the activity of the for-itself is not wholly negative. In a similar way Sartre writes that when we question the world and hold it at a distance we do not alter the being of the world, so this sense of negation carries with it no connotation of interference or destruction. "It is not given to human reality to annihilate, even provisionally, the mass of being which it posits before itself. What it can modify is its *relation* to this being."[88]

However, despite this positive angle, Sartre argues again and again that in order for there to be any consciousness of identity, any qualification of this identity, any response to it—the denial must be unqualified, the distance absolute. There is no such thing as a partial consciousness of ourselves. It may be hazy, we may be confused, but if something is present to consciousness, then there must be an absolute distinction and distance between the object of consciousness and the subject "who is" conscious—this is the original distinction contained in the notion of intentionality. Being-for-itself is not being-in-itself. To be conscious of something is to negate it, to deny that one is identical with it.[89] Negation is unavoidable.

Imagination and the Power of Negation

So far the discussion has been largely negative: We are *not* this identity, we are *not* this self. We are constituted by nothingness, by a negation in the heart of our being. We don't just lack external things, we lack ourselves.

85. *BN* 33; *EN* 68/70.

86. See R. D. Laing and D. G. Cooper, *Reason and Violence: A Decade of Sartre's Philosophy, 1950–1960* (London: Tavistock, 1964), 13–14.

87. Cf. the comments on Hegel and Derrida in Howells, *Sartre: The Necessity of Freedom,* 199–200.

88. *BN* 24; *EN* 59/61.

89. *BN* 123; *EN* 158/167.

Sartre's philosophy might seem to encourage a total deconstruction of the human being. Yet there is a constructive moment too, which is in fact inseparable from the negative one. This lack of identification with ourselves, this inner fragmentation, is the very thing that allows us to go beyond what we are and reach toward what we could be. It is only by recognizing what is not that we recognize what could be. We don't just deny ourselves, we surpass ourselves and make a choice about which self will be established in this movement. Negation frees us from the deterministic structures of being and makes room for freedom, possibility, imagination, creativity, and choice. It is only in prereflective self-consciousness that negation has a foundation, an origin. Any surpassing, any negation within the world must come from a being whose very nature is to surpass its own being. We can now look at how this positive aspect of freedom arises from negation.

Sartre is fascinated by negation. Mary Warnock has written that "it is impossible to exaggerate the importance which Sartre attaches to the power of denial, of negation, of asserting not only what is but what is not the case."[90] We have met a number of examples: someone cannot identify fully with his former resolution not to gamble; we cannot be sure how we will act on the cliff. As well as these instances arising from human activity, Sartre finds negation in the simplest realities such as distance, absence, change, otherness, repulsion, regret, and distraction, all of which "in their inner structure are inhabited by negation, as by a necessary condition of their existence."[91] Sartre calls them *négatités.*[92]

Negation reveals a peculiar twofold power that human beings have, which is first to conceive of what is not and then to compare what is with what is not. We do this so often we hardly notice. Sartre wonders where these negative conceptions come from. Two things strike him with great force. First, negation reveals something about the world, it lies in the heart of reality. These *négatités* are not just imposed on the world by our language or psychology, they tell us something essential about the world, and without them we could not even begin to understand and act. Second, absolutely nothing in the world as it is in itself, as *l'être-en-soi,* can account for this process of negation. In itself the world is dense with positive informa-

90. From her introduction to Jean-Paul Sartre, *The Psychology of the Imagination* (London: Routledge, 1972), xvi.

91. *BN* 21; *EN* 56/57.

92. See *BN* 21, translator's footnote 13.

tion; every sensation, every event, every encounter, reveals its own fullness. What, then, enables us to go beyond the purity and plenitude of our present experience and wonder what it is not? Sartre concludes that negation must come from ourselves: we reveal the negation that lies hidden in things. He associates the power to negate with our imagination, and he locates the source of that power in the negative structure of our consciousness.

It would be impossible to summarize Sartre's thinking about negation in a few pages—the relevant passages of *Being and Nothingness* contain some of his most complex ideas.[93] It will be enough to highlight one important observation that has already been made: human beings are able to conceive of what is not. This kind of conceiving, like so many things, is more puzzling than we usually think. It requires an ability to detach ourselves from what is and to think of something else as not existing. This is implied in the simplest act of *questioning*.[94] If we are simply caught up in a stream of positive experiences, in a constant flow of positive information telling us about the world, then how could we even ask a question? We could do no more than affirm and acknowledge.

If we question, then we are not sure of the answer.[95] Ignorance by itself is not an interesting phenomenon—it is knowledge of our ignorance that provokes Sartre. This knowledge, this doubt, presupposes that we have some kind of awareness that the world could surprise us. If we doubt, then we must have some kind of expectation that the world could turn out to be different from what we expect it to be.[96] This everyday presupposition is of huge significance since it means that we are often withdrawing from the fullness of what is given to us and relating it to what is not. "It is important therefore that the questioner have the permanent possibility of dissociating himself from the causal series which constitutes being and which can

93. Esp. *BN* part 1, 3–70; *EN* 37–106/37–111.

94. See esp. *BN* 21–25; *EN* 56–60/58–62.

95. Sartre's analysis of interrogation is similar to Heidegger's in *Sein und Zeit*, but Sartre is more concerned with the possibility of a negative answer and the implications of this for the relation of human beings to what is not. See Spiegelberg, *The Phenomenological Movement*, 505–6.

96. Sartre notes here his debt to Descartes (*BN* 25; *EN* 60/62) and acknowledges it more fully in Jean-Paul Sartre, "Cartesian Freedom," in *Literary and Philosophical Essays* (New York: Collier Books, 1962), 190, where he writes that Cartesian doubt implies the "power of escaping, disengaging oneself and withdrawing." It is "a breaking of contact with being," man's "permanent possibility of disentangling himself from the existing universe," and "the most magnificent affirmation of the reign of the human."

produce only being."[97] A negative reply tears us away from a wall of positivity that surrounds us, it is "an abrupt break in continuity which can not in any case *result* from prior affirmations."[98] Notice that Sartre's argument does not assume that the answer to a question will be without explanation. The answer may be a brute scientific fact with a perfectly comprehensible network of causes—"There is no milk in the fridge"; "It's three o'clock in the morning." What confirms our withdrawal from the causal series is the knowledge of our ignorance. The simplest question, the smallest doubt, shows that the totality of our experience is not enough and forces us to relate that experience with what is not.

> Being can generate only being and if human beings [*l'homme*] are enclosed in this process of generation, only being will come out of them. If we are to assume that human beings are able to question this process—*i.e.,* to make it the object of interrogation—they must be able to hold it up to view as a totality, i.e., to put themselves *outside of being* [en dehors de l'être].[99]

Questioning is one form of human behavior that reveals negation. Another is the power of imagination, which is a key term for Sartre.[100] In his language *une image,* an "image," is not just one type of mental perception, a "concrete and positive psychic fact,"[101] that somehow we subsequently judge to be unreal. Instead, it is of the nature of an image that it is *not* part of what we perceive, and that the object it refers to does *not* exist or is *not* here. We can see how this relates to the negation involved in questioning. To question is to allow for the possibility of a world beyond the fullness of what we experience in the present; to imagine is to conceive of something concrete that is not contained in the fullness of our present experience. The imagination is the very way that we refer to what is not.

> The image must enclose in its very structure a nihilating thesis. It constitutes itself qua image while positing its object as existing *elsewhere* or *not* existing. It carries within it a double negation; first it is the nihilation [*néantisation*] of the world (since the world is not offering the imagined object as an present object

97. *BN* 23; *EN* 58/59.

98. *BN* 11; *EN* 45–46/46.

99. *BN* 24; *EN* 59/60–61.

100. Although by the time of *BN* Sartre prefers the term "consciousness" to "imagination." Cf. *IM* 216 [358], where he writes that imagination "is the whole of consciousness as it realizes its freedom" ("c'est la conscience tout entière en tant qu'elle réalise sa liberté").

101. *BN* 26; *EN* 61/62.

of perception), secondly the nihilation of the object of the image (it is posited as not present).[102]

Sartre's explanations are very compact in *Being and Nothingness,* partly because he assumes that readers will be familiar with his earlier work on the subject in *L'Imaginaire.* In this work Sartre develops at greater length the fundamental distinction between objects as perceived and as imagined. Perception for Sartre does not just mean sensory perception; it embraces anything given within our experience, and could include feelings, fears, memories, etc., if they arise as positive facts within experience. Perception posits its objects as existing; the imagination posits its objects as absent or not existent. "This act of positing—and this is essential—is not superimposed on the image after it has been constituted. It is constitutive of the consciousness of the image."[103]

The characteristic of the intentional object of imaginative consciousness is that the object is not present and is posited as such, or that it does not exist and is posited as not existing, or that it is not posited at all.[104]

In order to see the picture as a picture *of Peter,* it is not enough just to look at the picture as it is; I have to imagine Peter as absent and allow the picture to become the means by which Peter appears to me as absent.[105]

Sartre's persistent concern is to undermine theories that suffer from the illusion of immanence.[106] In these theories our relationship with the world would be completely determined by the positive facts of what we experience, by our perceptions; our consciousness would be passive and "completely absorbed in its intuitions of the real,"[107] "engulfed in the real," "enmired in the world."[108] If everything were immanent there would be no way of accounting for the numerous ways in which we judge something to be absent, relate something to what it is not, question something about what it could be, and act for a future that does not yet exist. The imagination is this extraordinary human capacity to deal with what is not.[109]

102. *BN* 26; *EN* 61/63.
103. *IM* 12 [32].
104. *IM* 13 [34].
105. *IM* 25 [54].
106. *IM* 12 [32].
107. *IM* 208 [344].
108. *IM* 213 [353].
109. It is a philosophical concept, but Sartre's attraction to this concept undoubtedly reflected as well the instincts of his own heart as a writer. As Ronald Hayman has written: "Like Kafka, he never felt more free than when he was writing, creating an imaginary space. Paper as magic carpet; pen as wand"; see Hayman, *Writing Against: A Biography of Sartre,* 7.

Lack, Possibility, and the Projection of Values

With this understanding of negation in mind we can now return to the second theme introduced at the beginning of the chapter, that of the objective demands met in any given circumstances. It was suggested that normally when we explain an agent's actions we point to the agent's personal identity or to the objective demands met in a given situation. These demands, which Sartre calls values, seem to arise from the circumstances in which someone acts: a baby is hungry and needs feeding, a window is dirty and needs cleaning. Sartre's contention is simply put: We never discover any objective values simply by observing the world. It is the nature of any value that it is more than anything that can be discovered through objective observation. Values only exist because of our creative ability to see beyond the objective world and imagine a larger one.

Our actions are certainly motivated by our values. "A value" is taken here in the broad sense of "something worthwhile that we wish to achieve." We boil the pasta because it is not yet cooked; we teach the children because they do not yet understand. Whenever we act for a value we are acknowledging that something is not what it should be (an evaluative judgment), and this implies a prior acknowledgment that it is not what it could be (an empirical judgment). The idea that "this needs doing" presupposes the idea that "this could be *what it is not*." In other words, we cannot recognize values unless we have the ability to relate something that exists in the world with something that does not. This is the field of *le manqué* ("lack"). It seems unremarkable, until we remember that most of our thinking assumes that values exist in things as they are in themselves. A tire is flat and needs inflating; a visitor is late and needs to hurry up. This ordinary language provides a useful shorthand, but it disguises a subtle process of reasoning. We think that these adjectives (flat, late) are purely descriptive and that the situation so described necessarily calls for a certain response (inflation, speed). But in the common way they are used here, these adjectives contain both a description of fact and a judgment about the relation of this fact to what could be. On its own the tire is simply this irregular shape, and we only use the word "flat" to express its relation with another state that could be ("inflated"), a state we would like to bring about. In objective terms, the visitor will arrive at a certain time, and we only use the word "late" to express the relation between this time and the time we expected, a time that could have been.

We speak as if we are referring to objective demands and values found in the world, and we fail to notice the active role we take in constituting these values, the surreptitious move we make from fact to need. In pointing this out Sartre is not adopting an antirealist position. There is a real relation between what is and what could be, or between what is and what could have been: the tire really is flat and the visitor really is late. Sartre is merely highlighting the fact that these kinds of descriptions always require us to envisage an alternative reality and set the present situation against it. We have to compare what is happening with an alternative situation that *could* happen and then make a judgment that this alternative should happen. Our values always depend on the alternative realities we project. They are real, yet we have to create a context in which this reality can be acknowledged.

Lack cannot be found in what Sartre calls *l'être-en-soi,* in "being-in-itself." There is no lack in things as they are in themselves, as they are in their immediacy and objectivity, as they are outside the contexts given by human meanings and interpretations.[110] Sartre proposes an elegant schema:

> Lack does not belong to the nature of the in-itself, which is all positivity. It appears in the world only with the upsurge of human reality. It is only in the human world that there can be lacks. A lack presupposes a trinity: that which is missing or "the lacking" [*manquant*], that which misses what is lacking or "the existing" [*existant*], and a totality which has been broken by the lacking and which would be restored by the synthesis of "the lacking" and "the existing"—that is "the *lacked*" [*le* manqué]. The being which is released to the intuition of human reality is always *that to which some thing is lacking—i.e.,* the existing.[111]

In themselves, the things we perceive are complete ("all positivity")—they are what they are. Yet we register them as being incomplete, we compare them with an ideal—they are not what they could be. Only in this way are we led to the meaning *(le sens)* of what exists.[112] At first sight this is no more than a very general point about the human process of judgment and predication. Sartre's first examples of lack, therefore, are not especially to do with value or activity, they simply illustrate the way we understand

110. Cf. *BN* Introduction, section 6, xxxviii–xliii; *EN* 29–33/30–34. This summary account of *l'être-en-soi* will be elaborated later in chapter 3 below.

111. *BN* 86; *EN* 122/129.

112. *BN* 86; *EN* 123/130.

one thing ("the existing") in terms of its relation to what it could be ("the synthesis," "the lacked"). We understand this bright crescent in the sky as the moon because we relate it to our idea of the full moon; we can say that the Venus de Milo statue is broken only because we relate it to a complete statue of a human figure that includes both arms; we think our friend is a coward only because we have some conception of the courage we believe she could have. Judgments about value, however, also depend on the comparisons we make—comparisons that require us to go beyond the world as it is given to us, as we find it. The value we seek, the new thing desired (the "desideratum"), is indeed "an objective lack,"[113] it is not some subjective fancy imposed on a world unable to accept it; yet it is not present in the world—it is the world insofar as the world is not what it could be.

Sartre gives some examples. The emperor Constantine wants to build a new Rome in the eastern part of his empire.[114] Why? Because in the old Rome the taxes are collected badly, the city is insecure from invasions, its position as a Mediterranean capital is impractical, and its morals are corrupt. All these considerations are negative, they are value judgments about what is lacking in the city with respect to an ideal city. Not one observable fact forces Constantine to envisage this ideal, since "the most miserable situation can by itself be designated only as it is, without any reference to an ideal nothingness."[115] In itself Rome just has this position, this security, these morals—no more. It is the dreams of the emperor that help him see what is lacking in his city.

Sartre jumps from this example of a Roman emperor to that of a nineteenth-century French worker. Why does a certain worker not rise up in protest against his oppressive working conditions? One reason, Sartre says, is because his misfortunes seem natural, they seem to be an inevitable part of his condition and of his being. Suffering is not a demand that calls to him and motivates him, it just *is*. "He suffers without considering his suffering and without conferring value on it. To suffer and to *be* are one and the same for him."[116] Consciousness of suffering as intolerable does not emerge from the situation as he finds it, it only comes if he can contemplate it in relation to an ideal. This is the heart of Sartre's inversion of our commonsense view of values as things that exist plainly in the world.

113. *BN* 433; *EN* 478/508.

114. *BN* 433–34; *EN* 477–78/508–9.

115. *BN* 434; *EN* 478/509.

116. *BN* 435; *EN* 479/510.

Suffering cannot be a motivation for the worker's acts because it is only "when he has formed the project of changing the situation that it will appear intolerable to him."[117]

Once again, Sartre is not taking an antirealist position. He is not pretending that suffering does not exist until it is noticed, he is arguing that it has no practical significance, no regulative function, until it is compared with an ideal. This is true no matter how deeply held and universal the values are thought to be. Racism, infanticide, rape, genocide: a society condemns these only if it can generate ideals against which they are seen to be wanting. This does not take away the objectivity of value, it merely shows—as we shall see more clearly in chapter 3—that objectivity is itself dependent on the human projection of ideals. No factual state by itself can motivate any act whatsoever.[118] 'The motivation is understood only by the end; that is, by the non-existent."[119] It is worth citing an extended passage here:

> In so far as human beings are immersed in their historical situation, they do not even succeed in conceiving of the failures and lacks in a political organization or determined economy; this is not, as is stupidly said, because they are "accustomed to it," but because they apprehend it in its plenitude of being and because they can not even imagine that they can exist in it otherwise. For it is necessary here to reverse common opinion and on the basis of what is not to acknowledge the harshness of a situation or the sufferings which it imposes, both of which are motives for conceiving of another state of affairs in which things would be better for everybody. It is on the day that we can conceive of a different state of affairs that a new light falls on our troubles and our suffering and that we decide that these are unbearable.[120]

Normally, we take certain values for granted and they have an unquestioned urgency. The momentum of our action confirms their relevance,

117. *BN* 435; *EN* 479/510.

118. Olafson suggests that Sartre has much in common here with G. E. Moore, who used his "open question" argument against all forms of ethical naturalism. According to Moore, no matter what "natural" properties a thing or situation may have, this leaves open the question of whether it is good, whether it is valuable. He believed, however, that there are "nonnatural" properties that settle evaluative questions. Sartre pushes the open question argument further and shows that *no* property could possibly determine by itself the value of any thing or situation. See Olafson, *Principles and Persons: An Ethical Interpretation of Existentialism,* 126–27.

119. *BN* 437; *EN* 481/512. See chapter 5 for a proper discussion of *motive* and *motivation.*

120. *BN* 434–35; *EN* 478–79/509–10.

and our "acts cause values to spring up like partridges."[121] In the settled world of the bourgeois, for example, a pattern of respectable behavior reinforces both one's identity as bourgeois and the bourgeois values themselves. "Values are sown on my path as thousands of little real demands, like signs which order us to keep off the grass."[122] Then we may realize that these values have no foundation in the immediate being of the world, there is nothing necessary about them. This is another instance of anguish. We have to bring the values to light by envisaging an alternative world. "It follows that my freedom is the unique foundation of values and that *nothing*, absolutely nothing, justifies me in adopting this or that particular scale of values."[123] Lack, possibility, and value are all forms of negation that depend on the fundamental negation within consciousness. "The condition on which human reality can deny all or part of the world is that human reality carry nothingness within itself as the *nothing* which separates its present from all its past."[124]

We can return to some of the examples already given. How can the anguished cliff walker both desire to be safe in the future and fear that he could renounce this desire? Because "*I am the one which I will be, in the mode of not being it.*"[125] Why can't the reformed gambler cling onto his resolution definitively? Because "by the very fact of taking my position in existence as consciousness of being, I make myself *not to be* the past of good resolutions *which I am* [*je me fais* n'être pas *ce passé de bonnes résolutions* que je suis]."[126] Consciousness confronts its past and its future as "facing a self which it is in the mode of not-being."[127] The project of sincerity depends on an awareness within our consciousness that we are *not* who we are, that is, that we want to embrace an identity even while claiming that it already constitutes us.[128] The worker conscious of his oppression is able to take a new view on his sufferings. "This implies for consciousness the permanent possibility of effecting a rupture with its own past, of wrenching itself away from its own past so as to be able to consider it in the light of a non-being."[129] In all these ways, action implies negation, and negation depends on an inner fragmentation, a lack of identity, a nothingness, within the human being.

121. *BN* 38; *EN* 73/76.
122. *BN* 38; *EN* 73–74/76.
123. *BN* 38; *EN* 73/76.
124. *BN* 28; *EN* 63/65.
125. *BN* 32; *EN* 67/69.
126. *BN* 33; *EN* 68/71.
127. *BN* 34; *EN* 69/72.
128. *BN* 67; *EN* 102/108.
129. *BN* 436; *EN* 480/511.

We are able to hold any enterprise at a distance and question the values we have been pursuing. In that moment of reflection we realize that there is no necessity built into the world that requires us to get out of bed when the alarm rings or do what the boss orders or finish the book we are writing or even feed the starving baby. Some values may seem to have a greater immediacy or a more primal connection with our instinctive needs and biological nature (to eat, to talk, to love . . .), but all of them, if we reflect on them, can be questioned and then affirmed or denied.

Sartre is not promoting lethargy, or moral anarchy, he is merely drawing attention to the human foundation of value. We are not enslaved to the values of the world, rather we are free to release them. To deny this is to be *sérieux* ("serious"), a technical word that Sartre applies to anyone who resides "in the reassuring, materialistic substantiation of values" *(dans la substantification rassurante et chosiste des valeurs)* and pushes aside "*a priori* as impossible all enterprises in which [the person is] not engaged at the moment."[130] There will be much more to say in chapter 3 about how values are still objective, still real, but our concern here is just to appreciate the part we play in establishing values, the anguish we feel when we discover this, and the responsibility this calls us to.

The Self, Selfness, and Personhood

Human identity evolves. We have examined in this chapter the three stages of that evolution. They are distinct but intertwined. First, we recognize and accept the numerous factors that *do* make up our individual identity. This is the prereflective work of consciousness as we open ourselves to all that is and to all that we are. Second, we realize with anguish that this identity is precarious and cannot provide sufficient grounds for our forthcoming actions and for our unfolding identity. This is the result of consciousness reflecting on itself and appreciating its own insufficiency. Third, we have to determine for ourselves what our identity shall become by freely choosing to live and act for certain values. These values do not arise with any necessity from ourselves or from the world, they are chosen and projected by being-for-itself.

To put it very simply: Human beings have to move forward. We may be paralyzed momentarily by anguish and self-doubt. We may not be sure

130. *BN* 39; *EN* 74–75/77.

what to do or how to do it or why to do anything at all. But we must act, somehow, and our action as intentional must be *for* something. So as soon as we do act, we become a human being who values this end, we establish our identity as someone whose life is oriented to this goal. The identity that is reconstituted at each moment by this free adoption of values draws attention to a distinctive aspect of the human being. What is most significant is the self as projected and not as possessed; this is an identity we determine through action and not an identity that determines action. Sartre calls this *selfness* or *personhood.* We won't discover until chapter 5 exactly *why* a person's identity develops in the particular way it does, but we can finish this first chapter by looking briefly at the structure of personhood.

We have seen how everything human beings experience can be held at a distance because our very being is to exist at a distance from itself. There is a sense of bewilderment, but this traumatic fragmentation at the heart of the self is what allows us to be as human beings. We are being-for-itself as well as being-in-itself. We can always reflect on ourselves, and break the momentum that a certain activity may have generated previously. We have to keep moving forward and living for a freely chosen conception of the self, as if we had this identity. The identity for which we act is no longer a fixed foundation for our activity, it is the meaning we give to our life, freely chosen from all the possible meanings that reflection reveals to us. This identity is a future goal we are trying to achieve rather than a fixed self that we are; it is the evolving orientation of our life rather than its fixed essence. We cannot fully identify with anything in our past, and nothing in the present gives us our bearings, yet we cannot avoid setting before us an image of who we want to be. To reconstitute the self by seeking a self gives us selfness. To choose an identity and make this identity the goal of our actions makes us a person. This relationship we establish with a possible identity is what gives us personal identity. So we are much more than the passive presence-to-self of consciousness.

Sartre explains this in a short, crucial section of *Being and Nothingness* called "*Le moi et le circuit de l'ipséité.*"[131] The language of "person" has entered Sartre's vocabulary by the time of *Being and Nothingness.* In the years since *The Transcendence of the Ego* he has become interested in how we reestablish identity and not only in the denial of that identity. His purposes

131. *BN* 102–5; *EN* 139–41/147–49.

are also more constructive and less polemical.[132] There are two reflective movements that make us persons. The first we have already dealt with at great length: it is the presence to self of consciousness. In itself the ego (the "me," *le moi;* the "self," *le soi*) is not the conscious subject but an object that we are conscious of. As we have seen, nothing will constitute our identity unless we are conscious of it. Personal existence is conferred partly by this presence to ourselves, to the ego and all that we are. The second reflective movement that makes us persons Sartre calls *ipséité,*[133] for which Hazel Barnes substitutes the term "selfness." In selfness we become present not only to the identity that we *are,* but also to the identity that we *could be.* We understand ourselves in relation to a future identity that cannot be adequately derived from or determined by who we are now. Our being is to be present to what it is (through consciousness) and present-yet-absent to what we could be but are not yet (through selfness). Just as consciousness in the very structure of its being *refers to* an identity it denies, it also refers to a possible future identity.

> The for-itself is "self" *over there* [*Le pour-soi est soi* là-bas], beyond its grasp, in the far reaches of its possibilities. This free necessity of being—over there—what one is in the form of lack is what constitutes selfness [*l'ipséité*] or the second essential aspect of the person. In fact how can the person be defined if not as a free relation to oneself [*à soi*]?[134]

Sartre's study of consciousness and being-for-itself has so far been an analysis of "instantaneity," of what is contained in a single moment of consciousness. But now being-for-itself "under our observation, has been transcended toward value and possibilities," which is only possible "within a temporal surpassing."[135] This movement forward creates a "circuit of self-

132. Cf. the language about the impersonal and the prepersonal at *TE* 36 [19]. For an account of the shift in language from *TE* to *BN*, see Fretz, "Individuality in Sartre's Philosophy," esp 77–83; and Rhiannon Goldthorpe, "Sartre and the Self: Discontinuity or Continuity?" *American Catholic Philosophical Quarterly* 70, no. 4 (1996): 525–30. Sartre was influenced by his own experiences (an increasing engagement with the world brought about by the war) and by reading Gide (where a disintegration of the self is offset by its recovery through writing, creativity, and spontaneity).

133. *L'ipséité* is the translation of Heidegger's *Selbstheit,* a neologism Sartre attributes to Heidegger's French translator M. Corbin. See Thomas R. Flynn, *Sartre and Marxist Existentialism: The Test Case of Collective Responsibility* (Chicago and London: University of Chicago Press, 1984), 12 (endnote 27) and cf. *BN* 17; *EN* 52/53.

134. *BN* 103–4; *EN* 140/148.

135. *BN* 104; *EN* 141/149.

ness" *(circuit de l'ipséité)*[136] in which the world is understood in terms of our projects and our projects understood in terms of the world.[137] As well as consciousness *of* self, there is a "project toward self" that constitutes selfness.[138]

There are therefore two inseparable aspects to a human life: first, the life we possess in the present, the identity of which we are conscious; second, the life that unfolds through our activity, through the relationship between our present and our future. This second dynamic aspect initiates a "feedback" effect, since our present consciousness of our present identity (and the values we hold) partly depends on the goals we are striving toward. "My possible [*mon possible,* the future I freely choose] is reflected on my consciousness and determines it as what it is."[139] This is selfness, personhood. It is not an inner, static being that determines who we are and what we do; it is a unified, dynamic process in which our life is given meaning and purpose through a relationship with a specific and freely chosen future, and in which a future is simultaneously brought about by an action that gives orientation to our whole life. We create it and take responsibility for it, just as in Aristotle we take responsibility for our character by freely choosing to act in accordance with a certain image of virtue or vice: "[W]e become just by doing just actions."[140]

If we are conscious, then we are present to what is present. Then as persons having *selfness* we are present to what is absent—to what we decide is possible in the future—and this second presence is what defines us. We strive after a future self *(soi)* that never arrives because we always lack this identity. What is realized, however, "is a for-itself which is *designated* by the future and which is constituted in connection with this future."[141] This being-for-itself is the structuring of a whole life as it unfolds in time—a dynamic unity much greater than the static being of things in themselves.[142]

136. *BN* 102 and 198; *EN* 139/147 and 234/248.

137. *BN* 198–203; *EN* 234–40/248–54.

138. *BN* 198; *EN* 234/248.

139. *BN* 103; *EN* 140/148.

140. See Aristotle, *Nicomachean Ethics,* trans. Terence Irwin (Indianapolis, Ind.: Hackett, 1985), Bk2, 1103b1. For the relation between being-for-itself and Aristotelian "character," see Qizilbash, "Aristotle and Sartre on the Human Condition: Lack, Responsibility and the Desire to Be God," 31–32.

141. *BN* 128; *EN* 163/172.

142. This coherence of actions which comes from the future project is akin to Aristotle's notion of final cause: the end makes sense of the activity. See Phyllis Sutton Morris, "Self-

Sartre writes that we are like an ass pulling a cart and chasing a carrot that hangs from a stick attached to the cart:[143] our very movement causes the carrot (our goal) to draw us forward, which confirms the momentum created by the cart (our identity), and which makes it impossible that we shall ever reach the goal and realize this future identity.

So to return to the ideas suggested at the beginning of this chapter: We do act on the basis of an identity and an appreciation for the objective demands we meet in the world, but this identity does not exist before the activity as a determining cause, it exists as part of that dynamic reaching into the future that we are. Our activity determines our identity, our freedom determines our choice, our future determines our present. We are who we are through our verbs. As Ilham Dilman has written, our beliefs and projects belong to us only if we actively possess them:

> [A person] *holds* those beliefs, he *forms* his projects, he *makes* the promises and commitments he makes, he *maintains* his allegiances, he *dedicates* himself to their object. He is not just saddled with them.[144]

Nothing justifies the recognition of certain objective demands, the adoption of certain values,[145] yet the adoption of these values is what justifies and constitutes us as the active, unfolding being that we are. Sartre writes:

> The me with its *a priori* and historical content is the essence of the human being. [. . .] Human beings are always separated by a nothingness from their essence. [. . .] Essence is what has been. [. . .] It is the totality of characteristics which *explain* the act. But the act is always beyond that essence; it is a human act only in so far as it surpasses every explanation which we can give of it.[146]

We are temporal creatures whose being consists in crossing the gulf between present and future, in choosing to become through free acts what we are not by nature. This is Sartre's understanding of action and of being human; it is also that of Thomas Aquinas.

Creating Selves: Sartre and Foucault," *American Catholic Philosophical Quarterly* 70, no. 4 (1996): 542.

143. *BN* 202; *EN* 239/253.

144. Ilham Dilman, "Sartre and Our Identity as Individuals," in *Human Beings: Royal Institute of Philosophy Supplement: 29*, ed. David Cockburn (Cambridge: Cambridge University Press, 1991), 249.

145. *BN* 38; *EN* 73/76.

146. *BN* 35; *EN* 70/72.

Chapter 2

IDENTITY AND HUMAN INCOMPLETION IN AQUINAS

Plants, Animals, and Human Beings

Thomas Aquinas grew up in a Christian culture that took for granted the doctrine of creation. Etienne Gilson wrote that in the eyes of this culture the universe is "saturated with finality."[1] Everything is becoming something and going somewhere. In this dynamic universe, according to Aquinas, living things, such as plants and animals, have a special place. They move themselves and so are involved in a more intimate way in the progression of their own journey. The extraordinary thing about human beings is that within certain limits they can determine for themselves what their destination will be and how they will get there.

Aquinas examines these themes in a discussion about the life of God. He writes about the three types of movement that are associated with the three types of life we find around us: plant, animal, and human.[2] Plants move in accordance with

1. Etienne Gilson, *The Spirit of Mediaeval Philosophy,* trans. A. H. C. Downes (London: Sheed & Ward, 1936), 104. The full sentence reads: "Born of a final cause, the universe is necessarily saturated with finality, that is to say, we can never in any case dissociate the explanation of things from the consideration of their *raison d'être.*" This begs the questions of whether there is a single end for which things exist (see this chapter and chapter 6), and whether finality can be discovered without the knowledge that the universe is created (see the conclusion).

2. *ST* I.18:3. I am greatly simplifying this account.

their inherent nature, they grow and decay in a fixed way. Animal movements depend not just on their own nature but also on the nature of the things around them as they are apprehended through the senses. Plants, of course, are influenced by their immediate environment, but animals are more open to the world around them and influenced by things that remain apart from them. The goal of an animal, however, the direction of its movements, is still determined by its natural instincts. An animal's decision to fight or flee, for example, while it may involve highly complex mental processes, is ultimately determined by the animal's nature and the nature of its environment (the degree of danger, the possibility of escape, the needs of its offspring, etc.). Animals, as Stephen Brock writes, "only make themselves do what they are made to make themselves do."[3]

A third type of movement belongs to human beings, since we are creatures with intellect. Our life has much in common with that of plants and animals. Yet the distinctive thing about the movement of human beings is that "they move themselves to an end that they themselves propose."[4] The goals of our activity are not determined solely by our nature or by the nature of the world around us. Aquinas believes, in the terms of the previous chapter, that our actions cannot be explained solely with reference to an established identity or to the objective circumstances of our environment. Something else is involved. The direction of our life is somehow up to us. We choose our goals and in that choice we establish a meaning for our life and determine the person we will become. Human identity is not something fixed and definitive, it unfolds over time, and it constantly has to be appropriated, acknowledged, and re-created through our actions.

This whole book is an exploration of the nature of human identity, and only in chapter 6 will we look properly at Aquinas's understanding of how human beings constitute themselves through their free choices. In this present chapter we will examine two distinct aspects of the question of identity. First, Aquinas argues that human beings have a peculiar openness to the world around them because of their intellect. We can, in a certain sense, share in the being of other things. We are formed by what we understand, to the extent that our identity depends in part on what we identify

3. Stephen Brock, *Action and Conduct: Thomas Aquinas and the Theory of Action* (Edinburgh: T & T Clark, 1998), 35.

4. *ST* I.18:3c.

with. We *are* (through understanding other things) what we *are not* (by our own nature). Human identity, at any one time, is therefore a result of our willingness to go beyond ourselves and engage with what is other than ourselves through our understanding.

The second aspect of the question concerns the transformation of identity that takes place over time through our actions. In Aquinas's understanding, all things, nonliving as well as living, are in a process of development. In common with all things, we seek our own good, which is the perfection of our being. Human appetite is distinctive, however, because we determine for ourselves which goals to seek and what form our good will take. By seeking one particular good rather than another we ensure that one particular identity rather than another will emerge through our actions. We *are becoming* (as we seek our fulfillment in this goal) what we *are not* (since this goal is precisely an identity that is sought and not yet found).

There are startling similarities between the arguments of Aquinas and those of Sartre that were presented in chapter 1. I will not allude to these similarities much here—they will become clear as the argument develops. Human beings never lose their identity as human, yet this very identity consists of an ability to be transformed by our understanding of what is present and by our desire for what is future (and what is therefore absent). Aquinas, like Sartre, argues that we are what we are not (through the intellect), and that we become what we are not (through the will). Human identity is out there in other things and over there in the future.

It is worth making some preliminary notes here about "form" and "matter" since Aquinas's thinking is incomprehensible without some familiarity with these Aristotelian concepts. "Form" and "matter" are correlative terms. *Forma* ("form") is the inner principle that makes a thing to be what it is. A "thing" here, and throughout this book, is not just a physical object but anything that has its own unity. The English word is as broad and useful as its Latin equivalent, *res,* which has the following synonyms associated with it in one lexicon: thing, object, concrete being, matter, affair, event, fact, circumstance, occurrence, deed, condition.[5] So when we hear about understanding something or knowing the form of a thing we have all these possibilities in mind.

5. Roy J. Deferrari and Sister M. Inviolata Barry, *A Lexicon of St. Thomas Aquinas* (Washington, D.C.: The Catholic University of America Press, 1948), 968.

Substantial form gives a thing its fundamental constitution and shape and character—it makes it this kind of thing and not another (the form of an eagle or a tulip or a planet). Accidental forms modify or qualify a thing and give it an additional characteristic without altering its substantial form (the swiftness of an eagle or redness of a tulip or coldness of a planet). Things have different degrees of stability, yet all things must have at least some fundamental stability, some fixed form, if they are *to be* any one thing rather than being simply a random collection of other things that have no intrinsic unity and that only happen to be associated by circumstances for a certain time. Timothy McDermott writes that forms "are stable terminations or completions of processes of genesis, destinations of changes or movements, realizations tended towards or favoured."[6]

Materia ("matter") is that out of which the thing emerges, in which the form exists. It could be very loosely termed the material or parts out of which something is made. Yet this material does not exist in a pure state "before" the thing comes to be, like bricks waiting to be handled by the builder. A sealed bottle full of cream is shaken into butter: nothing enters or leaves the bottle, the same "stuff" is there, although "it" exists first as cream, then as butter.[7] An incinerator transforms wood into ash: "something" is continuous (the matter) even though two different things exist, one after the other. Scientists may identify the chemicals that underlie changes such as these, but the philosophical concept of matter allows one to refer to some element of continuity through every change even if one does not understand the specific nature of the continuity. The matter is the principle of continuity, the substratum that supports the change in structure, the "stuff" that endures as cream becomes butter and wood becomes ash. It is the subject of any change. Matter is open to being something, to being formed.

Neither matter nor form exist on their own. They are the two principles that combine to constitute every corporeal thing. In every substantial change there must be continuity of matter and change of substantial form. To say that something has a substantial form is to say that this thing is it-

6. Thomas Aquinas, *Summa Theologiae: A Concise Translation,* ed. Timothy McDermott (London: Methuen, 1989).

7. The butter example is from Anthony Kenny, who has a very helpful appendix on *Matter and Form* in Thomas Aquinas, *Summa Theologiae,* ed. Thomas Gilby, 60 vols. (London: Blackfriars/ Eyre & Spottiswoode, 1963ff), vol. 22, 124–25.

self and is not just the conglomeration of matter that went into it. Each substance, by virtue of its substantial form, has its own level of unity, stability, and structure. This form cannot be reduced to the constitutive matter nor separated from that matter—it is the concrete forming of this particular matter.

All things have a form. The form of living things is called *anima* ("the soul"),[8] which is the primary principle of life, that which makes something alive and not dead. A body can have eyes, legs, and lungs, but if it is not alive then the form of life is missing, and it does not have a soul. The human soul, as we shall see, is distinctive because of the nature of intellect and will.

There is no need to summarize here Aquinas's understanding of human nature since the four Thomistic chapters of this present study are in effect investigations into the main aspects of this question. We will reflect on the place of the human being in the natural world; on what we have in common with immaterial objects, with plants, with animals, with angels; on the distinctive features of human beings as creatures of intellect and will, whose freedom allows them to take responsibility for their lives and their goals; and on the constitutive ambiguity of a human nature that naturally seeks a perfect fulfillment that it cannot naturally find. It is worth making a final note, however, about one aspect of the human soul that does not receive a great deal of attention in this study; namely, its subsistence. Aquinas argues that the human intellectual soul, unlike the souls of plants and animals, is an incorporeal, subsistent principle,[9] which means that it is capable of continuing to exist after separating from its material body at death. There is therefore a double aspect to the human soul: it informs the human body, just as the soul of an animal does, yet it is also able to exist immaterially, as the angels do. This creates a host of philosophical problems for Aquinas—for example, about how the intellect can operate when it is not united with a body[10]—but it is the best way he can find

8. See *ST* I.75:1 and I.75:5.

9. *ST* I.75:2c.

10. See *ST* I.89:1; and the introduction by Thomas S. Hibbs to Thomas Aquinas, *On Human Nature* (Indianapolis, Ind./Cambridge: Hackett, 1999), vii–xxi. Hibbs writes: "The intellect's transcendence of the limits of its material conditions in its very act of knowing sensible substances seems simultaneously to allow for the intellect's separate existence and to undercut the possibility of its knowing anything in such a disembodied state" (xiii).

of holding onto his key insights about what it is to be a human being, and especially about the peculiarities of a material creature that has an intellectual nature. This topic is not the focus of my study, and I do not go into the complex debates about the subsistence of the human soul;[11] but it is good to bear in mind that for Aquinas the human soul by its very nature is open to a kind of existence quite distinct from that available to other corporeal creatures. We have a double kinship: with the angels as well as with the other animals.

Intellect, Knowledge, and Immateriality

The first distinctive aspect of human identity arises from our intellectual nature. In the *Summa theologiae,* Aquinas has a number of ways of expressing what happens when we come to know something. He explains that the form of the thing known is in the one who knows; the thing known is united with the soul of the one who knows; the intellect of the one who knows becomes what is known; the intellect abstracts the species of what is known.[12] His central insight, derived from Aristotle, is that knowledge is a relationship that in a particular way unites the knower with what is known.

Knowledge is not just an impression made upon us, like a poem carved on a tree trunk or a wound inflicted in a fight. It is not something with an extrinsic cause that nevertheless leaves us trapped within the isolation of our own being. This kind of "experience" Aquinas calls vegetative. Nor is knowledge just the immediate relationship animals have with the things in their experience. Their sensitive apprehension does take them outside their own being and unites them with what they apprehend so that they can relate to "every sensible body, not only the body to which the soul is united."[13] But animals, as far as we know, are unable to distinguish the apprehended thing from its embodiment in each concrete experience. Their apprehension is always clothed in their own instinctive responses to a thing, always colored by their desires and aversions. An animal apprehends *the thing as it belongs to this experience* or even *the experience of the thing* rather than *the thing itself.* Aquinas writes that an animal's senses "re-

11. I pay more attention to the soul's immateriality than to its subsistence (see the section "Intellect, Knowledge, and Immateriality" below, and elsewhere).

12. See the various references that follow.

13. *ST* I.78:1c.

ceive the form of the thing known, without matter indeed, but subject to material conditions."[14] Even though they can remember and plan ahead and instinctively make connections between means and ends, they cannot see that one thing within their experience can be more than their experience—that its form is distinct from the concrete conditions in which it is found.

Human beings, however, through intellectual knowledge, are present to things as they are in themselves, and not only as they are in this experience. This doesn't mean that things are present without the experience. We know "what is in individual matter" but "not as it is in such matter."[15] Aquinas uses the language of knowing something *absolute* ("absolutely," "as separated," "freed" from the limitations of sense experience) and *universaliter* ("universally," "in general," "not as individual"):

> Now a thing is known insofar as its form is in the knower. But the intellectual soul knows a thing in its nature absolutely: for instance, it knows a stone absolutely as a stone; and therefore the form of a stone absolutely, as to its proper formal idea [*secundum propriam rationem formalem*], is in the intellectual soul.[16]

We can relate to things, Aquinas believes, as they are for themselves and for other things in general and not only as they are for us in particular. We stand outside ourselves and affirm that the thing known does not depend on our understanding of it. In one sense it is unimportant that the knowledge is ours. Aquinas (following Aristotle) wants to show up the inadequacy of any explanations of knowing that would make knowledge a material effect produced on or within the knower. Ultimately these would define the known in terms of the one who knows and make it impossible to distinguish experience of oneself from experience of one's world. These are the problems encountered in idealism.

Intellectual knowledge, unlike the sensitive apprehension of animals, allows human beings to exist outside themselves, to be present to what they are not. We can be united with what we know while at the same time retaining the knowledge that we are *not* the thing known. Things with intellectual souls, like human beings, receive the forms of intelligible things, "so that the soul of the human being is, in a way, all things by sense and

14. *ST* I.84:2c.
15. *ST* I.85:1c.
16. *ST* I.75:5c.

intellect [*ut sic anima hominis sit omnia quodammodo secundum sensum et intellectum*]."[17] The soul, the human form, can become other things by knowing them. This means that our lives are given their distinctive shape by what we know. We are what we are not since the form our soul is given derives from what only exists outside ourselves in the world. There is a kind of austerity to Aquinas's theory of knowledge: human beings do not get in the way.

John Haldane has re-presented these Thomistic ideas in his "mind-world identity theory," and tried to draw out their relevance for contemporary debates about "realism" and "antirealism" in the analytic tradition.[18] For Haldane the two features of Aquinas's theory of cognition that have most bearing on the issue of epistemological realism are, "First, the insistence that the intellect engages directly with reality and not with some *tertium quid* intervening between them (concepts being the *means* and, apart from in reflection, not the *objects* of thought). And second, the striking claim that the forms or natures which give structure to the world, and the concepts which give 'shape' to thought, are one and the same."[19] A central epistemological idea in Aquinas, according to Haldane, is that "thought is constituted by the world" and that the intellect "is not to be regarded as a pre-existing cognitive mechanism but as a capacity to be informed by the structuring principles of the world. It is, so to say, 'not a something but not a nothing either'—in this case being a *potentiality* for the reception of form."[20]

When we come to understand something it is possible to say that nothing "happens," there is no "action," since no new form comes about. There is simply the same form of whatever exists, only now this form is a known form. The intellectual form that constitutes our knowledge is not affected by the form of the thing known, it *is* the form of the thing known. "The act of knowledge extends to things outside the knower: for we know things even that are external to us [*cognoscimus enim etiam ea quae extra nos sunt*]."[21] Timothy McDermott's interpretative translation of this last

17. *ST* I.80:1c.

18. See his "Mind-World Identity Theory and the Anti-Realist Challenge," in *Reality, Representation, and Projection*, ed. John Haldane and Crispin Wright (Oxford: Oxford University Press, 1993), 15–37.

19. Ibid., 21.

20. Ibid., 33.

21. *ST* I.84:2c.

phrase runs: "When we know a thing it remains other than us."[22] These are the same arguments and conclusions made by Sartre in his phenomenological account of intentionality. Human beings are not trapped in their own interiority, looking out at the distant world and wondering how they might make contact with it. The self *is* to exist beyond the self. We are "over there" in whatever we experience, essentially open to what we are not. We are constituted by our relationship with what is other.

The process of identification that takes place between the human being and what is known depends on the *intellectus possibilis* ("possible intellect," "receptive intellect"). Aquinas takes up Aristotle's description. The human intellect "is in potentiality with regard to things intelligible, and is at first 'like a clean tablet on which nothing is written,' as the Philosopher says in *De Anima* III."[23] He refers again to Aristotle in *ST* I.79:6 and notes that there is an identification between the possible intellect and the individual things it knows which (in a certain sense) actualizes it.[24] The possible intellect is said "to become all things, inasmuch as it receives the [intelligible] species of each thing [*fieri singula, secundum quod recipit species singulorum*]."[25] The thing understood is in the intellect by its own "likeness" *(similitudo)*.[26] This language might seem to imply that we have some kind of indirect representational knowledge. We are so used to imagining the mind as a "place" within us, and we slip into thinking that these forms are somehow within us too. The English phrase "to have something in mind" reflects this ambiguity—it can imply either a thought within or an external object of mental attention. The related phrase "to have something in sight" is more clearly Thomistic: the seeing is referred to the object as it is out there. When we say "I can't get my mind round this" we are suggesting that the thing we wish to understand is separate from the mind and the mind must somehow go out to it and embrace it. These phrases are useful because they help us to resist the idea that the form proceeds from the thing outside to the mind within. We mean instead that human beings, as intellectual, are able to exist out there in the forms of other things. Aqui-

22. Aquinas, *Summa Theologiae: A Concise Translation*, 130.

23. *ST* I.79:2c, citing Aristotle's *De Anima* 3:4, 430a1. For an English translation of the Aristotle, see J. L. Ackrill, ed., *A New Aristotle Reader* (Oxford: Clarendon Press, 1987), 196.

24. *ST* I.79:6c. Cf. Aristotle's *De Anima* 3:4, 429b5. For an English translation of the Aristotle, see Ackrill, ed., *A New Aristotle Reader*, 195.

25. *ST* I.79:6c.

26. *ST* I.85:2ad1.

nas is clear that having the form or likeness involves a formal identity between knower and known:

The thing understood is in the intellect by its own likeness [*per suam similitudinem*]; and it is in this sense that we say that the thing actually understood is the intellect in act [*intellectum in actu est intellectus in actu*], because the likeness of the thing understood is the form of the intellect [*similitude rei intellectae est forma intellectus*], just as the likeness of a sensible thing is the form of the sense in act.[27]

Intellectum in actu est intellectus in actu: the thing when it is understood *is* the understanding intellect.[28]

If the intellect is able to become other things in this way, it must have a different, nonbodily nature from the bodily things that it knows, otherwise its own bodiliness would interfere with and keep at a distance the things it wanted to know: "Whatever knows certain things cannot have any of them in its own nature; because that which is in it naturally would impede the knowledge of anything else."[29] Aquinas, like Sartre, uses the metaphor of transparency to describe the intellect. We cannot see the true colors of a liquid if the vase that holds it is not colorless and transparent, and a feverish tongue cannot distinguish tastes.[30] In other words, the intellect cannot be a body because its nature is to know other bodies. The nature of the intellect is to be an acknowledgment of other bodies by taking on their form and by not having the bodiliness that they actually are. We could say that the object of a faculty must have a different nature from the faculty itself: sounds, for example, are not heard by other sounds but by something that is affected by sounds (the hearing, the ear).[31] The immateriality of the intel-

27. *ST* I.85:2ad1.

28. There is an *active* aspect to the whole process of understanding which I do not pay much attention to in this chapter. The intellect has the power to "abstract" forms from the things it meets. Concrete experiences ("forms existing in matter"; "formae autem in materia existentes non sunt intelligibiles actu") are not actually intelligible, "we must therefore assign on the part of the intellect some power to make things actually intelligible, by abstraction of the species from material conditions" (*ST* I.79:3c). We have to light up and understand the immediate impressions *(phantasmata)* which things have made on us (*ST* I.79:4). For Aquinas's theory of abstraction and universals, see *ST* I.85.

29. *ST* I.75:2c.

30. *ST* I.75:2c.

31. There is a good discussion of this in Norman Kretzmann, "Philosophy of Mind," in *The Cambridge Companion to Aquinas,* ed. Norman Kretzmann and Eleonore Stump (Cambridge: Cambridge University Press, 1993), 132–33.

lectual soul is simply the ability of human beings to be formed by what they are not. Human life, as we have seen, is open to the presence of other things in a distinctive way, it is not limited by its own bodily form. In fact the form of its body, its very nature, is not to be a form limited by a particular material body, it is rather to be the form of what it understands. Our existence is larger than ourselves—this is why our intellect is said to be immaterial.

Herbert McCabe writes that the noncorporeal nature of understanding is meant to be obvious, it is a platitude and not an explanation of the process of understanding:

> It says "what I have in mind when I know the nature of a cow is the nature of a cow and nothing else." [To understand the nature of a cow] is to have this nature precisely *without* being a cow, and this is what is made clear by saying that one has the nature *in mind.* To have it in mind doesn't mean anything except that you have the nature without being the thing whose nature it is.[32]

If the intellect were a body, it would necessarily have a different sort of relationship with other bodies, one dependent on bodily change, which would never allow the intellect to go beyond each particular change and draw any wider conclusions through questioning and abstraction. Timothy Suttor writes that for Aquinas "thinking is *being* things," and Aquinas's proof of the nonbodiliness of human intelligence is intelligible "only in the light of this principle: to be able-to-be all bodies, a thing must not-actually-be any body."[33] The intellectual soul that becomes other forms must itself be "an absolute form, and not something composed of matter and form."[34]

The immateriality of the intellect and of the forms that are known should not be thought of as some sort of dualism that would take us away from the material world of human beings and the things they know. It is the individual, concrete, material things that are known through their forms. The nonbodiliness of the intellect allows us to look through or better still into the objects and situations we sense so that we can know what they are and not just what they are doing to us at this very moment. When we go beyond the instinctive delight we take in an object's shape and color

32. Herbert McCabe, "The Immortality of the Soul," in *Aquinas: A Collection of Critical Essays,* ed. Anthony Kenny (London and South Bend, Ind.: University of Notre Dame Press, 1976), 304.

33. Aquinas, *Summa Theologiae,* vol. 11, footnote b, 10.

34. *ST* I.75:5c.

and understand it to be a bird or a computer or a clock, our relationship with the object is no less real. But this grasping of its form though knowledge gives us an involvement with its being that cannot come from mere sense apprehension. We have *in*-sight as well as sight, *re*-cognition as well as cognition. This deeper, second glance can have no possible source in our own bodily nature since all bodies, even those of sophisticated animals, can only react to what they encounter—they cannot think about things.

The Openness of the Human Form

The intellect, then, takes on the form of what is known. Through our intellect we identify with what is known. Could this still mean that human beings have a fundamental substantial identity and in addition they identify with other things through the formation of their intellect? In other words, it might seem that human beings could have two forms: (1) their soul (which is the substantial form of the body, which makes them living human beings), and (2) the intellectual forms (taken from things known). Aquinas repudiates this possibility and insists that "there is no other substantial form in the human being besides the intellectual soul [*nulla alia forma substantialis est in homine nisi sola anima intellectiva*]."[35]

> We must assert that the intellect which is the principle of intellectual operation is the form of the human body. For that whereby primarily anything acts is the form of the thing to which the act is to be attributed: for instance, that whereby a body is primarily healed is health, and that whereby the soul knows primarily is knowledge; hence health is a form of the body, and knowledge is a form of the soul. The reason is because nothing acts except so far as it is in act; wherefore a thing acts by that whereby it is in act. Now it is clear that the first thing by which the body lives is the soul. And as life appears through various operations in different degrees of living things, that whereby we primarily perform each of all these vital actions is the soul. For the soul is the primary principle of our nourishment, sensation, and local movement; and likewise of our understanding. Therefore this principle by which we primarily understand, whether it be called the intellect or the intellectual soul, is the form of the body. This is the demonstration used by Aristotle in *De Anima* II.[36]

35. *ST* I.76:4c.

36. *ST* I.76:1c. Referring to Aristotle's *De Anima* 2:2, 414a4–19. For an English version, see Ackrill, ed., *A New Aristotle Reader,* 169.

This argument depends on an understanding of "form" as the principle that gives shape to an activity. The distinctive activity of the human soul is to know, and so knowledge is that which forms the soul. The distinctive activity of the whole human being is to live with understanding, and so this "knowing aliveness" (the intellectual soul) is the very thing that forms the human body. The intellectual soul, itself formed by what it knows, is what forms the human body. Who we are and how we act depends on what we know. Our lives are animated by our understanding and our whole bodily life and activity is shaped by our identification with the world through knowledge.

If we keep in mind Aquinas's conception of *form,* we will appreciate the radical nature of his thinking on this subject. The form of a thing is the inner principle that makes this thing to be what it is and gives it a particular constitution and shape and character. So Aquinas is saying that the inner principle of each human life, which constitutes it and gives it shape and character, comes from the nature of what we understand and not simply from our bodily nature. *Understanding* is used in its broadest sense here to encompass the multifarious ways that human beings conceive of things and make sense of them—it is not limited to the "head" knowledge of the logician or the scientist. Our individual identity, who we are, thus depends in part on what we understand (and the way we understand) and not just on our genes or our physiology or our instinctive temperament or any other factor that makes up the form of our animal nature.[37] When we

37. It could be objected that Aquinas's conception of *personhood* suggests a much more static understanding of individual human identity. There is no space here to explore properly his definitions of the word "person." See, e.g., *ST* I.29; *Commentum in quatuor libros Sententiarum Magistri Petri Lombardi,* in *Sancti Thomae Aquinatis Doctoris angelici ordinis predicatorum Opera omnia ad fidem optimarum editionum accurate recognita,* vols. 6–7 (Parma: *typis Petri Fiaccadori,* 1856–1858), I.25:1:1; and *De potentia,* in *Quaestiones disputatae,* vol. 2, ed. P. Pession (Turin/Rome: Marietti, 1953), 9:2. At this stage it is enough to point out that his use of Boethius's definition (*persona est rationalis naturae individua substantia;* "a person is an individual substance of a rational nature") does not in any way exclude the more developmental and open-ended account of individual identity presented in this discussion of the intellectual soul in *ST* I.76—indeed it prepares the way for it. In *ST* I.29:1c, for example, Aquinas argues that the point of putting the word "rational" into the definition of "person" is that particularity and individuality are found in a more special and perfect way in rational substances, "which have dominion over their own actions; and which are not only acted upon, like other things, but which can act of themselves [*sed per se agunt*]." So human action, which will include the remarkable ability of the intellectual soul to be transformed by what it understands, is one significant aspect of subsisting individual that is the person.

describe the character of others we often acknowledge this aspect of human identity by referring to their understanding. We talk about how people see the world, what their interests are, what they think about, what they care about, and if they have no interests or thoughts or cares we are hard-pressed to say who they are at all.

This is what Aquinas means when he says that we are formed by what we understand: we are what we attend to (with our understanding), and what we attend to influences everything significant about us. It's tempting to suggest instead that the forms of knowledge are merely accidental forms, and that the core identity of the human person is constituted by the unchanging substantial form of the body which is the human soul—as if we had a "substantial identity" (perhaps one described by the definition of "person"), and an "accidental identity" (which would develop as our understanding developed). But it bears repeating that "there is no other substantial form in the human being besides the intellectual soul";[38] and that "the likeness of the thing understood is the form of the intellect [*similitude rei intellectae est forma intellectus*]."[39] So the so-called core substantial form, our constitutive identity, is actually one with our changing understanding of things; it is fluid, dynamic, open—as open as the intellect itself. This does not mean that we cease to exist as individual substances when we are not actively understanding (all sorts of clarifications are needed here); but it does mean that as our understanding is transformed so our very being is transformed—since we are constituted in part by whatever form the intellectual soul has taken on.

The whole of a human life, and not just one part of it, is dependent on what someone is concerned with, and is given direction by it, and so the human form cannot be limited by the concrete nature of each life. The distinction here is not between a solid body and some kind of detachable spirit, it is between the given totality of a human life (body, psychology, history, etc.) and the fact that this human life can be given new meaning and purpose through its presence to other things. This new meaning that arises through our understanding could not be generated if we had a fully determined bodily form. It is the comprehensive understanding we have of ourselves and of the world that gives shape to our lives and determines

38. *ST* I.76:4c.
39. *ST* I.85:2ad1.

who we are. Our life has no shape apart from that given to it by our understanding. The form of the human being is the form of the world known to us. One could say that the human being *is* the world as understood. We are what we understand, and our body is therefore out there in what we know.

Further weight is given to this conclusion through Aquinas's contention that the intellect cannot know itself as an object of its own knowledge but only through its activity. It does not, in itself, have its own form (which might have given it a certain identity and allowed it to become an object of knowledge). Its only form is that taken from the things it knows. Considered in its essence "the human mind is potentially understanding" and does not have the power "to be understood" outside its activity of knowing.[40] Its essence is to have the ability to be other things through *their* form. To put it in more Sartrean language, the essence of the human intellectual soul is not to be or to be what it is not; it is not to have its own form but to have the forms of other things:

> But as in this life our intellect has material and sensible things for its proper natural object, as stated above [cf. *ST* I.84:7], so it follows that our intellect understands itself insofar as it is made actual by the species abstracted from sensible things, through the light of the active intellect, which not only actuates the intelligible things themselves, but also, by their instrumentality, actuates the possible intellect. Therefore our intellect knows itself not by its essence, but by its act. This happens in two ways: In the first place, singularly, as when Socrates or Plato perceives that he has an intellectual soul because he perceives that he understands. In the second place, universally, as when we consider the nature of the human mind [*naturam humanae mentis*] from knowledge of the intellectual act.[41]

This first type of self-consciousness or self-awareness is implicit in every act of understanding. It is not knowledge of a form (like all other knowledge). It is knowledge of an act (of knowing) and of a relationship (between knower and known). It is knowledge of an essence (the intellect) that does not have any identity except the identity it takes from other things. For this first type of self-consciousness "the mere presence of the mind suffices, which is the principle of action whereby the mind perceives

40. *ST* I.87:1c.
41. *ST* I.87:1c.

itself [*sufficit ipsa mentis praesentia, quae est principium actus ex quo mens percipit seipsam*], and hence it is said to know itself by its own presence."[42] The mind is knowing its own knowing, and so is in some way at the same time within that knowing as a participant and detached from that knowing as an observer—it is present to itself. This has an effect on the knowledge we have of things. If we are not only present to things but also present to our presence to things we are therefore conscious of the relationship between things and ourselves. This is why unlike that of animals, our knowledge has the kind of objectivity described above. We can take account of our place in the knowledge and factor it out and thereby acknowledge the reality of things as they are apart from their relation to us. Our intellectual presence to things as they are (and not only as they are for us) and our self-consciousness are one and the same thing. The "self" we are conscious of is not another "thing" (with a form) but a "nothing," a lack of form, a "not being" the form of what is known.

From this we can conclude that no amount of mental introspection will reveal our core identity. The only identity we have is actively constituted through that relationship we have with the world around us through understanding. The human form is therefore changing and is itself determined by the active knowing of each person. There is, as Sartre would say, no transcendental ego. We cannot *find* ourselves, we have to *make* ourselves by knowing other things. David Burrell, commenting on a different aspect of Aquinas's thought, comes to the same conclusion:

> I have remarked how Aquinas' analysis of action appears truncated. For it seems that the development of *habitus* as a proximate principle of activity demands one more step: to articulate what it is who acts. Such a step would carry us to the "transcendental ego." But Aquinas neatly avoids that problem by recognizing there is no step at all. The one who acts, as Aquinas views the matter, is articulated in the remote and proximate principles of action. Nothing more need be said because nothing more can be said: the self we know is known by those characteristics which mark it.[43]

42. *ST* I.87:1c.

43. David B. Burrell, *Aquinas: God and Action* (South Bend, Ind.: University of Notre Dame Press, 1979), 129. See Romanus Cessario, *Moral Virtues and Theological Ethics* (South Bend, Ind.: University of Notre Dame Press, 1991), 35–40, on how the personal development of *habitus* (character) transforms the very constitution of oneself.

In these two sections we have been examining a distinctive aspect of human identity that arises from our nature as intellectual creatures. We are formed by what we understand and we share in the being of other things. Our own identity depends on what we choose to identify with. We can now look at the human appetite, which allows us to reconstitute our identity over time in a more dynamic way. As willing creatures we pursue a particular good and through our actions determine which goal we shall seek and what form our good will take.

Being, Goodness, and Perfection

Aquinas approaches "the good," *bonum,* from two directions. First, the good is *something desired* in order to perfect whatever desires it. Second, the good is *a being insofar as it has been perfected.* The two approaches are brought together in this way: the good is *the perfection sought by a being through the attainment of what is desired.*[44]

Aquinas emphasizes the first approach to the good in *De veritate* 21:1. He asks whether the good "adds something" to being, which is a way of asking about the use and meaning of the term *bonum.* He quotes with approval Aristotle's preliminary definition of the good: "bonum est quod omnia appetunt" ("the good is that which all things desire [*or* seek *or* aim at]").[45] He goes on to say that the good adds something to being *secundum rationem tantum,* which means "in concept only" or "only according to reason" or "purely as an idea."

44. Aquinas often writes about one's goals, one's ends, the goods one desires, the values one seeks, the perfection one longs for. It sounds as if, in his philosophical system, human beings are inherently selfish, capable only of seeking their own fulfillment at the expense of that of everyone else. Yet it needs to be said very clearly that for Aquinas (and indeed for Sartre) "the good that we desire," "the fulfillment that we seek," *lies wherever we put it.* So we can find our good and fulfillment, for example, in the well-being of a spouse or a stranger or a community as much as we can in the pleasures of our own body or in the success of our own work. We can choose to make their good into our own end. Indeed we can find our good in absolutely anything that we choose. The good is simply what we seek, what we care about—even if it is not caring about "ourselves." The fact that we can seek things in a way that means something to us personally ("my good," "my perfection") is the very thing that ensures that our other-directed actions ("for you," "for them") are still our own actions. This is why love can be disinterested and personal at the same time. There is no contradiction in loving the other for one's own sake or in seeking the good of the other because it will make one happy. This meaning of "one's good" should be borne in mind throughout the book.

45. *DV* 21:1c, citing *Nichomachean Ethics,* 1:1, 1094a3. For an English version, see Aristotle, *Nicomachean Ethics,* trans. Terence Irwin (Indianapolis, Ind.: Hackett, 1985), 1.

The good is therefore not a constitutive and defining characteristic of a thing (it does not add to being "as limiting and determining it").[46] A horse is still a horse even if it is not a good horse. Nor is the good an additional characteristic that something might possess for a time and then lose (it is not "some reality which is outside the essence of the thing to which it is said to be added").[47] A horse is a horse whether it is awake or asleep, hot or cold, fat or thin. Instead, the concept that good adds to being is one of a certain kind of relation *(aliqua relatio)*. In this type of relation a first thing relates to a second thing even though the first thing is not affected by the relationship; one thing influences another thing without being influenced *by* that other thing in return.[48] Aquinas gives the example of human understanding. When we know the truth about something we have a certain relationship with it. In this case the thing known is not changed when it becomes known, even though the mind of the knower is changed through this relation with what is known. He then goes on to write about the good:

> Inasmuch as one being by reason of its being is such as to perfect and complete another, it functions as an end to that which is perfected by it [*habet rationem finis respectu illius quod ab eo perficitur*]. And hence it is that all who rightly define good put in its concept [*in ratione eius*] something about its status as an end.[49]

It is clear how wide ranging this use of "good" is. If the language of desire *(appetitus)* is never far away, one should remember that desire is an analogical term that applies to *all* relationships that involve attraction and perfection—from bodies falling and finding their "preferred" place of rest to spiritual beings willing and discovering their happiness.[50]

To say that something is good, therefore, is to point to a particular type of relationship it can have with something else. The house is good for those who live in it; the fire is good for those who are warmed by it; the music is good to those who listen to it. These things are good insofar as they

46. *DV* 21:1c.

47. *DV* 21:1c.

48. *DV* 21:1c, when "something is said to be referred which is not dependent upon that to which it is referred, but vice versa."

49. *DV* 21:1c.

50. Cf. David M. Gallagher, "Aquinas on Goodness and Moral Goodness," in *Thomas Aquinas and His Legacy*, ed. David M. Gallagher, Studies in Philosophy and the History of Philosophy (Washington, D.C.: The Catholic University of America Press, 1994), 38–40.

attract and perfect other things. Of course their goodness is inseparable from what they are in themselves. They are desired because they are desirable, and their desirability is absolutely dependent on their being. Yet if we know that something is good we know more than simply what it is. The good is coextensive with being but not synonymous with it.[51] "The essence of a thing considered absolutely suffices for the thing to be called a being [*ens*] on its account, but not thereby to be called good."[52] The good adds nothing to being except the concept of being an end. This *conceptual* addition, however, is no less real than the essence of what something is, since "to that concept something does correspond in reality [*isti rationi aliquid respondet in re*], that is, a real dependence of that which is directed to the end upon the end itself [*realis dependentia eius quod est ad finem ad finem ipsum*]."[53]

Aquinas takes the second approach to good (as the perfection of being) in *ST* I.5. *Perfectio,* "perfection," has many senses ("accomplishment," "finish," "attribute," "endowment," "excellence," etc.)—all of which imply some sort of completion. It may be the completion of a process or of the acquisition of a property or of the total fulfillment of all the possibilities of a given substance. Aquinas once again starts with Aristotle's definition of the good as that which all desire, but instead of discussing the desire one thing has for another, he begins with the desire each being has for its own perfection:

> The Philosopher says (Ethics 1): "Goodness is what all things desire [*bonum est quod omnia appetunt*]." Now it is clear that a thing is desirable [*appetibile*] only in so far as it is perfect; for all things desire their own perfection. But everything is perfect so far as it is actual. Therefore it is clear that a thing is good so far as it exists [*est ens*]; for it is existence [*esse*] that makes all things actual, as is clear from the foregoing [cf. *ST* I.3:4 and I.4:1]. Hence it is clear that what is good and what has being are one and the same thing. But calling it good expresses the aspect of desirableness, which saying it has being does not express [*Unde manifestum est quod bonum et ens sunt idem secundum rem, sed bonum dicit rationem appetibilis, quam non dicit ens*].[54]

51. See ibid., 40–42.

52. *DV* 21:1ad1.

53. *DV* 21:1ad9.

54. *ST* I.5:1c. Citing Aristotle's *Nichomachean Ethics* 1:1, 1094a3. For an English version, see Aristotle, *Nicomachean Ethics,* 1.

The good, therefore, is the completion or perfection sought by each thing, the existence that each thing seeks to achieve. But if the good and being are the same in things themselves *(secundum rem),* this raises a number of questions. How can something that already has being seek a being for itself that it does not have? Does this mean that it seeks to become what it is not, which suggests that it seeks its own annihilation?

These questions are answered implicitly in the reply to the first objection: "By its substantial being, everything is said to have being simply; but by any further actuality it is said to have being in a certain respect [*dicitur aliquid esse secundum quid*]."[55] The substantial being is what makes one thing *this* thing and not another, it allows us to identify it and distinguish it from whatever existed before it and from whatever exists around it: the child, the tree. The relative being, the "further actuality" *(actus superadditos),* is any further kind of existence that this substantial being can have: the child as kind, the tree as tall.[56] Relative being perfects substantial being, it makes something actual in this substantial being that did not exist before. This perfection is the extra or additional being desired by the substantial being. It is coextensive with the good of the substantial being.

Hence that which has ultimate perfection is said to be simply good; but that which has not the ultimate perfection it ought to have (although, in so far as it is at all actual, it has some perfection), is not said to be perfect simply nor good simply, but only in a certain respect [*non tamen dicitur perfectum simpliciter, nec bonum simpliciter, sed secundum quid*].[57]

So the choice is not between "being and not being," but between "being and more being." There is, however, one hugely important point to note. The perfection achieved, the additional being, is not like an external possession that leaves the substantial being indifferent and unaffected. The perfections do not stand to the substance as a hat on someone's head or a magnet on a fridge door. It is the substantial being itself that is perfected: *the child* is kind, and does not exist at this moment except as kind; *the tree* is tall, and tallness is not something added to an otherwise small tree, it simply *is* the present existence of this tree. At any moment there is only

55. *ST* I.5:1ad1.

56. Cf. *DV* 21:2ad6, "A thing can be called good both from its being and from some added property or state."

57. *ST* I.5:1ad1.

one actual being, which is this substantial thing perfected in these ways and existing in these forms.

We should at all costs avoid thinking that there is a core substantial being that remains unaffected by superficial changes. Aquinas wants to show how something can change and become *more* what it "is," without ceasing to be what it was all along, without losing its identity. There are always two ways of looking at anything: in terms of its unchanging identity (its substantial being), and in terms of what it could become (its perfection). This allows Aquinas to say something quite startling:

> In this way, therefore, viewed in its primal (i.e., substantial) being [*primum esse, quod est substantiale*], a thing is said to be simply and to be good in a certain respect (i.e., in so far as it has being), but viewed in its complete actuality [*ultimum actum*], a thing is said to be in a certain respect and to be good simply [*dicitur aliquid ens secundum quid, et bonum simpliciter*].[58]

In other words, in the light of what it could yet be ("its complete actuality," its unqualified goodness), a thing exists only *secundum quid,* in a certain sense: "a thing is said to be in a certain sense." So in relation to the good, each thing lacks being, it lacks itself as perfected. Someone could ask: Why say "lacks itself" instead of just saying "lacks perfection"? One could answer: Because what is lacked is the whole substantial being as perfected and not just the additional perfections themselves. The child doesn't just want to possess "kindness," the child wants *to be* a kind child, which it is not; the tree doesn't just strive to possess "tallness," it strives *to be* a tall tree, which it is not yet. Something becomes good through perfections in the accidental order, yet these accidents are not themselves good, rather they make the thing itself to be good. The imperfect wants to be more perfect. To seek one's good is, in one specific sense only, to seek to be what one is not.[59] As Aquinas will say later in Part I-II, "It happens with some things, that they have being in some respect, and yet they are lacking in the fullness of being due to them."[60] For this reason, even before considering

58. *ST* I.5:1ad1.

59. In *DV* 21:5 Aquinas uses the language of *generation,* which he defines as a "motion toward being." To receive substantial being is to be generated without qualification *(simpliciter);* to receive accidental being, that is, to be perfected, is to be generated in a certain sense *(secundum quid).* If something seeks its own good, it is seeking its own being, and this shows that in a certain respect it lacks its own being.

60. *ST* I-II.18:1c.

the special nature of the human appetite, we can see how at any given moment the identity of anything at all is unstable and open to development. The very being of anything can be changed and can be perfected or diminished, so nothing has a fixed and invulnerable identity—despite the continuation of its substantial form.

So there are two approaches to the good: it is *something desired by another* in order to perfect whatever desires it; and it is *a being in so far as it has been perfected.* The two approaches are brought together in this way: the good is *the perfection sought by a being through the attainment of what is desired.* The end which is sought through another being is always the perfection of the being which does the seeking. The "external" good always refers to the "internal" good of the one seeking. The root of all desire is not solely a desire for something else but a desire for the perfection of the seeker's being—to attain this perfection if it is not yet attained and to love or "enjoy" what is already possessed.[61]

The Will as Rational Appetite

We are now in a position to understand Aquinas's descriptions of appetite. The outlines of his thinking are presented in *ST* I.80:1.

> Some inclination follows every form: for example, fire, by its form, is inclined to rise, and to generate its like. Now, the form is found to have a superior existence in those things which have knowledge [*cognitionem*] than in those which lack knowledge. In anything lacking in knowledge we find only the form which determines that thing to its own one existence, namely its natural form. Therefore this natural form is followed by a natural inclination, which is called the natural appetite. But in those things which have knowledge, each one is determined to its own natural being by its natural form, in such a manner that it is nevertheless receptive of the species of other things: for example, sense receives the species of all things sensible, and the intellect of all things intelligible, so that the soul of the human being is, in a way, all things by sense and intellect; and thereby, those things that have knowledge, in a way, approach to a likeness to God, "in whom all things pre-exist," as Dionysius says.

61. Cf. *DV* 21:2c, "For whatever does not yet participate in the act of being tends toward it by a certain natural appetite. [. . .] But everything which already has being naturally loves its being and with all its strength preserves it."

Therefore, as forms exist in those things that have knowledge in a higher manner and above the manner of natural forms, so must there be in them an inclination surpassing the natural inclination, which is called the natural appetite. And this superior inclination belongs to the appetitive power of the soul, through which the animal is able to desire what it apprehends, and not only that to which it is inclined by its natural form. And so it is necessary to assign an appetitive power to the soul.[62]

It is thus a principle of Aquinas's philosophy that inclination is dependent on form: fire, for example, rises and burns. In things that lack "awareness" (*cognitio* is wider than intellectual knowledge) the significant factor is its natural form. This form leads to a fully determined inclination or appetite which will be fulfilled if there is no external impediment. This inclination constitutes a thing's natural appetite. Weeds grow, stones sink, footballs bounce. The kind of action and the kind of perfection depends on the kind of being something is, on its form.

Things with awareness, like animals, also receive the forms of other things,[63] so their inclinations are determined by two types of form: by what they are and what they apprehend, by their nature and their environment. Animals, of course, are reacting not just to what they apprehend through the senses as it is apprehended, they are reacting to what it means to them and how it relates to their own good. Their *potentia aestimativa* ("estimative" power) allows them to form intentions and see something as good or bad for their purposes. A sheep flees a wolf because it is dangerous (and not because its physical appearance is repulsive); a bird collects twigs because they are useful for nest building (and not because it takes pleasure in the sensation of carrying twigs). The "estimation" of danger and usefulness require more than mere sense perception. Here Aquinas allows to animals something that Sartre reserves for human beings, namely, the power to go beyond the positive information provided through sense about something's being in order to apprehend its usefulness. All these inclinations, which arise through the operation and interpretation of sense, constitute an animal's sensitive appetite.

Human beings, like all other animals, have a sensitive appetite. We are naturally inclined to react in a certain way to what we apprehend through

62. *ST* I.80:1c, citing Dionysius's *De divinis nominibus* 5.
63. *Species* is synonymous with *forma*.

our senses. This sensitive appetite has two aspects: we are concupiscent (we are attracted to what is good for us and repelled by what is harmful), and we are irascible (we resist those things that get in the way of our good or produce harm).[64] Love, hate, and aggression are perfectly natural passions, and like most animals we quarrel about things like food and sex.[65] Animals form these intentions "only by some natural instinct," while human beings gain them through the "particular reason" which makes a "comparison of individual intentions."[66]

Given that we have so much in common with other animals, a question remains: Is our inclination to a particular good determined solely by our natural form and by our environment as it is apprehended through the senses? Are we no different from other animals? Aquinas's answer is clear. Although the sensitive appetite (moved through the estimative power) determines the actions of animals, the extraordinary thing about the human sensitive appetite (moved through the particular reason) is that it is itself determined by other powers. Human beings are not controlled by the sensitive appetite, rather they control the sensitive appetite. First, the particular reason is "guided and moved according to universal reason" that draws "particular conclusions from universal principles." "Anyone can experience this in himself: for by applying certain universal considerations, anger or fear or the like may be calmed down or stirred up."[67] Second, the sensitive appetite does not move the human being unless it is commanded by a higher appetite, a rational appetite, namely, the will:

> For in other animals movement follows at once the concupiscible and irascible appetites: for instance, the sheep, fearing the wolf, flees at once [*statim fugit*], because it has no superior appetite which goes against it. On the contrary, human beings are not moved at once [*homo non statim movetur*], according to the irascible and concupiscible appetites, but they await the command of the will, which is the superior appetite.[68]

Our instinctive desires and fears, just like those of animals, are real (they belong to us) and immediate (we do not argue *to* them from abstract principles). Yet unlike other animals, we have a particular kind of dis-

64. These technical terms do not have the negative connotations of lust and irritability that they have today.

65. *ST* I.81:2c.

66. *ST* I.78:4c.

67. *ST* I.81:3c.

68. *ST* I.81:3c.

tance or detachment from them. They do not move us *statim,* "at once," "immediately"—instead there needs to be a process of mediation to make them effective. There is a gap between apprehension and action, between having a desire and being directed by that desire. This does not separate us from our immediate sensitive appetite—it still always belongs to us. But given a certain desire or fear or sense of anger we can do two things before we act: (1) we can think more deeply about what is really the case and (2) we can ponder more deeply what we really want. In both these ways we are able to put the immediate situation and our immediate reactions into a larger context. This context is discovered by our reason (whose job is to make a larger sense of what we already know from principles we already have), and this context is evaluated by our will (whose job is to seek our most complete good in the light of the possibilities this large context offers). It is the passivity of the sensitive appetite that marks it out—it is moved by whatever is apprehended. The rational appetite, in contrast, works out whether a particular thing apprehended leads to a more universal good.[69] Quite often one particular thing may lead to many more universal goods, and many different particular things may lead to the same more universal good. This is why, as we shall see, human beings are free to determine what they seek.

In this account human beings are not completely caught up within the momentum of their own seeking. It may seem a small thing for Aquinas to state that we question our desires and fears. But this means that within certain limits we question and therefore decide upon what our goals are and what our own good is to be. Rational creatures, as Aquinas wrote in the passage cited at the beginning of this chapter, "move themselves to an end that they themselves propose."[70] As far as we know, this doesn't happen with other animals. However sophisticated they are (and our appreciation of their sophistication has increased enormously since Aquinas's time), their agency is limited. Even when they execute their own actions and form them and seem to weigh up alternative paths they are still, in the words of Stephen Brock, "adjusting a predetermined inclination (desire) according to the perceived circumstances, in virtue of an equally predetermined regulative principle ('instinct')." He continues:

69. *ST* I.80:2c, I.80:2ad2, and I.82:5c.
70. *ST* I.18:3c.

What voluntary agents have, in addition to execution and formation, is the initiation or adoption of the very inclination itself, as a principle of movement, and the formulation of the rule or the criteria by which to judge among the things to be ordered to the object of inclination.[71]

The actual process of comparing one thing with another is the work of reason. In answer to a suggestion that the will, like the sensitive appetite, is necessarily moved by whatever the intellect apprehends (*ST* I.82:2obj3), Aquinas writes:

The sensitive power is not a power which compares different things with each other [*non est vis collativa diversorum*], as reason is, and it simply apprehends some one thing. Therefore, according to that one thing, it moves the sensitive appetite in a determinate way. But the reason is a comparison of several things together [*ratio est collativa plurium*], therefore from several things the intellectual appetite (that is, the will) may be moved, and not of necessity from one thing [*ex pluribus moveri potest appetitus intellectivus, scilicet voluntas, et non ex uno ex necessitate*].[72]

It may seem that an animal is "pulled in different directions" and inclined to many conflicting goods at the same time: a sheep wants to eat its supper *and* flee the wolf *and* laze around in the sun. It is true that in this case some sort of "judgment" has to be made, but in animals this judgment is made *ex naturali instinctu,* "from natural instinct."[73] The goods have a natural order and in the end one takes priority and overrides the others. In this sense the sheep does not ultimately have a doubt about which good to pursue. In the end, only one good is actually possible, and the sheep, for example, just runs. Even when a dog pauses on the shore and has to "decide" whether it is best to fetch the stick from the turbulent sea or to remain safely on the shore, this process of decision making takes place instinctively. The result has an underlying inevitably, given the individual animal and its particular circumstances, even if it is impossible for an observer or for the dog itself to predict what that decision will be. "All that share in one nature act in the same way."[74]

Human judgments are "from some act of comparison [*collatio*] in the

71. Brock, *Action and Conduct: Thomas Aquinas and the Theory of Action,* 38.
72. *ST* I.82:2ad3.
73. *ST* I.83:1c.
74. *ST* I-II.13:2ad3.

reason, therefore [a human being] acts from free judgment and can be inclined to various things. For reason in contingent matters may follow opposite courses [*Ratio enim circa contingentia habet viam ad opposita*]."[75] This topic will form the subject of chapter 6. We can say briefly here that reason allows us to hold together different goods without ordering them before there is even a scale of ordering. We have to compare them not with an external scale (which could only issue in one result) but with each other. The decision to pursue one in preference to the others *creates a scale* on the basis of which they are ordered. We could go to a restaurant or to the cinema or to the circus, each one is actually possible, each one would be reasonable. "Since the deliberating reason is disposed to opposite things, the will can go to either [*Quod ratio deliberans se habet ad opposita, voluntas in utrumque potest*]."[76]

Reason is a reflective power and rational agents can control their judgments.[77] "To judge about one's own judgment belongs only to reason, which reflects upon its own act and knows the relationships of the things about which it judges and of those by which it judges."[78] This is why "the root of all freedom lies in the reason [*totius libertatis radix est in ratione constituta*]."[79] Like other animals we discover goods and evils in the world that will affect us in different ways and we notice our own instinctive inclinations and aversions to these. Yet our actual response to each situation depends on which good we choose to seek and on how we choose to understand things. Intellect and will working together, as we shall see properly in chapter 6, allow us to determine our goals for ourselves. For this reason our unfolding identity is in part a consequence and not simply a cause of the choices we make about our goals. In other words, *we form ourselves.*

Human Beings Are Not Sheep

We have been looking at the two distinctive aspects of human identity. First, as intellectual creatures, we share in the being of other things and are formed by what we understand. Our identity is *out there* in the world.

75. *ST* I.83:1c.

76. *ST* I-II.6:2ad2.

77. For a very clear explanation of the relation between the judgment of reason and freedom, see David M. Gallagher, "Free Choice and Free Judgement in Thomas Aquinas," *Archiv für Geschichte der Philosophie* 76 (1994). See also chapter 6.

78. *DV* 24:2c.

79. *DV* 24:2c.

Second, in common with all things, our identity develops over time as we seek the perfection of our being. Furthermore, as creatures with a rational appetite, and not just a sensitive one, the course of this development is up to us, and we determine for ourselves which goal we shall seek and what form our good will take. Our identity is *over there* in the future. At this introductory stage it has been necessary to treat intellect and rational appetite separately, and this makes it hard to appreciate how closely connected their work is in the integrated life of the human being. We will go on to examine properly their interdependence as it manifests itself in the act of understanding (chapter 4) and in the act of choosing (chapter 6).

It might help to conclude this chapter by applying Aquinas's account of identity to two of Sartre's examples. Aquinas has used the example of fear to illustrate the role of both reason and will. The sheep flees the wolf as soon as it is afraid; the human being, equally frightened, nevertheless waits for the judgment of reason and the command of the will.[80] We can compare this with Sartre's reformed gambler.[81] Let's say that this man is motivated by a fear of gambling, which perhaps represents a wider fear of bankruptcy or of failure. He is, paradoxically, reassured by this fear; he depends on it and is defined by it. It keeps him safe. But then he realizes that he can put this very fear in question. The atmosphere of the casino beckons to him and he imagines himself beyond his fear in a paradise of riches and adulation. His response will be determined by whichever plans issue from his present thinking and desiring, and not simply by his initial instinctive reactions. Fear does not rule him, it is ruled (or measured or weighed) by him. His actions will depend on which measure he chooses.

Aquinas says as much in fewer words: we are not sheep. The sheep flees the wolf at once because it is afraid.[82] Aquinas's human being, call him the gambler, is different. When he is terrified by the "wolf" (the roulette wheel) Aquinas says that by applying "certain universal considerations" he may calm down or stir up his fear.[83] Perhaps he mulls over some universal considerations such as these: "Each time one goes to the table one has a real chance of winning"; "One's luck can increase as well as decrease"; "It is possible to mortgage one's house to pay one's debts." These indisputable

80. *ST* I.81:3c—see above.
81. See my chapter 1 and *BN* 32–33; *EN* 67–69/69–71.
82. *ST* I.81:3c.
83. *ST* I.81:3c.

truths allow him to resize and overcome his fear. Or he can simply direct his attention in a more focused way to the attractiveness of the goods he seeks and in this way sidestep the fear: he remembers the adrenalin rush as the wheel is spun; he thinks about the friendships he might make; he dreams of a life of risk, rebellion, and recklessness and curses his commuter-belt mediocrity. These goods might attract him more than financial security. By concentrating on them he avoids facing the fear of financial ruin.

Let us say that he decides to gamble. The goods he now seeks (excitement, friendship, rebellion) are also natural attractions caused by concupiscence: Aquinas doesn't say that when we change our goals the will pulls us away from our own natural desire. He writes elsewhere that "the man who yields to concupiscence acts counter to that which he purposed at first, but not counter to that which he wants now."[84] Yet by choosing his new goal the gambler determines for himself what his good will be and which identity will be formed. Sheep don't do all this. In Aquinas's scheme the sheep represents those who are *sincere* for Sartre: those who want to define themselves and their possibilities in terms of an unchanging nature that would determine everything they did.

Some interpretations of Aquinas emphasize the naturalness of human desires and underplay the responsibility we have to choose between them and decide our individual goals. Anthony Lisska, commenting on Aquinas's teleology, writes the following:

> An end is to be attained, not because of a subjective desire or wish on the part of the agent, but because the end itself determines the well-functioning of the human person. [. . .] Nature has "determined," as it were, the ends which lead to the well-being of the individuals of the natural kind. "To have been determined," however, means only that these particular ends are part of the development of the individual's essence.[85]

Aquinas would agree that *possible* ends are determined by nature (by concupiscence, etc.), but he would add that the choice of one end from among many is not determined by nature. Even those passages where he writes

84. *ST* I-II.6:7ad2.

85. Anthony J. Lisska, *Aquinas's Theory of Natural Law: An Analytic Reconstruction* (Oxford: Clarendon Press, 1996), 107.

about natural and universal human ends need to be read very carefully. In *De malo* 6c, for example, Aquinas distinguishes between habits and passions over which the will has some control, such as anger, and natural dispositions that are not subject to the will. If something appears good and suitable because of a natural disposition, then "the will prefers it from natural necessity [*ex necessitate naturali voluntas preeliget illud*], as all human beings naturally desire to be, to live, and to know."[86] But even these natural and universal goods do not move the will to choose them necessarily, since—as Aquinas explains just a few lines before—apart from the good of happiness, any good is capable of seeming less attractive when placed next to another good, either because the reason judges that the other good is objectively better, or simply because the person is enticed by thoughts that make the other good seem more attractive.[87]

Sartre gives a notable description of the human act: "The act is always beyond the essence; it is a human act only in so far as it surpasses every explanation which we can give of it."[88] Aquinas would support this description insofar as Sartre means that the natural explanation of the attractiveness of alternative goods (as determined by the sensitive appetite) will never be enough to explain why someone chooses one good rather than another (through the rational appetite).

Another of Sartre's examples can be read through the eyes of Aquinas. A young man whose brother has recently been killed in the German offensive is living in occupied France during the Second World War. He has to make a choice: he can stay in France in order to care for his bereaved mother or flee to England to join the Free French Forces.[89] There are thus two different ends (supporting a parent or fighting for one's country) with two different value systems (filial piety or patriotism). How does he decide? He speaks a particular language, he lives in a particular country with a particular culture, he has this character and this personal history, he has these strengths and weaknesses and aptitudes and preferences. It is tempting to say that his decision will be determined by all these factors. He is

86. *DM* 6c [470–72].

87. *DM* 6c [441–67].

88. *BN* 35; *EN* 70/72.

89. Jean-Paul Sartre, "Existentialism and Humanism," in *Jean-Paul Sartre: Basic Writings*, ed. Stephen Priest (London: Routledge, 2001), 33–34.

this person in these circumstances and therefore he will act in this way. Aquinas recognizes this appeal to an essential, natural identity and quotes Aristotle against himself in an objection to the possibility of human freedom:

Just as each one is, such does the end seem to him. But what kind of being we have is not in our power [*non est in potestate nostra aliquales esse*], for this comes to us from nature. Therefore it is natural to us to follow some particular end. Therefore it is not because of freedom [*Non ergo ex libero arbitrio*].[90]

Aquinas agrees that we naturally desire our last end, in general, but in his response to this objection he adds:

On the part of the body and its powers human beings may be such by virtue of a natural quality, inasmuch as we are of such a temperament or disposition due to any impression whatever produced by corporeal causes, which cannot affect the intellectual part, since it is not the act of a corporeal organ. And such as we are by virtue of a corporeal quality, such also does our end seem to us, because from such a disposition a human being is inclined to choose or reject something. But these inclinations are subject to the judgment of reason [*Sed istae inclinationes subjacent judicio rationis*], which the lower appetite obeys, as we have said [cf. *ST* I.81:3]. Wherefore this is in no way prejudicial to freedom [*Unde per hoc libertati arbitrii non praejudicatur*].[91]

So the many sensitive inclinations that arise from our nature and direct us to certain goals do *not* cause us to act. It is reason that will determine which goals we actually seek. We can apply this to our example. The young Frenchman does have an identity. There are many defining features about his life that make him who he *is* and motivate his actions. Yet this identity does not help him determine what he will *become* in the future. He can't find the answer by looking into the person he thinks he is. He can consider different things in the light of different ends. In this case he oscillates between two types of thinking. He is attracted to both goals and he recognizes that his identity could be defined in terms of either one. He thinks about the needs of his country, then about the needs of his depen-

90. *ST* I.83:1obj5. Citing Aristotle's *Nicomachean Ethics* 3:5, 1114b1. For an English version, see Aristotle, *Nicomachean Ethics*, 69.

91. *ST* I.83:1ad5.

dent mother. He considers his own desire for vengeance against his occupiers, then his own love for his mother. He judges his situation in the light of one's duty to one's country, then in the light of one's duty to one's parents. His intellect is free to hold both options simultaneously in mind, because they are both "abstract" possibilities that go beyond the immediate uninterpreted information he has from his sensitive apprehension. His particular circumstances, in other words, do not trap him within a single way of understanding those circumstances. The young man knows that his future will depend on which good he chooses. His actions will depend on which end he *allows* to become the object of his attention and the guiding principle of his life. But a theoretical goal only becomes an actual goal when he allows it to guide his thinking and when he allows himself to become the person who is formed by this goal.

This example shows us that the facts of our life and nature do not furnish us with a single scale of values against which we can make every decision. Ethics is more than psychology, morality more than metaphysics.[92] We have to acknowledge that our identity is insufficient and surpass it toward a new one. We will only exist as acting persons through the end that we set. Our actions depend on this unfolding identity and not on some preestablished essence.

For Aquinas, we are fulfilled by what we choose to seek. We are what we rationally desire. Our rational desire not only fulfills what we *already* are, it also creates new possibilities for who we can become. We can change the person we are, or it might be better to say that personhood lies in the fact that we don't have to be any particular person. We constitute ourselves as persons through freely chosen human action, even though we are constituted by other things in so many other ways (as we will see in chapter 6). For Aquinas, human beings are becoming what they are not, and this becoming is not determined by what they are. The future comes to exist, in some way, in their present, through their decision to orientate themselves to this particular future. Our being as persons, our personal identity, depends on a future that does not exist and which cannot be extrapolated with any necessity from the present. Our being, in this sense, echoing Sar-

92. A fierce criticism of moral theories that claim to be based on a certain metaphysics of human nature can be found in John Finnis, *Natural Law and Natural Rights* (Oxford: Clarendon Press, 1980).

tre, depends on nonbeing. It is created by our willingness to project one future in preference to a number of other possible futures.

Human identity, according to the arguments presented in this chapter, thus has two aspects. We *are* what we understand (through the intellect) and we *are becoming* what we decide to seek (through the will). Without this understanding our intellects would be blank and without this seeking our wills would be inert. In these ways Aquinas's account of human identity is very close to Sartre's.

Part Two

HUMAN UNDERSTANDING

Chapter 3

THE SUBJECTIVE NATURE OF OBJECTIVE UNDERSTANDING IN SARTRE

Being-in-the-World

In part one we explored the way human identity is constituted by the practical choices human beings make. In part three we will look more closely at how these choices are freely made. Here in part two we need to address a question that arises from the ideas developed so far. There have been hints in the previous two chapters that our personal commitments color the way we see the world, and that we only understand things in the way that we want to understand them. Sartre's *being-for-itself* and Aquinas's *will* seem to influence the way we interpret ourselves and our circumstances. There seems to be a suggestion that knowledge is subjective and that we can never grasp the truth of things as they are in themselves. If this is the case, then the choices we make will lack any objective foundation. Human beings make decisions about things, and if our perception of these things itself depends on our decisions, then the whole process will be hopelessly circular. Freedom will be a hollow kind of creativity without any external points of reference. Human life, cut off from any roots in objective reality, will just be a self-fulfilling fantasy, and a lonely one at that. So here in part two we ask this question: How do Sartre and Aquinas maintain that our understanding of the world is objective when it belongs to a human subject and when it in some way depends on this human subject?

Sartre is convinced that there are no neutral facts about the world. Everything we experience is understood in terms of ourselves, our perspectives, and our goals. This humanizing of the world, however, is paradoxically what allows the reality of the world to be revealed, since the world can only be known if it is placed in a particular perspective. One notion of objectivity (detached, inhuman, universal) is replaced by another (engaged, human, specific). Objective truth, to put it another way, is not endlessly deferred and out of reach, it is continually discovered within the irredeemably subjective activities of human beings. This subjective objectivity ensures that human decisions are based on an understanding of the world as it is and not just as we want it to be. Freedom and "facticity" are inseparable, and the concerns of both idealism and realism need to be taken into account if philosophy is to give a faithful account of human experience.

If we want to appreciate the theoretical framework that makes sense of this we will have to return to the opening sections of *Being and Nothingness.* Sartre is trying to develop a phenomenological ontology. This means that the foundation of his philosophy is concrete human experience. He tries to make no assumptions about what lies "behind" this experience. He wants to keep his focus on the experience and see what is happening within it. Metaphysics may concern itself with why this experience arose in the first place, what are its causes and grounds, but phenomenological ontology stays within the experience itself.

Human experience is, nevertheless, complex—it cannot be described in terms of a single principle.[1] In the introduction to *Being and Nothingness* Sartre scrutinizes our experience of phenomena in general, without alluding to concrete human behavior, and finds that it must refer to the correlative regions of being-in-itself and being-for-itself. We have touched on these ideas in chapter 1. The unified, concrete experience we have is "the relation" of these two "regions of being."[2] It is an "original bursting-forth [*un jaillissement primitif*]" which can't be reduced to anything more primary.[3] Being-for-itself represents that aspect of openness to what is experienced. Being-in-itself represents that aspect of openness to what is experienced.

1. See *BN* xxxvi–xliii; *EN* 26–33/27–34.
2. *BN* 4; *EN* 38/38.
3. *BN* 4; *EN* 38/38.

Consciousness is consciousness *of* something. This means that transcendence is the constitutive structure of consciousness; that is, that consciousness comes about *directed towards* a being which is not itself.[4]

If we try to divorce these two regions from each other, we will lose touch with them both. On the one hand, we never actually experience being-in-itself isolated from all human context and cut off from any relationship with us. What we experience is the phenomenon of this being, its place within experience, its status as meaningful. On the other hand, we are never directly conscious of our being-for-itself, we are only conscious of our consciousness of other things, and in this way we are implicitly conscious that this consciousness is ours.

In the body of *Being and Nothingness* (part 1 onward) Sartre builds on this highly abstract framework. He develops a term inherited from Heidegger and describes lived experience in terms of our *être-dans-le-monde,* our "being-in-the-world." We cannot experience being-in-itself, we can only experience being as it appears to consciousness, being-as-it-is-in-the-human-world, being as it is structured by our actions and our projects. Nor can we experience our own consciousness in isolation from a consciousness of something. The concrete world is the place where we start and where we actually exist. It is not a construction pieced together from two originally separate elements (a "pure" being-in-itself and a "pure" human consciousness), it is rather an original synthesis. We start by being-in-the-world, and then we may speculate about the regions of being that support this—our own being-for-itself and the being-in-itself of things.

The lived experience of acting human beings, which takes place in the world, is the main subject of *Being and Nothingness.* The relationship between human engagement and the apprehension of being is at the center of Sartre's understanding of the world. Negation, for Sartre, is the constitutive way in which things are revealed since they only take their place in the world when we isolate them, go beyond them, and relate them to what they are not. The world is the rising up of engaged human beings, the negation of being-in-itself by being-for-itself.

Sartre approaches this issue from different directions. He has a central insight that is expressed in different ways: the world is human; objectivity

4. *BN* xxxvii; *EN* 28/28.

is revealed through subjective purposes; being-for-itself reveals being-in-itself. In the course of *Being and Nothingness* he spirals around this insight, illustrating it with reference to different aspects of human experience. In each case Sartre tries to draw out the necessary subjective and objective element within experience, sometimes emphasizing one, then the other, but always referring to the original synthesis that constitutes our being-in-the-world. In this chapter I will describe some of these approaches in an unsystematic way, touching on perception, instrumentality and purpose, bodily perspective, and objective resistance. These different examples all illustrate the way that knowledge is human. One should bear in mind throughout this chapter that objects and things are not just physical objects but any unities that can become "objects" of our attention: events, deeds, groups, cultures, languages, properties, ideas, etc. So Sartre's theory provides a way of understanding how we constitute this human reality in many different contexts.

The Subjective Nature of Perception

Sartre was uneasy about theories of perception that overemphasized the role played by the intellect in the constitution of objects—he thought they were too influenced by idealist presuppositions. He was attracted to the gestalt school of psychology because it provided a corrective to these theories.[5] The gestaltists believed that we identify many objects in the world naturally and without learning.[6] They did not deny that learning affects the structures of our perceptual experience, but they said that perception is nevertheless based on an apprehension and categorization of objects that precedes the learning. Gestaltism was for its initiators and for Sartre a way of defending some form of philosophical realism. The segregation of visual things, wrote Wolfgang Köhler, is independent of meaning, and many objects and even complex figures (like some stellar constellations) are apprehended naturally, spontaneously, and universally.[7] They have a "constancy" because of their intrinsic unity and not solely because of the unifying judgments made by human beings. Köhler didn't deny that human understand-

5. For these various influences, see Adrian Mirvish, "Sartre on Perception and the World," *Journal of the British Society for Phenomenology* 14 (1983).

6. The German word *Gestalt* is roughly equivalent to the English *form* or *shape.*

7. See Wolfgang Köhler, *Gestalt Psychology: An Introduction to New Concepts in Modern Psychology* (New York: Liveright, 1947), esp. 136–72.

ing depends on the meanings we give to things through our purposes, but he wrote that "meaning follows the lines drawn by natural organization."[8]

So Sartre embraced "gestaltism" as a way of affirming the givenness and otherness of the world. We find objects, it argues, as they are. He does not, however, allow that these natural "figures" can be apprehended or understood outside the context of human choosing. The being (in-itself) of each figure does not depend on the choice of the for-itself, but this being is only encountered and revealed by the isolating power of the for-itself. We could express it in this way: We find what is there, yet it is only there through our finding.

Sartre argues that perceptual judgments depend in part on the direction of one's interest and attention. Choice has a role in the simplest act of perception. We choose to look at one thing rather than another, and different people looking in the same direction see different things. Each perceived thing has to be isolated from the undifferentiated perceptive field and viewed against it.[9]

> In perception there is always the construction of a figure [*une forme*] on a background [*un fond*]. No one object, no group of objects is especially designed to be organised as specifically either ground or figure; all depends on the direction of my attention.[10]

A constitutive aspect of something being there for us is that we have chosen to be interested in it. "In perception we constitute a particular object as a *figure* by rejecting another so as to make of it a *background,* and the other way round."[11] There is never a "figure" without this aspect of human selection. The world is what we actively uncover. This formal scheme is not just applicable to the perception of physical objects; it also applies to the perception of properties within a single object. We have to decide, for example, to attend to the weight or to the color or to the texture of a thing. "While I cannot make this fruit peel cease being green, it is I who am responsible for my taking it as a rough green or a green roughness."[12]

There is, therefore, a subjective and an objective element to every perception, and the one requires the other instead of undermining it. The ob-

8. Ibid., 139.

9. *BN* 316; *EN* 356/380.

10. *BN* 9; *EN* 44/44.

11. *BN* 20; *EN* 55/56.

12. *BN* 188; *EN* 224/238.

jective form is lit up by the subjective attention, and the subject can only attend to what is there. Sartre writes very simply that the relationship any particular thing has with its background is "both chosen and given."[13] On the one hand, we choose without any necessity to notice this thing, in the pursuit of our interests, and to see it in relation to its background. "I am free to look at *the book* on the table or at *the table* supporting the book."[14] On the other hand, *the givenness* comes from the relationship that things really have with each other. We can't change the "original distribution of *thises* [*distribution originelle des* ceci]" that make up the world.[15] It is an unavoidable fact that at this moment the book and the table have a specific relationship with each other. The decision to attend to one or the other of these objects is only possible because of this original givenness.

There is a certain ambiguity here, and a number of questions remain hanging: Are there any "natural" or universally acknowledged figures whose emergence does not depend on the interests of particular individuals or groups? Do the figures exist as figures before the choice made? Sartre is pulled in two directions. First, he is taking the side of realism and fighting against the idealistic notion that things are constituted solely in terms of the cognitive structures of the human subject.[16] Second, he nevertheless wants to affirm that perception and understanding are unavoidably human.

Instrumentality and Purpose

Why do we choose to notice one thing rather than another? Sartre says that it is because a thing is useful.[17] This does not mean, in a crude way, that we only perceive and understand things when we want to make im-

13. *BN* 316; *EN* 356/380.

14. *BN* 317; *EN* 356/380.

15. *BN* 316–17; *EN* 356/380.

16. He had been hostile to idealism ever since encountering it in some of the teaching at the École Normale Supérieur. He went on to believe that Husserl's whole phenomenological project was threatened by an unacknowledged idealism.

17. The thought of Husserl as much as Heidegger hovers in the background here. Husserl writes that in the natural attitude we find not only factual things but things with values and uses. These uses are not just additional characteristics we impose onto neutral facts. "Immediately, physical things stand there as Objects of use, the 'table' with its 'books,' the 'drinking glass,' the 'vase,' the 'piano,' etc. These value characteristics and practical characteristics also belong *constitutively to the Objects 'on hand' as Objects,* regardless of whether or not I turn to such characteristics and the Objects"; see Edmund Husserl, *Ideas Pertaining to a Pure Phenomenology and to a Phenomenological Philosophy. Book 1: General Introduction to a Pure Phenomenol-*

mediate practical use of them. It means that our broadest values and purposes define the kind of objects we give our attention to. Our purpose may simply be to understand something, or to contemplate something, or to honor something, or to move past something—but we have to have at least some reason for relating to it, some value we assign to our interaction with it. There is a reciprocal relationship between human desire and the instrumentality we attribute to things.[18] Sartre's examples here are more connected with sense perception and practical purposes, but he is making the wider point that any kind of knowledge or understanding must be related to some particular purpose, and ultimately to some overarching project—even if that purpose is aesthetic contemplation or a desire to satisfy one's intellectual curiosity.

When Sartre writes that objects are revealed to us in "a complex of instrumentality [*un complexe d'ustensilité*],"[19] he means that we only identify and understand something properly when we see how it works, how it functions, how it fits into the dynamic context in which it is situated. Things have a place in an active, unfolding world and not just in an abstract map of sensible objects. The instrumental place that things occupy only becomes apparent if we have some purposeful involvement in the world. "Sense perception is in no way to be distinguished from the practical organization of existents into a *world.*"[20] Everything refers, directly or indirectly, to our purposes and so to ourselves as the center of these purposes. There is always some relationship, however indirect, between what things are and what we do; and there is always some relationship between what we do and what we want.

Sartre puts it in this way: The place each thing has "is not defined by

---

ogy, trans. F. Kersten (The Hague: Nijhoff, 1982), 53. On the Heideggerian notion of *equipment* (*das Zeug:* instrument, tool, gear), see Martin Heidegger, *Being and Time,* trans. John Macquarrie and Edward Robinson (Oxford: Blackwell, 1962), 95–102, and translators' footnote 1 on 97. The "readiness-to-hand" of an instrument cannot be discovered by looking "theoretically," we have to look with the sight of "circumspection" (looking around *for* something) and notice what purpose the instrument is *for.* See *BN* 200; *EN* 236–37/250–51.

18. It's important to be aware that the language of "instrumentalism" has particular negative connotations for some contemporary philosophers. Charles Taylor, for example, uses it to refer to the loss of meaning and values that can occur in technocratic, consumerist societies. Sartre intends something different. See Charles Taylor, *Sources of the Self: The Making of the Modern Identity* (Cambridge: Cambridge University Press, 1989), 499–513.

19. *BN* 321; *EN* 361/385.

20. *BN* 321; *EN* 361/385.

pure spatial co-ordinates but in relation to axes of practical reference."[21] Thus our own activity determines the things we choose to find and also the way we understand them. To understand something, in whatever way, is to place it within axes of practical reference, in a context of meaning that is related to human interests and purposes. This doesn't imply that we simply create meaning or impose it onto a meaningless situation; it implies that meaning is only allowed to emerge once we are personally involved in a situation. Sartre gives two everyday examples.[22] First, we notice that a glass sits on the coffee table. Why do we notice this? It is not just a random sense perception. There are many other things we could notice now instead, and at other times in the past we did not notice the glass. In this case, for example, we want to move the table and are brought to consider what is on it so we don't break anything. Our perception of the glass is inseparable from our interest in moving the table. The glass is something we have to be careful with, it has a place in our practical purposes—even if we never actually move the table. Second, we spot the tobacco pouch on the mantlepiece. Why do we spot it? Because we want to smoke. Our apprehension of the location of the tobacco is inseparable from our desire for it. The tobacco is something we desire, it has a place in our practical purposes—even if we do not actually get round to retrieving it.

It may seem that Sartre is creating a big muddle of perception and purpose, of objective description and subjective meaning. Numerous objections spring to mind: Surely the glass is on the coffee table even if we are not interested in it? Surely other people may have different interests that bring this same fact to their attention? Surely the same truth can be described in objective terms without reference to human interests? The answer to all these questions is "Yes"; but this doesn't undermine Sartre's central contention that we only notice things in the first place if we have at least *some* interest in them. There are innumerable things to observe in any landscape, and our interests always determine what we find. In another passage Sartre summarizes his understanding in the following phrase: "In a word, the world gives counsel only if one questions it, and one can question it only for a well determined end."[23]

We can imagine another example.[24] Some people walk together through

21. *BN* 321; *EN* 361/385.

22. *BN* 321; *EN* 361/385.

23. *BN* 448; *EN* 492/524.

24. This is mine, not Sartre's.

a forest. They follow the same path at the same time, yet only one hears the birdsong, only one sees the snakes, only one smells the flowers. They have different fears, loves, instincts, hobbies, professions, etc., and these influence their perception. Even the "neutral" scientists in the group, who claim to have a greater objectivity, have chosen their own particular object of inquiry, be it the humidity, the temperature, or the river formation. And if the attention of all these people happens to converge on a single thing—say a scream from the other side of the river, or a tree fallen across their path—this convergence is inseparable from a convergence of their personal interests, and as soon as that interest wanes they will attend to other things. The members of this party even notice different "things" about the same "thing." An animal darts in front of them and they notice its color or speed or size or ferocity. There are innumerable properties to observe in any thing, and our interests always determine which we attend to. As soon as things are stripped of the meanings and references that purposeful human beings have given them, they vanish into abstraction. Our interest is like a light that illuminates things.[25] The light is not what it illuminates, yet nothing can appear without it.

Sartre returns to this relationship between objective fact and subjective purpose in a later section of *Being and Nothingness* entitled "My Place."[26] Here, aided by his discussions of freedom, Sartre admits that there is an "antimony." On the one hand, "human-reality originally receives its place [*place*] in the midst of things"—we find ourselves to be in a certain place and we have to accept that. On the other hand, "human-reality is that by which something such as place comes to things"—we give structure to an otherwise chaotic collection of things and organize them into a place by determining what they mean for us. In Sartre's use of the term there cannot be an abstract, nonhuman place, yet we "receive" our place without manipulating the things we find.[27]

His response to this antinomy is not so much to offer a resolution as to reinforce the necessity of this double truth. He revisits earlier arguments and shows how there is never a pure contemplation of objects or a disin-

25. Joseph Fell applies this metaphor to Sartre's account of instrumentality; see Joseph P. Fell, *Heidegger and Sartre: An Essay on Being and Place* (New York: Columbia University Press, 1979), 74.

26. *BN* 489–96; *EN* 535–41/570–76.

27. *BN* 491; *EN* 536/571.

terested apprehension of data. *Being there* in that placc is, for example, being near to something we remember or far from someone we love; being there is being able to reach the teapot or read in the light from the window; being there is waiting for my discharge from the army in a hundred and ten days; being there is being hidden from my enemies. These perspectives involved in "being there" are not additional meanings we give to a situation after we have cast a neutral eye over the landscape, they are part of the original data. Every aspect of place and time and environment and situation is somehow conditioned by the way we exist beyond being, by our freely chosen attitudes and plans and goals. "The future—a thrown-forward future [*un futur pro-jeté*]—intervenes everywhere."[28]

Try as we may to disentangle some independent data from our own purposeful schemes, we always fail. What we are really doing is replacing one human scheme with another. Sartre doesn't mention the example of science here, but one can see how even the movement to so-called scientific objectivity (detached, uninfluenced by human need) is actually the substitution of a more universal, more widely known purposeful scheme for that of an individual or local one. To observe, for example, how light reacts in an experiment reproduced in different laboratories throughout the world is still to understand light in a perspective of human purposes. There are reasons why these people are interested in light, why they experiment in this way, why they notate their results in this technical language and not another one, etc., and these reasons reflect their individual and communal purposes. This does not in any way undermine the utility of the scientific project, it simply reveals its true nature—which is to understand the world in the light of a particular collective human purpose. There is no neutral space where people act in a premoral way, there is no practical thinking that avoids the question of purpose and the good. There are no facts without values.[29]

28. *BN* 493; *EN* 538/574.

29. The philosophical difficulty is not the much debated one of how to get an "ought" from an "is," the real difficulty lies in trying to separate an "is" from an "ought." One's understanding of what *is* can never be separated from the values that drive one to understand. Our interest in truth, speculative as well as practical, is always intertwined with our understanding of what is good for us.

The Perspective of the Body

If human purposes give a certain perspective to experience, a much more literal kind of perspective comes from our nature as bodily creatures. In part 3, chapter 2, of *Being and Nothingness,* entitled "The Body," Sartre mounts an attack on what he calls "absolute objectivity" *(objectivité absolue).* He recalls his earlier conclusion that consciousness is consciousness *of* the world: We are aware that we are present to a world that is other than us. This might seem to provide the basis for an unqualified realism. Sartre adds, however, that the world we are conscious of is always understood from a certain perspective, from the point of view of an observer.[30] He does not say that things cease to exist when they are no longer placed in this perspective. He simply says that to have any understanding of their existence (as observed or not) there must be a specific point of view built into this understanding.

Consciousness does not fly over the world without perspective and contemplate it without a point of view. Each thing we observe has a specific orientation to a concrete reference point.[31] The glass is on the left or the right of the decanter depending on where the observer is sitting, and it is impossible to have any notion of position without referring to an observation point. Orientation "is a constitutive structure of the thing."[32] Even the most abstract spatial grid must somehow be rooted in the particular features of what is being surveyed. Without a point of view (on her right, on his left) nothing would remain, there would be "the total disappearance of *thises* at the heart of an original indistinction [*l'évanouissement total des* ceci *au sein d'une indistinction primitive*]."[33] Knowledge, thought, and language are situated, and there is always a context to our descriptions and our speaking.

Science may try and take an "abstract point of view,"[34] but for Sartre this is a contradiction in terms. The attempt to reach "absolute objectivity"[35]

30. The language of "perspective" recalls the *perspectivism* of Nietzsche and Ortega y Gasset. Frederick Olafson compares Sartre's version of perspectivism with William James's pragmatism; see Frederick A. Olafson, *Principles and Persons: An Ethical Interpretation of Existentialism* (Baltimore, Md.: John Hopkins University Press, 1967), 48–49.

31. *BN* 306–7; *EN* 345–46/368–70.

32. *BN* 316; *EN* 356/380.

33. *BN* 306; *EN* 346/369.

34. *BN* 307; *EN* 346/369.

35. *BN* 307; *EN* 346/369.

proves self-defeating. When things are described solely in terms of abstract characteristics and relations they drift free from reality and become merely formal representations. Scientific units of measurement (such as the measurement of speed) have to refer somehow to objects with specific dimensions, otherwise they have no meaning. Something moves in relation to a body of a given dimension.[36] Only the human being can specify these dimensions. If this world is to be understood it must be a world seen from a point of view by someone in particular—even if that someone is a scientist who can invite others to share this point of view. Sartre was pleased to discover that physicists such as Louis de Broglie and Werner Heisenberg were seeking to "reintegrate the observer into the heart of the scientific system."[37]

Human beings and the world are relative beings, "and the principle of their being *is* the relation."[38] To come into existence for me "is to unfold my distances from things and thereby to cause there to be things. But consequently things are precisely 'things-which-exist-at-a-distance-from-me.'"[39] Without these relations and concrete distances there could be no world to experience or speak about.[40] There is only a world in relation to situated and acting human beings.

> The point of view of pure knowledge is contradictory; there is only the point of view of *engaged* [engagée] knowledge. This amounts to saying that knowledge and action are only two abstract aspects of an original, concrete relation.[41]

"Knowledge," here, refers to the comprehensive way we understand and experience the world, and not just to the knowledge of the scientist or the logician. On the one hand, "It is absolutely necessary that the world appear to me *in order*." On the other hand, "It is wholly contingent that it should be *this* order."[42] Thus the world appears "as the necessary and totally unjus-

36. *BN* 307–8; *EN* 347/370.
37. *BN* 307; *EN* 346/370.
38. *BN* 308; *EN* 347/370.
39. *BN* 308; *EN* 347/370.
40. We exist, of course, in relation to other human beings, and we exist (first as children) in relation to *their* projects before we begin our own. Sartre doesn't discuss properly the social and cultural nature of human formation until part 3 (chapter 3) and part 4 of *BN*.
41. *BN* 308; *EN* 347/370.
42. Sartre does not mean that we can choose *any* order. We can't, for example, choose the submolecular order if we have no electron microscopes, or the Chinese cultural order if we only speak English. He simply means that whenever we do choose an order (from those available to us), this particular order is not necessitated by the world.

tifiable arrangement of the totality of beings [*comme agencement nécessaire et injustifiable de la totalité des êtres*]."[43] So things in the world have to appear in some particular perspective, and perspective as such is necessary. Yet the particular arrangement *(agencement)* that emerges depends for its form entirely on which perspective a particular human being happens to take on the world. It is contingent, not necessary. It is unjustifiable, in the sense that nothing in the world justifies the choice of this contingent perspective over another. "It is necessary that the book appear to me on the right or on the left side of the table. But it is contingent that the book appears to me specifically on the left"—because I could change my position and instead see it on the right.[44]

What is the bodily subject? Where do we ourselves fit into this order of things? What perspective can be taken on the one who gives the perspective? Sartre's answer is that we cannot be objects *within* this order, instead *we are* this ordering. "It is absolutely necessary that the world appear to me *in order.* And in this sense this order *is me* [*cet ordre* c'est moi]."[45] This is a difficult concept to grasp. Sartre takes the example of human sensation and shows that in our own personal experience we are never aware of a sense sensing a sensation. We sense objects in the world, and we do not, for example, observe our own eye seeing visible sensations. The eye is the point where the visual lines of perspective meet.

> Thus the perceptive field refers to a center objectively defined by that reference and located *in the very field* that is oriented around it. Only we do not see this center as the structure of the perceptive field considered; *we are the center.* Thus the order of the objects in the world perpetually refers us to the image of an object which on principle can not be an object *for us* since it is what we have to be.[46]

This object that *we are* is "the contingent upsurge of one orientation among the infinite possibilities of orienting the world."[47] The specific orientation of my world indicates a center that is myself. Sartre calls both the orientation of the world and the center of orientation my body, and concludes that my body is both coextensive with the world and at the same time "condensed into this single point which all things indicate."[48]

43. *BN* 309; *EN* 348/371.
44. *BN* 317; *EN* 356/380.
45. *BN* 309; *EN* 348/371.
46. *BN* 317; *EN* 357/381.
47. *BN* 317; *EN* 357/381.
48. *BN* 318; *EN* 358/382.

The implications of this will become apparent as this chapter develops. A human life is not something in addition to the ordering of this world—it is the fact that the world is ordered in this particular way at this moment. What makes a human being this human being (and not another) is the fact that the things of this world are seen in this distinctive way (and not another). A human life can't be separated from the world. To exist as a human being is to "allow" the world to exist in a particular form. One's existence is, for example, the room observed from this angle, the noises from the street heard in this way, the conversation understood in this manner, the pain felt to this degree. The uniqueness of the person depends on the uniqueness of the perspective, and there is no disembodied human existence apart from this perspective. A human being does not have a perspective, a human being *is* this perspective. The corresponding truth, already discussed, is that each thing in the world cannot be abstracted from its place in the order we bring.

It bears repeating that this does not mean that things cease to exist when we cease to observe them, or that we are incapable of imagining things in different situations, or that we cannot communicate things to other people with a different perspective. It simply means that the very notions of continuing existence or imagination or communication require a concrete perspective. The *decentering* of my world, for example, which takes place when I realize that I am an object for another person's subjectivity, is always a *recentering* around the concrete perspective brought by this other person.[49] The public perspectives given to me when I enter a city (street signs, price tags, etc.) still have to be appropriated by me in order to become meaningful: I make my perspective fit with the perspective of the social order.[50] Perspective is a constitutive part of each thing. There is nothing in our world that does not have a concrete relation to a living, acting, seeking human being. There are many other relations between things that we can't understand, but at present these are closed to us. We can't even imagine such relations without imagining them in the perspective of our world.

49. See *BN* 254–56; *EN* 293–95/311–13.
50. See *BN* 509–12; *EN* 554–57/591–94.

The Objective Resistance of the World

The fact that we bring a human perspective to the world does not mean that we can interpret the facts of experience in any way that we choose. Our purposes may determine which things we are interested in, but it is the things themselves that determine whether our purposes can be fulfilled. Sartre explains this aspect of objectivity in terms of the resistance offered to our projects by the world. In his descriptions of resistance Sartre was deeply influenced by Gaston Bachelard and Max Scheler.[51] Bachelard criticized the phenomenologists for exaggerating the role played by the intellect in human experience. Intentionality, according to Bachelard, is not just about our intellectual relationship with known things, it is about the multifarious ways in which we interact with the world. There is a dynamic and a material "intention" through which we meet objects in their force, their resistance, their materiality.[52] Scheler places cognition in the context of the "lived body" and shows how it is constantly meeting resistance from its material environment.[53] For both these philosophers human beings have to apply force to their environment, they have to be sufficiently "offensive," in order to get to grips with the world and see how it reacts.

Sartre develops this theme of resistance and writes that things have a "coefficient of adversity" that cannot be avoided.[54] At the same time he wants to show that objective resistance itself is only discovered and interpreted through our free projects. Without our subjective involvement there would be nothing to notice. The coefficient of adversity in things is only met because of our desire for certain ends. In itself, this large rock formation is neutral, there is nothing about it that can help or hinder our lives. Only when we think about climbing it do we realize how impossible this is: the rock is revealed as "too difficult to climb" only because we questioned whether it was "climbable."

Thus although brute things (what Heidegger calls "brute existents") can from the start limit our freedom of action, it is our freedom itself that must first con-

51. For their views and their influence on Sartre, see Mirvish, "Sartre on Perception and the World."

52. *BN* 324 and footnote 3; *EN* 364/388 and footnote 1.

53. Sartre refers to Scheler at *BN* 330; *EN* 370/395.

54. *BN* 481; *EN* 527/561. Sartre borrows Bachelard's term.

stitute the framework, the technique, and the ends in relation to which they will manifest themselves as limits.[55]

Sartre is careful *not* to say that our free action constitutes the things themselves or their limits. Instead it constitutes the framework, the technique, and the ends *(le cadre, la technique et les fins)* through which the limits are revealed. A "technique" is the particular type of human endeavor or cultural practice in which someone is involved. So here the difficulty of the rock is only revealed because those dedicated to climbing (which is the framework) want to scale the rock (to achieve this end) using their skills and climbing equipment (which is their technique). In itself, the notion of "difficulty" is meaningless, yet when we seek to climb the rock it reveals itself "*as it is* (i.e., resisting or favorable)."[56] There is no contradiction between creativity and discovery: each requires the other. "There is no obstacle in an absolute sense, but the obstacle reveals its coefficient of adversity across freely invented and freely acquired techniques."[57]

Despite these nuanced passages about the resistance we meet when we engage with the world, Merleau-Ponty still believed that Sartre gave too little weight to the objective reality of the world and to our concrete being. It is worth examining some of his criticisms in order to appreciate what Sartre was really doing. Merleau-Ponty accepted that the central thesis of intentionality was meant to preserve phenomenology from idealism. The subject is not trapped within the structures of the mind since consciousness is transparent to what is other than itself. But he drew attention very early on to some dangers inherent in Sartre's notion of transparency.[58] Merleau-Ponty believed that Sartre held to a kind of Cartesian dualism that did not allow for an "interworld"—a world between the transparent subject and the impenetrable object, a world between one human subjectivity and another.[59] In this interworld things would carry a weight from elsewhere, they would suggest and sometimes impose their own meanings. The "flesh" of others and of the world would intrude into our compre-

55. *BN* 482; *EN* 527/562.

56. *BN* 488; *EN* 533/568.

57. *BN* 488; *EN* 533–34/569.

58. See M. Merleau-Ponty, *Phenomenology of Perception,* trans. Colin Smith (London: Routledge & Kegan Paul, 1962), esp. the final section on freedom, 434–56. Merleau-Ponty reacts to Sartre's ideas without mentioning him by name very often.

59. See Monika Langer, "Sartre and Merleau-Ponty: A Reappraisal," in *The Philosophy of Jean Paul Sartre,* ed. Paul A. Schilpp (La Salle, Ill.: Open Court, 1981), esp. 304–9.

hension more forcefully than Sartre allows. Without the interworld, consciousness would be rootless and isolated.

Merleau-Ponty picks up Sartre's example of fatigue, and agrees that it is not an objective motive that causes us to halt on a journey. We have to decide freely to give in to it. But there is nevertheless a kind of "sedimentation" of our life; some attitudes have a "favored status" and become more "probable."[60] Freedom presupposes a situation whose meaning we have not chosen. Two passages express this insight very clearly.

> We therefore recognize, around our initiatives and around that strictly individual project which is oneself, a zone of generalized existence and of projects already formed, significances which trail between ourselves and things and which confer on us the quality of man, bourgeois or worker.[61]

> The choice which we make of our life is always based on a certain givenness. My freedom can draw life away from its spontaneous course, but only by a series of unobtrusive deflections which necessitate first of all following its course—not by any absolute creation. [. . .] I am a psychological and historical structure, and have received, with existence, a manner of existing, a style. All my actions and thoughts stand in a relationship to this structure.[62]

These are penetrating criticisms, and if they are correct they will undermine Sartre's philosophical project. The key question is this: Is the phenomenology of *Being and Nothingness* irreparably idealistic or does it already allow for the intrusion of an "interworld" into human consciousness?

Sartre's answer is straightforward: There are many ways in which we are already formed, many ways in which our actions depend on a momentum and direction we have not freely given them, many occasions when we participate without reflection in the projects of others. Yet all of these, if they are to have any significance for us in our world, have to be given a personal meaning in the light of our purposes and projects. We have to make sense of them for ourselves. This is not a denial of the dense givenness of ourselves and of the world, it is the very way that we appropriate this givenness and ensure that it does not sit unacknowledged on the fringes of consciousness.

60. Merleau-Ponty, *Phenomenology of Perception*, 441.
61. Ibid., 450.
62. Ibid., 455.

Sartre often highlights the fundamental givenness of experience. He notes that "far from being able to modify our situation at our whim, we seem to be unable to change ourselves."[63] A later section where Sartre is unambiguous about the intrusion of externally formed meanings into our personal world is called *Mon prochain,* "My neighbor" or "My fellow human being." The world contains meanings I have not given it, which are inherited and *"already mine."*[64] In a city I meet an "innumerable host of meanings which are independent of *my* choice": streets, buses, directions, warnings, sounds, etc.[65] I have a factual belonging to an already meaningful world. This is one manifest part of Sartre's "interworld." Sartre's sole and all important qualification is that this penetration of concrete reality into our free subjectivity can only occur when human beings seek their own goals in the world—it is never passive. The interworld just is, it is inert and ineffectual, unless we live and act in it, and even the external meanings it carries to us need appropriating and responding to.[66]

Sartre uses the word "exist" as a transitive verb to stand for our purposeful appropriation of the concrete world we inherit. "The only positive way which I have *to exist my factual belonging* [exister mon appartenance de fait] to these collectivities is the use which I constantly make of the techniques which arise from them."[67] The fleshly meaning of the interworld itself needs to be given meaning by our freedom. Simone de Beauvoir was right to accuse Merleau-Ponty of conflating Sartre's notion of a transparent, contemplative consciousness (apparent in the introduction to *Being and Nothingness*) with a *subject* that develops, for example, in relationship with others, in the context of the world. She writes that Merleau-Ponty neglects Sartre's work on facticity, and doesn't acknowledge that for him consciousness is always incarnate.[68] In the end, I believe that the

63. *BN* 481; *EN* 526/561.

64. *BN* 510; *EN* 555/592.

65. *BN* 510; *EN* 555/592.

66. Sartre recognized an interworld but did not want it to be used as an excuse for passivity. It was not just for phenomenological reasons that Sartre emphasized our need to take responsibility even for the meanings and purposes that seem to be an unavoidable part of our fleshly existence. In an interview given a few years after *BN* (which was written between 1941 and 1943) he said that the war undoubtedly influenced his outlook. In Sartre's eyes it was impossible *not* to make a fundamental decision about one's life in occupied France. One had to decide to resist or not to resist. See Jean-Paul Sartre, "The Itinerary of a Thought," in *Between Existentialism and Marxism* (New York: Pantheon Books, 1974), esp. 34.

67. *BN* 512; *EN* 557/594.

68. Simone de Beauvoir, "Merleau-Ponty et Le Pseudo-Sartrisme," *Les Temps Modernes* 10, nos. 114–15 (1955): esp. 2074–75.

views of Merleau-Ponty and Sartre on freedom are closer than Merleau-Ponty recognized.[69]

The use of language provides a paradigm for this question of how we can give personal meaning to the world even when meaning seems to be thrust upon us, of how we can play a part in forming our world even when we are formed by the world. Sartre briefly suggests how a philosophy of language might be developed.[70] He writes that to learn a language is to understand and belong to a culture. In theory this could imply that we are restricted by the language and culture, and that the personal meanings we express through our use of the language are limited by the meanings that are embodied in the culture. But Sartre says that the meaning of speech depends on structured sentences and not only on words alone, and the sentence refers us to the "*speaker* [discoureur] as the concrete foundation of speech."[71] The reality of spoken language "is the *free act* of designation by which I choose myself as *designating*."[72] Speech is not a language that speaks all by itself and meanings are not predetermined or limited by the words. Speech refers us to the free intentions and overall purposes of those who speak as they interpret and go beyond their inherited situations. Sartre writes that this theory of speech applies to any "technique" in which human beings are involved. It could provide a basis for a philosophy of culture and allow one to see how new cultural and historical projects can arise even within tightly determined structures. It also explains his well-known opposition to structuralism.[73]

Knowledge Is Human

In this struggle to integrate the subjective influence of human perspective and the objective givenness of the world Sartre is trying to integrate two distinctive strands of phenomenology: the more personal-subjective philosophy of Husserl and the more impersonal-objective philosophy of Heidegger. In Husserl's phenomenology one's first outlook on life is the *natural attitude.* With this initial attitude, Husserl writes, "I continually find the

69. Despite insisting that human life has its own momentum and direction, Merleau-Ponty still gave the final word to freedom: "As long as we are alive, our situation is open, which implies both that it calls up specially favoured modes of resolution, and also that it is powerless to bring one into being by itself"; see Merleau-Ponty, *Phenomenology of Perception,* 442.

70. *BN* 512–21; *EN* 557–65/594–603.

71. *BN* 515; *EN* 560/598.

72. *BN* 516; *EN* 561/598.

73. For further comments on this point, see chapter 5.

one spatiotemporal actuality to which I belong like all other human beings who are to be found in it and who are related to it as I am. I find the 'actuality,' the word already says it, as a *factually existent actuality and also accept it as it presents itself to me as factually existing*."[74] This is not a world merely of facts and affairs, it is at the same time a world of values, a world of goods, a practical world. When we perform the *epoche* and "bracket" this natural attitude we realize that these facts, values, and meanings are dependent on the structures of understanding brought by the human subject.[75] We still attend to the same "world," to the same facts, values, and meanings, but we no longer accept them in an unreflective way, we realize that their force depends on their place in our subjective processes. Thomas Busch writes that in Husserl's *epoche* "objects, thus reduced to the status of meanings *for* consciousness, are further grasped as constituted *by* the meaning-giving acts of consciousness."[76] There are risks here which even the most sympathetic phenomenologist such as Robert Sokolowski acknowledges. This emphasis on subjective constitution leaves Husserl "with the content of constitution as an unexplained residuum, a pure facticity which escapes the principles of his philosophy."[77] This is why Sartre's reading of Heidegger in the late 1930s proved so timely. Heidegger's *Dasein* rerooted him in the givenness of the world (the very givenness that attracted him to Husserl in the first place). It gave him a corrective to Husserl's subjectivity, even though Sartre persisted quite consciously in using the more subjective phrase *réalité-humaine* as a substitute for the impersonal *Dasein.*

Did Sartre's project of integrating Husserl and Heidegger succeed? Was he able to present a convincing picture of a subjective objectivity that preserves both the human nature of experience and its objective foundations in the world? Some commentators, such as Ronald Aronson, criticize him

74. Husserl, *Ideas Pertaining to a Pure Phenomenology and to a Phenomenological Philosophy. Book 1: General Introduction to a Pure Phenomenology,* 56–57.

75. On the *epoche,* see, e.g., Edmund Husserl, *Cartesian Meditations: An Introduction to Phenomenology,* trans. Dorion Cairns (The Hague, The Netherlands: Martinus Nijhoff, 1960), 18–22.

76. Thomas W. Busch, "Sartre's Use of the Reduction: *Being and Nothingness* Reconsidered," in *Jean-Paul Sartre: Contemporary Approaches to His Philosophy,* ed. Hugh J. Silverman and Frederick A. Elliston (Pittsburgh, Pa.: Duquesne University Press, 1980), 19.

77. Robert Sokolowski, *The Formation of Husserl's Concept of Constitution* (The Hague, The Netherlands: Martinus Nijhoff, 1964), 218.

for not giving enough weight to the structures of consciousness. Human beings are too transparent to the world. "Sartre ejects into the world everything that 'idealism' explains through recourse to the structured activity of subjectivity. And therewith, the world becomes a moody, implacable given." Aronson writes that he tries in vain to remove subjective structures from consciousness:

> The for-itself negates the in-itself—presumably in regular, patterned, predictable ways—and so there emerges an ordered, structured world and a consciousness that comprehends it. But what is this if not the hidden return of preconscious constituting processes.[78]

In effect Sartre is accused of a naïve realism. In my own view Aronson does not pay enough attention to the enormous part consciousness plays for Sartre in structuring experience. Consciousness does structure the world, but consciousness is not itself structured by prior structures—it *is* the dynamic structuring of the world. The only way Sartre can avoid idealism is by insisting that consciousness adds nothing to being, but reveals what is there through negation. So the emergence of the world is wholly dependent on the structuring of consciousness but not on its structures. If we ask why there is this structuring, Sartre's answer is that this just is the particular shape given now to the world through the actions of a free human being. The structuring of human beings and their freedom to rethink themselves and to surpass the world are one and the same reality.[79]

The more serious doubts about Sartre's project come from those who believe he failed to escape from the idealist presuppositions of Husserl's phenomenology. This line of criticism accuses him of importing unproven metaphysical notions into his system in order to buttress the weaknesses of his ontology. Sartre is charged with failing to establish the independent reality of being-in-itself. This failure follows inevitably from his decision to develop an ontology out of phenomenology. Klaus Hartmann, one of Sartre's most perceptive critics, writes that Sartre's ontology "is unable to ac-

78. Ronald Aronson, *Jean-Paul Sartre: Philosophy in the World* (London: Verso, 1980), 96–97.

79. It is interesting that in his serious and wide-ranging study Aronson makes hardly any references (only three) to part 1 of *BN*, "The Problem of Nothingness" (which deals with the structuring imposed by the for-itself through negation), and not one of these references concerns negation.

count for what is there *per se* from an objectively ontological perspective, namely, individual things and individual persons."[80] Sartre starts within a correlativistic epistemology where subject and object define each other in the unity of experience, and for this reason he struggles to explain the origin of the discreteness and individuality that negation reveals. He has no higher ontological principles or categories (like essence or existence) that will elucidate being-in-itself. Joseph Fell echoes these concerns.[81] He sees that the idea of being-in-itself is developed to support a kind of realism against the idealism latent in Husserl. At the same time he wonders whether Sartre has created an idealism of meaning in which all distinctions lie in the realm of consciousness. To search for the extrahuman foundation of differentiation is to enter the area of metaphysics, which—on the whole—Sartre refused to do,[82] even though at the end of *Being and Nothingness* he recognized the legitimacy of metaphysical questions.[83]

In my opinion there is no contradiction in trying to assert the presence of two complementary principles in our experience of the world. This is Sartre's very limited and extremely valuable project in *Being and Nothingness*. Sartre returns to this again and again, and formalizes it in a few pages at the end of part 2 ("Being-for-itself"). The section is entitled "Knowledge,"[84] where knowledge is used in a broad sense to indicate all that is within the human experience of the world. Sartre tries to clarify what his own position does and does not have in common with the philosophical traditions he labels "idealist" and "realist." He grants to idealism that in human experience there is an unavoidable association between the being of the world and our knowledge of this being. This is what has led some thinkers to reduce being to a function of knowledge and therefore to reduce the objective world to the level of a human construct. This might be possible if we could envisage a human subject that first existed and knew

80. Klaus Hartmann, *Sartre's Ontology: A Study of Being and Nothingness in the Light of Hegel's Logic* (Evanston, Ill.: Northwestern University Press, 1966), 135.

81. Fell, *Heidegger and Sartre: An Essay on Being and Place,* esp. 71–81.

82. On Sartre's occasional references to a purer, more metaphysical conception of being-in-itself, see Thomas W. Busch, *The Power of Consciousness and the Force of Circumstances in Sartre's Philosophy* (Bloomington: Indiana University Press, 1990), esp. 23–30. Busch believes that the very notion of the in-itself is a muddled one "because Sartre fluctuates, in presenting the notion, between a pure phenomenological ontology and a speculative metaphysics" (23).

83. See *BN* 619; *EN* 667/713.

84. *BN* 216–18; *EN* 253–55/268–71.

itself and then knew the world in relation to itself and in terms of its own understanding. But for Sartre "the for-itself does not exist in order subsequently to know [*le pour-soi n'est pas pour connaître ensuite*]."[85] There is no human subject that has knowledge. "Knowledge is nothing other than the presence of being to the for-itself, and the for-itself is only the *nothing* which realizes that presence [*le pour-soi n'est que le* rien *qui réalise cette présence*]."[86] Knowing is an absolute and primitive event, "it is the absolute upsurge of the for-itself in the midst of being and beyond being [*c'est le surgissement absolu du pour-soi au milieu de l'être et par delà l'être*]."[87]

The idealist position needs reversing (and therefore abandoning). It is more accurate to say that we, through knowledge, are absorbed in being than to say that the being of the world is trapped within the structures of our knowing. There is only being, and the relation of the for-itself to the in-itself is "a fundamental ontological relation."[88] The in-itself is affirmed through the self-negation of the for-itself. This affirmation exists only *for* the for-itself, but it is not *in* the for-itself, since it is an *ek-stase,* a being present out there. In a later passage Sartre defends what he describes as "something like an ontological conditioning of freedom," "a kind of ontological priority [*une préséance ontologique*] of the in-itself over the for-itself."[89] As Sartre writes in the conclusion to *Being and Nothingness,* the for-itself has no reality except that of being the negation of being, and "its sole qualification comes to it from the fact that it is the nihilation of an individual and particular in-itself and not of a being in general."[90] The idealist dilemma (how to unite world and mind) is unnecessary. "Therefore we have no business asking about the way in which the for-itself can be united with the in-itself since the for-itself is in no way an autonomous substance."[91]

Sartre, in this light, grants to realism that being is present to consciousness in knowledge and that "the for-itself adds *nothing* to the in-itself except the very fact that *there is* in-itself; that is, the affirmative negation."[92] Although there are many ways in which being seems to be "structured" by human experience, they all arise through negation and none of them

85. *BN* 216; *EN* 253/268.
86. *BN* 216; *EN* 253/268.
87. *BN* 216; *EN* 253/268.
88. *BN* 216; *EN* 253/268.
89. *BN* 484; *EN* 529/564.
90. *BN* 618; *EN* 666/712.
91. *BN* 618; *EN* 666/712.
92. *BN* 217; *EN* 254/269.

"modify the pure being which is revealed through them."[93] Everything is given; nothing of what we see comes from us. "*Representation,* as a psychic event, is a pure invention of the philosophers."[94] Yet realism, by insisting on the primacy of being, does not take adequate notice of the negation that makes being *there* and makes us *present to* being. The for-itself "knows being *such as it is* [tel qu'il est] when the 'such as it is' cannot belong to being."[95] This "such as it is" does not belong to being unless it is in relationship with the for-itself, and so we are always implicitly aware of what we bring to being—even if it is only negation. Realism cannot account for this. The realism thus rejected by Sartre is a crude kind of naturalism in which the thing known has a causal influence on the knower, in which known and knower belong to the same kind of being.[96] Realism may affirm being and even affirm the immediate presence of the for-itself to being, but it cannot account for the negation of presence, the denial of identity, which brings about an infinite distance between the for-itself and being. "Knowing has for its ideal being-what-one-knows and for its original structure not-being-what-is-known."[97] The world of experience, the only world that we know, is human.

Knowledge puts us in the presence of the absolute, and there is a truth of knowledge. But this truth, although releasing to us nothing more and nothing less than the absolute, remains strictly human.[98]

In each of Sartre's examples there has been an original synthesis that is subsequently abstracted through reflection into two complementary parts. Experience is the synthesis of being-for-itself and being-in-itself. Truth is neither relative nor absolute, it is the relationship itself between the absolute and human beings which makes up the world. Objectivity depends on the subject. This will be a good place to turn to Aquinas. For him, we can only know what we desire, yet neither the knowledge nor the desire detract from the immediacy of our union with being—they are the condition of that union.

93. *BN* 217; *EN* 254/269.

94. *BN* 217; *EN* 254/269.

95. *BN* 217; *EN* 254/270.

96. It would be quite possible, according to Herbert Spiegelberg, to consider Sartre's philosophy as "realist" in a wider sense, as committed to the independence of what is known from the knower; see Herbert Spiegelberg, *The Phenomenological Movement,* 3rd ed. (The Hague, The Netherlands: Martinus Nijhoff, 1982), 509.

97. *BN* 218; *EN* 254/270.

98. *BN* 218; *EN* 255/270.

Chapter 4

THE SUBJECTIVE NATURE OF OBJECTIVE UNDERSTANDING IN AQUINAS

Objectivity and the Human Subject

As creatures with intellect, human beings are open to the world around them and transformed by what they understand. As creatures with will, we desire what is good and seek our own perfection. Within certain limits we can choose our goals and in doing so choose who we will become. These are the conclusions Aquinas led us to in chapter 2. It appears that human desire must be based on a prior understanding of what is good. Our decisions about ends and action, it seems, must have a rational foundation in the objective reality of the world as it is understood by the intellect, and the detached and disinterested work of the intellect must precede the more personal and purposeful work of the will.

Aquinas's thinking about the relationship between intellect and will, however, is highly nuanced. He argues that the loving will and the knowing intellect always involve each other. The true is something good and must be desired if it is to be known. The good is something true and must be understood if it is to be desired. At every level, intellect and will influence each other. Nothing can be understood unless it is sought, and nothing can be sought unless it is understood.

The technical Scholastic vocabulary can obscure the full significance of what Aquinas is doing here philosophically. He is exploring at different levels what we might today call the question of *objectivity;* or, to see it from the other side, the question of *the subject.* (A) At the level of epistemology he wants to affirm that our understanding is inescapably human. The desire of the will influences everything. Our purposes and preferences determine when we understand, whether we understand, what we understand, and how we understand. Understanding is thoroughly subjective—this is what makes it personal. Yet at the same time we understand only what is there and nothing more. It is the intellect that understands, not the will, and it is the nature of the intellect to be formed by the being of whatever is understood. So understanding is thoroughly objective as well as subjective. The emergence of objectivity in fact depends on subjectivity. (B) At the level of action theory and ethics Aquinas wants to affirm that the goods we seek, which determine our actions, are freely chosen by the human subject. No good (apart from the final end) is so good that it cannot be seen in a different perspective. We can choose which perspective to take on each good, so that the subjective attractiveness of the good depends on our choice, and our actions follow from this choice. Yet at the same time we can only be attracted to what is actually a good, since it is the intellect alone that understands what is good in this personal perspective.

In both epistemology and action theory Aquinas thus proposes a kind of subjective objectivity. Objective truth is unveiled through its encounter with a purposeful subject, and the subject only grasps this truth in the terms of its own subjective preferences. It is still, nevertheless, completely objective. The truth, as Sartre says, is strictly human.[1]

At this stage the notion of subjective objectivity may seem unconvincing. In this chapter we will revisit Aquinas's descriptions of human intellect and will. Each has its own clear function. The richness of his account comes from the fact that there is a reflexive aspect to every human act, so that human beings know their own knowing and their own willing, and they will each act of knowing and each act of willing. In this context, objectivity takes on a different meaning. The search for foundations is still possible, but much more nuanced. It will help to bear in mind that this rather technical-sounding discussion about intellect and will concerns these broad questions of objectivity, subjectivity, and the nature of human experience.

1. *BN* 218; *EN* 255/270.

I will not pay much attention in this chapter to the differences between Aquinas's earlier and later writings on intellect and will because I believe that these differences are not of great significance. There is an ongoing debate about the development of Aquinas's thinking.[2] Odon Lottin proposed that Aquinas moved from a kind of intellectual determinism (in *De veritate*) to a more voluntarist conception of human action that highlighted the dynamic freedom of the will (in *De malo* 6).[3] This fits with R. A. Gauthier's contention that during his second regency in Paris Aquinas underwent some kind of personal conversion that affected his writing and mitigated an excessive intellectualism displayed in earlier texts. This change in outlook could have been due to the growing influence of Augustine or to the theological/political situation in Paris in 1270 when there were suspicions that the Thomistic intellectualist position led to a denial of the freedom of the will.[4] But Kevin Flannery, as I have already noted in the historical introduction, through a textual comparison of *De malo* 6 and *De veritate* 24:1, judges that the article in *De veritate* is a rewrite of at least parts of *De malo* 6.[5] This would make *De malo* 6 quite an early work. My only concern here is to show how difficult it is to draw conclusions about the development of Aquinas's thinking in this area. I accept Daniel Westberg's conclusion that the differences are in emphasis rather than in matters of substance: There is a consistent picture of the interdependence of intellect and will, a picture in which every action takes place for the sake of a good that is both understood and desired; and the earlier writings—if they are indeed earlier—pay great attention to the place of the will in the exercise of human freedom.[6]

2. See Jean-Pierre Torrell, *Saint Thomas Aquinas, Vol. 1: The Person and His Work* (Washington, D.C.: The Catholic University of America Press, 1996), 244–46; and Daniel Westberg, "Did Aquinas Change His Mind about the Will?" *The Thomist* 58 (1994): esp 41–60.

3. See Odon Lottin, "Libre arbitre et liberté depuis saint Anselme jusqu'à la fin du XIIIe siècle," in *Psychologie et morale aux XIIe et XIIIe siècles,* vol. 1, 2nd ed. (Gembloux: J. Duculot, 1957), 11–389. Note that there is still a dispute about the dating of *De malo* 6 itself; see the Historical Introduction above, in the section "Aquinas: Historical and Intellectual Background."

4. See James A. Weisheipl, *Friar Thomas D'aquino: His Life, Thought, and Works* (Washington, D.C.: The Catholic University of America Press, 1983), 244–45; and Westberg, "Did Aquinas Change His Mind about the Will?" 60.

5. Kevin L. Flannery, *Acts Amid Precepts* (Edinburgh: T & T Clark, 2001), 247–49.

6. Westberg writes: "Free choice is a matter of choosing, on the part of both reason and will, the *bonum intellectum*. This never changes in Thomas." But in his later works "he came to express more precisely that final causality had to do with the *bonum* aspect, and formal causality with *intellectum*"; see Westberg, "Did Aquinas Change His Mind about the Will?" 56.

It is worth making a final introductory note about the soul and its powers. Aquinas writes about the relationship that the human soul has with the world. The soul *(anima)* in general, as we learned in chapter 2, is the primary principle of life for any living thing.[7] A soul forms any living body. It is the "shape" of each body insofar as it has this characteristic of being alive about it.[8] The *human* soul forms the human body. It is the "shape" of the human body insofar as it is alive in a distinctively human way. So when Aquinas writes that the soul relates or knows or wills we must not be misled into thinking that some faculty is working of its own accord in isolation from the life of the whole human being. Aquinas means that human beings, insofar as they are acting in distinctively human ways, are doing these things. It is not distinctively human to digest or snore or flee a predator—many other animals do these things. Yet it is distinctively human to understand things and to act on the basis of this understanding.

In the same way, we must not treat intellect and will as if they were separately functioning substances or even biological individuals that assist the soul in its thinking or acting, like talkative passengers in the backseat of a car.[9] Intellect and will are instead powers of the soul, which means that they are the soul itself insofar as it is capable of acting in certain ways and relating to certain objects.[10] So to say that the intellect takes in or the will goes out is simply to say that living human beings are doing these distinctively human things. David Gallagher writes that "it is not the powers—reason, will, appetite, etc.—which act, but the individual human person."[11] This is a holistic way of understanding the human being that still allows one to analyze the distinct elements involved in human action.

7. *ST* I.75:1c.

8. *ST* I.75:5c.

9. Simon and Donagan warn against these dangers, without using this metaphor. See Yves R. Simon, *Freedom of Choice* (New York: Fordham University Press, 1969), 97; and Alan Donagan, "Thomas Aquinas on Human Action," in *The Cambridge History of Later Medieval Philosophy,* ed. Norman Kretzmann, Anthony Kenny, and Jan Pinborg (Cambridge: Cambridge University Press, 1982), 654.

10. See *ST* I.77:1.

11. David M. Gallagher, "Free Choice and Free Judgment in Thomas Aquinas," *Archiv für Geschichte der Philosophie* 76 (1994): 276.

The Interdependence of Intellect and Will

There are a number of places where Aquinas describes the intellect and the will and their complementary functions. In an article about angels Aquinas makes some distinctions that apply to human beings as well as to angels.

> [The will] cannot be the same thing as the intellect of angel or human being. Because knowledge comes about in so far as the object known is in the knower, so that the intellect stretches out to what is outside it, inasmuch as what (in its essence) is outside it is in some way suited to being within it [*illud quod extra ipsum est per essentiam, natum est aliquo modo in eo esse*]. On the other hand, the will stretches out to what is outside it, inasmuch as by a certain inclination it tends, in some way, to the external thing itself [*quodammodo tendit in rem exteriorem*]. Now it belongs to one faculty to have within itself something which is outside it, and to another faculty to tend to a thing outside it. Consequently intellect and will must necessarily be different powers in every creature.[12]

Human beings thus relate to the world in two distinctive and complementary ways. Through the intellect they take in what is outside them. This "bringing inside" is actually a way of describing the intellect as it "extends itself to what is outside it"—so there is no danger of forgetting that knowledge is a relationship we have with things and not just an internal possession of thoughts about things. Through the will human beings go out *in rem exteriorem,* "toward the external thing." Willing is a movement that brings about a change in our active relationship with the world and not just in our understanding. We involve ourselves, as Aquinas writes in *De veritate,* with "the being that the thing has in itself" and not just with its being as it is understood.[13]

Human beings take things in through the intellect and go out to them through the will; they think and they act; they understand the world and they try to achieve things in this world. There seems to be a natural progression from understanding to willing, and in a number of places Aquinas writes in a straightforward way about the dependence of the will on the intellect. We touched on this topic in chapter 2. We share with all animals an ability to be moved by what we apprehend in our environment.

12. *ST* I.59:2c.

13. *DV* 22:11c.

"An animal is able to desire what it apprehends, and not only that to which it is inclined by its natural form."[14] The will depends, moreover, on reason to supply its object.[15] Three passages illustrate this point.

The will does not do the ordering, but tends to something as it is ordered by reason. Consequently this word "intention" indicates an act of the will, presupposing the ordering of the reason as it orders something to the end.[16]

The goodness of the will depends properly on the object. Now the will's object is proposed to it by reason. Because the good as it is understood [*bonum intellectum*] is the object of the will proportioned to it.[17]

If then we consider the movement of the powers of the soul on the part of the object specifying the act, the first principle of motion is from the intellect, for in this way the good as it is understood [*bonum intellectum*] moves even the will itself.[18]

In this scheme it is the intellect that first understands what is good and the will that consequently seeks it. There are so many fitting examples one could imagine: A woman sees that a job advertised in the newspaper has a high salary, so she puts in an application for the post. A man catches sight of a particularly striking painting in a gallery, so he sits down to contemplate it. A child is learning to read, so her parents help her with her homework. There are objective goods here—money, beauty, literacy—and they have to be understood by the intellect before they can be sought by the will. While there is certainly much more to acting than simply understanding, nevertheless we cannot desire or act unless we already have an objective understanding of the goods before us:

The object of the intellect is more simple and more absolute than the object of the will, since the object of the intellect is the very meaning of desirable good [*ipsa ratio boni appetibilis*]; and the desirable good, whose meaning is grasped by the intellect [*cuius ratio est in intellectu*], is the object of the will.[19]

14. *ST* I.80:1c.

15. Reason *(ratio)* and intellect are the same power in human beings, though they work in different ways. Through intellect we apprehend intelligible truth; through reason we build on this truth and connect it with other truths and so arrive at a deeper intelligible truth. See *ST* I.79:8.

16. *ST* I-II.12:1ad3.

17. *ST* I-II.19:3c.

18. *DM* 6c [339–43].

19. *ST* I.82:3c.

It is difficult to translate this passage fairly, yet the main idea is clear. In order for the will to be attracted to a good, the intellect must first take in the fact that something *is* good and desirable [*ipsa ratio boni appetibilis*], it must comprehend its *ratio,* its meaning.

The will, therefore, depends on the intellect. The intellect takes priority. In *ST* I.82:4, however, Aquinas tries to look at the question in another way. In the first articles of question I.82 Aquinas accepts that the will moves human beings toward their *beatitudo* (happiness), toward their perfect good (art. 1), by seeking certain particular goods (art. 2), in response to the understanding that the intellect has of what is good (art. 3). *Bonum enim intellectum movet voluntatem,* "the good which is understood moves the will."[20] Then, in article 4, Aquinas shifts to another level and asks whether the will moves the intellect. At first sight this is a surprising and perhaps unnecessary question. One might think that Aquinas has already resolved the question of the order of intellect and will. The will, he has already shown, is the movement of human beings toward the good as it is presented by the intellect. Now, strangely, Aquinas asks whether this process of understanding is itself something that we have to want. This is a reflexive question about whether the act of the intellect, which furnishes the will with its object, is itself something that we desire, something that we actively seek, something for which we are responsible.

Reflexivity is a hugely significant issue, and it will allow us to return to the subject of self-consciousness that we touched on in part one. It is worth looking at *ST* I.82:4 in depth, together with the related articles *DV* 22:12 ("Does the will move the intellect and the other powers of the soul?"), *ST* I-II.9:1 ("Whether the will is moved by the intellect?"), and certain passages in *DM* 6. The insights it provides might help us to answer some of the questions that were left hanging at the end of part one: How are we conscious of our consciousness of things? How are we present to our presence to things? How can we at one and the same time affirm and question our identity and our understanding of the world?

The objections to the reflexive thesis of *ST* I.82:4 all revolve around the problem of priority. I will paraphrase the three short arguments. Objection 1: It has already been established (in art. 3) that the intellect precedes and

20. *ST* I.82:3ad2.

moves the will by its understanding of the good. (In *DV* 22:12obj1 Aquinas cites Augustine: "For nothing is loved or desired unless it is known.")[21] Objection 2: It is the nature of the will to move (the human being) after it has been moved (by the good that is understood), and it is the nature of the intellect to move the will (by understanding the good) on the basis of something that does not move (the apprehended good). In other words, there is a nonmoving foundation to movement, a source of movement, which in this case is the goodness of the object understood. In other words, the reality of the world is what founds our understanding and therefore our desires. Objection 3: Aquinas will not allow any room for some kind of unmotivated, purposeless, irrational willing. The will is precisely the rational appetite, and "we can will nothing but what we understand."[22] So if the will does move us to understand, it must have a reason to do this, and so we must already think that it is good to understand at this moment. This willing (of the process of understanding) must be on the basis of some prior understanding, by the intellect, of the goodness of this act of understanding. This prior understanding would itself have needed willing, "and so on indefinitely, which is impossible."[23] In other words, if willing is to be rational, there must be at least some foundation in the intellect for the initial act of willing.

All three objections argue that the priority of the intellect is essential to the whole structure that Aquinas has been working to build. Without this priority: (obj1) our understanding has no objective foundation in the world, (obj2) our willing has no objective foundation in what is understood, and (obj3) a vicious circle of understanding and willing is created in which there is no beginning and no possibility of justifying any thought or action.

Exercise and Specification

In the body of *ST* I.82:4 Aquinas makes some distinctions and begins to explore the reflexive nature of the soul. We can relate his answers here to those he gives in the related articles *DV* 22:12, *ST* I-II.9:1, and *DM* 6. There are two ways in which one thing can move another thing.

21. *DV* 22:12obj1.
22. *ST* I.82:4obj3.
23. *ST* I.82:4obj3.

> First, as an end; for instance, when we say that the end moves the agent. In this way the intellect moves the will because the good understood is the object of the will, and moves it as an end.[24]

Aquinas never renounces this principle that the will can only ever seek what the intellect presents to it as good. The "end that moves" gives shape and direction to the movement. In *DV* 22:12 Aquinas characterizes this end as the *ratio agendi,* the *ratio movendi:* it is the reason for acting, the pattern or meaning or sense of this particular movement. He clarifies this issue by saying that the *ratio agendi* is "the form of the agent by which it acts." This form "is in the agent by way of intention," through its reception by the intellect, and "not according to the existence it has of its nature [*non secundum esse naturae*]."[25] The intellect, therefore, grasps the goal to be achieved and presents it to the will, it *praeconcipit* ("conceives beforehand") the *ratio* of the end.

The second way in which one thing is said to move another thing is this:

> A thing is said to move as an agent, in the way that what causes an alteration moves the thing it alters, and what pushes moves what is pushed [*sicut alterans movet alteratum, et impellens movet impulsum*]. In this way the will moves the intellect and all the powers of the soul.[26]

Alterare has the general sense of altering, changing, or making different; *impellere* has a slightly more specific sense of instigating, inciting, or initiating the process of change. *DV* 22:12 gives a simple explanation of this. Action and movement concern things as they are in themselves, in the world, and not as they are spiritually in the soul by way of intention. It is the will that relates to things in this way, which inclines human beings to real things in the world and not just to intentions in their minds. We could paraphrase this by saying that no amount of theorizing will actually make anything happen. Aquinas offers a terse example: The idea of heat never kept anyone warm ("it is not heat in the soul which heats, but that which is in fire").[27]

In *ST* I-II.9:1 (and in *DM* 6) Aquinas identifies these two types of movement by distinguishing between the exercise or use *(exercitium vel usus)* of

24. *ST* I.82:4c.
25. *DV* 22:12c.
26. *ST* I.82:4c.
27. *DV* 22:12c.

an act and its determination *(determinatio)* or specification *(specificatio).*[28] He uses the analogy of sight. To see anything at all we have to exercise our sight, we actually have to be seeing. If we are then exercising our sight, what we actually see (the objects, the colors, the distances) is determined by the world we are looking at and not by ourselves. "The first of these is on the part of the subject, which is sometimes acting, sometimes not acting, while the other is on the part of the object, by reason of which the act is specified."[29] Aquinas recalls the language of "form" from *DV* 22:12 and writes that the determination specified by the object is a type of formal principle, and "the first formal principle is universal 'being' and 'truth,' which is the object of the intellect."[30]

So there are two types of movement: exercise, which gets the whole process going; and specification, which determines how the process will develop. The intellect, like other powers of the soul, has its own proper object, its own good, which is the truth of things. Once it is acting, the activity of the intellect is governed by its proper object, but this intellectual activity itself needs activating—it does not just happen. Intellectual activity is not an independent, uncontrollable vegetative function (like sweating) since we can choose not to understand something. Nor is it an essential aspect of being human that occurs simply by virtue of our being human (like being alive), since we are still human even if we are not understanding.[31] Intellectual activity, with its particular ends, needs activating by the will, which seeks the more universal human good (which is happiness).

Aquinas continues in the body of *ST* I.82:4:

> Now the object of the will is good and the end in general, and each power is directed to some suitable good proper to it, as sight is directed to the perception of colour, and the intellect to the knowledge of truth. Therefore the will as agent moves all the powers of the soul to their respective acts, except the natural powers of the vegetative part, which are not subject to our decision.[32]

28. In *ST* I-II.9:1 and *DM* 6c "determination" and "specification" are synonymous and used interchangeably. In *ST* I-II.10:2 Aquinas writes only of "specification."

29. *ST* I-II.9:1c.

30. *ST* I-II.9:1c.

31. This is why Aquinas writes that the intellect is a *power* of the soul (which can be acting or not acting) and is not to be identified with the essence of the soul (which simply *is* as long as the human being is alive). See *ST* I.77:1.

32. *ST* I.82:4c.

There are a number of points to note here. The will activates an act of understanding but does not specify the content of the understanding. This activation is for the sake of an end, which is the universal good that the human being seeks, and so the activation is itself based on a prior understanding of the universal good. Yet there is not a vicious circle, since the prior understanding of happiness that motivates the will is not the same as the particular understanding which the intellect achieves now in this particular act of understanding.

A similar argument is put forward in *DM* 6:

> But if we consider the movement of the powers of the soul on the part of the exercise of the act, in this way the principle of motion is from the will. For the power to which the principle end pertains always moves to act the power to which pertains that which is for the end, for example the military art moves the bridle-maker to operate. And in this way the will moves both itself and all the other powers: for I understand because I will to, and likewise I use all the other powers and habits because I will to do so.[33]

The implications of this are profound. All human understanding is for the sake of something larger, which is our ultimate goal in life—whatever that may be.[34] We are not trapped in the immediacy of our present experience. We do not just automatically understand the world and automatically seek what we understand. We also decide whether we want to understand or not, we determine when we shall understand, on the basis of a larger understanding and an already established commitment to a larger goal. In other words, we have a reflective distance from those acts that seem to be a constitutive part of our experience. On the one hand, we understand and evaluate the world to which we are present; there is an immediacy and transparency that creates a kind of identification between self and world and values and actions. On the other hand, we are also understanding and evaluating this very process of understanding and evaluating the world, in the light of a deeper understanding of who we are and what we seek.

Before analyzing the responses Aquinas gives to the objections to *ST* I.82:4, it is worth pausing to remind ourselves that intellect and will are powers of the soul, and that it is the integrated human being who acts.

33. *DM* 6c [343–52].

34. We will look at the question of how this ultimate goal is determined by each human being in chapter 6.

The faculties are not separate agents. Although we can identify the distinct stages involved in this mutual determination of intellect and will, there is a unified process taking place. David Gallagher explains it this way:

> When we say, in a kind of shorthand, that the will moves the intellect or the intellect moves the will, we always mean that the *person* voluntarily exercises his capacity to know or that the person, through an act of knowing, determines himself to choose one act or another.[35]

The exercise of the intellect's act and the specification of the will's act occur together, as part of a single process with distinct aspects.

Reflexivity of Intellect and Will

The reply to the first objection of *ST* I.82:4 is a substantial reflection on the interrelation of intellect and will and is like a continuation of the body of the article. Aquinas's key insight is that there are two ways of considering intellect and will. First, one can consider these powers in terms of their general object, "as apprehensive of universal being and truth," as "appetitive of universal good."[36] Second, one can consider the intellect or the will *secundum quod est quaedam res, et particularis potentia habens determinatum actum,* "as a thing of a certain sort and a particular power having a determinate act." We can, as it were, stand within the functioning of intellect or of will, looking out at their objects, or we can stand outside these processes and see them as objects of investigation or of desire in themselves, as observable things, powers, and acts. Human beings are not only within their experience of understanding and wanting, looking out to the world, transparently concerned with the true and the good. We are not just completely caught up in our own activity, unaware of ourselves. We are also aware of our own understanding and wanting, because these are acts that we can view taking place within our "world" as well as vantage points on that world. We are conscious of the act of our own consciousness of the world, and thus we are implicitly conscious of and present to ourselves. The soul, of which intellect and will are powers, is not just formed by the world and attracted to what it finds, it is also formed by its own understanding of *itself-being-formed* and attracted by its understanding of *itself-*

35. Gallagher, "Free Choice and Free Judgment in Thomas Aquinas," 276.
36. *ST* I.82:4ad1.

being-attracted. It may seem tendentious to draw so much meaning out of a straightforward distinction, but the reflexive nature of intellect and will is brought out with great clarity in the second half of this first reply:

> If, however, we take the intellect as regards the common nature of its object and the will as a determinate power, then again the intellect is higher than and prior to the will, because under the notion of being and truth [*sub ratione entis et veri*] (which the intellect apprehends) is contained both the will itself, and its act, and its object. Wherefore the intellect understands the will, and its act, and its object, just as it understands other species of things, as stone or wood, which are contained in the common notion of being and truth. But if we consider the will as regards the common nature of its object, which is good, and the intellect as a certain thing and a particular power, then the intellect itself, and its act of understanding, and its object, which is truth, each of which is some species of good, is contained under the common notion of good, as one particular instance of it [*sub communi ratione boni continetur, velut quoddam speciale*]. And in this way the will is higher than the intellect, and can move it.[37]

So, in some respects, the will is an object for the intellect, and in other respects, the intellect for the will. There is no suggestion, however, that one consideration excludes the other. The simultaneous reflexivity of intellect and will is a perpetual possibility, as Aquinas implies in the conclusion to this reply, which repeats a thought from *ST* I.16:4ad1.

> From this we can understand why these powers encompass each other in their acts [*hae potentiae suis actibus invicem se includunt*], because the intellect understands the will to will, and the will wills the intellect to understand [*quia intellectus intelligit voluntatem velle, et voluntas vult intellectum intellegere*]. In the same way good is contained under truth, inasmuch as it is an understood truth, and truth is contained under good, inasmuch as it is a desired good.[38]

When this same argument about the mutual influence of acts of intellect and will on each other is referred to in *ST* I-II.17:1 Aquinas adds the following seemingly paradoxical conclusion: "The result is that an act of reason precedes an act of will, and conversely [*actum voluntatis praeveniri ab actu rationis, et e converso*]."[39]

37. *ST* I.82:4ad1.
38. *ST* I.82:4ad1.
39. *ST* I-II.17:1c.

At this point it could be objected that none of this is properly reflexive, since the intellect can be an object for the will, and the will an object for the intellect, but it has not been established that each can be an object for itself. A preliminary answer, staying within the bounds of *ST* I.82:4, could rightly refer to the unity of the soul. It is the soul that reflects on itself, through the operation of these two powers. There is only one soul, which wills its understanding and understands its willing. This idea alone would provide a remarkable foundation for an understanding of self-consciousness, self-possession, and freedom. *DV* 22:12, however, goes further and provides a much more explicit statement of the capacity of each power to reflect on itself as well as on the other powers. Aquinas cites the immateriality of the soul as a reason for this.

The higher powers of the soul, because immaterial, are capable of reflecting upon themselves. Both the will and the intellect, therefore, reflect upon themselves, and upon each other, and upon the essence of the soul, and upon all its powers [*reflectuntur super se, et unum super alterum, et super essentiam animae, et super omnes eius vires*]. The intellect understands itself and the will and the essence of the soul and all the soul's powers. Similarly the will wills itself to will, and the intellect to understand, and wills the essence of the soul, and similarly the other powers [*Intellectus enim intelligit se, et voluntatem, et essentiam animae, et omnes animae vires; et similiter voluntas vult se velle, et intellectum intelligere, et vult essentiam animae, et sic de aliis*].[40]

These statements about reflexivity could not be clearer, but they raise the question of what it means for something to act on itself. In *ST* I-II.9:3 Aquinas addresses this question by asking how the will can move itself. He concludes that in willing an end it can will the means to this end, although in this case something that is actual (the will already willing the end) brings about a new willing (the will willing the means) that was only potential, and so the will does not move itself to move "in respect of the same" *(secundum idem)*.[41] This clarification of a necessary order within the reflexive activity of each power is what stops Aquinas's claims descending into absurdity; in chapter 6 we will look at the hierarchy of goods and truths that stabilizes human action. Yet we should not shy away from that element of

40. *DV* 22:12c.
41. *ST* I-II.9:3ad1.

circularity that haunts these discussions about reflexivity and which Aquinas readily acknowledged:

Since there is in reflection a certain similarity to circular motion, in which what is last in the movement is what was originally the beginning [*Cum in reflexione sit quaedam similitudo motus circularis in quo est ultimum motus quod primo erat principium*], we must so express ourselves in regard to reflection that what was originally prior then becomes posterior.[42]

A final citation on this subject leaves no doubt about the reflexive processes involved in something like choice:

Choice precedes use, if they be referred to the same object. But nothing hinders the use of one thing preceding the choice of another. And since the acts of the will react on one another, in each act of the will we can find both consent and choice and use; so that we may say that the will consents to choosing, and consents to consenting, and uses itself in consenting and choosing [*voluntas consentit se eligere, et consentit se consentire, et utitur se ad consentiendum et eligendum*].[43]

These are huge claims, as radical as anything in Sartre, about the capacity we have to take a view on ourselves and on our involvement with the world. Aquinas seems to go even further than Sartre by stating that the intellect can even reflect upon the essence of the soul (see above, *DV* 22:12c). He proposes all this without any danger of dualism, without any suggestion of a separate self.

What is the point of introducing this reflexive second level to the functioning of the soul? Is it not enough for human beings to relate to the world without relating to their own powers? What is the difference, for example, between willing and willing to will, between knowing and knowing that one knows? Why the duplication? The answer is that it will allow Aquinas to explain how human beings are free. If we apprehend our own involvement with the world we can assess what we are doing and why we are doing it, we can judge what we wish to understand and whether we want to act. Aquinas believes that we have a presence-to-self through this presence to our acts of intellect and will. Without this we cannot be free. His central contention,

42. *DV* 22:12ad1.
43. *ST* I-II.16:4ad3.

repeated time and again, is that human beings do not just take in the world through knowledge and reach out to it through desire, we also know our own knowing and desiring, and desire our own knowing and desiring.

Understanding, therefore, is an act of the intellect that only takes place when it is wanted by the will. There are different levels to this. To understand anything at all, to understand in general, we have to want to understand in general, we have to want the intellect to function. To understand this object, we have to want to understand this object. To understand this aspect of this object, we have to want to understand this aspect of this object. This never means that the will is determining the nature of what is understood, since this formal determination is specified solely by the object and apprehended by the intellect. Yet it means that whenever we understand anything we have to think that it is good to understand, and good to understand this object, and good to understand this object in this way. Each level of understanding is an act that needs willing, although the different acts may be implicitly willed in a single act.

There are many unresolved issues here, and I will leave most of them hanging. I will return to the problems of circularity, priority, and the foundation of our ultimate goals in chapter 6 on freedom. But one note needs to be made at this stage about *ST* I.82:4ad3, which seems to undermine the thesis I am presenting here, and indeed the arguments Aquinas has put forward in the rest of the article. The third objection was concerned with the infinite regress that seems to be established if the will moves the intellect to understand, and if that very willing requires some prior understanding, and so on. Aquinas replies:

> There is no need to go on indefinitely, but we must stop at the intellect as having priority [*sed statur in intellectu sicut in primo*]. For some apprehension must precede every movement of the will, whereas not every apprehension is preceded by a movement of the will [*Omnem enim voluntatis motum necesse est quod praecedat apprehensio, sed non omnem apprehensionem praecedit motus voluntatis*]. But the principle of counselling and understanding is an intellectual principle higher than our intellect, and this is God [*Sed principium consiliandi et intelligendi est aliquod intellectivum principium altius intellectu nostro, quod est Deus*]—as Aristotle says in the *Eudemian Ethics*. And in this way he shows that there is no need to proceed indefinitely.[44]

44. *ST* I.82:4ad3; referring to Aristotle's *Eudemian Ethics* 7:14, 1248a18ff.

Taken out of context, the central phrase seems to deny the interdependence of intellect and will: "... not every apprehension is preceded by a movement of the will."[45] It appears to contradict Aquinas's argument earlier in the same article that, as far as the activation of the intellect is concerned *(per modum agentis),* "the will moves the intellect and all the other powers of the soul"; and that, as far as the powers include each other in their acts, "the intellect understands that the will wills, and the will wills the intellect to understand."[46] But the reply needs to be read carefully. It is not at all clear in what respect the intellect has priority, or what kind of apprehension is at issue here. Does Aquinas mean that sometimes the intellect functions in isolation from the will, as if we have two distinct modes of knowing (one willed, the other not); or two distinct objects of knowledge (one kind willed, and the other not)? Such an interpretation would seem to run counter to the body of the article and to the response to the first objection, and it would leave us with acts (of knowing) that were not truly human acts, in the terms set by Aquinas, since they would not include the active involvement of the human person which is signified by the will.

Or perhaps there is some initial apprehension at the beginning of any process of deliberation when a possible goal "comes to mind," not because we have decided to investigate it, but because of external circumstances or because of the "internal" workings of our memory or imagination or subconscious. Sometimes things just happen, sometimes thoughts just "happen," and we have to determine whether to focus our attention on them and pursue them, or whether to let them fall away. Eleonore Stump, in considering this third reply, gives the example of hearing the telephone ring when one is immersed in another activity.[47] We hear the telephone; we reflect on whether to answer it or not; and then we stop what we are doing and go to answer it. There is no question of an infinite regress here, since this particular process of decision making began with an unexpected event

45. It is striking how often this phrase is quoted in isolation as a kind of proof-text. See, e.g., P. S. Eardley, "Thomas Aquinas and Giles of Rome on the Will," *Review of Metaphysics* 56 (2003): 845–46; and T. H. Irwin, "The Scope of Deliberation: A Conflict in Aquinas," *Review of Metaphysics* 44 (1990): 23–24, where Irwin refers to the passage, and concludes that "intellect is prior to will and independent of it" (23), and that "the intellect operates independently of the will and initiates the motions of the will" (24)—which seems to be drawing far too much from Aquinas's few words.

46. *ST* I.82:4c and *ST* I.82:4ad1.

47. Eleonore Stump, *Aquinas* (Abingdon, U.K.: Routledge, 2003), 282.

and an uninvited apprehension of that event. This is uncontroversial, and says nothing more than the fact that knowledge is rooted in experience. But notice that the initial apprehension is not a knowledge that determines which choice we shall actually make—it is the very thing that causes there to be a choice in the first place. We have to attend to that apprehension (or not), weigh up the different possible responses (or not), make a choice (or not), and do what we have chosen to do (or not). All of this involves both the will and the intellect; and none of it is determined by the initial apprehension. From the very moment when we first take notice of the initial apprehension, intellect and will are involved inextricably in that reflexive process described so fully in the rest of the article. So on this reading, in a restricted sense, some kinds of knowledge do arise without any movement of the will, and provide a foundation for the whole willed process that ensues. But this does not mean that for Aquinas every movement of the will is directed with any necessity by a prior determination of reason.

On another reading, we should note that Aquinas relates whatever this "unwilled" apprehension is to the *principium consiliandi et intelligendi,* to the principle or source or foundation of our deliberating and understanding; and this he identifies with an intellectual principle higher than our intellect, namely, God. Notice that he does not say that the *principium consiliandi et intelligendi* is caused by God, or has its foundation in God; he says that it *is* God—which suggests that the *principium* is not so much a first principle that we use within our deliberating and understanding, but is rather a transcendent foundation of our deliberating and understanding. Aquinas thus shifts the focus of his response away from the question of whether, within our rational activity, the intellect or will has priority (he has dealt with this in the response to the first objection), and he turns it toward the larger question of whether our whole rational activity has some foundation in intellect. And he answers, Yes—but it is God's intellect not ours. This is what saves the whole intellectual-volitional structure from an infinite regress.

So perhaps the unwilled apprehension referred to is not so much a particular unsought item of knowledge (which then founds a particular act of the will), but is instead the more fundamental orientation of the intellect to the truth, which must have its external foundation in God.[48] The men-

48. This interpretation would create a parallel with *DM* 6c (390–91), which tackles the apparent circularity of willing and taking counsel, and concludes that the will must be moved "by

tion of the *Eudemian Ethics* makes this interpretation plausible, since in other places where Aquinas refers to the same text it is because he is concerned with God as an exterior, foundational principle for our knowing and willing, and not as a source of particular interior acts of supposedly (unwilled) knowing or (unknown) willing. In *ST* I-II.9:4c, for example, he refers to the *Eudemian Ethics,* and concludes that "the will advanced to its first movement in virtue of the instigation of some exterior mover."

In conclusion, it is not clear exactly what Aquinas is saying in this difficult response to the third objection of *ST* I.82:4. If only he had given some examples of the unwilled apprehensions he is describing. Perhaps he has in mind some very specific convictions or principles of reason that are planted in us by nature (and ultimately by God); perhaps he is pointing to the initial apprehensions that catch our mind unexpectedly when we are focused on other things; perhaps he is referring, as he does in the response to the first objection and in the previous article, to the different ways in which the intellect can be considered higher than and prior to the will—knowing that the will, in other ways, must also be considered higher than and prior to the intellect; perhaps he is arguing that the whole work of deliberating and understanding relies on a transcendent foundation that is itself intellectual; perhaps there are other issues here. The one thing that is clear from this statement about the priority of the intellect is that Aquinas is not undermining the carefully constructed arguments made in the rest of the article about the interdependence and reflexivity of intellect and will.

The Will Activating the Intellect

The main concern of this present chapter is to notice the implications for Aquinas's concept of objectivity. We have learnt that through the intellect human beings are open to the world. We are present to the objective reality of things and transformed by them. But now the functioning of this intellect seems to depend on the human will. Despite Aquinas's reassurances that the understanding of the intellect is formed solely by its object, we are left with the suspicion that our own desires *determine* our understanding. If this is true, it is a strange and very human notion of objectivity. I will

something external, by the impulse of which the will begins to will [*ab aliquo exteriori, cuius instinctu voluntas velle incipiat*]"—namely, God.

sketch some ways in which Aquinas's idea of objectivity is indeed thoroughly *human,* and make some links with the views of Sartre outlined in the previous chapter.

Aquinas has likened understanding to sight.[49] We have to open our eyes "before" we can see anything; we have to "exercise" our sight, to get it working, "before" this sight can be specified by the objects we see. This is true even though the exercise and specification are simultaneous—the opening of the eyes coincides with the beginning of seeing. So we can't begin to see in general without actually seeing anything in particular, but we must want to see in general in order to see anything in particular. In the same way the intellect, "before" it can be specified by its objects, needs to be exercised. In terms of this exercising, "no object moves the will necessarily, for no matter what the object be, it is in our power not to think of it, and consequently not to will it actually."[50] If we stop thinking about something, then we will stop desiring it, so if we want to desire anything in particular we have to have the more general desire to think at all. Human beings can't understand anything unless they have an interest in understanding. The functioning of the intellect is an act that must be willed. This may seem a trivial point. We need to have a brief digression on the subject of the human end in order to appreciate its significance—even though the subject will be dealt with more fully in chapter 6.

In the first question of Part I-II of the *Summa* Aquinas discusses the nature of our final end. It will help to summarize the relevant conclusions: (*ST* I-II.1:1) Human actions are those in our control that proceed from a deliberate will. The will seeks an end, a good, and so human actions are those done for an end. (1:3) Actions are specified by this end, which preexists in one's intention. (1:4) There must be a final end, a first thing that attracts us in the order of intention, for the sake of which an action takes place, otherwise no good would actually move our appetite. (1:5) Each individual can have only one final end at any moment. We cannot direct our will to various final ends at the same time since we are integrated beings who seek a single fulfillment in our perfect good—whatever that may be. (1:6) Whatever we desire, it must be desired for the sake of our last end, because we wish all goods to contribute somehow to our perfect good, and

49. See the comments on *ST* I-II.9:1, above.
50. *ST* I-II.10:2c.

our will could not be attracted to a particular good unless we were seeking our greatest good through it. (1:7) All human beings share in this desire for their own fulfillment, but they do not all agree about which good will satisfy this ultimate longing. Some desire riches, some pleasure, others something else.

So all human actions take place for the sake of the ultimate good of the one who acts. We can now combine this conclusion with the earlier conclusion that the functioning of the intellect is an act that must be willed. This means that *all* our understanding has to occur within the framework of our goals and desires. No understanding is neutral or passive, it never just comes to us, even though the content of understanding comes from the object. There is therefore always a personal stake in human understanding, it depends on a commitment to our final goal, and it only takes place if we judge that understanding is a good that helps us achieve our final goal. This has nothing to do with the distinction between the speculative and the practical intellects.[51] All acts of the intellect, speculative as much as practical, are *acts* that have to be wanted and willed because they are good and because they help us to achieve our final goal. Acts both of the speculative and the practical intellect have to be judged (by the practical intellect) to be worthwhile.

Objective knowledge therefore requires the personal commitment of the subject, and each single act of understanding has to be wanted as a means to our happiness. In this sense our objective understanding of the world reflects our subjective attitude to the world. Understanding is still not in any way specified by the desires of the subject, but the fact that there is any understanding at any moment is completely dependent on our deepest personal desire. Our desire to understand (or not) influences the way the world is revealed to us, and different human worlds emerge, depending on the interest of the subject. This is true even before we take into account what our specific interests are. The measure of our interest as such affects the world we allow ourselves to encounter. We can take an example. Some tourists visit London together. One doesn't want to learn anything because he is tired from the journey; one hates learning because she associates it with dull school lessons; one is hungry for knowledge so he can

51. See *ST* I.79:11, where Aquinas explains that they are the same power directed either to consideration of the truth or to operation.

use it to impress people at home; another wants to understand all she sees in order to please the tour guide. They have different reasons for understanding or not understanding the world they are in, for exercising their intellect. Their desire will determine whether they take in this world or not, yet the world they take in will not depend on them at all. In this sense the world that each of them discovers is a human world and depends completely on the ultimate goal that motivates them. David Burrell writes of Aquinas's view:

> Knowledge or information can be assimilated only in the measure we have sought it. This is not to say, of course, that we find only what we're looking for! We may well be surprised. But at least we have to be probing in the area which yields the unexpected knowledge.[52]

If understanding *in general* needs exercising, it is also the case that *each particular act* of understanding needs exercising. We cannot see unless we are willing to open our eyes *and* to pay attention to the particular object within our sight. The willing of the general exercise is included in the particular exercise, but it is nevertheless distinct. This is apparent when we have a desire to see a particular object which is frustrated by an unwillingness to see in general (e.g., we want to watch the film but we are too tired to keep our eyes open), and when we have a desire to see in general which is frustrated by a failure to see anything in particular (e.g., we want to see but there is a power outage and it is pitch black). We can recall the following passage already cited:

> But if we consider the will as regards the common nature of its object, which is good, and the intellect as a certain thing and a particular power, then the intellect itself, and its act of understanding, and its object, which is truth, each of which is some species of good, are contained under the common notion of good, as particular things. And in this way the will is higher than the intellect.[53]

So the will has to want each particular act of understanding. Put another way, we can only understand something if we think it is good to understand. It is vital to remember that it is the goodness of the act of under-

52. David B. Burrell, *Aquinas: God and Action* (South Bend, Ind.: University of Notre Dame Press, 1979), 121.

53. *ST* I.82:4ad1.

standing that is in question at this reflexive level, and not the goodness of the object of understanding, which is determined by the being of the object itself. The intellect alone discerns the goodness of a thing.[54]

The Possibility of Different Points of View

If the exercise of the intellect by the will influences our understanding of the world, it is also true that the manner in which the intellect is exercised influences our understanding as well. The intellect approaches its object in different ways, from different perspectives. It does not just take a cold, neutral view of the world. The particular view it takes colors the nature of the good that it discovers, so that the personal approach adopted by the intellect, as much as the character of the object itself, determines which good the will is attracted to. This may seem to undermine Aquinas's contention that the good is specified solely by the object, and that the will is necessarily attracted to a good object. There are two articles in Part I-II that will help us clarify these questions.

In *ST* I-II.10:2 Aquinas asks whether the will is moved by its object of necessity. First, as we have already seen, Aquinas writes that no object moves the will to the exercise of its act necessarily, since it is in our power not to think of it and so not to be actually attracted to it. We would then expect Aquinas to say that at the level of specification, when the will is confronted with a particular object, the movement will be necessitated by the object. The will should either be attracted to the object or not, depending on the nature of the object. We have learnt that the goodness of a thing, its attractiveness, depends on its being, which is apprehended by the intellect. So there should be a necessity about the will's movement (or lack of movement) toward an object. Yet Aquinas doesn't quite say this. He does confirm our expectations by insisting that "if the will be offered an object which is good universally and from every point of view [*universaliter bonum et secundum omnem considerationem*], the will tends to it of necessity, if it wills anything at all; since it cannot will the opposite."[55] How could we not want the perfect good? But then he introduces a fascinating analogy with sight and says that we can decide whether we are moved by some-

54. We shall see in chapter 6 why a good object does not necessarily move the will even when it is understood by the intellect.

55. *ST* I-II.10:2c.

thing by deciding in what way we attend to it. As Sartre says, it is we who determine in what perspective the world is seen, and this perspective has a great significance.

Aquinas develops the analogy in this way: Sight is concerned with what is visible. It is "illuminated color" *(obiectum coloratum in actu)* that moves the sight.[56] If we are actually looking at something which is illuminated, if our sight is being exercised and we do not turn our eyes away, we cannot fail to see it.

> But if sight were confronted with something only partially illuminated [*quod non omnibus modis esset color in actu*], and with one part lit up, one part in darkness [*sed secundum aliquid esset tale, secundum autem aliquid non tale*], then sight would not necessarily see such an object, for it might direct its attention to that part of the object in darkness [*qua non est coloratum in actu*], and thus it would not see it.[57]

Aquinas imagines that part of an object is hidden in shadow. Let's say that a bright scarf is carelessly placed in an open drawer, with one end dangling out over the front. When we look at the end hanging in the light of the room, we see it quite clearly. But if we peer into the back of the drawer we can hardly see the scarf—its color and even its outline are indistinct in the darkness and we cannot distinguish it from the gloves and T-shirts. Aquinas wants to make a subtle distinction on which his whole philosophy of freedom depends. There is a difference, he believes, between (A) not looking at something and (B) looking at something without seeing it—even though in both cases we fail to see the thing. In the first case, we turn our gaze away from something. In the second case, we turn our gaze to a different part of the same thing, and this shift of attention means we are unable to see the object because of the nature of the object or of the circumstances.

This slightly strained analogy allows Aquinas to say that it is possible for us to see an object in a different way, and even to see "something" different, even though we are looking at the same thing. We have different

56. The analogy is difficult to follow. Aquinas writes that the color of an object can be *in actu* or not. The sense seems to be that the surface of an object can be illuminated and visible, or in darkness and therefore invisible. I have translated the texts quite freely with this meaning in mind.

57. *ST* I-II.10:2c.

apprehensions not because the formal specification given to sight by the color *of* the object changes, but because the nature of the attention given by the subject changes. So there is a real difference in what is seen that depends on the subject who sees even though what is seen is still specified solely by the object itself. Aquinas is struggling to express how a change in the subject can bring about a change in what is perceived without undermining the objective nature of the perception. Having made these distinctions in this example from the world of sensation, Aquinas then applies them to the powers of the soul.

Now just as illuminated colour is the object of sight, so is good the object of the will. Wherefore if the will be offered an object which is good universally and from every point of view, the will tends to it of necessity, if it wills anything at all; since it cannot will the opposite. If, on the other hand, the will is offered an object that is not good from every point of view [*quod non secundum quamlibet considerationem sit bonum*], it will not tend to it of necessity. And since lack of any good whatever brings an aspect of non-good [*quia defectus cuiuscumque boni habet rationem non boni*], consequently, that good alone which is perfect and lacking in nothing, is such a good that the will cannot not-will it, and this is Happiness. Whereas any other particular goods, in so far as they are lacking in some good, can be regarded as non-goods [*inquantum deficiunt ab aliquo bono, possunt accipi ut non bona*], and from this point of view, they can be set aside or approved by the will, which can tend to one and the same thing from various points of view [*secundum diversas considerationes*].[58]

The same thought is present in *De malo* 6:

If, however, there is a good of such a nature that it is not found to be good according to all the particular aspects that can be considered [*non inveniatur esse bonum secundum omnia particularia que considerari possunt*], it [the will] will not be moved of necessity even in regard to the determination of the act: for a person will be able to will its opposite, even while thinking about it, since perhaps it [the opposite] is good or fitting according to some other particular consideration; as, for instance, what is good for health is not good so far as enjoyment is concerned, and so on in regard to other things.[59]

58. *ST* I-II.10:2c.
59. *DM* 6c [441–49].

We have here one of the most striking conclusions from the discussion so far: *Any other particular goods, insofar as they are lacking in some good, can be regarded as nongoods.* This is going to be the foundation of Aquinas's defense of freedom in chapter 6. It's easy to think of examples. We look at a cake and can consider either how tasty it is or how fattening it is; we investigate a new business venture and can consider either the benefits it could bring or the financial risks it presents; we bump into a friend and can call to mind either her past generosity or her past impatience. Our response in each situation will be determined by the specific consideration we make, and not just by the object in view. The important thing to realize is that in each example the intellect can see both points of view. Both are true. Both truths are specified by the object. It is as if there are two rival acts of the intellect, two potential thoughts. But in fact they are both held at the same time. Either truth can be set aside or approved by the will. When the will does approve one truth it is not determining what is true, it is determining that a truth shall be noticed, by exercising a specific act of the intellect. The will is not determining what is good, it is determining which aspect of the good is understood. The reflexivity of the powers of the soul is essential here, since the will is exercising and so controlling the act of the intellect and not the specification of the good.

It is important to appreciate the significance of what Aquinas is doing here. He is trying to find a third way between intellectualism and voluntarism. Let us take each of these in turn. (A) *Intellectualism:* If the specification of the good depends solely on the object and our intellectual apprehension of that object, then the will must inevitably follow that good. It has no leeway, it cannot reinterpret the good, since the intellect is formed by the object alone. Intellectualism leads to determinism. (B) *Voluntarism:* If, alternatively, the will can specify what is good without being bound by our intellectual apprehension of the object, then we will certainly have more control over our goals and our actions, but our desires will not be rooted in the objectively apprehended reality of the world. Voluntarism leads to irrationalism. (C) *Aquinas's Third Way:* If, however, we can apprehend with our intellect a single object but view that object in different ways, the different views might attract or repel us in different ways. Intellectual determinism is avoided, because we are freely choosing to see this aspect of something rather than another aspect, and our actions will depend on our willingness to attend to the goodness of one aspect or the other. Equally, an irrational voluntarism is avoided because the nature of the aspect of the good which *is* seen depends solely on the specification provided by the object as it forms the intellect. In other words, what we desire is actually good. The will does not specify the good, it simply determines that one aspect of the good can or cannot be specified. The will determines the perspective in which the objectively determined good is seen.

These themes are deepened in *ST* I-II.13:6. Aquinas is writing about the freedom to choose. The body of the article reinforces the argument about perspective from 10:2, and explains how it is the reason that allows us to alter our point of view (our "consideration"). Human beings can will and not will, act and not act; and they can will this or that, and do this or that. This is possible because of the power of reason, which apprehends the good toward which the will tends. Surely, we assume, this apprehension depends on the object? Aquinas's answer is double-edged. The perfect good alone is always apprehended as good by the reason, since it lacks nothing, and it is therefore not possible to take a point of view on it (a "perspective") that would reveal it to be not-good. However:

> [Reason], in all particular goods, can consider the aspect of some good [*potest considerare rationem boni alicuius*], and the lack of some good (which has the aspect of evil), and in this respect it can apprehend any single one of such goods as to be chosen or to be avoided [*potest unumquodque huiusmodi bonorum apprehendere ut eligibile, vel fugibile*].[60]

So the reason changes its consideration and in this way the will is brought to seek a certain good. It is usually a bad thing, for example, to be cut open with a knife, but the patient accepts this at the hands of the surgeon who is trying to remove a tumor. The farmer wants to rejoice when it rains after a long drought but he is sad that the school sports day is ruined. A child falls into a surging river and a stranger hesitates on the bank, thinking alternatively of the danger of jumping in and of the duty of helping. This does not mean that human beings can change their final good, which is always the complete perfection of happiness. The particular goods that we are reinterpreting at any moment are always a means to our ultimate end. The necessity of our final end is one element of Aquinas's scheme that saves it from circularity and absurdity. Yet in each example the particular good under

60. *ST* I-II.13:6.

consideration will only be appreciated and sought if the will wants to consider it.

These two articles from Part I-II allow Aquinas to draw a startling conclusion. Every single particular good can be freely apprehended as not-good, without compromising in any way the objectivity of good and the openness of the intellect to truth. Every single particular good can thus be willed or not willed, depending on the point of view we take on it.

An Example: People in a Station

Aquinas has come to a number of conclusions: Understanding in general has to be willed. Every particular act of understanding has to be willed. Every object can be seen from different perspectives. Every good object can be seen to be bad in certain respects. An object can only be willed if it is seen to be good. It can only be seen to be good if the will approves and exercises this act of understanding it as good. This means that we cannot understand anything unless we think it is good to understand it, and that we will refuse to understand if we think that this understanding is bad for us. So our understanding of the world is entirely dependent on what we think is good for us, which is in turn dependent on the overall orientation of our lives to a final goal. We only see "what we want to see." Yet it bears repeating the proviso Aquinas has already made. It is the good of the act of understanding this object (an internal, reflexive good) that is at issue here, not the good of the object which is understood (which is determined entirely by the being of the object as apprehended by the intellect).

We can imagine an example. Five people are waiting in a station. One has an important exam the next day and is completely caught up in revising some texts. Another is daydreaming and oblivious to the surroundings. We can ignore these first two characters now. They have no interest at all in their environment. Their understanding, as far as it concerns the station, is not being exercised at all. The "world" of the station does not even figure in their conscious lives.

So we are left with three people who are alert and aware of their surroundings. They look around the same space but all notice different things. One surveys the architecture, another looks at the clothes of those milling around, another stares at the clock. This has nothing to do with whether the architecture is good or the clothes attractive. They look at different things because they have different interests. They have different views about what it is good to be interested in. They see different worlds, and the type of world they see depends on the type of world they want to see, even though the actual building or clothes or time they discover is determined by the nature of what they find in this world.

If they all look at the clock at the same time, will they see the same time? Of course they will. But they will only look at the clock if they have a reason to, and so their common discovery of a common time in a shared world will only take place if their individual interests converge on the same "object" (which is "the clock as timekeeper" and not just "the clock as beautiful object"). This is true even if their reasons for wanting to know the time are different. So the commonness of the time is not some neutral reality that unites them despite their disparate interests—it only unites them if their interests unite them around this common subject.

Is it possible for something to capture their attention and unite them in a commonly understood world? Is it possible to take them outside the realms of their personal interests? It might seem so, but this would be deceptive. Say that a passing stranger screams and falls to the ground clutching her heart, and all three of them look to see what is happening. It's true that something outside their immediate interests has caught their attention, but it is not divorced from their wider personal interests. They have an interest in paying attention to unexpected disturbances in public places for the sake of their own safety, or a concern for their fellow human beings, or a curiosity about the unknown. These interests are not impersonal and they are certainly not universal. There may be others in the station who don't "notice" the sound of screaming for different reasons. Some may have learnt to filter out inconvenient sounds, perhaps because of a deep selfishness; others may have lived in a war zone, which made them immune to signs of human suffering; others may have chosen to listen to music on headphones with the express purpose of insulating themselves from their environment.

Once they are looking toward the scene, the three are not united in a neutral world that has startled them away from their personal worlds, rather they are brought together by a common interest, which is to answer the question "How shall I respond to this?" Suddenly they share the same conception of what is good: "It is good to understand what has happened and decide how I should react." We can only understand something if we want to understand it. How do they react to the same situation? One goes to help, another opens the newspaper, another pulls out a camera and starts to take photographs. They see the same situation but their personal interests determine which aspect of the situation they see: they see it from different perspectives. This is stronger than saying that they interpret the same thing in different ways. They actually *see* different things. One sees a sick person who needs help; another sees a growing crowd of people that might delay the train; another sees a journalistic scoop for a local newspaper. All these things are true, they are specifications made by the object and apprehended by the intellect, and in theory any human being could understand the same truth. But in Aquinas's scheme, we can't understand anything unless we think it is good to understand this thing, and unless we are attracted to this way of understanding.

There are no neutral descriptions of what has happened. Even the seemingly objective statement "This person has had a heart attack" is a medical description that requires a commitment to a certain worldview. If everyone in the station adopts the medical point of view and shares in the interests of medics, then of course everyone can understand this description and enter this world. But there is no medical understanding without a medical interest, and one could take alternative scientific viewpoints on the same incident that would reflect different interests: acousticians, for example, could study the sound of the scream, physicists the fall of the body. In other words, there is no such thing as purely neutral knowledge. Knowledge without an interested, attentive, motivated knower is not knowledge at all.

The three characters in this example think and observe and act in different ways because their intellects consider a common object (the station, the collapsed person) in different ways. This in turn depends on the fact that the will commands the exercise of the intellectual act. Human beings have to allow themselves to start thinking and to continue thinking along a certain line of thought, even though the understanding itself is specified by the object under consideration. This act of the will is the foundation of all reasoning, and it saves Aquinas from an intellectual determinism that would insist there is only one way in which a given object or circumstance can specify our good.

The root of liberty is the will (which is where freedom lies [*sicut subiectum*]) but it is the reason that is its cause. For the will can tend freely towards a variety of things, because the reason can have various conceptions of good [*voluntas libere potest ad diversa ferri, quia ratio potest habere diversas conceptiones boni*].[61]

Aquinas is not a "compatibilist," one who believes that accounts of voluntary action are compatible with deterministic causal explanations.[62] David Gallagher draws attention to the reflexive roots of Aquinas's thinking on this matter. It is not enough to assert that the will can be moved without necessity by a number of alternative particular goods presented to it by the intellect. The crucial question is "how the intellect comes to consider an object in one way and not in another such that the will's act with respect to the object is specified as it is."[63] How, in other words, do we choose to dwell on one good rather than another? We do this by willing *the consideration of this good* (a reflexive act), which has to take place "before" we will *this good* (an act in the world). This two-stage explanation can seem to be a form of compatibilism, because our action in the world (the second stage) *is* determined solely by the good that is understood. The will necessarily moves toward the good that is understood in the world, which seems like a form of determinism. The decisive factor, however, is that the consideration of this good (the first stage) has to be willed. This willing is a reflexive movement that depends on the soul's ability to observe and judge its own acts. Our willingness to consider this good is not determined in any way by the objective nature of the good itself, which is why Aquinas's account is not compatible with determinism. Gallagher summarizes this clearly:

The *exercise* of the intellect's act is something voluntary. I may think of the utility of a murder and suppress the thought of its wickedness, or I may consider it in the opposite way. According as the intellect considers an action one way or another it will judge it to be either good or bad. But whether or not it considers one way or another is determined by the will. This is where the will's capacity either to command or to stop the exercise of reason is decisive. The judgment of an action's goodness or evil depends on how the agent considers it, and this consideration falls under the control of the will. [. . .] An act of choice is specified by the object which reason supplies. But which object reason supplies, or

61. *ST* I-II.17:1ad2.

62. See Norman Kretzmann, "Philosophy of Mind," in *The Cambridge Companion to Aquinas,* ed. Norman Kretzmann and Eleonore Stump (Cambridge: Cambridge University Press, 1993), 147–48.

63. Gallagher, "Free Choice and Free Judgment in Thomas Aquinas," 266.

better, under which aspect a particular action is judged, depends upon how the will exercises the intellect's act in its regard.[64]

Aquinas's genius lies in the fact that he locates freedom in the reflexive procedures that establish how the world is understood. Once this world is established, with its presently understood goods, he never needs to argue that the will asserts its "voluntariness" or "freedom" by going against what it understands to be good. Aquinas preserves the twin foundations of a "deterministic" intellectual specification of what is good and a "voluntaristic" exercise of the particular consideration that allows this specification. He holds onto his cake and eats it too.

All this begs a series of further questions: What is the reason for wanting to understand something in one way rather than another? What makes the will approve of one intellectual perspective and so notice one good rather than another? What, in other words, is the ultimate foundation of willing and understanding that saves Aquinas's system from circularity? These questions bring us to the issue of freedom, which will be discussed properly in chapter 6.

Understanding as a Subjective Objectivity

Each aspect of Sartre's "human world" is mirrored in Aquinas's account of the reflexivity of intellect and will. (A) Sartre says that the world of experience as such is only brought to light by the purposeful involvement of being-for-itself. Aquinas says that there must be an initial willingness of the will to understand anything at all. Even before the world reveals its particularities this general willingness gives a certain shape and rhythm to the appearance of the world, which depends on one's desire for truth and understanding. At any moment the will can think or not think about anything at all, for many different reasons. The pattern of thinking and not thinking decides the pattern of the appearance of the world. (B) Sartre says that human beings determine exactly which objects are given their attention. Their interests decide which "figures" will emerge from a field of possible understanding and which will recede into the "background." In Aquinas this is the willingness of the will to see some types of understanding as "good" and worthy of interest and to ignore others. We cannot understand anything

64. Ibid., 267.

unless we value the activity of understanding in question. Any good can be seen as not-good from a certain perspective, and any act of understanding can be seen as not-good from a certain perspective. (C) Sartre wrote about paying attention either to the roughness of the green peel or the green of the rough peel—these properties stand like figures against a background. Aquinas would agree that our understanding of any one kind of property is a good that must be sought by the will. The multifarious properties and characteristics of any object reveal themselves only if someone is interested in them.

For Aquinas, as for Sartre, every single thing understood is objective—whether we are considering the world as a whole, the objects within it, their orientation within its structure, or their characteristics. Our understanding is specified by the nature of what is understood. Yet this objectivity is only revealed through the interests of human beings, through the activation of the will as we seek specific, concrete goods (including the goods of understanding) in our quest for our ultimate good. The objective resistance of things is only met through the pressure of purposeful activity.

Objectivity, we could say, is subjective. We don't need to pretend that we stand in some neutral space outside our personal experience in order to begin the process of understanding the objective world. We act within a culture and a language, guided by a set of personal and communal goals, and as we act we come up against the objective. This is against the view, held with such force by someone like Karl Popper, that objective understanding is somehow adulterated by the presence of the subject. He went to great lengths to protect scientific knowledge from the errors of psychologism and could even assert that some forms of knowledge are totally independent of anyone's claim to know. "Knowledge in the objective sense is *knowledge without a knower:* it is *knowledge without a knowing subject.*"[65]

Aquinas, through his Averroist adversaries, confronted an analogous philosophical project to Popper's and took it seriously. The so-called Averroists argued, broadly speaking, that if a common truth is understood and

65. Karl R. Popper, "Epistemology without a Knowing Subject," in *Objective Knowledge, an Evolutionary Approach* (Oxford: Clarendon Press, 1979), 109. On the other hand, Popper's view connects with Sartre's convictions about the transparency and impersonality of unreflective consciousness and Aquinas's understanding of the openness of the intellect to the forms of other things.

shared by diverse people it must be because a unique, separate intellect is shared.[66] In other words, if there is one objective truth it must be that there is only one way of knowing it, which implies that there is only one intellect that understands. They believed that there can only be one way of knowing the one truth, and the individual knowing subject must not get in the way. We can glimpse the way Aquinas responds in a short passage from *De unitate intellectus contra averroistas*, chapter 5:

> It is therefore one thing which is understood both by me and by you. But it is understood by me in one way and by you in another, that is, by another intelligible species. And my understanding is one thing, and yours, another; and my intellect is one thing, and yours, another.[67]

Aquinas, like Sartre, thus makes understanding radically personal, without losing the objectivity of truth. We have to make things true in the sense that all understanding is something we have to do. Understanding is an act that has to be done for an end. What matters is how we conceive the world to be, where "conception" can imply both "thinking about what is" and "creating something new" (as in the conception of a baby). *Invenire* is another word that provides a useful double meaning: in contemporary English "to discover" and "to invent" have opposing senses, but in Latin a single word stands for both.

Aquinas and Sartre each emphasize the constructive work that needs to be done by each individual intellect in order to place the truth of things in the perspective of human understanding. Truth is not just found, ready-made—it has to be personalized. To think that we have to become more detached in order to become more objective is an illusion, in any area of understanding. Yet this is in no way a denial of universality or objectivity, because the truth gained by each person *is* the truth of things. The subjective element does not blur but reveals the being of things. The ontological

66. See, e.g., Weisheipl, *Friar Thomas D'aquino: His Life, Thought, and Works*, 250–54, and Edward P Mahoney, "Aquinas's Critique of Averroes' Doctrine of the Unity of the Intellect," in *Thomas Aquinas and His Legacy*, ed. David M. Gallagher, Studies in Philosophy and the History of Philosophy (Washington, D.C.: The Catholic University of America Press, 1994).

67. Thomas Aquinas, "De Unitate Intellectus Contra Averroistas," in *Sancti Thomae De Aquino Opera Omnia*, Iussu Empensaque Leonis XIII P. M. Edita, vol. 43 (Rome:Editori di San Tommaso, 1976). For an English translation, see Thomas Aquinas, *On the Unity of the Intellect against the Averroists*, trans. Beatrice H. Zedler (Milwaukee, Wis.: Marquette University Press, 1968), chapter 5, #112.

priority of things is what founds the universality of our particular modes of understanding. It is not the unicity of the intellect that guarantees the shared objectivity of truth, as the Averroists believed, but the unicity of the world as understood in different ways.

It will become clearer in the next two chapters how in both philosophers this personal construction of truth is the foundation for human freedom and responsibility. We are free to act because we are free to understand the world in different ways. If one starts with the assumption that there is only a single (and therefore determined) way of understanding the world common to all human beings, one's view of freedom will inevitably become voluntaristic. This is because freely made personal preferences, if they are not linked to a personalized understanding of the world, must therefore be made by an irrational will that turns against the shared and determined understanding.

In one sense, Aquinas would say, people live in the same "world" because the being that specifies *what* they understand is the same being, and their interests are always capable of overlapping and coinciding and determining *that* they understand this same being. In another sense, people live in different "worlds" since their interests vary slightly, or greatly, and they are forever understanding different aspects of different things for different purposes. This is why Aquinas could agree with Sartre when he writes:

> Knowledge puts us in the presence of the absolute, and there is a truth of knowledge. But this truth, although releasing to us nothing more and nothing less than the absolute, remains strictly human.[68]

Truth, according to Aquinas and Sartre, is not found by trying to escape from our personal interests. These interests give us a purchase on truth. Knowledge depends on desire, on love. If we come to share a larger truth it is because our interests and love have expanded and not because we have abandoned them for some impersonal neutrality.

68. *BN* 218; *EN* 255/270.

Part Three

HUMAN FREEDOM

Chapter 5

FREEDOM, CHOICE, AND THE INDETERMINATION OF REASON IN SARTRE

The Intentional Structure of the Act

Sartre and Aquinas, as we found in part one, have a shared understanding of how human identity is constituted by the free choices human beings make. We create ourselves and establish our goals through our actions, and these actions are not determined by any preexisting self. In part two we learnt how both thinkers believe that our interests and purposes determine how we understand the world, yet this personalised understanding still makes us present to a truth that is other than us. The subjective perspective we bring to things reveals their objectivity. Now in part three we need to ask about the foundation of this whole process of acting and understanding. What is happening when we act? Why do we choose to act in one way rather than another? How can our choices have any rational foundation if our understanding is itself based on our choices? What, in other words, is the nature of human freedom? In this chapter we can look more closely at Sartre's analysis of the human act and at the projection of ends that establishes the act.

The first chapter of *Being and Nothingness* part 4 concerns freedom. Sartre makes explicit the structure of the human act. The defining feature of a human act is that it is *intentional,* which means that it is for the sake of a known end.[1] We know

1. *BN* 433; *EN* 477/508.

what we are doing in this act (even if we are doing other things at the same time); we foresee a certain result (even if there may be other unforeseen results too); and we try to bring about this result (even if we do not succeed). Sartre gives the example of an explosion at a quarry which was *an act* (and not just an accident) because the worker "intentionally realized a conscious project" when he set off the dynamite.[2] He wanted to achieve this end, unlike another worker who carelessly discarded a cigarette and unintentionally set off another explosion. An intention involves an active commitment toward an end, a first step toward its realisation (this is what distinguishes it from a dream or a wish), even if it is not achieved. The prisoner, by trying in some way to escape, learns that he has an intention and not a mere wish to escape.[3] In this dynamic structure of intention there are always three inseparable aspects: (A) each *act* (B) has an *end* (C) that refers to a *motive.*[4] These aspects relate to the structure of temporality: (A) each act in the present (B) takes place for the sake of a future (C) which makes sense of and fulfills a past.[5] So this is the structure of intention: motive-act-end.

Sartre dismisses the idea that human actions, in order to be free, need to be without motives. Proponents of this view "can only end up by rendering the act absurd."[6] We should note from the start Sartre's opposition to a view of freedom in which free acts are gratuitous and arise without explanation and without reference to one's convictions or values. He has more sympathy with determinists who stress the role of prior motives and believe that acts arise quite predictably if a certain person is in a certain situation. But the problem with deterministic philosophies (and with much of our everyday thinking) is that they reify motives. Motives are treated as brute, incontrovertible facts that drive the human being in a predetermined direction. De-

2. *BN* 433; *EN* 477/508.

3. *BN* 483–84; *EN* 529/563–64. John Atwell writes that "for Sartre it is not self-contradictory to say 'I intended to do *X*, but I didn't do it'; but it is self-contradictory to say 'I intended to do *X*, but I didn't do anything toward doing (i.e., accomplishing) *X*.'"; see John E. Atwell, "Sartre and Action Theory," in *Jean Paul Sartre: Contemporary Approaches to His Philosophy*, ed. Hugh J. Silverman and Frederick A. Elliston (Pittsburgh, Pa.: Duquesne University Press, 1980), 72.

4. Here I use the English word "motive" to stand for the complex of objectively found motives *(motifs)* and subjectively felt motivations *(mobiles)* which seem to "cause" an action. The distinctions are not important at this stage. See *BN* 446; *EN* 491/522–23.

5. *BN* 436–37; *EN* 480–81/511–12.

6. *BN* 437; *EN* 481/512.

terminists extrapolate from these "psychic givens" and assume that there is an unbroken continuity between the motive, the act, and the end.[7] In deterministic psychological theories, for example, Gustave Flaubert's whole life and work might be explained in terms of his innate ambition—as if the discovery of this "ambition" left nothing else to be said.[8]

In Sartre's eyes the fundamental mistake is to assume that "the motivation provokes the act as the physical cause its effect." In this false view "everything is real, everything is full"; "motive, act, and end constitute a 'continuum,' a *plenum*."[9] This is the misconception we looked at in chapter 1, where one's identity and one's values are taken to be indisputable features of reality which generate a certain pattern of events. Sartre argues that factual states of affairs cannot by themselves give rise to values that would necessitate action. He exposes the contradictions inherent in a deterministic appeal to motives. He argues that since motives *understood as motives* must be objects of our reflective consciousness, they must therefore be questionable. If we are reflecting on them, then we are able to hold them at a distance, and their power automatically to direct our conscious acts is nullified. This, once again, is the experience of anguish.

In Sartre's view a motive is not discovered before the act, it is constituted by the act. In the formulation of each act, there is a necessary moment of negation. The agent must recognize an end, a "desideratum," whose counterpart is an "objective lack" or "*négatité*."[10] We must go beyond the determined facts in front of us and decide what is missing and what could be desired. The emperor Constantine, for example, as we saw in chapter 1, conceives of the establishment of a new Christian city in the East of his empire to counter the decadence of Rome. This decadence is only revealed to be a lack that motivates if it is held up against a projected ideal. Nothing in the city of Rome by itself actually constitutes a motive and prompts the projection of a new city. A motive lies in the realm of "nonbeing," that is, it cannot be discovered in the being of the world.

> From the moment of the first conception of the act, consciousness has been able to withdraw itself from the full world of which it is consciousness and leave the level of being in order frankly to approach that of non-being.[11]

7. See *BN* 440; *EN* 484/515–16.
8. See *BN* 560; *EN* 605/646.
9. *BN* 440; *EN* 484/516.
10. *BN* 433; *EN* 478/508.
11. *BN* 434; *EN* 478/509.

The possibility of a new city *that does not exist* is what reveals that the old city is lacking something, and Constantine's consciousness of this motivation, his dissatisfaction with the decadence of Rome, is inseparable from his projection of a new possibility. Before the new ideal came to mind the "decadence" of Rome was just considered to be an ordinary and acceptable part of urban life. Similarly, a worker in the oppressive conditions of early nineteenth-century Lyon does not necessarily see his suffering as a motive for action. He has no contemplative distance from suffering and cannot understand it as good or bad—it just *is*. "To suffer and to *be* are one and the same for him."[12] His suffering only becomes a motive when he is able to envisage a better future that does not exist. The projection of an ideal society achieved by revolution is what allows him to see that his present situation is not what it could be. There is a double negation here: a future that is not the present (and which cannot be extrapolated from the present with any necessity) and a present that is not this future. Sartre draws two conclusions, one about the act, another about the work of consciousness, and these shed some light on his understanding of freedom:

> (1) No factual state whatever it may be (the political and economic structure of society, the psychological "state," etc.) is capable by itself of motivating any act whatsoever. For an act is a projection of the for-itself toward what is not, and that which is [*ce qui est*] can in no way determine by itself that which is not. (2) No factual state can determine consciousness to apprehend it as a *négatité* or as a lack. Better yet no factual state can determine consciousness to define it and to circumscribe it [as an isolated system].[13]

We saw in chapter 3 that the very identification of a specific object of interest depends on negation. Now we see that negation also underlies the identification of any lack. Both these processes are one with the movement of consciousness as it withdraws from the "plenitude of being" (*plénitude d'être)* of the historical situation in which it is immersed, isolates a single object of attention, and surpasses it toward an ideal.[14] Consciousness can effect a rupture with its past and present and give them a meaning by relating them to a projected future. This is how, from a great range of potentially motivating factors, a single one is actually given priority and experi-

12. *BN* 435; *EN* 479/510.

13. *BN* 435–36; *EN* 479–80/511.

14. *BN* 434; *EN* 479/510.

enced as a motive. "The motivation is understood only by the end; that is, by the non-existent."[15]

Indetermination and the Projection of Ends

Given that every act is motivated, and that the notion of an unmotivated human *act* is absurd, Sartre's description could seem like a form of determinism. Sartre, it seems, would be able to draw a causal line back from any action to the circumstances that preceded it—whether these were objective motives in the world or subjective motivations in the mind and heart of the agent.

It is true that we can draw a causal line *back* from any initiated action to its prior causes. The crucial point to make, however, is that we cannot draw a causal line *forward* from a present set of circumstances to the initiation of a future action.[16] Insofar as we are aware of multiple possible meanings and futures, then we are by definition in a state of indetermination. Anguish is the realization that our circumstances do not determine our understanding or values or actions. There is a gap, a need to interpret and choose and act, and this makes us aware of our freedom. By insisting otherwise the determinist ignores the experience of anguish and brings a prejudice to the phenomenological evidence.

The indetermination we experience is that of not knowing how to think about the future. The totality of our experience does not provide enough. We experience an awareness simultaneously of two (or more) possibilities, two directions in which everything could go, two interpretations of this totality, two motives. We can, for example, give away the cash or keep it for ourselves, we can be polite or be rude, we can propose in marriage or escape to New Zealand.[17] With all the facts at our fingertips we are conscious that there is still a choice to make. This is a primary and irreducible experience for Sartre. His whole philosophy stands or falls by the truth of this experience: that when we observe and assess the totality of what is within view of our consciousness, we cannot discover a necessary meaning, a de-

15. *BN* 437; *EN* 481/512.

16. In this regard, as John Atwell believes, Sartre should be associated with those twentieth-century action theorists who draw attention to the impossibility of characterizing an agent's goals as causal events that exist prior to an action; see Atwell, "Sartre and Action Theory," 63–66.

17. These are my examples, not Sartre's.

termined future, an inevitable course of action. Everything depends on the relation of the totality to an end, and an end simply cannot be found. This is not because we do not yet know enough. However much or little we know there is always, by definition, a wider context, an ideal one, that will frame the whole and provide for its interpretation. We have a direct experience of *not* experiencing a single ideal, a single end.

Sartre's position is not undermined if a determinist points out that there are hidden causes or unobservable details that are influencing the future outcome of events. This is because "external" events, even those within our psyche, are different from intentional acts. Sartre never suggests, for example, that human beings are unable to make predictions about chemical reactions or planetary orbits on the basis of scientific knowledge. It is the subjective, internal, phenomenological future that concerns him. In the experience of anguish we are simply unable to discover what our future will be, what will be the future for which we are now responsible through our intentional acts. We experience the lack of a predetermined future. This is enough to establish human freedom. Indeterminism is not a theory about the mechanics of the universe, it is an experience, and it is inseparable from consciousness itself.

It is by the choice of one end out of many that an action is determined. By acting we allow the present to be determined by one future rather than another one. Freedom is the foundation of all human activity and of all the reasons, motives, and values that arise through that activity. No deterministic description of human action can account for the surpassing of what is that lies at the center of all distinctively human behavior. The heart of being human is transcending the given and turning it toward a freely chosen future. The oppressed worker already mentioned above can interpret his suffering in two ways: as a natural and unavoidable part of a cosmic order, or as a prelude to a revolution. Neither thought is demanded by his circumstances, neither is necessary. His circumstances become a motive (for inaction or for action) only because the worker can distance himself from his circumstances and understand the whole in the light of something greater.

> This implies for consciousness the permanent possibility of effecting a rupture with its own past, of wrenching itself away from its past so as to be able to consider it in the light of a non-being and so as to be able to confer on it the mean-

ing which it has in terms of the project of a meaning which it does not have. Under no circumstances can the past in any way by itself produce an act; that is, the positing of an end which turns back upon itself so as to illuminate it.[18]

The peculiar status of the end is what preserves the whole scheme from determinism. An end is something that influences the interpretation of these circumstances even though it exists only in our intention and not in reality. Circumstances produce results, not ends. Ends, on the other hand, produce circumstances, or at least they change the relationship which the circumstances have with the future. This effects a change in the meaning and orientation of the circumstances themselves. Ends, values, motives, and meanings are not found in the world but only in the understanding of a being-for-itself that can conceive of a world beyond the world of immediate experience.

Ends are not, as Sartre writes, ready made and prehuman, coming "from God, from nature, from 'my' nature, from society."[19] Even the "impulsive" decision to save one's life and flee from mortal danger requires a commitment to the value of one's life, which is a commitment not everyone chooses to make.[20] The goal, however fixed it seems, is always chosen, if it is a conscious intention that forms part of a human act. We cannot *receive* our ends, "either from outside or from a so-called inner 'nature.'"[21] If we are acting, if we are seeking to bring about a particular future, then we must have at least some reflective awareness that this future is not fixed and does not arise inevitably from our present. The fact that we can ask "What am I doing? What am I seeking to achieve here?" shows that we are conscious of the lack of necessity about our goal and our distance from it. In Sartre's scheme we can only act if we realize that the end is *not* given to us in our present experience. The condition of intentional action is that we are simultaneously aware of the end as a reason for acting *and* of the end as a value that we freely choose to sustain. Human reality is unavoidably

18. *BN* 436; *EN* 480/511.

19. *BN* 440; *EN* 484/516.

20. *BN* 443; *EN* 487–88/519–20.

21. *BN* 443; *EN* 488/519. This sounds very different from the Thomistic view, but we must remember that for Sartre a possible goal only becomes an "end" once it has been chosen and incorporated into the structure of an act. Aquinas is certainly aware of the goods to which all human beings are naturally attracted (such as existence, life, and knowledge), but he insists at the same time that the will is not determined to any particular goods. In this sense, he could agree with Sartre that we cannot "receive" our ends *as actual ends* but only as possible ends. See chapter 6 below, in the section "The Indetermination of Particular Goods."

aware of its role in choosing the ends that guide its activity. "It chooses them and by this very choice confers upon them a transcendent existence as the external limit of its projects."[22]

Sartre does not imagine that we are always in the process of establishing new ends. We are often doing things in the present that we decided to do in the past. We often take for granted a prior motive.[23] This is what gives continuity to each human life. But if we are conscious of and present to this motive, then like all intentional objects it becomes separated from us by a nothingness. "It can act only if it is *recovered;* in itself it is without force."[24] All motives, all values, all ends—however definitive we took them to be in the past—need to have a value continually conferred on them in the present. Their past meaning needs to be maintained in existence, or rejected, or appreciated in a new way. The end we choose *now* is absolutely decisive for our interpretation of all that has influenced us in the past. The French word *sens* is useful because it signifies both "meaning" and "direction." Sartre writes that it is the meaning/direction of the past (which includes our past motives and values) that must be decided by us at each moment. "I decide it precisely and only by the very act by which I pro-ject myself toward my ends [*je me pro-jette vers mes fins*]."[25]

Sartre argues that ends are chosen even when we react to a situation in what seems to be an impulsive, unreflective, emotional manner. Emotions, for Sartre, are intentional—they make up part of our project and we allow them to steer us toward freely chosen ends. It does not make a difference for Sartre whether the end we project is grasped by the will in a deliberated, reflective mode, or by the passions in an emotional, symbolic mode. In both cases we are freely choosing how to respond to the world and to go beyond it toward certain values.[26] It does not matter whether we understand the reason for acting to be an objective motif ("motive") discovered in the facts of the world or a subjective mobile ("motivation") lying in our desires and emotions. Each reflects in its own way a value projected by freedom.[27] "Motives and motivations have only the weight which my project—that is, the free production of the end and of the known act to be realized—confers upon them."[28]

22. *BN* 443; *EN* 488/520.
23. *BN* 449–50; *EN* 493/525.
24. *BN* 450; *EN* 494/527.
25. *BN* 450; *EN* 495/527.
26. *BN* 441–45; *EN* 485–89/516–21.
27. *BN* 445–51; *EN* 489–95/521–27.
28. *BN* 450–51; *EN* 495/527.

Choice and Self-Constitution

So, given any act, we will discover motives and ends, and there will a kind of necessity about the elements within the whole process. We might say of someone: "Of course this person, with these values, in these circumstances, with these motives, acted in this way." But this deterministic description doesn't go far enough. It fails to explain the existence of the total process. It assumes without evidence that the circumstances of the world and the nature of the agent provided for only one course of action. It ignores the fact that motives and ends refer to ideals that do not exist in the facts of the present and that need to be sustained by some negating power. Before the commencement of the act, these motives have only a theoretical power and do not actually motivate anything. Motive, act, and end, writes Sartre, are all constituted in a single upsurge. "But the organized totality of the three is no longer explained by any structure."[29] In an attempt to find a foundation for this totality Sartre writes: "It is the act which decides its ends and its motives, and the act is the expression of freedom."[30] The active projection of a goal determines the whole process. There is no foundation outside the act itself. As David Jopling puts it, "[T]his is another way of arriving at the idea that the radical choice is a groundless ground."[31] In other words, the human act is self-determining.

The young man in *Existentialism and Humanism,* for example, finds it impossible to find a definitive reason either for joining the resistance or caring for his mother.[32] He can't prioritize his motives. Each motive emerges from a different understanding of his life; each understanding is incompatible with the other. Jopling writes that in this situation, "the conflict of duties, responsibilities, and moral intuitions is ultimately a conflict between two ways of life, and not a conflict between moral claims within a single way of life."[33] What we are really concerned with is an explanation for the whole way of life in which we allow these motives to make sense.

29. *BN* 438; *EN* 482/513.

30. *BN* 438; *EN* 482/513.

31. David A. Jopling, "Sartre's Moral Psychology," in *The Cambridge Companion to Sartre,* ed. Christina Howells (Cambridge: Cambridge University Press, 1992), 118.

32. Jean-Paul Sartre, *L'Existentialisme Est Un Humanisme* (Paris: Gallimard, 1996), 41–46, translated as Jean-Paul Sartre, "Existentialism and Humanism," in *Jean-Paul Sartre: Basic Writings,* ed. Stephen Priest (London: Routledge, 2001), 33–34.

33. Jopling, "Sartre's Moral Psychology," 119.

Questions of moral and rational justification are necessarily *internal* to a way of life (or to the project or basic moral framework), but as a whole, a way of life does not afford external rational justification.[34]

Sartre believes that there "is" no single answer to the young man's question that sits out there in the world of being. The dilemma comes about for the very reason that there are two incompatible answers that can arise from the same circumstances. They are incommensurable. Each of them is "right" in its own terms. The young man's past does indeed recommend a future of heroic patriotism, but also of heroic filial piety—and it cannot in this case recommend both together. Each response would have a rational and sufficient motive for the particular response it would motivate. Yet neither has a greater right than the other to claim the attention of the man and to become established as a cause of his actions. There are no cross-project or metaproject reasons that would allow one to compare the two fundamental options.

Sartre's advice to the young man in *Existentialism and Humanism* is to say, "You're free, choose, that is, invent."[35] Choose whether to be a dutiful citizen or a dutiful son. Personality will be manifested in the priorities that guide a life, and these priorities are seen here to be a consequence and not a cause of one's free decisions. With this word "invent," *inventer,* Sartre draws attention to the creative aspect of choice, which brings about what would not have existed without the choice. It is an act of origination. Yet it is also, as the Latin root of *inventer (invenire)* suggests, an act of discovery, of meeting what is really there. Thomas Flynn explains that the original choice at the heart of a decision is "criterion-constituting and hence is without antecedent reason or necessity."[36] This is not far from Aristotle's idea that the reasonableness of any virtuous activity can be fully recognized only from within the practice bounding it, to the eyes of one experienced in and engaged in that activity.[37] The active free choice establishes a structure in which the components (motive-act-end) have a place. Every-

34. Ibid., 118.

35. Sartre, "Existentialism and Humanism," 34; Sartre, *L'Existentialisme Est un Humanisme,* 46, "Vous êtes libre, choisissez, c'est-à-dire inventez.".

36. Thomas R. Flynn, *Sartre and Marxist Existentialism: The Test Case of Collective Responsibility* (Chicago and London: University of Chicago Press, 1984), 8.

37. See Aristotle, *Nicomachean Ethics,* trans. Terence Irwin (Indianapolis, Ind.: Hackett, 1985), Bk2, 1103a14–09b27; and J. McDowell, "Virtue and Reason," *The Monist* 62 (1976).

thing within the structure has a meaning, but there is no "external" meaning that will justify the structure itself. "Thinking" cannot work out which of many incompatible "ways of thinking" is the best. There must be a suprarational foundation for a given mode of rationality and action. It is in this sense that Sartre characterizes choices as "absurd." He is not just using audacious language for its own sake.

> Choice is not absurd in the sense in which in a rational universe a phenomenon might arise which would not be bound to others by any *reasons*. It is absurd in this sense—that the choice is that by which all foundations and all reasons come into being [. . .] . It is absurd as being beyond all reasons.[38]

Sartre believes that the "external" foundation of action lies in the existence of human freedom itself, and he identifies this with the very being of the for-itself. Questions of action and personhood are inseparable. The surpassing of identity we looked at in chapter 1 is what founds the totality "motive-act-end." "This ensemble is ultimately myself as transcendence; it is me in so far as I have to be myself outside of me [*c'est moi en tant que j'ai à être moi-même hors de moi*]."[39] Freedom is not just one of many human capacities that we happen to activate now and then, it is the "stuff" *(l'étoffe)* of one's being.

So if we ask the question "Why did we do this rather than that?" or "Why did we value this rather than that?" the answer refers us to the person we are. And if we ask "Why, though, are we this person?!" there is no answer beyond the fact that we are becoming this person through our actions. When Sartre was a conscript testing his ideas about freedom on his fellow soldiers one of them gently reminded him that he must "take people as they are," and his impatient reaction was to say, "Yes, but I know in my bones that people aren't, they do."[40] Personhood, as we saw in chapter 1, lies not in a substantial self that is a cause or explanation of the person, it lies in the perpetual going beyond the self required by our consciousness of self. Our human existence is more than our essence. There is nothing more fundamental to which we can refer. The only "explanation" for the shape of our actions and our existence is the fact that our being-for-itself is an original

38. *BN* 479; *EN* 524/559.

39. *BN* 437; *EN* 481/513.

40. "[. . .] les gens ne *sont* pas, ils *font*"; Jean-Paul Sartre, *Lettres Au Castor,* vol. 1 (Paris: Gallimard, 1983), 382.

and irreducible event. It is the single thing (in our phenomenological experience) that is not caused by something else, because its nature is precisely to project itself beyond causes toward an end.

For the for-itself, to be is to nihilate the in-itself which it is [*Etre, pour le pour-soi, c'est néantiser l'en-soi qu'il est*]. Under these conditions freedom can be nothing other than this nihilation. It is through this that the for-itself escapes from its being as it does from its essence; it is through this that the for-itself is always something other than what can be *said* of it.[41]

Sartre thus returns to themes from the beginning of *Being and Nothingness*. The intentional act that establishes the structure "motive-act-end" is one with this unavoidable movement beyond identity that constitutes our very being as self-conscious creatures. So for Sartre these are not different areas of discussion. The intentional act itself, freedom, being-for-itself, and the choice of ends are all one thing. The "unjustifiable" adoption of one course of action is associated with the negation that takes place at the very heart of human consciousness.[42] Freedom is "equivalent to my existence."[43] Each intentional complex of action needs an external foundation, and this is inseparable from the movement in which we go beyond the present and relate it to a future that does not exist. We are free to act because we have to deny our identity and choose how to reconstitute it. "Human reality is free because *it is not enough*."[44] It is wrenched away from what it is.

Human beings are free because they are not self but presence to self [*L'homme est libre parce qu'il n'est pas soi mais présence à soi*]. The being which is what it is cannot be free. Freedom is precisely the nothingness which *is-been* [est été] at the heart of the human being and which forces human-reality *to make itself* instead of *to be*. As we have seen, for human reality, to be is to *choose oneself*.[45]

So to the ultimate question "Why this choice, this end, this purpose in life?" there is no answer. This choice, this end, this purpose *is* the person who exists in this moment. There is nothing more fundamental to which we can point. Any other explanation would deny the phenomenological evidence, which shows that the choice of one's ends and the constitution of

41. *BN* 439; *EN* 483/515.
42. *BN* 464; *EN* 509/542.
43. *BN* 444; *EN* 488/520.
44. *BN* 440; *EN* 485/516.
45. *BN* 440; *EN* 485/516.

one's identity are one with each other, and that they are originating, foundational events that cannot be reduced to anything else. It is not true to say, "She sought this thing because she is this kind of person." Sartre would instead say, "She is this kind of person because she is seeking this thing," or better still, "This person *is* the seeking of this thing; this human being *is* the surpassing of this world for the sake of this end." The choice and projection of one end, which determines the whole meaning of our life, is not determined by an already existing personal identity—it *is* the person who exists in this moment in relation to this end. There is no Bergsonian "deep self" *(moi-profond)* hidden away somewhere, distinct from the manifestation of the person that takes place through action.[46] Even though Sartre paid more attention in his later works to the practical limits of freedom and the influence of one's environment on the formation of the self, he never lost this basic philosophical conviction that we determine our being by going beyond what we are. Ronald Aronson summarizes Sartre's thesis in this phrase: "We make ourselves from what has been made of us."[47] In other words, it is not enough just to be ourselves: we have to adopt ourselves and take responsibility for who we are becoming. There "are" no ends; they are not out there waiting to be discovered.

In the search for explanations, there is nowhere further back to go than the original choice of ends that takes place when we become aware of the inconclusiveness of the present. It is foundational and self-constituting since it is precisely the response we have to make to the insufficiency of all previous foundations. To put it in a slightly different way: Our free response to the foundations we discover becomes foundational for the future. A phrase that became an existentialist slogan ("existence precedes essence") only makes proper sense in the context of *Being and Nothingness.* Sartre refuses to grant that descriptions of *essence* can ever account for the freely projected *existence* of human beings, where "essence" stands for all that is and "existence" stands for the dynamic orientation of all that is to what it is not.[48]

46. *BN* 444; *EN* 488/520.

47. Ronald Aronson, *Jean-Paul Sartre: Philosophy in the World* (London: Verso, 1980), 78.

48. If Sartre concentrates on analyzing the individual, it should become clear that these categories will help us to understand the developments that take place within a community, a society, a language, a narrative. In each case an inherited "essence" may be negated and surpassed in the light of freely chosen values.

> Freedom is existence, and in it existence precedes essence. Freedom is an upsurge that is immediately concrete [*la liberté est surgissement immédiatement concret*] and is not to be distinguished from its choice; that is, from the person himself.[49]

We interpret the present by choosing a future. We act in the world by going beyond it toward an end. We constitute ourselves by going beyond ourselves. Freedom is thus one with our existence as conscious human beings.

The Reasonableness of the Project

It is clear, then, that ends are not constituted by the given circumstances. Sartre is not a determinist, even though he has argued that all actions are motivated. There is a line from the past to actions that have already begun, but not yet from the present to future actions. This raises another set of questions: Is the free choice of each project irrational? Is everything within each project therefore without rational foundation? Sartre thinks not. He is not a voluntarist, as we shall see, and each project has its own rationality. Even though he characterizes freedom as an "unanalyzable totality," he recoils against the suggestion that it is "a pure capricious, unlawful, gratuitous, and incomprehensible contingency."[50]

It is interesting to note Sartre's thoughts about Camus's novel *L'Étranger* in a review of September 1942.[51] Sartre comments on the indebtedness of Camus's prose style to Hemingway. Events are recorded in short sentences, without explicit connections, such that their overall significance is opaque and we are unable to profit from the momentum of the narrative. The isolated phrases of the text communicate the isolated moments experienced by the protagonist and help the reader to enter into the absurdity of a life without meaning. Only the immediacy of the present counts. At the end of the review Sartre confesses himself reluctant to classify Camus's work as a novel *(un roman)* because he believes that in a novel it should be obvious that time is irreversible. Camus replaces the causal order one expects to find in a novel with a mere chronological series of incidents. We have a sense that Sartre feels let down, as if the novelist has a duty to describe lives that are full of purpose, lives that make sense. There seems to be some sort of contradiction here: How can Sartre defend his radical view of free-

49. *BN* 568; *EN* 613/655.

50. *BN* 452–53; *EN* 497–98/529–30.

51. Reprinted in Jean-Paul Sartre, *Situations I* (Paris: Gallimard, 1947), 92–112.

dom and still suggest that there is some kind of overarching meaning to each human life?

It might be helpful to consider one example of voluntaristic thinking from the history of philosophy and see how far Sartre's thinking is from this. Servais Pinckaers describes the "freedom of indifference" that is proposed by traditions influenced by William of Ockham.[52] He contrasts this voluntaristic view of freedom with a "freedom for excellence" proposed by Aquinas. For our purposes it doesn't matter whether Pinckaers is fair to Ockham or not (or to Aquinas). I am using his presentation of voluntarism to provide a contrast with Sartre's position.

"Freedom of indifference" drives a wedge between freedom and reason. Ockham argues that freedom resides in the will, which can respond to the conclusions of reason by accepting them or rejecting them. Freedom is an indetermination or a radical indifference in the will regarding contraries. Actions are produced in a wholly contingent way without having any necessary orientation to the good as it has been understood by reason. Love for the good and rational desire are replaced by a self-determining domination. Freedom chooses without reference to one's ultimate goal in life or to one's past actions. Decisions take place in an isolated present moment, disconnected from each other. Pinckaers explicitly mentions Sartre as a figure who stands (perhaps unconsciously) in this voluntaristic tradition, although one suspects that he does not know Sartre's work well.[53]

There is an order in the voluntaristic system described by Pinckaers. First we understand the world and ourselves, and then we choose how to act. The will functions in a context determined by reason and it chooses whether to accept or reject the good that reason proposes. Freedom determines what we do, but it does not determine how we think about things or how we understand the world—it takes this understanding from the reason. If the will chooses *against* a value assigned by reason, this is not because the will *values* this "countervalue," since it is only the reason that can judge that something is valuable. There can be no reason for choosing the

52. Servais Pinckaers, *The Sources of Christian Ethics,* trans. Sr. Mary Thomas Noble (Edinburgh: T & T Clark, 1995), 330–42.

53. Ignatius Eschmann is another reputable Thomist who uses Sartre as a voluntarist foil against which he can set the more rational ethics of Aquinas; see Ignatius Theodore Eschmann, *The Ethics of Saint Thomas Aquinas: Two Courses* (Toronto: Pontifical Institute of Mediaeval Studies, 1997), 53.

countervalue—it is precisely what is *against* reason and what does not fit in to a rationally established order of values and goals. This is all quite different from Sartre. I will summarize some of the features of Sartre's scheme that contrast with the voluntarism described by Pinckaers, and then I will give some examples from *Being and Nothingness.*

(A) For Sartre, choices about action are always comprehensible in the light of what we understand to be good. We can only do what we understand to be worthwhile and valuable. In this sense the "will" (in the language of Ockham) is tightly integrated with the "reason" and cannot go against its conclusions. Motive, act, and end make up an unbreakable complex of reasons, actions, and values that refer to each other and depend on each other. If someone is capricious or an action gratuitous then that person, according to Sartre, has not acted freely. There is no such thing for Sartre as an arbitrary human *action,* one without a motive or an end—although there are many things we do accidentally (or incidentally) for which our freedom is not responsible. This is therefore quite different (to take another example of voluntarism) from Kierkegaard's teleological suspension of the ethical, where obedience to God's particular commands can take someone outside the sphere of the ethical and into an activity that is at odds with one's system of understood moral values.[54] Kierkegaard and Ockham allow the will to move against the recommendations of reason—creating what could be called a nonethical freedom, or alternatively an irrational ethic. Sartre's human being *has to be ethical.* In his scheme we have to live for values that are comprehensible and make sense of our life.

(B) The freedom that founds an intentional complex does not function *within* the reasoning determined by this complex—it is "prior" to it. This is why freedom cannot go against reason. It is, rather, the foundation of one line of reasoning. In the moment of choice there are no necessary goals proposed by a rational assessment of our situation, so freedom is not moving against any rational recommendations. It is not indifferent to "the" good that is understood, because in the moment of choice there are no rationally persuasive values to which it can be indifferent. As we discovered in chapter 3, the subjective involvement of human beings is what allows the objective truth about the world to be revealed. There can be no reasons

54. See Frederick A. Olafson, *Principles and Persons: An Ethical Interpretation of Existentialism* (Baltimore, Md.: John Hopkins University Press, 1967), 28–30.

(no motives or ends) unless we have freely chosen to establish a particular project by acting in a certain way. Sartre wants to defend us from "the illusion which would make of original freedom a *positing* of motives and motivations as *objects*, then a *decision* from the standpoint of these motives and motivations."[55] The motives and motivations do not exist before the commitment of freedom, so they cannot be rejected or accepted.

(C) Much thinking and action does take place within a framework of reasons provided by an ongoing project. We often weigh up different means, using a rational scale, to see which will best achieve a preestablished goal. Yet if, having been committed to project A, we then reach a point of crisis and have to choose between project X and project Y, the rationality of project A cannot always determine which of the two possible future projects will be most reasonable. Sometimes one comes to a point where, as Phyllis Sutton Morris puts it, "what counts as a reason must be decided upon before one can begin the process of decision making on the level of particular acts."[56] Both new projects (X and Y) make sense of A, and the point is that each one makes a different kind of sense of project A and the reasons contained within it. Each one could justify the decision to choose it. The decision cannot be made solely within the terms of project A, nor within some higher or abstract structure of reasoning. The decision is the living of a certain life (X or Y) within which the earlier life (A) makes a new kind of sense. We are not simply discovering, through rational investigation, who we already are. We are deciding who we shall become and what will define us. This decision creates something completely new that has never existed before, which is at the same time a rational continuation of the life up to this point. This original choice is one with the consciousness we have of ourselves.

And as our being is precisely our original choice, the consciousness (of) the choice is identical with the self-consciousness which we have [*la conscience (de) choix est identique à la conscience que nous avons (de) nous*]. One must be conscious in order to choose, and one must choose in order to be conscious. Choice and consciousness are one and the same thing.[57]

55. *BN* 462; *EN* 506/539.

56. Phyllis Sutton Morris, *Sartre's Concept of a Person: An Analytic Approach* (Amherst: University of Massachusetts Press, 1976), 108.

57. *BN* 462; *EN* 506/539.

So there is no voluntaristic, irrational rejection of the goods that have been significant for the agent, there is instead a prerational or suprarational choice about future goods that preserves and transforms the rationality that has sustained the initial project. Once again, freedom does not work against reason.

Sartre gives a concrete and apparently trivial example of a group of hikers out on a tiring walk.[58] After several hours one hiker gives up because he is tired. His exhaustion is given as a reason for stopping. He judges that his tiredness is unbearable and gives a decisive value to resting. His companions, who are equally tired, judge their tiredness to be endurable and even embrace it as part of the experience of conquering the mountain. The different decisions reflect different attitudes to hiking and to life in general.

Sartre goes on to analyze the total worldview and original project that is expressed through each choice. In each case we are still within a given complex of motive-action-end. The one who gives up the hike values the comfort of the city more than the others, and he has a low appreciation of the value of overcoming difficulties. These are the things that motivate him to stop walking. Could he do otherwise? Yes he could. He is not constrained to stop, and he does not actually collapse against his will through exhaustion. The real question is this: What price would he pay for making another decision? To stop walking is to reaffirm his quest for a comfortable, stress-free, urban existence—this is the "ultimate and initial possible" that drives him, the value that forms his project.[59] Sartre speaks for him in the first person:

> I can refuse to stop only by a radical conversion of my being-in-the-world; that is, by an abrupt metamorphosis of my initial project—i.e., by another choice of myself and of my ends. Moreover this modification is always possible.[60]

The "cost" of making a different choice would be abandoning one's previous goals and motives and structuring one's life in a new way. It would be a new way of being.

Sartre's description of freedom might still seem to suggest that human actions are gratuitous, but in fact it is the one explanation that can save the free act from being gratuitous. If we admit that there are motives for actions, based on the understanding and values we have, then we are faced

58. See *BN* 453–55 and 464–65; *EN* 498–500/530–32 and 508–10/542–44.

59. *BN* 464; *EN* 509/542.

60. *BN* 464; 509/542.

with two other unsatisfactory alternative explanations. (i) Motives are fixed and determine our actions completely. We cannot act otherwise and so we are not free. (ii) Free acts are those that go against our motives, that is, they are irrational and gratuitous. Sartre describes a third way in which we have a choice because we can allow ourselves to be moved by *different* motives, by changing the understanding and values we have, and by becoming a different person. We do not go against reason, we refound it. We rethink reason itself. To put it another way: We can act differently because we can adapt, expand, and transform our rationally appreciated desires. We are free to do something different because we are free to be someone different, and in this way the free act is always integrated with our understanding and our rational goals and our identity. This is far from voluntarism.

It still begs the question, of course, of whether this choice to allow oneself to be moved by different motives is a fully rational choice. Sartre would say that this very question misses the point: The decision to let ourselves be guided by certain motives is the very thing that allows us to be rational; it is the foundation of rationality. There is no abstract set of reasons lying outside our intentional frame of reference. We can only reason in a particular way because we have experienced, perhaps only in anticipation, the inner logic of this choice, and been attracted by this logic. Why do I choose to do this? Because I want to; because it makes sense; because it is reasonable. That's all there is to say. And if someone then asks, "Ah, but why do you to choose to do this rather than something else?" I still give the same answer: Because I want to; because it makes sense; because it is reasonable. I don't have to say, I choose this because it makes more sense than the alternatives—since that answer only becomes true once I have chosen it. They all make sense, that's why I have to choose. The fact of choosing then becomes a part of what allows us to make sense of what we have chosen, not as an additional reason, but as the act that brings to light the reality of this intentional path.

I know that the other courses of action are also reasonable (in different ways). Acts are free, *and* once they are unfolding they make perfect sense in the light of our motives. So *acts* are never gratuitous. The gratuitousness is now moved to a different level, to that of the person, of the being of the human agent. The reason why this person is this person lies in his or her being, which is identical with the choice one makes about one's existence. To be a human being is to be free to be who one chooses to be (within the factual limits of one's circumstances)—anything else would run against the phenomenological evidence of anguish. So the gratuity of the act is avoided in favor of the gratuity (or absoluteness or self-constitution) of the person. This ongoing fundamental choice of oneself is necessarily unconditioned, since it is the negation and foundation of conditions.

We know that we can "reverse steam" and abruptly invert this choice. We are perpetually threatened with the negation of our present choice in the future.[61] But this fragility is part of the absolute, foundational nature of the choice—it is attendant on the fact that we are free to be ourselves in the present, and on the fact that we are not free to abandon our freedom by fixing some determinate choice for the duration of the future. Freedom and a lack of integration go hand in hand. It is as if the perpetual possibility of "otherness" is interiorized and there is a simultaneous experience of disintegration and reintegration. Anguish, writes Sartre, is "the fear which I have of being suddenly exorcized, that is, of becoming radically other [*de devenir radicalement autre*]."[62] Our reality is *interrogative* and our being is always *in question,* "since it is always separated form itself by the nothingness of otherness [*puisqu'il est toujours séparé de lui-même par le néant de l'altérité*]."[63]

Sartre is happy to call the choice of oneself "absurd." The absurdity lies in the fact that the necessity of choosing oneself is an unavoidable given for each human being. We have to choose who we are but we are not the foundation of the being which has to make this choice.

> We apprehend our choice—i.e., ourselves—as *unjustifiable.* This means that we apprehend our choice as not deriving from any prior reality but rather as being about to serve as foundation for the ensemble of significations which constitute reality.[64]

We could say that for Sartre we establish the form of our existence but not the fact of our existing. Human beings do not create their whole being from nothing, and in this sense they share in the unjustifiability and incomprehensibility of *everything:* "By this being which is *given* to it, human reality participates in the universal contingency of being and thereby in what we may call absurdity."[65]

61. *BN* 465; *EN* 509/543.
62. *BN* 475; *EN* 520/555.
63. *BN* 619; *EN* 667/713.
64. *BN* 464; *EN* 509/542.
65. *BN* 479; *EN* 524/559.

Temporality, Conversion, and the Unity of Life

Despite all that has been said about the continuing role of motives, a serious misunderstanding is possible here. It might seem that the unjustifiability of the choice creates a structure in which the act has no rational justification in the past or in the identity of the agent. It might seem that the continuing possibility of remaking the choice and undermining it will destroy the coherence and continuity of any life project. Sartre recognizes that the possibility of a meaningful life is radically undermined if original choice is thought of as "producing itself from one instant to the next."[66] His answer is to affirm the importance of temporality. Just as the act founds the end and the motive, the present founds the future and the past. The choice in the present is not an arbitrary event that interrupts an already established orderly progression from past to future, it is the very thing that makes the unity of past and future possible. This is a subtle idea that needs some explanation.

We have to keep returning to the phenomenological roots of this investigation: anguish, presence to self, the denial of identity, the insufficiency of the past. If the past simply explained the present and justified a certain future, there would be no questions to ask about freedom. The problem is that we have a direct experience of the insufficiency of the past, of its lack of meaning, and precisely of its lack of an established continuity with our present and future.

We can return to the reformed gambler of chapter 1. He stands at the casino door and is torn between two irreconcilable desires: to gamble and not to gamble.[67] He remembers his vow never to gamble again. It is a past that does not give him direction because of the fact that he can consider it and that its implications are necessarily ambiguous. "By the very fact of taking my position in existence as consciousness of being, I make myself *not to be* the past of good resolutions *which I am.*"[68] His past identity is disintegrating before his eyes. The vow faces him as a dead, free-floating fact without any orientating relation to his present actions. It could be the vow of another person—until he makes a choice and acts. The crisis arises because the vow has no fixed meaning, it doesn't lead him to anything—

66. *BN* 465; *EN* 510/543.

67. *BN* 32–33; *EN* 67–68/69–70.

68. *BN* 33; *EN* 68/71.

there is no steady line of continuity. Only when he chooses and acts does the vow take its place in a temporal succession of meaning. If he walks away from the casino, the vow becomes the source of that resolution that keeps him away. If he enters the casino, the vow becomes a pointless moment of heroism in a life otherwise wholly given to gambling. The action in the present fixes and orientates the event in the past.

The important point to grasp is that before he acts, when he experiences the anguish of having to choose, the vow has no fixed meaning. It is a memory without force, an event without significance, and it has no meaningful place in his personal history. This changes when he acts—however he acts. By giving it meaning (in the present) he gives it a secure place in his past. So temporality is established by and not broken by the unjustifiable upsurge of the present choice. Consciousness is not a succession of instantaneous moments isolated from each other—it is the foundation of temporality. To be conscious is to allow an understanding of oneself to emerge in a framework of time. Sartre puts this beautifully: To choose ourselves is "to cause a future to come to make known to us what we are by conferring a meaning on our past."[69] Our orientation to a future allows us to unify the self that is seeking this future. We are "self-creating selves," as Phyllis Sutton Morris puts it, where the created self (who we are in the light of our past) is formed by the creating self, which is nothing other than the conscious bodily agent acting in the present.[70]

The original choice continually made in the present is in one sense an unjustifiable foundation for all temporality, just as the act founds the motive and end. Yet in another sense the choice, no matter how radical and spontaneous, is always an essential part of a reinterpreted temporal progression. This is why it is impossible to isolate a "new" choice from the life it manifests. Freedom always has the two faces of sheer originality and plodding necessity. A "new" choice, for example, is certainly an integral part of the newly begun totality—it explains the direction of the future. It is less obvious, but equally true, that the new choice necessarily determines itself "*in connection* with the past which it has to be."[71]

Whatever the decision, we have to understand it in terms of our past,

69. *BN* 465; *EN* 510/543.

70. Phyllis Sutton Morris, "Self-Creating Selves: Sartre and Foucault," *American Catholic Philosophical Quarterly* 70, no. 4 (1996).

71. *BN* 466; *EN* 511/545.

even if the new decision makes us realize how wrong we were before. Our new "rightness" is a correction and in some ways a culmination or fulfillment of the "wrongness" that guided us in the past. If we do something completely unconnected with our past identity, without any reference at all to what went before, this is not freedom—we call it madness or amnesia. The radical, unjustifiable choice has to justify itself and interpret itself in the perspective of the past. Whether we fight the enemy or flee, remain in our marriage or leave, eat the chocolate or diet, work for a multinational corporation or travel the world—in each case we will understand the choice in terms of the past and see our past as building up to it and explaining it. In each case the immediacy of the present choice, which seems to shatter all continuity, is actually the very moment that establishes continuity. Even the many "noncrisis" things that we do without much reflection—feeding our children, traveling to work, watching the TV—are original choices, in the sense that they perpetuate and reestablish for the present a specific temporal project (that is already under way). We give them our implicit consent, and there is always an implicit possibility of not doing them.

If we make a radical change, then the decision to change is what gives new meaning even to the past choice that is rejected. The new choice is "on principle, a decision to apprehend as past the choice for which it is substituted."[72] This is why it is a grave misunderstanding to think that Sartre's view of original choice implies a series of discontinuous changes and arbitrary repudiations of one's past. A "new" choice is not "a global flip-flop,"[73] nor a wild, empty leaping of the will away from one's established personality and one's present reasoning.[74] Consciousness takes the past as an object and "evaluates it and takes its bearings in relation to it."[75] Sartre later puts this in a succinct phrase: "It is the future which decides whether the past is living or dead."[76]

Every memory is an interpretation and a certification. An event as uncontroversial as a childhood illness depends on a thousand present projects to sustain it. Sartre's memory of having whooping cough as a four year old depends on his commitment to a social order that uses a certain calen-

72. *BN* 466; *EN* 511/545.

73. Jopling, "Sartre's Moral Psychology," 126.

74. Cf. Iris Murdoch, *The Sovereignty of Good* (London: Routledge, 2001), 26–40.

75. *BN* 467; *EN* 512/546.

76. *BN* 499; *EN* 544/580.

dar, to the trustworthiness of the adults who recounted it, to the medical science that defines the condition.[77] We could object that there is simply a brute fact lodging in his memory. Sartre would say that we cannot get at this fact—cannot select it, locate it, describe it, understand it—without the structures of interpretation provided by our present commitments. This doesn't mean that we can always control which memories come to mind and when they do (although our consent is often more important than we admit). It does mean that whatever the memory is, it must be understood in the light of our projects. We could also object that this overarching social order is not something one can realistically opt out of. A young boy like Sartre brought up in early twentieth-century France did not have the option of dating his birth by the Egyptian or Mayan calendar. Sartre would still say that we are giving assent to the pervasive social order, and aligning our personal project with the larger social one, even if there are not many live alternatives. We may not be responsible for the values of our society, but we are complicit in them. It is worth remembering that all societies have had those who have chosen to reject aspects of the social order through voluntary exile or rebellion.

Phyllis Sutton Morris suggests that for Sartre remembering is *remembering-as*. In this respect he agreed with the Freudians in saying that a principle of selection operates in memory. Yet for Sartre the principle is one with our present projects, it is not some hidden influence determining us despite ourselves. His phenomenology of freedom is not divorced from psychology. Morris writes: "We are not, then, at the mercy of the past, and we cannot excuse present actions on the basis of inexorable memories of the past." Sartre's discussion of memory "is directed against those psychological determinists who would claim that memories of the past compel or coerce present action and that men are therefore not responsible for their acts."[78] Nevertheless, we have to keep reminding ourselves that the influence of a past that is given meaning by our project in this way is real, it exists in the past and not just in the imagination of the one who acts, it is what the agent discovers.[79]

77. *BN* 498; *EN* 543/579.

78. Morris, *Sartre's Concept of a Person: An Analytic Approach*, 64, see also 55–64.

79. In *BN* Sartre is usually concerned with the individual human being, but one can apply his analysis of time and consciousness to other "subjects": to groups, institutions, communities, etc.

So our free acts in the present structure our past and our future and allow us to interpret them. Sometimes these acts reinforce our previous interpretations. Sometimes a new way of acting gives rise to a new interpretation—which is still, nevertheless, in continuity with one's past. "Conversion" is Sartre's preferred word to stand for the radical modification of one's project that brings about a new continuity. A converted atheist is not simply a believer, "he is a believer who has denied atheism for himself, who has turned the project of being an atheist into an aspect of the past in him [*qui a passéifié en lui son projet d'être athée*]."[80] His previous atheism is not simply ignored, it becomes a part of his new religious story. His religious conversion—far from being capricious—makes perfect sense when set against the atheist background. Sartre is at his most eloquent when he points to some of the great conversions in literature: Gide's Philoctetes casts off his hate, Dostoyevsky's Raskolnikov decides to give himself up.

> These extraordinary and marvellous instants when the prior project collapses into the past in the light of a new project which rises on its ruins and which as yet exists only in outline, in which humiliation, anguish, joy, hope are delicately blended, in which we let go in order to grasp and grasp in order to let go—these have often appeared to furnish the clearest and most moving image of our freedom.[81]

Sartre himself delighted in experiences of crisis and conversion. After strenuous resistance he finally supported (if only for the next four years) the pro-Stalinist Communist Party (the PCF) in the summer of 1952 in the face of much derision. He was mocked by its enemies and suspected by its members. Yet for him nothing was more thrilling or enjoyable than these moments "in which he believed with all the fervency of the convert that until now he had been totally wrong but now he was totally right."[82]

The exhilarating heart of freedom, however, is not necessarily found in conversion. It is in the free choice of one's project, and this is found as much in the free preservation of a project as in its rejection. A lifelong devotion to a duty inherited from birth can be an expression of freedom as

80. *BN* 467; *EN* 511/545.

81. *BN* 476; *EN* 521/555.

82. Ronald Hayman, *Writing Against: A Biography of Sartre* (London: Weidenfeld & Nicolson, 1986), 280.

long as it is accepted and undertaken as a personal commitment and not as a necessity that "sincerity" imposes. Sartre's examples focus on moments of drama and change, but this should not make us lose sight of his central contention that freedom lies in one's personal commitment to a project, whatever it is. Projects that are dutiful, common, or dull have as much significance in Sartre's scheme as those that are reckless, extraordinary, or dazzling—as long as they are freely chosen.

The most beautiful description Sartre gave of the twofold face of freedom is in a passage about the graceful body.[83] A moment of grace has both continuity and originality—and these aspects do not in any way contradict each other. "The graceful act has on the one hand the precision of a finely tuned machine and on the other hand the perfect unpredictability of the psychic."[84] It is perfectly understandable if one considers what has elapsed, it has a kind of aesthetic necessity, yet it remains unpredictable and awaits an unforeseen illumination from a future goal. The graceful movement of a hand seems to be both required by the situation, summoned, and to be the very origin of its being. Grace is an image of the inseparability of necessity and freedom in human life.

Facticity and the Limits of Freedom

Sartre has used a number of characters to exemplify his theories: the hiker, the gambler, the oppressed worker, the emperor, the affronted patriot who is also a dutiful son. All of them have to decide who they will become. They have to choose to act for an end on the basis of selected motives. Does this mean that they can choose anything at all? What are the constraints of freedom? How can there be any limits if the limits are themselves interpreted in the light of one's acts?

It should be clear from the discussion of objectivity in chapter 3 that for Sartre factual limits are only discovered within a personal project, yet they remain just that: factual *limits* that reveal the objective nature of the world. We have to obey nature in order to command it, and if we wish to act, then we have to accept a network of determinism. There is a givenness to everything we encounter, a resistance, a "facticity." This makes it possible for us, within a given project, to distinguish truth from falsehood and realistic in-

83. *BN* 400; *EN* 440/470.
84. *BN* 400; *EN* 440/470.

tentions from fantasies. It also makes it possible for us, within a given project, to find objective foundations for that project. Mountain climbing, for example, makes no sense without mountains, and only when we decide to climb will we discover if a given obstacle is climbable or not.[85]

In *Being and Nothingness* Sartre discusses the various forms of facticity under five headings: one's place, past, environment, fellow human being, and death.[86] These are some of the richest sections of the work. The weight of facticity appears in many forms. Climate, earth, race, class, language, history, heredity, childhood, habits, and the small and great events of life all press in and form us.[87] One of the most indisputable facts confronting human beings, mentioned in an earlier section of *Being and Nothingness,* is the biological unity of each human organism, our "shocking solidarity with the foetus."[88]

Sartre therefore recognizes that we appear *to be made* more than *to make ourselves.*[89] He goes on to argue, however, that the factual limits of our actions are not limits to existential freedom, they actually make freedom possible, since freedom is the way we go beyond all that is to a not-yet-existing end. "Only the ensemble of real existents can separate us from this end—in the same way that this end can be conceived only as a state to-come [*état à-venir*] of the real existents which separate me from it."[90] Being-for-itself is the negation of these "real existents." It depends on them. "There can be a free for-itself only as engaged in a resisting world."[91] So freedom is nothing without our presence to the facticity of existence. Given this facticity, we can notice three ways in which the "absoluteness" of human freedom is qualified.

First, freedom is an essential aspect of conscious human life, but it is not the whole of human life. There is more to the human being, to human reality, than being-for-itself. It is actually only one element of an original synthesis. Human reality is the negation and reconstitution of a particular being-in-itself, through the presence to self of being-for-itself, in a total context of one's being-in-the-world—with an awareness of one's being-for-others.[92] This is what saves Sartre from a rootless freedom that would have

85. *BN* 482; *EN* 527/562.
86. *BN* 489–553; *EN* 535–98/570–638.
87. *BN* 481–82; *EN* 527/561–62.
88. *BN* 139; *EN* 174/185.
89. *BN* 481–82; *EN* 527/561–62.
90. *BN* 483; *EN* 528/563.
91. *BN* 483; *EN* 528/563.
92. There is not space in this book to deal adequately with being-for-others.

no relationship with an embodied human life. In Sartre's philosophy it is not true to say "The human being *is freedom.*" We should instead say "The human being *is free,*" since the human being is not an abstract freedom but the free reconstitution of a concrete bodily life.

A second sense in which freedom is not absolute stems from the contingency of freedom itself. We did not freely choose to be free. Our freedom is a contingent fact about our being, a given that we have to accept. The absoluteness of freedom does not therefore imply that freedom is its own foundation, as if we could decide whether to be free. Sartre famously writes that we are "condemned to be free"—a strangely negative phrase that simply means that freedom is the starting point for our existence, part of the facticity that defines our life.[93] This language of "condemnation" is Sartre's exaggerated way of expressing the very humble thought that we do not create our existence as such even though we have to create the form that this existence will take through our project.

A third sense in which freedom is not absolute will require some explanation, since it is so often ignored. The "absoluteness" of freedom has nothing to do with naïve notions of human omnipotence. Nowhere in *Being and Nothingness* does Sartre suggest that human beings, blind to the constraints of their circumstances, can achieve all that they wish to achieve through a kind of Promethean will to power. Practical questions about the effectiveness of human activity are simply not the main concern of this work. Sartre makes a very clear distinction between the "empirical and popular" concept of freedom, which is "the ability to obtain the ends chosen," and the "technical and philosophical" concept of freedom, which is the "autonomy of choice."[94] We could also call this a distinction between practical freedom and ontological or existential freedom. If all his readers had paid attention to this distinction he would have been spared a great deal of misunderstanding.[95] Sartre explains:

> "To be free" does not mean "to obtain what one wanted" but rather "by oneself to determine oneself to want" (in the broad sense of choosing) [*"se déterminer*

93. *BN* 485; *EN* 530/565.

94. *BN* 483; *EN* 528/563.

95. For an account of various misunderstandings, see David Detmer, *Freedom as a Value: A Critique of the Ethical Theory of Jean-Paul Sartre* (La Salle, Ill.: Open Court, 1988), esp. 36–38 and 55–56.

à vouloir (au sens large de choisir) par soi-même"]. In other words success is not important to freedom.[96]

We should note that Sartre does not say that practical success is not important in itself (he cared deeply about practical matters), he says that it is not important to freedom. In other words, we are still free even if we fail to achieve our ends. We should also remember that the self-determination of our wanting is strictly limited by our situation, since "choice" in Sartre's technical language means undertaking a project and not just dreaming about an alternative reality.[97] Sartre never implies that human beings can conjure up *any* project they like for themselves, irrespective of their past, their personality, their commitments, their actions. A single sentence that encapsulates Sartre's thinking about the contingent limits of freedom could be the following: "To be free is not to choose the historic world in which one arises—which would have no meaning—but to choose oneself in the world whatever this may be."[98] Historic world stands here for that immensely complex set of facts and circumstances that constitutes one's present reality. It all has to be accepted and surpassed, affirmed and denied.[99] Sartre gives the example of the prisoner.

We shall not say that a prisoner is always free to get out of prison, which would be absurd, nor that he is always free to long for release, which would be an irrelevant truism, but that he is always free to try to escape (or to get himself liberated); that is, that whatever his condition may be, he can project his escape and teach himself the value of his project [*il peut pro-jeter son évasion et s'apprendre à lui-même la valeur de son projet*] by beginning some action.[100]

96. *BN* 483; *EN* 528/563.

97. See Sartre's distinction between a wish *(un souhait)* and a free choice. A wish is a desire *not to be* in this situation, a free choice is a decision to transform this situation by seeking an end. See *BN* 482–83; *EN* 527–28/562–63.

98. *BN* 521; *EN* 566/604.

99. This suggests that truthfulness (at least to oneself) is a requirement for freedom. Truthfulness is not a project, it is a precondition for all projects. Sartre could have added that for this we will need certain intellectual aids: language, discernment, a critical eye, the advice of others, a cultural respect for truth, etc. We will also need certain moral virtues: honesty, humility, courage, perseverance, etc. If we are free we will seek to cultivate the intellectual and moral virtues necessary for leaning the truth about ourselves and our situation and holding to that truth.

100. *BN* 485; *EN* 529/563–64.

The "choice of oneself" which Sartre refers to so often is highly nuanced: I have to choose myself "not in my being but in my manner of being."[101] This is the heart of freedom: the fact that *within* being, being itself is given a new orientation through its relationship with a freely created end that does not exist in being. Human beings determine *their manner of being.*

If there seems to be a just balance in Sartre's thought between accepting the contingent facts of one's circumstances and freely choosing one's ends, we should not think that the raw facts can be appreciated before the ends are chosen. They are never apprehended outside the interpretation given by freedom. Facts and circumstances are only understood in the light of one's freely chosen goals. This seems to reintroduce the problem of circularity: We choose our goals on the basis of the facts, but the facts are interpreted in the light of our goals. Sartre admits that this seems to be a "paradox," but he insists that it represents the reality of the human situation.[102] We are always being confronted by facts we have not chosen, yet we only understand them in the light of our ends, and our ongoing commitment to new ends makes us reinterpret and surpass these facts.

> There is freedom only in a *situation,* and there is a situation only through freedom. Human-reality everywhere encounters resistance and obstacles which it has not created, but these resistances and obstacles have meaning only in and through the free choice which human-reality *is.*[103]

Freedom and facticity therefore require each other. There is no contradiction between the two. In a later passage he restates the same idea:

> Just as the situation is neither objective nor subjective, so it can be considered neither as the free result of a freedom nor as the ensemble of the constraints to which I am subject; it stems from the illumination of the constraint by freedom which gives to it its meaning as constraint.[104]

One can see why Sartre had such an ambiguous relationship with the structuralism that became popular in French philosophy. He insisted as much as anyone on the impossibility of encountering unmediated facts and on the omnipresent influence of human structures. But his other two convictions are inseparable from this. First, he is convinced that the objec-

101. *BN* 548; *EN* 593/633.
102. *BN* 489; *EN* 534/569.
103. *BN* 489; *EN* 534/569.
104. *BN* 551; *EN* 596/636.

tive reality of the world is revealed through these structures and claims its rightful meaning within them. Second, he is convinced that the structures are not static, they are constructed and kept in being only through the purposeful activity of human beings as they go beyond what they encounter. In other words, Sartre believed in truth and freedom as well as structure, and far from thinking that these were threatened by the constraints of structure he believed that all three concepts depended on each other for their significance. Many years after *Being and Nothingness* he wrote: "There is no doubt that structure produces behaviour. But what is wrong with radical structuralism [. . .] is that the other side of the dialectic is passed over in silence, and History is never shown producing structures."[105]

The question of structures relates to the broader question of the relationship between individual freedom and human culture. There is no doubt that Sartre paid more detailed attention to cultural factors in his later works, where the concept of the *vécu* ("lived experience") becomes central.[106] Influenced by figures such as Freud, Lacan, and Marx, he is much more aware of the opaque forces of family and history that structure a human life. "A simple formula would be to say that life taught me *la force des choses*—the power of circumstances."[107] Yet Sartre does concern himself with the subject of culture in *Being and Nothingness*. The long section entitled "Freedom and Facticity: The Situation" is a philosophy of culture in all but name.[108] Sartre analyzes the numerous ways in which the reality of the world is mediated to us through humanly constructed frameworks.

As I have already suggested in my introduction, the formal relationship between facticity and freedom remains fundamentally the same in his earlier and his later work, and there is a change of emphasis and tone rather than a new philosophy. In later years Sartre defines freedom as "the little movement that makes of a totally conditioned social being a person who does not return in its entirety what he received from his conditioning."[109]

105. Jean-Paul Sartre, *Situations IX* (Paris: Gallimard, 1972), 86.

106. On the shift in his thinking, see Christina Howells, "Conclusion: Sartre and the Deconstruction of the Subject," in *The Cambridge Companion to Sartre*, ed. Christina Howells (Cambridge: Cambridge University Press, 1992), esp. 335–43; and Thomas W. Busch, *The Power of Consciousness and the Force of Circumstances in Sartre's Philosophy* (Bloomington: Indiana University Press, 1990), esp. 41–42 and 95–101.

107. Jean-Paul Sartre, "The Itinerary of a Thought," in *Between Existentialism and Marxism* (New York: Pantheon Books, 1974), 33.

108. Part 4, chapter 1, section II.

109. Sartre, *Situations IX*, 101–2.

He writes that the project is a "mediation between two moments of objectivity" (between what forms us and what we form), and he proclaims his enduring interest in "the perpetually resolved and perpetually renewed contradiction between the-human-being-as-producer and the-human-being-as-product, in each individual and at the heart of each multiplicity."[110] None of these statements contradicts the overarching thought of *Being and Nothingness,* which proves to be programmatic for all his later works.

The Persistence of Existential Freedom

Perhaps the hardest and most illuminating question to ask is whether freedom can ever be taken away from a human being. There are "soft" versions of this question that highlight the apparent lack of existential freedom experienced in everyday life. Gregory McCulloch thinks that some of Sartre's talk about choice is overblown and that he ignores the phenomenon of *drift.* We have many broad preferences determined, for example, by our biological facticity, and even though we can question them they are hard to change and the alternatives remain stubbornly dead.[111] Phyllis Sutton Morris draws attention to the many ordinary people who seem unable to decide what they most want, or who are unable to organize their decisions into a life project, or who are living a number of irreconcilable projects at the same time. "The perpetually confused and the chronically inadequate do not appear to be describable as individuals who have made a choice of fundamental project."[112]

Sartre's account allows for these states. *Being and Nothingness* is alive to the reality of drift—it goes by the name of bad faith, or seriousness, or sincerity, and it can be confused with an ongoing commitment to a free project. He would use his existential psychoanalysis to show that confusion and indecision are often deeply engrained ways of approaching the world that reflect subtle choices about our sense of self.[113] At the same time he recognizes that a weight of facticity limits the full functioning of many minds, hearts, and bodies. But he would remind us that existential free-

110. Jean-Paul Sartre, *Critique de la Raison Dialectique, Vol. 1: Théorie des Ensembles Pratiques, Bibliothèque des Idées* (Paris: Gallimard, 1960), 67–68 and 158.

111. Gregory McCulloch, *Using Sartre: An Analytical Introduction to Early Sartrean Themes* (London: Routledge, 1994), 66–69.

112. Morris, *Sartre's Concept of a Person: An Analytic Approach,* 117.

113. See his description of the inferiority complex at *BN* 459; *EN* 504/537.

dom lies in the necessity of taking a view on these limitations and not on the possibility of overcoming them. Someone confused, broken, seemingly powerless—*if the person is conscious*—has to choose how to understand his or her state and how to respond to it, as much as those who are in the full possession of their powers.

This brings us to the "hard" version of the question about whether freedom can be taken away. Sartre seems to suggest that even in situations of grave oppression human beings are still free. Whatever the "coefficient of adversity" it is "senseless to think of complaining since nothing foreign has decided what we feel, what we live, or what we are."[114] This is the point at which, according to Herbert Marcuse, his treatise on human freedom reaches the point of self-abdication. Marcuse writes:

> If philosophy, by virtue of its existential-ontological concepts of man or freedom, is capable of demonstrating that the persecuted Jew and the victim of the executioner are and remain absolutely free and masters of a self-responsible choice, then these philosophical concepts have declined to the level of a mere ideology, an ideology which offers itself as a most handy justification for the persecutors and executioners—themselves an important part of the "réalité humaine". [. . .] The free choice between death and enslavement is neither freedom nor choice, because both alternatives destroy the "réalité humaine" which is supposed to be freedom. [. . .] Behind the nihilistic language of Existentialism lurks the ideology of free competition, free initiative, and equal opportunity. Everybody can "transcend" his situation, carry out his own project: everybody has his absolutely free choice.[115]

Sartre has made numerous distinctions that need to be borne in mind when considering these questions—distinctions between empirical freedom and existential freedom, between obtaining what one wants and deciding what one wants, between choosing the reality of one's being and choosing the manner of living this reality. His thoughts about the prisoner are in one sense a test case for existential freedom.[116] Of course those enslaved or in prison are not free to wish themselves out of their situation and create a new reality if there is no material prospect of this ever happen-

114. *BN* 554; *EN* 598/639.

115. Herbert Marcuse, "Existentialism: Remarks on Jean-Paul Sartre's 'L'être et le néant,'" *Philosophy and Phenomenological Research* 8 (1948): 322.

116. See above and *BN* 483–84; *EN* 529/563–64.

ing. Sartre recognizes that this is an absurd proposition. But what would it mean to say that the oppressed have no freedom, no choices to make, no possibility of interpreting the weight of their situation?

The main argument of *Being and Nothingness* is phenomenological. Sartre points to the experience of oppression. He will not admit that this forms a category of experience outside the intentional structures analyzed in the early parts of the work. It is a fact of experience that the oppressed, if they are conscious human beings, have to face their experience and work out what it means and how to react to it. Being-for-itself has to see beyond the brute givenness of the circumstances and ask what it means in the light of a freely chosen end. The oppressed, as much as their oppressors, suffer from anguish and have to ask: Who am I? What is important to me? What shall I do?

Many people are indeed so brutalized that they are unable to think and choose—they lose their "existential" consciousness even though they are technically "conscious" and still awake. They can be overcome with fear or pain and respond solely through a kind of animal instinct. They can be drugged into oblivion. They can lose their "presence to self" just as we do when we sleep. Many, tragically, are killed. But if they are aware of their experience, then they have to interpret it and respond to it—this is an existential fact that Sartre will not let go of. Whatever their concrete circumstances, they have at least some choices to make, some moments when they realize that an action or an attitude is not determined and is "up to them." In the very narrow confines of their historical situation, all human beings have to decide to some small extent how they will act in the circumstances they inhabit, how they will form the form of life that has been given to them. Sartre is not suggesting that people can escape their lives, he simply believes that all people have some personal responsibility for how their life is lived. Existential freedom cannot be a product of education or opportunity, it is part of the human condition, however terrible the material conditions in which one lives.

It is also a historical fact that the oppressed have always interpreted their oppression in different ways, and these interpretations have led to vastly different responses. However terrible their oppression, some have fought openly, some have engaged in subterfuge, some have accepted their lot silently, some have collaborated behind the scenes, some have joined the ranks of the oppressors. Anyone who has seen a documentary such as

Le Chagrin et la Pitié, about the Nazi occupation of France, will have been struck by the variety of responses chosen by free human beings in the face of a situation of terrible oppression.[117] Sartre knew as well as anyone that violent circumstances can take away the *practical* freedom of entire peoples, yet he didn't balk from describing the heightened sense of responsibility each person faces in these circumstances.

There is also a metaphysical or anthropological argument implicit in *Being and Nothingness* that Sartre doesn't quite spell out—one that has political consequences. If we accept that the oppressed have had their ontological freedom taken away from them, then what is there left to defend in their lives? There is no project, no freedom, no presence to self, and there is consequently no recognizable human being to harm, no right to be defended, no dignity to be preserved. The reason we recoil at injustice and oppression, even when someone seems to have had the very humanity crushed out of him, is because we believe there is still a trace of humanity present, a life to be lived. Sartre expressed this in a later essay when he took issue with a Marxist conception of political liberation that assumes that structural changes can take away (and restore) the inherent freedom of human consciousness.

> But, say the Marxists, if you teach man that he is free, you betray him; for he no longer needs to become free; can you conceive of a man free from birth who demands to be liberated? To this I reply that if man is not originally free, but determined once and for all, we cannot even conceive what his liberation might be.[118]

David Detmer brings this argument together in a very clear way.

> Thus, the slave, the unemployed worker, and the prisoner are free in one sense of the word, that designated by such expressions as "freedom of choice" and "ontological freedom," but relatively unfree in another sense, that designated by "freedom of obtaining" and "practical freedom." Moreover, according to Sartre, it is precisely *because* the slave, the unemployed worker, and the prisoner are free in the first sense, that it is possible to (1) describe them as being free in the

117. *Le Chagrin et la Pitié* [documentary film], written by André Harris and Marcel Ophüls, directed by Marcel Ophüls (1969).

118. Jean-Paul Sartre, "Materialism and Revolution," in *Literary and Philosophical Essays* (New York: Collier, 1962), 244.

second sense, (2) condemn those who render them unfree in this sense, (3) encourage them to become free in this sense, and (4) help them to do so.[119]

Without the persistent ontological freedom there is simply no one to liberate. If there is no one to liberate, then those who are working for the liberation of the oppressed must have some notion that they are creating the free humanity of the oppressed through their work of liberation. For phenomenological reasons alone Sartre would have found absurd this idea that we can create some new pocket of human freedom by transforming political structures. There must be some kernel of freedom in those who are being liberated, otherwise there will be nothing to liberate.

In all these debates the central argument is the same phenomenological one that Sartre has pursued throughout *Being and Nothingness.* Human beings are not just the totality of all that they are, of all that they have become, they are also a presence to all this. They have to go beyond it, make sense of it, relate it to a future that is not, and transform it through action. At this level, there is no difference between oppressor and oppressed, rich and poor, the famous and the forgotten. All human beings, whatever their nature or circumstances, have to make a life out of what they have been given. If our practical options are extremely narrow in relation to those of other human beings we are still existentially responsible for the self we aim to become. This may seem to be a callous view that ignores the huge constraints imposed upon those, for example, who are poor or oppressed. In reality, it is the only way of defending the dignity as persons of those who are poor or oppressed. They are still responsible for themselves and their choices, and this is why we can honor the choices they make now and wish that they had greater practical and political scope for choosing in the future.

In itself Sartre's philosophy is actually a defense of the human against all dehumanizing forces. He accepts without flinching the total situatedness of the self, the comprehensiveness of one's historical conditioning, the relativity of all understanding, yet by insisting on our presence to this totality he allows us to transcend it and transform it. Ontological freedom becomes an argument against passivity, despair, and the reification of the self. It provides a counterweight to structuralist philosophies that seek to undermine the possibility of subjectivity or agency. In this sense, Sartre was a humanist.

119. Detmer, *Freedom as a Value: A Critique of the Ethical Theory of Jean-Paul Sartre,* 63.

At least some of Sartre's contemporaries understood correctly the political implications of existentialism. Ray Davison, reporting the views of Pierre Verstraeten at a colloquium in 1993, has noted how much *Being and Nothingness* was wedded to the historical moment. France was weighed down with a growing feeling of culpability about the Vichy regime, an oppressive sense of historical destiny or fate. With Sartre the opposite was true:

"Contingence" and "surgissement perpétuel" were notions capable of fragmenting the structures of historical confinement and releasing the self from reification and passivity. In this sense, Sartre was a philosopher of liberation and a force of progress right from the original formulation of the ontology.[120]

To claim that the prisoner is as free as the persecutor is not a justification for oppression but an appeal to prisoner and persecutor alike: things do not have to be this way, the prisoner is more than his sufferings, the persecutor is more than his oppressive power. Yet the "more than" is something that needs to be freely chosen because it cannot be found in the constraints of the present situation.

Human beings are free because they have to live beyond the present. We act for a freely chosen end. The choice that we make gives meaning to everything we experience and constitutes our very being.

120. Ray Davison, "Sartre Resartus: The Circuit of 'Ipséité' from London to Clermont Ferrand. 'L'être et le néant' at 50," *Journal of European Studies* 24 (1994): 154.

Chapter 6

FREEDOM, CHOICE, AND THE INDETERMINATION OF REASON IN AQUINAS

Desire for the End

Sartre and Aquinas agree that human actions are characterized by their end. According to Sartre, there is an insufficiency about everything we find, and we have to go beyond it and interpret it in the light of a particular chosen future. This future allows us to make sense of the past and the present, but it can in no way be derived from the facts of the past and the present. Ends cannot be *discovered* in the world or in ourselves. We are indeed formed by many factors (our human nature, our individual psychology, our circumstances, etc.), but these do not force us to dedicate our lives to the pursuit of any single particular goal. This is what Sartre means when he writes that we cannot receive our ends "either from outside or from a so-called inner 'nature.'"[1] The heart of Sartre's existential freedom lies in the fact that we have to choose a goal and orientate our life to this goal through action. We are free because we can choose our ends, and in so doing we determine for ourselves who we are, where our life is going, and what actions we undertake in the world.

For Aquinas, it would seem, things are much tidier, human

1. *BN* 443; *EN* 488/519.

nature is more solidly established, choices are more rational, and ends are more accessible. In his view, all human beings seek a common goal, which is determined by their nature. He calls this goal the *finis ultimus* ("the last end") or *beatitudo* ("happiness"). We are free to choose how we reach this goal, and we have many short-term goals that allow us to achieve it, but we have no say in the nature of the final end itself.

Unlike Sartre, therefore, it may seem that Aquinas has a very restricted view of freedom. Our deepest desire is imposed upon us, our ultimate goal is determined for us, and freedom extends only to "technical" questions about which "means" we can employ to get there. It's as if we are ordered to visit London and given the choice of whether we take the train or the bus, or forced into a marriage and invited to select which color wallpaper will go in the dining room. This seems a far cry from Sartre's *liberté,* which is a completely undetermined decision to form a unique personal identity by pursuing a freely chosen set of purposes. For Sartre we are artists and visionaries—responsible for ourselves and for our world. For Aquinas, it seems, we are bureaucrats and managers—responsible for fulfilling the tasks we have been given, perhaps with some originality or aplomb, but without much room for maneuver.

In reality, however, the scope Aquinas gives to human freedom is almost limitless, and is certainly as wide as Sartre's. This is because the final end we seek is the good *in general,* without any further specification; it is happiness *in principle,* without any further conditions. "Under the good in general are included many particular goods, to none of which is the will determined."[2] We don't just choose the means to an already established end, we also choose the particular form that this end takes for us. We cannot seek good or happiness in general without making a particular choice to seek a particular type of good. In this sense the concrete goal that we seek, the good that embodies our perfect happiness, is completely up to us. Aquinas, like Sartre, believes that the constitution of practical goals always depends on human freedom.

The first point to make in this chapter is about the scope of human choice. Despite what is often assumed, Aquinas believes that we have to choose all of our ends—except the final one. It's easy to miss this and overemphasize other aspects of Aquinas's thought. He writes so clearly about

2. *ST* I-II.10:1ad3.

the necessity of seeking the final end, and about the instinctive needs and desires of our human nature, that one could get the impression that the scope he gives to human choice is minimal. Yet he also states that within the circumstances of our life we are completely free to determine which particular goods we seek and which particular form our final end will take. We freely determine, therefore, who we are, since our identity depends on what we seek to become through seeking our end.

Having established the scope of human choice, the main argument of this chapter then concerns the act itself of human choosing. Aquinas says that choices are made by the will and reason working together. The will accepts and affirms one possible line of reasoning. This is because in practical matters the reason is often undetermined since it arrives at many simultaneous conclusions. All these conclusions derive from the objective circumstances of the world; each one would give rise to a different rationally justified course of action; yet only one can be acted upon, and sometimes the reason cannot decide between them. We have to decide to follow one conclusion by actively accepting the reasonableness of one single course of action with our will. This is why a choice is always rational *and* personally willed—which is what makes it free. Human beings seek (through the will) a good (understood by intellect and reason)—the two elements of choice are inseparable, yet they are also distinct. In this way we freely constitute our own identity since we are the concrete seeking of one way of life.

It is vital to keep in mind the meaning of the technical vocabulary used throughout this chapter, as it was explained in chapter 2, so that the full significance of Aquinas's vision of the human being becomes clear. When he writes about "intellect" and "reason," he is referring to our openness as human beings to other things. Understanding makes us present to other things and one with them. Through understanding we go beyond ourselves and our interests and share in the reality of other things. We are transformed by them and in some sense we take on their identity. We are internally displaced so that we have a center outside ourselves. When Aquinas writes about "will" he is referring to our ability to go beyond ourselves in a further way. Whenever we act we are seeking to attain a good thing or to bring about a good situation. This means that we recognize an insufficiency about the present state of things and want to transform our situation into something that it is not. The good situation we want to produce is precisely something that does not yet exist and that could exist. Even in the most insignificant willed action we therefore re-create the world and take it beyond what it is. At the same time, to seek a good thing is to seek our own good through the achievement of that good thing. We recognize that our own being is not complete, not sufficient, and we seek a perfection for ourselves that we do not yet have. This means that we are transforming ourselves into what we are not and creating a new identity through our activity. So there are various levels of identification, transformation, and re-creation associated with the philosophical vocabulary of Aquinas.

Now, in this chapter, we will see how all the goods that human beings seek (apart from the final one) are freely chosen. This means that at every level the transformation and re-creation of our identity is completely up to us. We freely determine what we are (through understanding), what will become of the world (through actively seeking the good), and who we are becoming (through actively seeking our own perfection in this good). These are the radical conclusions Aquinas comes to, and they are easily masked by the language. Throughout this chapter it will help to bear in mind these large ideas which form the background to many apparently simple words: intellect, reason, will, etc.

A final introductory note about language. As has been mentioned in the historical introduction, contemporary English-speaking philosophy tends to discuss questions of human freedom and action under the heading "freedom of the will." Aquinas inherits a tradition that refers to similar issues under the heading *liberum arbitrium,* which is preserved in the contemporary French *le libre arbitre.*[3] The Latin does not contain the word "will," *voluntas.* It was a matter of debate whether the will was free, or the reason, or some other faculty, or none at all.[4] For these reasons it seems prejudicial to the debate to continue using the traditional translation of "free will" for *liberum arbitrium.* Various alternatives have been suggested and used: "free choice," "free judgment," "free decision."[5] I have chosen

3. The term goes back to classical literature and legal formulations where it indicates the "power to decide" or "freedom of action." See Daniel Westberg, *Right Practical Reason: Aristotle, Action, and Prudence in Aquinas* (Oxford: Clarendon Press, 1994), 81–82; and Charles H. Kahn, "Discovering the Will: From Aristotle to Augustine," in *The Question of "Eclecticism": Studies in Later Greek Philosophy,* ed. John M. Dillon and A. A. Long (Berkeley and Los Angeles: University of California Press, 1988), 250.

4. See J. B. Korolec, "Free Will and Free Choice," in *The Cambridge History of Later Medieval Philosophy,* ed. Norman Kretzmann, Anthony Kenny, and Jan Pinborg (Cambridge: Cambridge University Press, 1982), 630–34.

5. See Westberg, Korolec, and also Timothy Suttor in Thomas Aquinas, *Summa Theo-*

to use the single word "freedom" to stand for the Latin phrase.[6] This is not just to create a convenient parallel with Sartre's language. *Liberum arbitrium* is often used by Aquinas as a synonym for *libertas* (see, e.g., *ST* I.83:1ad3). "Freedom" is an English term that can stand for both, and using it helps us to see that Aquinas is interested in a range of philosophical concerns that go beyond what might be suggested by a translation such as "free judgment." Like the Latin phrase, it leaves open the question of how the human being is free and where that freedom lies; it emphasizes neither an intellectual nor a volitional interpretation; and it indicates the subject of the argument and not its conclusion. I hope this will facilitate the development of ideas in this chapter.[7]

The Indetermination of Particular Goods

The purpose of this section and the following one (about "goods" and "ends") is to show that, apart from the formal idea of the final end, Aquinas does not believe them to be predetermined. We have to choose which particular goods we will seek and which end will perfect us. I will allude to a number of texts, without going into too much detail, in order to present a broad picture of Aquinas's position, and prove that for him our goals and actions are not determined by our nature. Once this is clear, we can look in more detail in the following sections at the nature of freedom as it is manifested in the act of choice.

We should recognize at the very start that there are many ways in which human life *is* determined. We are contingent, bodily creatures with a certain nature who live in particular environments. It is worth alluding to some of the passages where Aquinas describes the extent to which human life is determined.

We have many instinctive desires that are part of our sensitive appetite *(appetitus sensitivus)*.[8] We thus instinctively want to seek what is suitable

---

logiae, ed. Thomas Gilby, 60 vols. (London: Blackfriars: Eyre & Spottiswoode, 1963ff), vol. 11, 237, footnote a.

6. See, e.g., Timothy McDermott's usage in Thomas Aquinas, *Summa Theologiae: A Concise Translation,* ed. Timothy McDermott (London: Methuen, 1989), 128–29.

7. This does not rule out the fact that there are other senses of freedom for Aquinas that lie outside the range of meanings included in *liberum arbitrium* and *libertas,* such as the free will *(libera voluntas)* that inclines us to our final end, even though it excludes any choice and involves a kind of natural necessity. Cf. *DV* 24:1ad20.

8. *ST* I.81:2.

to our human nature and to flee what is hurtful to it—this is our concupiscible appetite *(appetitus concupiscibilis).* We also want to defend ourselves against things that thwart these aims—this is our irascible appetite *(appetitus irascibilis).* We are bodily creatures, and our bodiliness takes a particular form that we have not chosen and that is constantly influenced by other bodily influences outside our control.[9] This bodiliness gives each of us a certain inherent temperament *(complexio)* or disposition *(dispositio)* that colors the way we see things and inclines us toward certain goals.[10] We also have various acquired habits and passions that incline us to one thing or another. And whether we like it or not, as Aristotle has pointed out, hearts beat and genitals stir—as if they were independent creatures with their own principle of life guiding them.[11]

Human beings are enmeshed in a great web of forces and causes that determine everything from the global environment to the quirks of our individual physiologies. These forces are represented in medieval cosmology by the movement of the heavenly bodies, *motus coelestis corporis.*[12] This cosmology allows thinkers like Aquinas to propose a sophisticated and contemporary-sounding view of our ecological situatedness. These diverse influences stir us in numerous ways. Aquinas gives the simplest example: "When it gets cold, we begin to wish to make fire."[13] He even allows for what we would now call a kind of genetic determinism when he describes the conception of a child through the union of "the semen and the matter of the one conceived."[14] This genetic mixing is part of what ensures that the soul "is in some sense made prone to choose something inasmuch as the choice of the rational soul is inclined by the passions."[15]

We are determined furthermore by the paucity of practical options available to us at any moment.[16] However radical the notion of "choice" seems, it can only be about possible things—things that can realistically be achieved through our actions. And even the actions we undertake with some realistic hope of success may be frustrated from the very beginning.[17] We may wish various things, but as soon as we try to command one of our

9. *ST* I.83:1ad5.

10. *DM* 6c [468–82].

11. *ST* I-II.17:9ad2–ad3; cf. Aristotle, *De Motu Animalium,* trans. Martha Craven Nussbaum (Princeton, N.J.: Princeton University Press, 1978), 11, 703b5.

12. *ST* I-II.9:5ad2.

13. *ST* I-II.9:5ad2.

14. *DV* 24:1ad19.

15. *DV* 24:1ad19.

16. *ST* I-II.13:5c.

17. *ST* I-II.6:4c.

powers to act, "the will can suffer violence, as regards the commanded acts of the will, insofar as violence can prevent the exterior members from executing the will's command."[18]

All of these influences contribute to our "facticity" for Aquinas; we are always already "in situation." These Sartrean phrases are entirely appropriate here—they emphasize the extent to which we are made in Aquinas's philosophy. We seem so unfree. Numerous influences press upon us from without and from within, and human life seems thoroughly determined by forces over which we have no control.

There is another way, however, in which we have a great deal of control over our lives. Aquinas does not just describe our human nature, he goes on to explain how this nature is under reason. We have to respond to our determined nature and decide what we will make of ourselves. We have to respond to our determined situation and decide what we will make of it. The irascible and concupiscible appetites are subject to reason and will.[19] The instinctive assessment we make of what is best, an assessment that all animals are able to make through their estimative power *(vis aestimativa),* is itself "naturally guided and moved according to universal reason" as it "directs the sensitive appetite."[20] So we are not just driven by our instincts, we also direct them according to our deepest understanding of what is true and what is good. This kind of directing, as we shall see as this chapter develops, depends on the freedom of the individual agent.

The *rational* appetite is completely undetermined as regards the concrete goods that it seeks.[21] This is the disconcerting heart of Aquinas's account of the will. We freely choose which goods will perfect our life and give it purpose. We are obliged to find our perfection in something (which is what it means to seek the universal good), yet there is no necessity for us to find our perfection in anything in particular.[22] Aquinas is unambiguous about this. In a question about the will in the *Summa* he writes: "As the capacity of the will regards the universal and perfect good, its whole capacity

18. *ST* I-II.6:4c.

19. *ST* I.81:3c.

20. *ST* I.81:3c.

21. John Bowlin gives a particularly fine account of the "contingency of the human good" in Aquinas in chapter 2 of his *Contingency and Fortune in Aquinas's Ethics* (Cambridge: Cambridge University Press, 1999), esp. 56–66.

22. Not even in God. See *ST* I.82:2c and Ignatius Theodore Eschmann, *The Ethics of Saint Thomas Aquinas: Two Courses* (Toronto: Pontifical Institute of Mediaeval Studies, 1997), 53.

is not subjected to any particular good [*non subiicitur eius possibilitas tota alicui particulari bono*]."[23] When discussing the manner in which we will in Part I-II he states: "Under good in general are included many particular goods, to none of which is the will determined [*ad quorum nullum voluntas determinatur*]."[24] This is despite the fact that in the body of the same article he argues that various particular goods are naturally wanted by the will insofar as they "belong to the willer according to one's nature" and "relate to [one's] natural well-being [*respiciunt consistentiam naturalem*]."[25] The fact that there is a kind of spontaneous desire for what is naturally beneficial does not mean that the will actively seeks these objects with any necessity.[26] There is not a single particular good to which the whole human being is naturally, necessarily directed with some kind of integrated wanting. So although it seems that there are many natural human ends, in fact there is no natural end for the person. It is not enough for us to want a good, we have to choose to make that good a part of the universal good to which we are directing ourselves—it has to become an embodiment of our deepest desire.

Sometimes, for example in *DV* 22:5c, Aquinas suggests that human beings necessarily will some goods, such as life or knowledge, because they have a necessary connection with our final end. Yet in a parallel question in Part I of the *Summa*, which is composed later than *De veritate*, he is much more cautious. He still believes that some goods have a necessary connection with happiness and with our adherence to God, in whom alone true happiness consists. But he recognizes that we can be ignorant of these connections, and for this reason there are *no* goods at all that human beings have

23. *ST* I.82:2ad2.

24. *ST* I-II.10:1ad3.

25. *ST* I-II.10:1c. Cf. *ST* I-II.94:2c ("Does natural law contain many precepts or only one?") where Aquinas says that reason naturally apprehends as good those things to which we have a natural inclination.

26. In the *Summa* Aquinas grants to the will a natural desire for particular goods, for those things that belong to the willer as befits his or her nature (*ST* I-II.10:1); but a *natural* desire should not be confused with a *necessary* desire, and the movement of the will is not itself necessary (*ST* I-II.10:2). Cf. *DM* 6c, where Aquinas acknowledges that certain goods are naturally desired by all human beings (such as existence, life, and knowledge), and states that "the will prefers [them] from natural necessity [*ex necessitate naturali voluntas preeliget illud*]" [468–72, at 470–71]; but in the same section he argues that all goods (apart from happiness) can be considered in such a way that they will seem less attractive than some alternative goods [441–62]. Cf. David M. Gallagher, "The Will and Its Acts (Ia IIae, Qq. 6–17)," in *The Ethics of Aquinas*, ed. Stephen J. Pope (Washington, D.C.: Georgetown University Press, 2002), 77–78.

to will. "Yet until through the certitude of the Divine Vision the necessity of such connection be shown, the will does not adhere to God of necessity, nor to those things which are of God [*Sed tamen antequam per certidudinem divinae visionis necessitas huiusmodi connexionis demonstretur, voluntas non ex necessitate Deo inhaeret, nec his quae Dei sunt*]."[27] The parallel between the two passages is not exact, but there is certainly a refusal to allow that in this present life there are any particular goods that are necessarily willed.

The extraordinary thing about human beings is not that we are uninfluenced by our nature or our environment, but that we have to determine for ourselves how to respond to the sum total of these influences. However many things form us, we are still capable of asking "What is happening? What do I want? What shall I do?" It is true that the sensitive appetite continually influences us: We naturally want to eat, to talk, to discover things, to be warm, to play, to have families, etc. These things are human goods, and we often seek them without much reflection, like a moth seeking light or a lion chasing a gazelle. Yet we have an additional ability to question these instinctive goods and to make our own priorities among them. This process presupposes an extraordinary ability not to identify with our natural desires and not to identify with the "person" who seeks these goods. At one and the same time we recognize (i) that we *are* this person who *does* want these things, and (ii) that we *could be* a "different" person who would want other things. If we question one of our present goods (this meal, this job, this holiday, this family), we are necessarily questioning the person who is seeking these goods—since a good is precisely something desired for the sake of the perfection of the one who seeks it. To question the good is to question oneself. This is the deepest significance of the rational appetite.

Animals, of course, have priorities. One desire may override another. A bird, for example, might refrain from swooping down on the crops if it knows that the farmer has a gun, in which case self-preservation takes priority over being fed. Yet the peculiar thing about human beings (and other creatures with rational appetite) is that we decide how the priorities are set, we decide for ourselves what is most important.[28] We can find our perfection in different ways in different goods, and the good we eventually

27. *ST* I.82:2c.

28. See John Finnis, *Natural Law and Natural Rights* (Oxford: Clarendon Press, 1980), 90–95, on the difficulty of prioritizing natural goods. For an excellent discussion of the relation-

seek is up to us. Animals have to work out how to get the goods they already seek and so how to perfect the creatures they already are; human beings have to work out which goods to seek and in that way work out which persons we will allow ourselves to be.[29] This is what it is for human nature to be under reason.

The Indetermination of Ends

Our ability to choose which goods we seek is inseparable from our ability to choose our end. There are some passages in the works of Aquinas where he flatly denies that ends can be chosen, and taken out of context they might convince some readers that the emphasis I put on choice in this present chapter is misplaced. In *ST* I-II.13:3, for example, Aquinas writes that "the end, as such, is not a matter of choice" because it is the principle, the starting point, of any action, which gives the action meaning.[30] Yet in the same article he qualifies this statement by saying that an end in one activity may be achieved for the purpose of achieving something else ("may be ordered to something as to an end").[31] In this way any end, apart from our final end, can be a matter of choice, because we may decide that it is not a suitable means to a further end. It should be borne in mind throughout this section that whenever we choose between ends we are choosing between means to a further end.

In a passage from *De veritate* Aquinas meets head on the possibility that our ends and therefore our desires are determined by the stable identity we have received at birth and through the forces of circumstance.[32] The objection he meets runs like this, and it could stand as an eloquent example of a contemporary argument for determinism:

According to the Philosopher in *Ethics* 3, "the way we see the end depends on what we are like [*qualis unusquisque est, talis finis videtur ei*]." But it is not in our power to be like this or like that [*non est in potestate nostra quod sumus tales*

---

ship between particular goods and the final end of the person, see R. Mary Hayden, "Natural Inclinations and Moral Absolutes: A Mediated Correspondence for Aquinas," *Proceedings of the American Catholic Philosophical Association* 64 (1990).

29. In this sense, for Aquinas as for Sartre, existence precedes essence, since the identity we are coming to have (our "essence") depends on the free response we make (our "existence") to what has determined us.

30. *ST* I-II.13:3c.

31. *ST* I-II.13:3c.

32. *DV* 24:1ad19.

vel tales], since what one is like is given at birth and it depends, as some maintain, upon the arrangement of the stars. It is therefore not in our power to approve this or that end.[33]

Aquinas's answer is a blunt restatement of our absolute freedom to choose particular ends, despite the facticity which makes us who we are:

Neither from the heavenly bodies nor from anything else do human beings acquire from birth immediately in the intellective soul any disposition by which they are inclined with necessity to choose any end; except that there is in them from their very own nature a necessary appetite for their last end, happiness. But this does not prevent freedom, since different ways to attain that end remain open to choice [*cum diversae viae remaneant eligibiles ad consecutionem illius finis*]. The reason for this is that the heavenly bodies do not have any immediate influence upon the rational soul.[34]

So no matter how extensive the network of intangible forces that conspire to shape us ("the heavenly bodies"), they do not touch our rational soul. In other words, the many causes that determine who we are do not in any way take away our ability to reason and will. Our being, our identity, can be determined, but our understanding of that identity (our intellect), our ability to reinterpret that identity (our reason), and our desire to transform that identity (our will) can in no way be determined.

Aquinas touches more fully on the indeterminateness of the human end at the beginning of Part I-II of the *Summa*. He writes about the last end of human life, which is *beatitudo*, "beatitude" or "happiness."

We can speak of the last end in two ways: first, considering only the idea of last end [*secundum rationem ultimi finis*]; secondly, considering the thing in which the idea of last end is found [*secundum id in quo finis ultimi ratio invenitur*]. So, then, as to the aspect of last end, all agree in desiring the last end: since all desire the fulfilment of their perfection, which is the idea of the last end consists, as stated above [see 1:5]. But as to the thing in which this aspect is realized, all human beings are not agreed about the last end: since some desire riches as their consummate good; some, pleasure; others, something else.[35]

33. *DV* 24:10obj19. Citing Aristotle's *Nicomachean Ethics* 3:5, 1114b1. For an English version, see Aristotle, *Nicomachean Ethics*, trans. Terence Irwin (Indianapolis, Ind.: Hackett, 1985), 69.

34. *DV* 24:1ad19.

35. *ST* I-II.1:7c. Thomas Gilby's translation distinguishes between *what happiness means*

On the one hand, the idea of happiness is something all human beings seek, since we all want to be fulfilled. Aquinas expresses the same point in a later question: "To desire happiness is nothing else than to desire that one's will be satisfied, and this everyone desires" (*ST* I-II.5:8c).[36] It is essential to note that in Aquinas's view this is the only thing that we necessarily seek by nature. On the other hand, human beings are not all agreed about "the thing in which the idea of the last end is found [*id in quo finis ultimi ratio invenitur*]," about "where" the last end is found. Just as we seek our good in different ways, in different particular goods, so we do not all agree about which particular thing will perfect us. There is a radical indetermination about human desire.[37]

So the fact that we are all necessarily seeking happiness does not determine for us what thing we actually seek, what the last end is for us. Happiness can take many different forms. In this first question of *ST* I-II Aquinas is not judging the respective worth of various possible final ends. He doesn't say "some people desire riches as their final end (but they are wrong . . .)" or "some desire pleasure (yet this is only part of the story . . .)"—these issues follow in question 2. Here in *ST* I-II.1 Aquinas is writing about the nature of human action and its orientation to an end. Aquinas believes that those who desire riches or pleasure as their consummate good are seeking to be perfected through these goods. The purpose and direction of our whole life is determined by the end we seek—whatever that may be.[38] In the *sed contra* to *ST* I-II.1:5 he writes, "That in which human beings rest as in their last end, is master of their affections, since they take from that the rule of their whole life," and he applies this to gluttons who make the satisfaction of their belly the dominating end of their whole existence.[39] Once again, Aquinas is not at this stage making moral judgments about human choices, he is simply noting that we *can* seek different ends and choose to

---

and *that in which it is realized,* and he comments that this is the difference between "the idea of happiness and the happy-making thing; approximately happiness in the abstract and in the concrete." See Aquinas, *Summa Theologiae,* vol. 16, footnote b, 27.

36. *ST* I-II.5:8c.

37. It could be instructive to translate *finis ultimus* as "*a* last end" rather than "*the* last end." The indefinite article would remind us that in seeking these particular things we are seeking *an end, our end,* and not "that end" which everyone else has.

38. This does not mean that all particular ends are equivalent nor that all human beings are able to *find* happiness in the ends they seek. See *ST* I-II.5:8.

39. *ST* I-II.1:5 sed c.

find fulfillment in different places. Aquinas is explicit in *De veritate* that different ways are legitimate and possible: "There are many ways of reaching the last end, and for different people different ways prove suitable"[40]; and he writes in *De malo* 6: "we can attain happiness in many ways."[41] David Gallagher summarizes Aquinas's position well:

> It is important to emphasize here that the object of the will's natural inclination is not some specific good but a general formality, since this fact provides the ultimate basis for the will's freedom. [. . .] Because the will tends toward beatitude in general or toward the perfect good in general, it remains free with respect to any specific form of beatitude or good. Each person must choose what specific good will be, for him, his ultimate end.[42]

A sentence from *ST* I-II.1:7ad2 expresses this well: "Different ways of devoting oneself to living [*diversa studia vivendi*] arise from the various things in which the idea of complete good is sought."[43] In other words, there is no universal meaning to human life—apart from the search for happiness. The only common meaning to each human life is the need to have a meaning (a final end *secundum ratione ultimi finis*): *where* that meaning will be found *(id in quo finis ultimi ratio invenitur)* is up to each individual. In a question concerning sin later in Part I-II Aquinas makes it explicit that the decision we make about our final end is a decision about our self and our identity. Our first decision about our last end takes place in childhood when the child begins to reason and "to deliberate about itself" *(deliberare de seipso).*[44] Jacques Maritain draws attention to this article and comments that "each time that a man takes himself in hand in order to deliberate over his ultimate end and to choose his destiny, he recovers in this act something of the absolute beginnings of his childhood."[45]

Our decisions about goods and ends, therefore, are fundamental. Many aspects of human life are determined by nature and circumstances, yet we are still responsible for choosing which particular goods we will seek, and which object our last end will be found in. We are responsible, ultimately,

40. *DV* 22:6c. 41. *DM* 6ad9.

42. Gallagher, "The Will and Its Acts (Ia Iiae, Qq. 6–17)," 74.

43. *ST* I-II.1:7ad2. 44. *ST* I-II.89:6c.

45. Jacques Maritain, "The Thomist Idea of Freedom," in *Scholasticism and Politics* (London: Geoffrey Bles: The Centenary Press, 1945), 99. See also David M. Gallagher, "Desire for Beatitude and Love for Friendship in Thomas Aquinas," *Mediaeval Studies* 58 (1996): 6.

for ourselves. Aquinas believes that we are sources and centers of our activity. Our life is our own and that is why we are held responsible for it. When searching for the explanations and causes behind human behavior there is nowhere further back to go than the existence of the human being in question. However many external and internal factors influence the action, it is impossible to leave out this aspect of personal commitment that gives a center to the action and makes it human. Human actions ultimately refer to and derive from the integrity of this individual human being. We can now investigate the nature of this freedom that allows human beings to make decisions about goods and ends.

Freedom, Choice, and Preference

There are many passages in the *Summa* concerned with freedom and choice (in relation to God, to angels, and to human beings), and we will look into some of them in this section. It would take a great deal of space just to outline Aquinas's well-known analysis of the structure of the human act in *ST* I-II.8–17.[46] In this section I will introduce the concept of freedom. In the rest of the chapter I will focus on its heart, which lies in the self-movement of the will toward one way of reasoning from among many possible ways.

Freedom is not, for Aquinas, a third power that underlies or complements the work of intellect and will, it is the unified functioning of these two powers. Freedom is simply the working of intellect and will. We are free because we understand and desire. It will help to begin looking at one of the more systematic accounts. In question 83 of Part I Aquinas asks specifically about the nature of human freedom. He takes it for granted that human beings are free, appealing—as we might now say—to the witness of sociologists, lawyers, psychologists, and parents ("otherwise counsels, exhortations, commands, prohibitions, rewards, and punishments would be in vain").[47] Then, by explaining how we are free, he also explains what

46. Good pieces that comment on these questions include Gallagher, "The Will and Its Acts (Ia Iiae, Qq. 6–17)"; Alan Donagan, "Thomas Aquinas on Human Action," in *The Cambridge History of Later Medieval Philosophy,* ed. Norman Kretzmann, Anthony Kenny, and Jan Pinborg (Cambridge: Cambridge University Press, 1982); Westberg, *Right Practical Reason: Aristotle, Action, and Prudence in Aquinas;* and John Finnis, "Object and Intention in Moral Judgments According to Aquinas," *The Thomist* 55 (1991).

47. *ST* I.83:1c.

freedom is. It is the fact that the human being, unlike other animals, "acts from free judgment and retains the power of being inclined to various things [*potens in diversa ferri*]."[48] Freedom is thus our ability to seek *different things* because we can think about things *in different ways.* Actions are concerned with contingent, concrete matters, and "in such matters the judgment of reason may follow opposite courses [*ad diversa se habet*], and is not determinate to one. And forasmuch as human beings are rational is it necessary that they be free."[49]

Aquinas takes up the definition of "what is free" *(liberum)* from Aristotle's *Metaphysics,* cited in the third objection of the same article. "What is free is *sui causa*" ("cause of itself" or "self-determining").[50] He clarifies this in his response. "Freedom is the cause of its own movement, because by their freedom human beings move themselves to act."[51] These themes are repeated in the first question of Part I-II, and one citation brings them together very succinctly: "Those things that have reason, move themselves to an end, because they have dominion over their actions through their freedom, which is *the faculty of will and reason.*"[52]

These, then, are some of the ideas associated with freedom: a judgment that is not determined, the ability to seek different things, the indetermination of reason, having control over one's actions, self-movement, self-determination. In the third article of *ST* I.83 Aquinas makes more explicit what is at the heart of each of these characterizations of freedom: *choice.* "The proper act of freedom is choice [*electio*]: for we say that we are free because we can take one thing while refusing another, and this is to choose."[53]

Now two things concur in choice: one on the part of the cognitive power, the other on the part of the appetitive power. On the part of the cognitive power, deliberation [*consilium*] is required, by which one thing is judged [*diiudicatur*] to be preferred to another; and on the part of the appetitive power, it is required that the appetite should accept the judgment of deliberation.[54]

48. *ST* I.83:1c.

49. *ST* I.83:1c.

50. *ST* I.83:1obj3. Citing Aristotle's *Metaphysics* 1:2, 982b25. For an English version, see Aristotle, *The Metaphysics: Books I–IX,* ed. G. P. Goold, trans. Hugh Tredennick, The Loeb Classical Library (Cambridge, Mass.: Harvard University Press, 1933).

51. *ST* I.83:1ad3.

52. *ST* I-II.1:2c. He cites Peter Lombard, II *Sent.,* 24, 3. Cf. *ST* I.83:2obj2.

53. *ST* I.83:3c.

54. *ST* I.83:3c.

So there are two elements to any choice: a rational preference and a willing acceptance. Choice always involves a double movement: it is (i) judging what is to be preferred and (ii) accepting the judgment. Or to put in another way, it is the unified movement of allowing the judgment of preference through its acceptance. It seems, to put it crudely, as if the cognitive power first does all the hard work of determining what is best to do, and then the will just rubber stamps this. We should not, however, be misled by the description of this sequence. It does not imply that the "choice" of which path to follow is made solely by the judgment of deliberation, as if the intellect can always provide us with sufficient reason to prefer one course of action rather than another, and the will simply ratifies this irrefutable judgment. Aquinas is insistent that choice is a function of the cognitive and appetitive powers working together, and nothing is actually chosen unless the will accepts what is understood to be preferable. His reply to the second objection is highly nuanced.

> Judgment [*iudicium*] is a sort of conclusion and termination of deliberation [*consilium*]. Now deliberation is terminated [*determinatur*], first, by the sentence [*sententia*] of reason; secondly, by the acceptance of the appetite: whence the Philosopher says in Ethics 3 that, "having formed a judgment by deliberation, we desire in accordance with that deliberation." And in this sense choice itself is a kind of judgment [*quoddam iudicium*] from which freedom [*liberum arbitrium*, "free decision"] takes its name.[55]

At first sight this text might seem to confirm the sequential description of understanding and willing introduced in the body of the article: the will (inevitably) follows the reason. Yet two enormously important qualifications are made here. First, deliberation, which might seem to be an independent rational process, is not in fact "terminated" or "determined" *(determinatur)* without the intervention of the will. In one sense it is still true to say that the reason determines the final deliberation, since (if the deliberation takes place) there is nothing apart from the sentence of reason for the will to accept. But on the other hand, without the concluding acceptance of the will, there is no deliberation, and the reason remains ineffective. In this sense, it is possible to say that the will determines the deliberation, since it determines *whether* any particular judgment of rea-

55. *ST* I.83:3ad2. Citing Aristotle's *Nicomachean Ethics* 3:3, 1113a12.

son ultimately becomes effective. Deliberation is not complete (and therefore a preference is not made) until the will accepts the sentence of reason. So the function of the will is not simply to accept (or reject) the conclusions of deliberation, it actually plays a part in bringing deliberation to a conclusion about what is preferable. The integrated work of choice, which involves reason and will, is what brings the deliberation to a close. The second qualification made in this response is that choice (effected by the understanding *and* the will) is itself a kind of judgment, and it is not just the carrying out of a previous judgment made by the understanding in deliberation.

The background assumption to this article is that the sentence given by reason is inconclusive, which is why it can only be concluded and determined if it is finally accepted by the will. This is not true of *all* decisions. We often make a decision without choosing, if we rationally work out that one solution is clearly the best. Yet when we face a choice, we find that two or more options are acceptable according to the sentence of reason. They may be acceptable in different ways, but they are nevertheless both rationally acceptable. This is the very reason we have a choice. The "reason" we have to choose is that there are no compelling reasons to act, or put another way, that there are too many conflicting reasons to act. We can think of trivial and serious examples: we have to choose between eating an apple or a pear, between watching the sport or the comedy on television, between giving oneself up to the police or escaping into lifelong exile, between forgiving someone or hating that person. In each case our reason can see the sense of each alternative action and may be unable to decide between them on rational grounds alone. We have to make a choice, which involves actually accepting one option when both are acceptable in theory, which involves actually preferring one option when both are preferable in theory.

These nuances from *ST* I.83 are apparent in the question about choice in *ST* Part I-II. Choice, Aquinas writes, involves both reason and will. "The will tends to its object, according to the order of reason, since the apprehensive power presents its object to the appetite."[56] This implies an orderly sequence, and might suggest that the reason compares the various options and determines which single option is preferable, as if there were a kind

56. *ST* I-II.13:1c.

of rational necessity involved for anyone who is thinking properly. But the whole point is that we have to make choices when one option is not obviously better, when numerous options all make sense, and when each one could reasonably be chosen. John Finnis emphasizes this and is highly critical of theories that might obscure the fact that for Aquinas choice is between rational, viable alternatives. "Any deliberation which ends in choice must have yielded, not one judgment affirming the choiceworthiness of an option awaiting adoption by the will, but (at least) two judgments."[57] Aquinas makes this clear in the following article when he repeats what we have already learnt, that the will, unlike the sensitive appetite shared with animals, is "indeterminate in respect of particular goods."[58]

Since choice is the taking of one thing in preference to another it must of necessity relate to several things that can be chosen [*necesse est quod electio sit respectu plurium quae eligi possunt*]. Consequently in those things which are altogether determinate to one there is no place for choice.[59]

Kevin Flannery draws attention to the fact that for Aquinas, and not for some of his neo-Scholastic interpreters, there is still a choice to make even after the intellect has made all the judgments that it can:

If the process of practical reasoning truly leads to choice [*electio*], at the threshold of choice, there must yet exist options among which the agent chooses. The scholastic ordered pairings *consilium-consensus/iudicium-electio* suggests that the job of *voluntas* is to deliver propulsion (by *consensus* and *electio*) to what is decided only in intellect *(consilium* and *iudicium)*. The genuinely Thomistic order, on the other hand—*consilium, iudicium, consensus, electio*—makes it apparent that the entire moral agent is present right at the very threshold of going into action.[60]

The Inconclusiveness of Reason

So freedom is associated with choice, and choice with indetermination. Aquinas thus has a very distinctive explanation of our freedom to choose: it derives from the fact that *in* practical matters reason itself is undeter-

57. Finnis, "Object and Intention in Moral Judgments According to Aquinas," 5–6.
58. *ST* I-II.13:2c.
59. *ST* I-II.13:2c.
60. Kevin L. Flannery, *Acts Amid Precepts* (Edinburgh: T & T Clark, 2001), 163.

mined. In this central respect, Aquinas's thinking about freedom is identical to that of Sartre, who believes that we are free because there are different, irreconcilable ways of thinking about the reality of our present situation. This does not make freedom irrational.

Aquinas links freedom with the indetermination of reason in a number of key passages. In the first article of *ST* I.83, for example, he argues that our practical judgments are free and that we can incline ourselves to different goods because we are reasoning about particular, contingent things. This type of reasoning, like dialectical and rhetorical argument, does not lead to a single, scientifically demonstrable conclusion.

> In such matters the judgment of reason may follow different courses, and is not determined towards one [*iudicium rationis ad diversa se habet, et non est determinatum ad unum*]. And insofar as the human being is rational is it necessary that the human being be free.[61]

Aquinas's view is startling: Practical reasoning about contingent things is necessarily inconclusive. So when, for example, we examine our lives and the situation before us, taking into consideration all the relevant facts, trying to work out what we shall do, we will *always* find that no single answer presents itself. The most meticulous analysis of all the available data, the most clear-sighted view of the issues involved, will be inconclusive and will leave us facing alternative courses of action. This will not be because we have missed something, it is part of the nature of paying full attention to the situation and thinking about it carefully. A single present allows for multiple possible futures; a single human situation allows for multiple possible actions. This is exactly the way that Sartre understands the experience of anguish. Existential anguish is not some kind of primeval terror in the face of life or panic in the face of commitment, it is simply one's appreciation of the inconclusiveness of reason. In anguish we realize that when we examine our past and our present they cannot guide us into a single future and determine our actions. Knowledge of what is always proves to be insufficient. In Sartre's language, human existence cannot be determined by essence, by our nature or the nature of the world. When we confront the totality of being, and bring to bear the full resources of our intellect and reason, we find that there are further unresolved questions about how we should exist.

61. *ST* I.83:1c.

The inconclusiveness of reason in practical matters concerns above all the determination of which good we shall seek and what our end should be. In *ST* I-II.13:6c Aquinas gives the reason unlimited flexibility in its ability to see particular things (but not the perfect good which is happiness) as desirable or not.

Now the reason can apprehend as good, not only this, "to will" or "to act," but also this, "not to will" or "not to act." Again, in all particular goods, the reason can consider the aspect of having some good, and the lacking some good, which has the aspect of bad [*potest considerare rationem boni alicuius, et defectum alicuius boni, quod habet rationem mali*]: and in this respect, it can apprehend any single one of such goods as to be chosen or to be avoided.[62]

This is a huge claim—that any concrete thing at all can always be seen as good in one way, or as not good. Choice is not just about those rare moments when we stand before two finely balanced and incompatible options. Aquinas says that we can always see more than one way of acting, because we can always see an aspect of good and an aspect of bad in any option, and therefore we can always discover reasons for doing it and reasons for not doing it. It is part of the nature of reason for Aquinas that it can observe present reality in different ways. The world has multiple possible meanings. The particular situations we encounter always and necessarily give rise to more than one conception of what is good, more than one practical option, more than one possible future. It can't be emphasized enough that it is *reason* that does this. Reason discovers that there is no necessity about any single interpretation of the good—this is not because of a failure of reason.

Aquinas addresses this question of necessity in the same article (13:6). The second objection is very forceful, and he accepts its argument: If there is a necessity about the prior judgment of reason, then it seems there will be a necessity about the choice. In other words, if we have to think that something is good, then we will inevitably choose it. In the body of his reply he restates his central contention. "The human being does not choose of necessity. And this is because that which is possible not to be, is not of necessity [*quod possibile est non esse, non necesse est esse*]."[63] In other words, we can choose, without necessity, because of the possible *not-being*

62. *ST* I-II.13:6c.
63. *ST* I-II.13:6c.

of the options. What makes them options is their conditionality, the fact that they could be and therefore that they are not, the fact that they do not come about as a necessary consequence of the being of the world that is. "Being" (the reality of the present situation) gives rise to "nonbeing" (the possible futures that are not yet determined) through the mediation of reason. The element of negation is as important for Aquinas as it is for Sartre. When we face a choice we face options that precisely do not exist, they do not flow out of the present constitution of the universe with any necessity. These options have to be made to be through the choice, and that is why it is not possible for there to be any necessity in the reasoning involved in a choice. David Gallagher writes about how important it is for Aquinas that human beings are free to understand things in different ways and not just free to act:

> Does the agent have control over how the options appear? This question cuts to the heart of the matter. If we say that choice and action depend upon how various goods appear to a person, and if a person does not control how these goods appear, then the person's action will not truly be free—able to be otherwise—nor will the person be morally responsible for it. If goods simply appear to an agent as they appear, then to characterize the will as rational appetite leads us into a form of psychological determinism, a determinism incompatible with freedom and responsibility.[64]

Gallagher explains that for Aquinas the agent exercises control over the very act of reason that governs his or her choice. "How objects appear, in terms of good or evil, is not simply a question of those objects taken independently of a particular agent, but rather depends in large measure on the agents themselves." An agent's "contribution" to the appearances is always to some extent voluntary or willed.[65]

Aquinas's specific replies to the first two objections of *ST* I-II.13:6 contain two remarkable glosses on the nature of the type of reasoning that takes place in practical judgments. The first response runs:

> The conclusion does not always of necessity follow from the principles, but only when the principles cannot be true if the conclusion is not true. In like man-

64. David M. Gallagher, "Free Choice and Free Judgment in Thomas Aquinas," *Archiv für Geschichte der Philosophie* 76 (1994): 248.

65. Ibid., 249.

ner, the end does not always necessitate in the human being the choosing of the means, because the means are not always such that the end cannot be gained without them; or, if they be such, they are not always considered in that light.[66]

One end can be achieved in different ways. One set of principles can lead the reason to a number of different conclusions. The reason by itself cannot "decide" which of these reasons is to be followed, because they are all reasonable. The second response adds:

> The reason's decision or judgment of what is to be done is about things that are contingent and possible to us. In such matters the conclusions do not follow of necessity from absolutely necessary principles [*non ex necessitate sequuntur ex principiis necessariis absoluta necessitate*], but from principles necessary only given a condition [*sed necessariis solum ex conditione*]; as, for instance, "If he is running, he is in motion."[67]

So in these cases when there are many legitimate conclusions, multiple futures, the only way that a single conclusion is reached is when a condition is inserted that turns the principle into the kind of principle that requires a single answer. In other words, we have to create the conditions in which one conclusion will make sense.

Let's say that a woman has to choose whether to take option A or option B in order to achieve the goal X. Let's accept that these are viable options, they arise from the reality of her situation and the possibilities available to her. X is the end, the guiding principle, which serves as the principle in a practical judgment. Perhaps she wants a salary and has to choose between being a teacher or a car mechanic; perhaps she wants a holiday and has to choose between traveling to Brighton or Bournemouth. She already knows that both options (A and B) lead to X—this is the very reason she has a dilemma. If she chooses A, all the specific benefits of A will accrue (together with the goal X); if she chooses B, all the specific benefits of B will accrue (together with the goal X). She cannot come to an unconditional conclusion on the basis of reason alone. She can only conclude that A is the correct conclusion if she first decides to build the conditions of A into the very principle X from which she is trying to derive A. A will be the conclusion that derives from her desire for X only if she sees the problem (and

66. *ST* I-II.13:6ad1.
67. *ST* I-II.13:6ad2.

the solution) in terms of A, and decides to appreciate the specific benefits arising from A. There is a fundamental insufficiency about X.

This radical insufficiency of reason to come to a practical conclusion actually reflects a superabundance and not an insufficiency of viable options.[68] It manifests itself when we find we have consented to more than one option:

> It may happen that through deliberation several means have been found conducive to the end, and since each of these meets with approval, consent is given to each [*in quodlibet eorum consentitur*]; and from the many options that are approved, we give our preference to one by choosing it [*sed ex multis quae placent, praeaccipimus unum eligendo*].[69]

Aquinas could not be clearer here about the remarkable fact that we can approve of and consent to many options at the same time. "Since each of these meets with approval, consent is given to each [*dum quodlibet placet, in quodlibet eorum consentitur*]." In these cases the reason alone is not able to find a preference. In fact, a preference is not something that is found, it is made or given to one option *by choosing* or *in the very choosing (eligendo).*

The similarities with Sartre's understanding of freedom are striking. A reasoned analysis of the situation produces many possible courses of action. None of them arises from the facts before one with any inevitability, none of them makes a claim on us with any necessity. Reason alone is insufficient for determining our ends. The characters in *Being and Nothingness* are confronted with many options: to gamble or to walk away, to continue the journey or to give up, to suffer in silence or to rebel. They are aware that nothing determines the future for them—nothing about themselves or their situation. The totality before them gives rise to alternative possible outcomes. They have to go beyond this totality and freely project themselves into a specific future that is not determined. They determine it for themselves by choosing to act for one good out of many possible goods. They allow themselves to be motivated by one set of reasoning by acting for a specific end, and this free choice to seek one end is what gives le-

68. This is one reason why Yves Simon insists that the key to Thomistic freedom is *superdetermination* and not *indetermination;* see Yves R. Simon, *Freedom of Choice* (New York: Fordham University Press, 1969), 152–53.

69. *ST* I-II.15:3ad3.

gitimacy to this specific set of reasons. They can do this because they are not trapped within being-in-itself. Their being is to exist beyond being as being-for-itself. In Aquinas's scheme it is reason that allows us to see the alternative possibilities for good within being, and the will that allows us actively to project ourselves toward one of these possibilities. The reason liberates us from necessity and the will re-creates a kind of conditional necessity that is based on the freely chosen end.

In the view of both Aquinas and Sartre, we are free to act (in one way rather than another) because we are free to reason and to understand the good (in one way rather than another). An English phrase captures this nicely: the act of choosing is often called "making up one's mind."[70] The judgment of preference takes place in the very choosing, and one's will *is* one's capacity to shape oneself by responding to reasons.[71] This means that in their choices human beings are freely deciding how they will understand the world, what they will prefer, and where their lives are going. We should note that Aquinas's account of choice, like Sartre's, does not just apply to those dramatic "Moments of Decision" when we hesitate before an agonizing dilemma that will determine the direction of our life and the quality of our character.[72] Whenever an action is "up to us,"[73] whenever we could have done otherwise, we then have to choose to do it. Both the seasoned Mafia hit man and the loyal charity worker may go about their business without much reflection or hesitation, but they are still freely choosing to do their work and fully responsible for it. They could have done otherwise, if only by not acting.

Aquinas connects the fact that there are alternative contingent solutions to practical dilemmas with our ability to deal with universals. Human knowledge is not tied to particular, material things, and for this reason we can—as it were—direct and apply our ideas to various things by our free choice. If an architect had only a particular material form of a house in mind, one that was already individualized, then he would not be able to

70. See Joseph M. Boyle, Germain Grisez, and Olaf Tollefsen, *Free Choice: A Self-Referential Argument* (South Bend, Ind., and London: University of Notre Dame Press, 1976), 13.

71. See John Finnis, *Aquinas: Moral, Political, and Legal Theory* (Oxford: Oxford University Press, 1998), 66–70.

72. See Flannery, *Acts Amid Precepts,* 162–66. The examples that follow are based on Flannery's.

73. See Aristotle, *Nicomachean Ethics,* 3:5, 1113b6.

build any other type of house, since there would be only one concrete idea determining his thinking and motivating his actions. (For example, if an architect were using some off-the-shelf plans for a three-bedroomed, two-story house made of wood and glass that had already been constructed a hundred times.) But architects usually start with universal forms (e.g., "a family home," "an office block") that can be realized in different concrete ways. Aquinas explains this in *De malo* 6:

An intellectual form is a universal, under which many things can be comprehended [*Forma intellecta est universalis, sub qua multa possunt comprehendi*]. Hence, since acts are concerned with singulars, among which there is none that is equal to the potentiality of the universal, the inclination of the will remains indeterminately related to many things [*remanet inclinatio voluntatis indeterminate se habens ad multa*]; for example, if an architect conceives the form of a house in a universal, under which houses of different shapes are comprehended, his or her will can be inclined to build a house that is square or circular or of some other shape.[74]

The same building analogy is used in a question about the divine will in *De veritate,* but here Aquinas connects the universality of human reason not only with the architect's ability to embody universal ideas in different particular ways, but also with the architect's ability to decide whether to build the house or not.

Because the form of the house in the mind of the architect is the idea of the house taken absolutely [*ratio domus absoluta*], of itself not disposed any more to existence than to non-existence or to existence in one particular way rather than in another [*magis ad esse quam ad non esse, nec ad sic quam ad aliter esse*], as far as the accidental features of the house go, the architect's inclination in regard to making the house or not remains free.[75]

Once again, the future is not determined by the being of the present. The *ratio absoluta* of the house is not disposed more to existence or to nonexistence, nor to one kind of embodiment rather than another. So knowledge gives us an indifference to being, an ability to decide whether something shall be or not be. The fact that we can abstract immaterial forms

74. *DM* 6c [287–96].
75. *DV* 23:1c.

and think about things in general is what allows us to go beyond the totality of the present and envisage *what does not have to be,* which is another way of saying that we envisage *what could be.* Possibility and the conditional tense only emerge through this process of stepping back from concrete being (making a deeper sense of it, through knowledge) and stepping forward beyond concrete being (seeing the possibilities, through practical reasoning about human action). We don't just know *that* the future is open and undetermined—it is our knowledge that *makes* the future undetermined. Human knowledge introduces the potential being of multiple human actions through the actual nonbeing of the single understood form. Our ability to deal with universals which do not exist in concrete reality is what frees us from necessity and determination. Alan Donagan summarizes Aquinas's view in this way:

> [Freedom] is wholly a matter of the non-necessity of any judgment a man can arrive at by his natural powers as to the goodness of an end or the suitability of a means. Even when will seems to fly in the face of intellect, there is always a (foolish, perhaps vicious) judgment which directs it.[76]

Donagan points out that to his immediate successors Aquinas seemed to be affirming the priority of intellect over will, but as we shall now see there is a particular kind of priority that belongs to the will.

The Influence of the Will over Reason

If reason itself cannot determine what is to be done, what does? If in questions of human action "the judgment of reason may follow opposite courses, and is not determinate to one,"[77] what finally determines that a certain judgment be made? Aquinas believes it to be the will. One has to be extremely careful about the way this is phrased in order to avoid misinterpreting him. The will determines that a certain judgment be made, while the reason determines the nature of the judgment actually made. The will and reason working together in this way constitute our freedom. We have seen that the acceptance by the will of a set of reasoning is what completes a choice. In practical matters, which are necessarily open-ended, we prefer something by willing one understanding of the good. Now in this sec-

76. Donagan, "Thomas Aquinas on Human Action," 652–53.
77. *ST* I.83:1c.

tion we can investigate this movement of the will that concludes the act of choice.

Aquinas touches on the activating power of the will in a number of articles, some of which we have looked at in chapter 4. The will as an efficient cause [*per modum agentis*] moves the intellect and all the powers of the soul, "because wherever we have order among a number of active powers, that power which regards the universal end moves the powers which regard particular ends."[78] With respect to their exercise, the will moves the other powers of the soul to their acts, "for the end and perfection of every other power is included under the object of the will as some particular good," and the will moves the other powers to their particular ends as it seeks the universal end.[79] As to the exercise of its act, "no object moves the will necessarily, for no matter what the object be, it is in one's power not to think of it, and consequently not to will it actually."[80] This is true even of the universal good of happiness, because a person "is able not to will to think of happiness at a certain moment, since even the very acts of the intellect and the will are particular acts."[81]

ST I-II.10:2 contains perhaps the most unambiguous description of the decisive role of the will in determining human action. The question concerns whether the will is moved by its object of necessity. Aquinas writes:

> If the will be offered an object which is good universally and from every point of view, the will tends to it of necessity, if it wills anything at all; since it cannot will the opposite. If, on the other hand, the will is offered an object that is not good from every point of view, it will not tend to it of necessity. And since lack of any good implies some non-goodness [*quia defectus cuiuscumque boni habet rationem non boni*], consequently, that good alone which is perfect and lacking in nothing, is such a good that the will cannot not-will it: and this is happiness. Whereas any other particular goods, in so far as they are lacking in some good, can be regarded as non-goods [*alia autem quaelibet particularia bona, inquantum deficiunt ab aliquo bono, possunt accipi ut non bona*]: and from this point of view, they can be set aside or approved by the will, which can tend to one and the same thing from different points of view [*quae potest in idem ferri secundum diversas considerations*].[82]

78. *ST* I.82:4c.
79. *ST* I-II.9:1c.
80. *ST* I-II.10:2c.
81. *DM* 6c [438–40].
82. *ST* I-II.10:2c.

We can notice the following points: (A) If the will is actually in the process of willing, then it is not free *not* to seek the perfect good in happiness. So there is a general necessity about willing our final end. (B) Apart from the perfect good, absolutely any other good at all can be viewed as good or as not good. In other words, even though Aquinas insists that the object specifies the act and the reason determines what is good, nevertheless the object and the reason alone can never "specify" which specification of the good will motivate the act. Reason supplies too much information—it can never present the will with a single, indisputable possible good (apart from the perfect end). (C) Particular goods can be either set aside or approved *by the will (possunt repudiari vel approbari a voluntate).* This is crucial. Even though Aquinas sometimes simplifies his account and suggests, as we have seen, that the cognitive power alone (through deliberation) judges what is preferable,[83] nevertheless deliberation itself is not terminated without the acceptance of the will,[84] and a preference cannot be given without the affirmation of the will that closes choice.[85] (D) When the will sets aside or approves a particular object, when it accepts one good rather than another, this is because it sets aside or approves of a point of view which is reasonable, which is one legitimate way of understanding this object. So the will is not going against reason; rather the will is selecting one reason from among many. The act is still specified solely by the goodness of the object as presented by reason. It is the object that moves and determines the act as its specifying principle, the object that makes it this act and not another.[86]

In a passage from *De malo* 6 Aquinas gives three factors that might incline the will to consider a good in one way rather than another, three "reasons" why we might take one point of view on an issue rather than another:

> That the will is drawn to that which is presented to it more according to this particular condition rather than another, can occur in three ways. In one way, inasmuch as one condition is of greater weight [*in quantum una preponderat*], and then the will is moved according to reason; as, say, when a person prefers

83. *ST* I.83:3c.
84. *ST* I.83:3ad2.
85. *ST* I-II.13:2c and I-II.15:3ad3.
86. The object of the intellect is "universal being and truth" *(ens et verum universale),* as Aquinas writes in *ST* I-II.9:1c.

that which is useful for health rather than what is useful for pleasure. In another way, inasmuch as a person thinks about one particular circumstance and not about another, and this often happens because some situation comes about, either from within or from without [*per aliquam occasionem, exhibitam vel ab interiori ab exteriori*], in such a way that such a thought occurs to him. In a third way, this occurs on account of a person's disposition [*ex dispositione hominis*]: because as the Philosopher says, "as each one is, so does the end appear to him." Hence the will of an angry person and the will of a calm one are moved to something in different ways, because the same thing is not suitable to each; just as food is regarded in different ways by a healthy person and a sick one.[87]

The three factors that might influence my will are thus: (i) the objective importance of the options before me (their "weight"); (ii) my particular situation insofar as it influences my way of thinking (where this situation includes what is happening in my inner life as well as the world in which I exist); and (iii) my character. I might buy a cake either because I am hungry and need some nourishment; or because [externally] I happen to be walking past a shop with an enticing advertisement for cakes outside; or because [internally] I am daydreaming about a cooking program I saw on television; or because I am gluttonous and want to satisfy my gluttony.

Aquinas says that only in the first case is the will moved according to reason. This fits with our everyday assumptions—that when we are being enticed by advertisements, or swayed by external pressures, or driven by a particular character trait, we are not being completely rational. But this has to be read carefully. Aquinas does not mean that in the other two cases the option chosen is not rational. He has already explained that the very reason why we can consider something to be good and still decide not to will it is that other things, at the same time, can also be considered good or fitting. With regard to any good (apart from the complete good of happiness), "a person will be able to will its opposite, even while thinking about it, since perhaps it [the opposite] is good or fitting according to some other particular consideration; as, for instance, what is good for health is not good so far as enjoyment is concerned, and so on in regard to other things."[88] So even when, against the objective advice of reason, the will considers a lesser good, and inclines to that instead, it is still some-

87. *DM* 6c [450–467]; quoting Aristotle's *Nicomachean Ethics* 3:5, 1114a32–b1.
88. *DM* 6c [444–49].

thing that reason understands to be good in the terms of the particular consideration at hand. In this sense, the will is not being irrational when it chooses pleasure over health (cf. Aquinas's example), or excitement over safety, or the short term over the long term—it is simply allowing reason to consider another particular object as good and suitable in another light. Nor does Aquinas suggest that the will is less free when influenced by the circumstances of the moment or by one's character.

The whole point of this section of *De malo* 6c [418–84] is to show how there is no necessity in the movement of the will, even with regard to the specification of the act. The will can allow itself to be inclined to a "weighty" long-term good that has been prioritized by reason; or to a good that has a special attraction to it in these circumstances; or to a good that appeals in a particular way to a person of such a character. In neither of these three cases is the will drawn with any necessity or compulsion; and in all three cases the particular end under consideration can be presented in such a light that it seems good or fitting *(bonum vel conveniens)* to reason.

In an article about choice from *De veritate* Aquinas is slightly fuller in his description of the distinctive role of the will and its relation to the "weighing up" done by reason. He is discussing the nature of choice:

> Choice is the final acceptance [*ultima acceptio*] of something to be carried out. This is not the business of reason but of will [*quod quidem non est rationis, sed voluntatis*]; for, however much reason puts one ahead of the other, there is not yet the acceptance of one in preference to the other as something to be done until the will inclines to the one more than to the other. The will does not of necessity follow reason [*Nam quantumcumque ratio unum alteri praefert, nondum est unum alteri praeacceptatum ad operandum, quousque voluntas inclinetur in unum magis quam in aliud: non enim voluntas de necessitate sequitur rationem*]. Choice is nevertheless not an act of the will taken absolutely but in its relation to reason, because there appears in choice what is proper to reason: the putting of one next to the other or the putting of one before the other [*conferre unum alteri, vel praeferre*]. This is found in the act of the will from the influence of reason: reason proposes something to the will, not as useful simply, but as the more useful to the end.[89]

89. *DV* 22:15c.

Once again it must be emphasized that the reason is not proposing a single reasonable plan of action that is automatically approved by the will. Sometimes alternative plans of action cannot be ordered by the reason, they are all equally reasonable, and the reason "puts them next to one another" *(conferre)*. Sometimes the reason puts one plan before the others *(praeferre)*—but without losing sight of the viability and reasonableness of the alternatives. In neither case is the will obliged to prefer one alternative as ground for action *(ad operandum)* rather than another. The inclination of the will to one rational plan, which is the ultimate cause of action, is *not* necessarily determined by the order given by reason. There couldn't be a clearer statement of the determining influence of the will. Aquinas's own words, however, could mislead us here. When he writes that the will does not of necessity follow reason he means here that it does not follow *the ordering (praeferre)* which reason gives among rival plans. It still, however, follows the reasonableness of the chosen option. As he goes on to say, choice is always an act of the will in relation to reason, and the option preferred by the will is always therefore a reasonable one that has been proposed (even if it is a lower ranking proposal) by reason.

Stephen Brock draws attention to the role of the will in making the preference.[90] When we reason about possible actions, "it can happen that both "measure up" *and* that neither is a clear winner." If taking one excludes the other, then the decision is simply "up to you."

> You refuse one when all conditions needed for your accepting it are present, and you accept the other when all conditions needed for refusing it are present. [. . .] The will moves toward one thing *despite* a sufficient attraction toward something excluding it; this is a choice, a taking one thing in the face of another, a preference. This is not at all to say that the choice is not informed by a judgment. The chooser must have formed a judgment declaring the preferability of what he chose. Only, he also formed a judgment declaring the preferability of the alternative he rejected. Nor are these two separate judgments; it is one judgment, declaring one alternative preferable in some respect, and the other preferable in another respect.[91]

90. He is commenting on *ST* I.83:3.

91. Stephen Brock, *Action and Conduct: Thomas Aquinas and the Theory of Action* (Edinburgh: T & T Clark, 1998), 170, footnote 75.

So there are multiple practical truths, multiple possible acts, which all make sense in different ways. Let's call them different lines of reasoning. Reason cannot decide between them, since reason is the very faculty that has brought them to light. It is up to the will to prefer one way of reasoning and acting. This is free choice. It is simply the way that we activate a reason. Note that it does not involve an additional, alternative, nonrational apprehension of good. Stephen Brock puts it this way:

> [The will is not] an *additional* source of objects or specificatory principles, outside or apart from those given by the intellect. Rather, the will plays a role in the determination of its object precisely by playing a role in the process by which the intellect comes to provide it with an object.[92]

The will is not determining what is good (the reason does this), it is determining that one way of looking at one good should be activated, that one project be followed. The only reason for doing X is X itself—as judged by the reason. The movement of the will is necessarily in accord with the good as it is presented by reason, but *the movement itself* is not caused by the understanding of the good—it is caused by, indeed it *is,* the will's very attraction to this good. A choice is rational, indeed there is no such thing as an irrational choice (since it must be between reasonable options)—yet a choice is not *rationally made.*

The will, for Aquinas as for Sartre, is not against reason, it is what establishes it as something with practical relevance. The exercise of the will is what gives momentum to the reasonableness of one way of reasoning, which up to this moment had only a theoretical power. Why did we go to the cinema instead of the bowling alley? Eat Italian instead of Mexican? Talk about football instead of politics?

On the one hand, the action brings about its own explanation—we act for the objective good sought. The only reason for eating Italian food is because Italian food is good. But why do we not follow other reasons? Because of the reasonableness of the reasons that we do choose. There are no further reasons to put into the equation. This is not voluntarism, for the simple fact that the movement of the will toward this good is explained by the objective rationality of the good in question. The fact that other goods could also have been reasonably chosen does not alter this.

92. Ibid., 170, see 61–72.

On the other hand, there is no explanation beyond the freedom of the one who acted.[93] The goodness of Italian food is not enough to explain the choice since Mexican food is equally good. We freely determine ourselves to act in this way, to follow these reasons. I do this because I choose to: that is the reason. There is something irreducible about the movement of the will that results in a choice being made. It is a kind of unanalyzable fact. A choice creates something new. This is still not voluntarism, since the movement of the will is never made against reason or in isolation from reason—it is the very thing that allows me to use my reason.

By choosing one way of reasoning we are giving priority to one notion of good and orienting our life to a particular goal. Through our choices, big and small, we are giving shape to our identity. John Finnis gives an example of a scholar dedicated to the pursuit of the truth who abandons this for a new cause such as fighting for his community or caring for his sick wife (perhaps there are echoes of Sartre here). His new commitment has not somehow become *more reasonable;* rather, the change in his chosen life-plan has made the reasonableness of this new commitment more persuasive.

> That chosen plan *made* truth more important and fundamental for him. His new choice changes the status of that value *for him;* the change is in him. Each of us has a subjective order of priority amongst the basic values.[94]

So Aquinas is neither an intellectualist nor a voluntarist. He believes that we creatively determine which understanding of the good will motivate our personal actions even though each understanding is determined solely by the nature of the good as understood by reason. In other words, the objectively understood good can be deeply personal. This is the kind of moral synthesis so many contemporary thinkers struggle toward. Charles Taylor, for example, is acutely aware that some ethical theories can depersonalize human action. Choices are based on the objective values that our disengaged reason discovers. Yet he knows that other theories that appeal to the language of self-realization and subjective fulfillment run the risk of losing sight of the objective good. Caught between rationalism and romanticism, Taylor pursues a "search for moral sources outside the subject

93. See Gallagher, "Free Choice and Free Judgment in Thomas Aquinas," for a particularly fine account of all these issues.

94. Finnis, *Natural Law and Natural Rights,* 93, see chapter IV, 81–97.

through languages which resonate within him or her, the grasping of an order which is inseparably indexed to a personal vision"—he wants value to be both objective and subjective.[95] Aquinas describes just this "resonance" in the language of intellect and will. The objective good must be subjectively accepted; the reasonableness of a right action must be personally willed by the agent. Aquinas's action theory thus allows for a concept of human autonomy that does not separate personal responsibility from a rational understanding of the objective good.[96]

We are left not so much with the mystery of freedom as the fact of freedom. To bring in the word "mystery" at this stage would not only be a fudge, it would also be inaccurate—since it implies that something is being kept secret. It suggests that in the moment of choice there is some deep knowledge philosophers can't quite get to, some hidden piece of psychological machinery we can't quite pry open. But for Aquinas this is simply untrue. The whole point of his account is to show that when absolutely everything has been explained, when every factor has been taken into account, when every possible point of view has been considered—both out there in the world and in our own inner experience—then we are still left with alternative rational possibilities, and the only way we can move forward is by making a decision. The will is not something that finds out more (it is rather the reason that finds things out), it is our ability to make a choice, to take a decision, in the absence of higher reasons that would make the decision inevitable. It is, ultimately, our ability to live a particular life and give it a particular shape.

There is nowhere further back to go than the very act of choice, which establishes the agent as one who is now acting for this goal. The frustrated questioner still wants to know why we make this choice, but this very desire to know betrays a misunderstanding of the dilemma of choosing. In the moment of deliberation, we don't yet know what to do. We don't know (in the present) what we will choose (in the future) until we do actually make the choice. We can't look somewhere else for an answer. It is fair to say that there simply is no answer—until we choose. There is no answer

95. Charles Taylor, *Sources of the Self: The Making of the Modern Identity* (Cambridge: Cambridge University Press, 1989), 510.

96. This idea of autonomy in Aquinas is brought out in Martin Rhonheimer, *Natural Law and Practical Reason: A Thomist View of Moral Autonomy* (New York: Fordham University Press, 2000), see esp. viii and 143.

for the agent about to decide, nor for the philosopher trying to analyze the prehistory of the agent's eventual decision, since both the agent and the philosopher are trying to investigate the same thing. Choosing brings about an answer that did not exist before, except as one possibility among many. The recurring demand for more philosophical clarity here is understandable but misplaced, since it denies the very fact of freedom. The inquisitive philosopher is always trying to collapse this "future" choice into the determinations of the past and present. But once again, the disconcerting heart of Aquinas's view is that the present, as it is understood by reason, is not enough (because reason is undetermined), or rather it is too much (because reason sees alternative possibilities), and it can only be determined by an unanticipated movement of the will in the future choice—which will still be perfectly explicable in terms of the end that is actually chosen.

Intellectualist Readings of Aquinas

This whole approach to understanding the relationship between intellect and will in Aquinas has been questioned by a number of recent commentators who follow a more "intellectualist" line.[97] Broadly speaking, they deny this so-called voluntarist interpretation, in which the will has some kind of final control over its own activities, and they insist instead that its activities are controlled by the intellect.[98] So in the particular situation of choosing between alternative rational goods it is not the will that inclines us to one good (or to one consideration of the good) rather than to another; or if it is the will, then this will is following the conclusions of the intellect about which good is to be rationally preferred. This is not the place for a line-by-line rebuttal of these intellectualist arguments. I hope that my own reading of the Thomistic texts will have made another interpretation more attrac-

97. See, e.g., Jeffrey Hause, "Thomas Aquinas and the Voluntarists," *Medieval Philosophy and Theology* 6 (1997); P. S. Eardley, "Thomas Aquinas and Giles of Rome on the Will," *Review of Metaphysics* 56 (2003); and Robert Pasnau, *Thomas Aquinas on Human Nature* (Cambridge: Cambridge University Press, 2002), esp. section 7.4, 221–33.

98. It is almost impossible not to use the words "voluntarist" and "intellectualist" when discussing these arguments since these are the labels used in the literature to characterize rival interpretations. So I reluctantly adopt these terms in this discussion. But one of the main points of my own position is that even though Aquinas is not an intellectualist, this does not make him a voluntarist, insofar as the good eventually chosen is always completely specified solely by the intellect.

tive. But at least I can point out some of the shortcomings of some these other approaches.

Jeffrey Hause argues that Aquinas is a thoroughgoing intellectualist:

On Aquinas's view, the will cannot, by any innate capacity, direct the intellect's attention, keep the intellect from issuing judgments about what one ought to do, or keep itself from willing what the intellect has determined what one ought to do. Nor can it select one from among a variety of alternatives unless the intellect has first settled on that one as the alternative to be pursued. Which, if any, of a set of objects the will wills, and whether it wills anything or nothing at all, depends not on any voluntaristic capacity of the will, but on how the intellect judges the object in question.[99]

He distinguishes between various kinds of voluntarism, highlights some false assumptions in the voluntarist position, and points to some apparently intellectualist texts. His main arguments, however, are more general ones: (i) Yes, Aquinas admits that the will sometimes influences the intellect even before the intellect passes judgment; but in this case the act of the will is linked to previous judgments of the intellect.[100] (ii) Aquinas never says unambiguously that the will, without direction from practical reason, selects from among the options presented to it.[101] (iii) Yes, Aquinas frequently attributes to the will control over which rational plan is chosen, with no mention of any contribution by reason; but this is because "speaking of the *will's* control is a useful shorthand for speaking of the *human being's* control."[102]

There is some truth in these statements, but there is also something slightly inconclusive in an appeal to what Aquinas doesn't say and to what he might be suggesting in shorthand. The real problem for Hause's argument is that in the texts where Aquinas is specifically analyzing the relationship between intellect and will, their interdependence and their particular functions, he does give the will a power of control over the intellect and its considerations, and he doesn't say that this control is itself dependent on the prior deliberations of the intellect. Hause insists that reason's role "is to evaluate goals and means and to make plans in accordance with

99. Hause, "Thomas Aquinas and the Voluntarists," 168.
100. Ibid., 175.
101. Ibid., 177.
102. Ibid., 178.

its evaluations. [. . .] The will always chooses in accordance with reason's decisions, and it always executes those decisions in accordance with reason's commands."[103] He pays too little attention, however, to the passages where Aquinas explains that the reason is not always fully determined, and that sometimes it finds that different options are equally preferable, or it finds that the will rejects its rational priorities (and inclines to an object that is good in another rational way).[104]

In this respect, Hause's interpretation of *ST* I-II.13:6ad3 betrays his own intellectualist inclinations. The question is about whether we choose out of necessity or freely. The third objection proposes that a choice cannot be free because from several objects we will necessarily choose whichever appears to be best. Aquinas replies (in Hause's translation):

> If two things are proposed (to the will) which are equal in one respect, nothing prevents our considering in one of them some quality which makes it stand out, and (so nothing prevents) the will's being inclined to the one rather than to the other.

Hause's gloss on this "intellectualist reply" is: "Reason's determination of some point of superiority in one option over another is a necessary condition of the will's choosing."[105] This is true in one sense, if it means that the will can only incline to a good that the reason judges to be superior in a certain respect—since the reason and never the will specifies its object. But Hause intends us to understand that when faced with a range of options, one of them will be superior, and the reason will determine this superiority, and the will will then choose this predetermined superior option. He wants to tie the movement of the will to the decision of the reason. This interpretation cuts right against the very point Aquinas wishes to make. It's important to recall the objection: "If two or more things are available, of which one appears to be more eligible [*inter quae unum maius appareat*], it is impossible to choose any of the others. Therefore that which appears to be best [*quod eminentius apparet*] is chosen of necessity." We should hold in mind that this is the objection. So Aquinas needs to find a reply against the necessity of choosing whatever seems to be (rationally) best. The whole point of the article, and of this third response, is to show that when numer-

103. Ibid., 178.

104. See *DV* 22:15c; *ST* I.83:1c; *ST* I-II.13:6; *DM* 6c; and my comments on them above.

105. Hause, "Thomas Aquinas and the Voluntarists," 180.

ous things are available, and one seems to be best, we still do not choose out of necessity, because the reason can consider different things to be superior in different ways. It is about the indetermination of reason, and the fact that the will is free to move in different directions precisely because the reason has not come up with any necessary conclusions, and is still capable of entertaining various alternative considerations. The will is not determined by the reason here; it is the will that "determines" which of the many possible rational determinations will prevail. This is why, to return to the third objection, a hungry man can choose one appetizing dish rather than another; it is also why he can choose what does *not* appear to be best *(eminentius apparet),* and eat the tablecloth, or not eat at all.

P. S. Eardley, another interpreter in the "intellectualist" line, presents a fair summary of David Gallagher's argument that for Aquinas, when an object and an act can be considered by the reason in different ways, it is the will that controls which consideration will take priority, independently of a prior determination of reason.[106] Eardley argues that this view, however, should not be attributed to Aquinas, but that it fits more with the teaching of Giles of Rome, one of his pupils.

On Thomas's account, the will can never act independently of a prior judgment of reason, either as regards exercise or as regards specification. If the will desires one object over another, this is because reason has apprehended it as better and specified or determined the will's act accordingly. Furthermore, whether or not the will exercises its act or the other powers of the soul is also determined by a prior act of the intellect.[107]

Yet Eardley provides very little evidence for rejecting Gallagher's conclusions. He appeals once to Hause, without referring to his actual arguments.[108] And, in another place, like Hause, he accepts hypothetically the main thrust of the "voluntarist" argument, only to insist that a thoroughgoing intellectualism would nevertheless lie behind it: "Even if the will has the ability to control how the object is ultimately regarded by the intel-

106. P. S. Eardley, "Thomas Aquinas and Giles of Rome on the Will"; commenting on David M. Gallagher, "Free Choice and Free Judgement in Thomas Aquinas," *Archiv für Geschichte der Philosophie* 76 (1994).

107. P. S. Eardley, "Thomas Aquinas and Giles of Rome on the Will," 846.

108. "Aquinas cannot, as Gallagher would have it, be considered a voluntarist as regards the self-motion of the will. Rather, as Hause has shown, he should be regarded as a thoroughgoing intellectualist"; see Eardley, "Thomas Aquinas and Giles of Rome on the Will," 847.

lect, nonetheless, any such act has to have been itself determined by a prior judgment of the intellect."[109] The evidence for this statement is the passage from *ST* I.82:4ad3, which I have already discussed in chapter 4 ("[But] not every apprehension is preceded by a movement of the will").[110] Whatever Aquinas is doing in this difficult passage, he is certainly not talking about prior judgments of the intellect which might control how the will then controls the considerations made by the intellect.[111]

Eardley continues his interpretation with a misreading of *ST* I-II.9:4. Aquinas writes that "even with regard to its being moved to exercise its act, it is necessary to posit that the will is moved by some external principle."[112] Eardley writes that "such an 'external' principle is deliberation *(consilium),*" and uses this understanding to conclude that "the intellect both determines whether the will should elicit an act or not and also what it should will."[113] But the "external principle" referred to in this article is quite clearly not *consilium*—it is instead God. In the body of the article Aquinas explains that we can only come to will the means to an end through a process of deliberation, and that this process of deliberating and willing cannot stretch back indefinitely; and for this reason the original willing of the will must come "by the impulse of some exterior mover [*ex instinctu alicuius exterioris moventis*], as Aristotle concludes in a chapter of the *Eudemian Ethics*."[114] So the reference is to the transcendent cause of our willing, which lies in God, and not to any particular (intellectual) principle within us. The reference to the *Eudemian Ethics* makes this very clear.[115]

Robert Pasnau gives a spirited intellectualist reading of various Thomistic texts.[116] The main problem is that by the end he loses spirit himself, and becomes uneasy about the deterministic implications of this reading, and about whether such implications are really true to Aquinas. He believes that Aquinas's theory of free decision is *compatibilist,* and gives two sub-

109. Ibid., 845.

110. See the section "Reflexivity of Intellect and Will."

111. See my comments on this passage in chapter 4 above, in the section "Reflexivity of Intellect and Will."

112. *ST* I-II.9:4c; Eardley's translation, in P. S. Eardley, "Thomas Aquinas and Giles of Rome on the Will," 845–46.

113. P. S. Eardley, "Thomas Aquinas and Giles of Rome on the Will," 846.

114. *ST* I-II.9:4c.

115. *Eudemian Ethics* 7:14, 1248a18ff.

116. Robert Pasnau, *Thomas Aquinas on Human Nature* (Cambridge: Cambridge University Press, 2002), esp. section 7.4, 221–33.

tly different definitions of compatibilism. It means (i) that "freedom can coexist with cognitive and volitional systems that function in entirely deterministic ways, necessitated by the sum of prior events"; and (ii) that human freedom can be explained "without any recourse to an uncaused, undetermined act of will or intellect—as if only an uncaused decision could count as a free decision."[117]

Pasnau is not at all simplistic in his intellectualist account. He pays attention to passages where a more "voluntaristic" reading seems required—for example, to *ST* I-II.13:6c (there is no necessity in choice because "a human being can will and not will, do and not do, and can also will this or that, and do this or that"); and to *DV* 22:15c ("[. . .] the will does not follow reason of necessity").[118] He moves the argument to the level of higher order volitions, to the broader interests and longer term goals that guide our everyday decision making. It is these higher level beliefs and desires that give us a measure of control over our immediate judgments that is denied to animals. He shows how the will can influence the intellect at this higher level—for example, how some fixed dispositions and desires of the will might override the more short-sighted dictates of reason.[119] He sees the relationship between reason and will in Aquinas as "a back-and-forth exchange, extending over the course of our lives."[120] He recognizes that, in his compatibilist reading, even though we control our acts through higher order judgments and higher order volitions, this just moves the problem back a step, and ultimately we have to say that our current choices have been determined by the prior events and forces that have shaped us.[121]

117. Ibid., 221. In my understanding, Aquinas could certainly not support the first statement because a lack of necessity in freedom is one of his constant refrains; but he could possibly support the second statement because he does not say that freedom is uncaused or undetermined, since the intellect always determines the object of free decision (so the act itself is never undetermined), and since freedom does not exclude various kinds of causes (e.g., the transcendent cause of our natural desire for happiness).

118. Pasnau's translations; ibid., 224 and 227.

119. Ibid., 228–29.

120. Ibid., 229.

121. Thomas J. Loughran gives a sophisticated defense of Aquinas's apparent compatibilism in his "Aquinas, Compatibilist," in *Human and Divine Agency: Anglican, Catholic, and Lutheran Perspectives*, ed. Michael F. McLain and Mark W. Richardson (Lanham, Md.: University Press of America, 1999). He argues that what makes acts of human intellect and will *contingent*, rather than necessary, even when they are determined by a full set of causal antecedents, is the fact that the antecedents themselves are contingent, and that they are beyond the grasp of the agent. In other words, our acts are fully determined, but because the contingent determining

How—the libertarian asks—could we then be free? The compatibilist has no defense against this line of attack, other than to suggest that it is a mistake to suppose ourselves so in control of our choices. It just is true that the causes of our actions extend beyond our reach.[122]

This kind of response, Pasnau admits, seems to run against Aquinas's repeated insistence that the movement of the will is in no way necessary. He finds "hints" that Aquinas understands necessity in a way weaker than libertarians would want; and then suggests that human beings are only subject to a "conditional necessity" that results from the contingent circumstances of our environment and our history: "Given the entire state of the universe, including an individual's higher-order beliefs and desires, a certain choice will inevitably follow"; "Human beings must make certain choices, given (a) their natures, (b) the surrounding circumstances, and (c) their higher-order beliefs and desires."[123] Pasnau finishes this section in a slightly wistful manner:

> It would be absurd to deny that animals do, in some sense, determine their own actions. It would be equally absurd to deny that we determine our own actions, in a fundamentally deeper way. Perhaps we too do not escape the chains of causal necessity. But if we are determined, we are determined by our own beliefs and values, not simpy by the brute design of nature and the happenstance of events. This difference, for Aquinas, makes all the difference.[124]

The problem, on this compatibilist account, is that we *are* ultimately determined by the brute design of nature and the happenstance of events.[125] This is not just unfortunate (for us and for our freedom), it also denies the repeated statements by Aquinas that there is no necessity in our willing, and

---

forces are so diffuse and beyond our comprehension, we understand ourselves to be acting independently and without necessity. "Human beings experience independence from any measure of the causal antecedents to choice which they can comprehend" (15).

122. Robert Pasnau, *Thomas Aquinas on Human Nature,* 231.

123. Ibid., 232.

124. Ibid., 233.

125. Loughran draws the same conclusions. "The compatibilist model leaves human beings with exactly the measure of independence from proximate causal orders which reflection on human experience reveals [. . .] . But that independence from proximate causal orders, freedom from necessity in that sense, in no way implies independence from the entire order of created causality." He goes on to acknowledge that, for libertarians, this kind of freedom "will seem plainly insufficient to preserve freedom; worse, it seems irrelevant"; see Thomas J. Loughran, *Human and Divine Agency,* 18.

that we do not choose out of necessity.[126] I am not giving a detailed response here to Pasnau's large work. I am simply trying to expose the difficulty that lies at the heart of any more intellectualist and compatibilist reading of Aquinas's act theory. The difficulty is that, however faithful such a theory may seem to be to some of Aquinas's arguments, it is not ultimately faithful to his larger and often-stated concerns about freedom and the nonnecessity of human choices that this freedom must involve. Pasnau recognizes all this. He tries to show that there is some kind of freedom left in our ability to determine for ourselves our long-term goals. But then he gives up:

> The libertarian will rightly object that for a compatibilist these goals and values cannot *really* be up to us: they too must be determined by our nature and by the surrounding circumstances. Adding higher-order links in the chain only prolongs and perhaps obscures the inevitable necessity of any particular choice.[127]

There is a valuable compatibilist action theory here. All I want to show is that it is not Aquinas's. By the end of this section, Pasnau seems to have admitted as much as he resigns himself to accepting that his reading involves "the inevitable necessity of any particular choice."

The Self-Movement of the Will

When the will prefers one plan of action by inclining to it, there is no prior reason for this inclination (beyond the good sought)—it is the very exercise of our freedom. "The proper act of freedom is choice: for we say that we are free because we can take one thing while refusing another; and this is to choose."[128] Aquinas's explanation for this is simple, and it is more a description than an explanation: the will moves itself. The will can "pass or not pass into the act of willing with regard to anything at all" because "animate things are moved by themselves" [*moventur a seipsis*].[129] Self-movement gives us control over our actions and independence from the totality of causes which press upon us.

> Those things that have reason, move themselves [*seipsa movent*] to an end, because they have dominion over their actions through freedom, which is the *faculty of will and reason.*[130]

126. *ST* I.82:2; *ST* I-II.10:2, *ST* I-II.13:6; DM6; etc.
127. Robert Pasnau, *Thomas Aquinas on Human Nature,* 233.
128. *ST* I.83:3c.
129. *DV* 22:6c.
130. *ST* I-II.1:2c, citing Peter Lombard, II *Sent.,* 24, 3.

Self-movement belongs properly to the will and not to the intellect, since the intellect is moved by the will to act, "but the will is not moved by another power but by itself."[131] The idea of self-movement implies that the fact of movement has no cause outside the occurrence of the movement itself. Aquinas states that "freedom is the cause of its own movement [*causa sui motus*], because by one's freedom one moves oneself [*seipsum movet*] to act."[132] There is a kind of "immanent" operation here, which must, as Stephen Brock explains, "be an activity which is immediately and simultaneously able to effect either one thing or its contrary."[133] It is no exaggeration to say that self-movement is a kind of self-creation, since the self is constituted by its ends, and we choose our ends and therefore our self by moving ourselves toward them.[134]

On this question of the will's self-movement, *De malo* 6 is particularly helpful.[135] Aquinas is writing about the exercise of the act (i.e., whether an end that is already understood by the reason in a particular way will actually be pursued), rather than the specification of the act (i.e., whether an end will be understood by the reason in one way rather than another).[136] He explains that "the will is moved by itself [*voluntas movetur a se ipsa*]: for just as it moves the other powers, so also does it move itself [*se ipsam movet*]."[137] He recognizes that this seems to imply a contradiction, since moving something normally involves one thing that is not in motion being moved by another thing that is in motion. How can the will be both not in motion and in motion at the same time? He writes that in this case the will is not "both in potency and in act with regard to the same thing."[138] For just as our knowledge of one thing leads us on an investigation that results in some new knowledge, so the fact that we already will one thing (such as health) leads us to will another thing (such as the taking of some medicine).

131. *DM* 6ad10.

132. But this doesn't exclude God being the first cause of our freedom; see *ST* I.83:1ad3 and below.

133. Brock, *Action and Conduct: Thomas Aquinas and the Theory of Action*, 40, footnote 79.

134. This does not mean, as we shall see below, that the will is without a transcendent cause that explains its original ability to move.

135. See *DM* 6c [360–415].

136. But it is important to remember that the will's control over the exercise of an act also has some bearing on the act's specification, since any specification depends on a particular act of the intellect that itself needs activating.

137. *DM* 6c [361–63].

138. *DM* 6c [364–65].

Aquinas then makes two striking clarifications. First, we only will a particular means (such as medicine) if we are willing to take counsel *(consiliari)* about how to achieve an already established end (such as health). And given that the will moves itself by counsel, and "council is a kind of investigation that is not demonstrative but involving opposites, the will does not move itself of necessity."[139] So the lack of necessity, the freedom, flows from the fact that a will that is already willing a certain end can continue willing that end in different rationally valid ways. The willing of a concrete good (such as medicine) is thus never a new and self-generating act, it is always part of an already established movement toward some greater goal. This is what preserves both its freedom and its rationality.

The second clarification is about the transcendent cause of the will's overarching movement.[140] Aquinas writes that even the act of taking counsel must be willed, and that this act of will requires its own act of taking counsel, which seems to lead to an infinite regression. Aquinas concludes that the will must be moved "by something external, by the impulse of which the will begins to will [*ab aliquo exteriori, cuius instinctu voluntas velle incipiat*]."[141] Given that the rational soul is immaterial, this initiating force cannot be material—it must be something above the will and the intellect, namely, God.[142] But in this case God "moves the will according to its condition: not from necessity but as indeterminately relating to many things [*voluntatem movet secundum eius conditionem, non ex necessitate set ut indeterminate se habentem ad multa*]."[143] So the will is not the cause of its own initial or originating movement. Aquinas's whole theory rests on this Aristotelian assumption that there is an "external" or "transcendent" source of the will's dynamism.[144] But the will is moved according to its "condition" or "nature" [*conditio*], which is to be open to many things in a way that is indeterminate. It is, to use a slightly strained phrase, necessarily indeterminate. In other words, the transcendent foundation of the will (in God) does not take away from its freedom to move itself to different possible goods.

139. *DM* 6c [378–81].

140. Cf. *ST* I-II.10:4 and I-II.109:2ad1.

141. *DM* 6c [390–91].

142. Aquinas refers to Aristotle's conclusions in the chapter *De bona fortuna* of Aristotle's *Eudemian Ethics,* 8:2, 1248a16–29.

143. *DM* 6c [412–15].

144. Freedom, as Sartre has put it, is not its own foundation: we are "condemned to be free"; see *BN* 485; *EN* 530/565.

To the suggestion that an external principle behind the will brings with it some kind of coercion, Aquinas replies: "The will contributes something when it is moved by God, for it is the will itself which acts [*ipsa enim que operator*], although moved by God."[145] God makes the will to be what it is, which is an inclination to happiness that can be embodied and fulfilled in many different ways—and the decision about which way depends on the human person and not on God. In a discussion of what happens when the will makes a new choice, he writes that this change is effected by two movers, "insofar as the will itself moves itself to act and insofar as it is also moved by an external agent, namely God [*in quantum ipsa voluntas movet se ipsam ad agendum et in quantum etiam movetur ab alio exteriori agente, scilicet Deo*]."[146] There is no contradiction for Aquinas between our radical dependence on God as the transcendent foundation of our freedom, and the radical independence of that freedom insofar as it allows us to determine our goals and thus constitute ourselves. To be human is to have the possibility of creating a future that has not been predetermined; it is to go beyond the bounds of necessity.

In *ST* I-II.6:1 Aquinas relates the possibility of the will's self-movement more specifically to knowledge of an end. He writes that a stone does not move itself downward, even though the principle of this movement is intrinsic to the stone (and we might therefore be tempted to say that through its own heaviness the stone thrusts itself downward). "But those things which have a knowledge of the end are said to move themselves because there is in them a principle by which they not only act but also act for an end."[147] Irrational animals have an imperfect knowledge of their end and consequently their acts have a kind of voluntariness [*voluntarium*]. Yet these animals apprehend the end "without knowing it under the aspect of the end, or the relationship of an act to an end."[148] Aquinas continues:

> Perfect knowledge of an end goes with voluntary activity in its complete sense; inasmuch as, having apprehended the end, a human being can, from deliberating about the end and the means thereto, be moved, or not, to gain that end.[149]

145. *DM* 6ad4 [512–14].
146. *DM* 6ad17 [637–39].
147. *ST* I-II.6:1c.
148. *ST* I-II.6:2c.
149. *ST* I-II.6:2c.

We should notice the connection here between knowledge of an end and self-movement. Aquinas could have said: We know the end, therefore we can choose between various means. Instead he says: We know various means to an end, therefore we can choose whether to seek the end or not. It's important to see that one deliberates here about the end as well as the means, although the sense is that one deliberates about whether the end of this action is desired as a means to a further end.[150] In the reply to the second objection Aquinas draws attention to the main theme of this chapter, the fact that the movement of the will is not against reason but is fully in accord with the disposition of the reason. The significant point here is that there is no *single* disposition. The deliberating reason is indifferently or equally disposed to opposite things *(se habet ad opposita)*, and on account of this the will can be inclined to either *(in utrumque potest)*.[151]

We have come full circle in the argument of this chapter. We started by investigating human goods and ends. Now we find that the self-movement involved in free choice depends on understanding the relationship between a means and an end. Our knowledge of ends and our freedom are, in fact, the same thing. We are free because at any one moment we can see different valid ways of acting, different goods, different selves—any of which would make sense of the objective understanding we have of the world and allow us to achieve our final end. This is Sartre's "anguish." Our present identity does not give rise to a single future identity. Why does one choose to do this rather than that? Because one chooses to be this person. But why does one choose to be this person rather than that one? Because one *is* this person—through the choice. Aquinas believes that no further answer is possible. The choice doesn't depend on something else, it *is* oneself—it is the self-constitution of the person who seeks perfection in this goal and not another. As David Burrell explains, "[T]he human self becomes itself by acting in the way it does, and these ways come to stamp an individual with his or her particular character."[152] The person one be-

150. Cf. *ST* I-II.13:3c, where Aquinas explains how the end in one operation can be a means to bring about a further end.

151. *ST* I-II.6:2ad2.

152. David B. Burrell, *Aquinas: God and Action* (South Bend, Ind.: University of Notre Dame Press, 1979), 128. There is no space here to discuss the huge topic of character in Aquinas. It is enough to say that even though character *(habitus)* can become a principle of human actions (see *ST* I-II.49:3), it develops *as a consequence* of human actions (see *ST* I-II.51:2–3). There

comes through choosing this goal did not *exist* before the choice was made. The human person *is* the one who creates oneself through seeking specific goals. The choice itself is self-constituting. David Gallagher formulates this in a startling way:

> The judgment of choice which determines the will's motion arises in the choice, a choice which occurs only when it is willed. Hence the will influences, in the act of choice, the very judgment it follows in that act.[153]

There is no actual circularity here, since choice is a single human act of an individual person. In that one act, by means of two powers, we determine ourselves to a particular action *and* establish that one judgment of the good (out of many possible judgments) is governing that action.[154]

It will help to recall once again the significance of Aquinas's vocabulary. Intellect and will are not detached, independent faculties that happen to be associated with our being, like wristwatches or personal computers. We *are* our understanding and willing.[155] To ask the question "Who are we?" is to ask what we understand, what we think, what we love, what we live for. *We* identify with other things and are transformed by our personal understanding of them (this is what it means to be an "intellectual" creature). *We* seek perfection by seeking what is good, by acting in the world, by transforming ourselves and our world (this is what it means to be a "willing" creature). This integrated process of understanding and willing *is* our unfolding "self."

This means, for Aquinas, that when we face a choice about goods and ends, whether small or large, we face a choice about ourselves. Before the moment of choice, our reason discovers that there are different ways of interpreting the matter in hand, different ways of understanding the good, all of which arise from the present reality of the world and of our self. So our identity, which is formed by our understanding and by the goods we seek, is in question. We are not sure who we are because we are not sure

---

is a feedback effect in which actions produce dispositions and dispositions produce actions. The ultimate foundation of the process lies in the individual choices that produce action.

153. Gallagher, "Free Choice and Free Judgment in Thomas Aquinas," 256.

154. Ibid., 276.

155. In a passage about how one can attribute the activity of parts of a substance to the activity of the whole, Aquinas writes: "We may therefore say that the soul understands, just as the eye sees; but it is more correct to say that the human being understands through the soul [*homo intelligat per animam*]" (*ST* I.57:2ad2).

how to understand or what to seek. Our reason has discovered that there *is* no single objective way of understanding things, no single set of necessary goals. We are paralyzed. Then, at the moment of choice, our will approves of one specific way of understanding things by actually seeking one specific good. The will *as it brings about one possible way of understanding things* constitutes the freedom of the acting person. We go beyond the indeterminate world of possibility and create a single determined future through action. So our identity, which is constituted in relation to the goods that we actually seek, is established. We become sure of who we are by crystallizing one way of understanding the world and our self, and orientating our whole being to this good. We create ourselves by seeking *this* form of perfection in *this* good.

So the undertaking of one project (understanding in this way, desiring in this way, being this person) *is* the self. There is no other "self" that exists outside or before the willing of one goal, as its cause or explanation. There is no "deep self" that is a prior foundation for the choice we make of one project from among many. We constitute ourselves through our free choices. Our goals constitute our personhood, yet they are themselves constituted by the person we choose to be. Even if we never reach the goal in the future, an identity is still created in the present. What matters is the direction in which we are actually moving and our personal understanding of the significance of that direction. We are a longing, a direction, a project—not a finished product. To be human is to be *in via,* to be on the way. To be free is to choose the way, and in choosing the way, to choose the end at which we hope to arrive.

Part Four

HUMAN FULFILLMENT

Chapter 7

THE POSSIBILITY OF HUMAN HAPPINESS IN SARTRE

The Goal of Happiness

In the action theories of Sartre and Aquinas human beings are creatures who seek particular concrete things: food, pleasure, success, security, fame, friendship, etc. We are not disembodied creatures who have some abstract notion of human fulfillment. Desire takes us beyond who we are, in all its particularity, to the person we hope to become, in all its particularity. Nevertheless, both thinkers hold that within these concrete goals, or through them, there is a more universal good that we are seeking. This universal good is the fulfillment we find in achieving our goals, whatever they may be. It is not another "greater" good to which we direct our lives, it is the underlying fulfillment that we seek as we seek concrete goods. It explains why we are motivated to seek anything at all.

We desire a particular thing because we want to find fulfillment in general in particular things. We have a general desire for fulfillment that allows us to understand why we seek particular types of fulfillment. I will use the English word "happiness" to refer to this general goal that lies at the heart of all particular human seeking. There is some warrant for this in the language of both the writers we are concerned with. Aquinas calls the last end that motivates all desire *beatitudo,* which is usually translated as "happiness."[1] Sartre writes that human reality is by nature a *conscience malheureuse,* "an unhappy consciousness," since we are constantly frustrated in our desire to find fulfillment in a stable and freely chosen identity.[2] The suggestion, however slight, is that this fulfilled identity would be a state of happiness. I won't pretend that "happiness" is a key term for Sartre—as we shall see, he prefers the obscure neologism *l'en-soi-pour-soi.* I simply want to have one English word to stand for this universal goal that plays such a significant part in the philosophy of both thinkers. The main question to ask here in part four is this: Given the understanding of freedom discussed in the previous chapters, can we ever be happy?

The single most important difference between the philosophy of Aquinas and that of Sartre is that Aquinas thinks that human beings can find happiness and can rest in it and enjoy it. We are not perpetually dislocated and permanently moving on. At the same time, Aquinas insists, just as Sartre does, that finding perfect human happiness in this life is nevertheless an impossible ideal. We should not therefore be too quick to conclude that Aquinas's views about happiness create a gulf between his thinking about the nature of human life and Sartre's. The impossibility of finding happiness in this life is in fact a final idea that they share.

Before launching into the texts I want to remind the reader about a point made in the preface. Aquinas is a theologian through and through.[3] Yet he is also able to make philosophical arguments that make sense in their own right without the need for theological convictions or faith in revelation. His analyses of intellect and will, of human action, and of the desire for happiness do not depend on faith in God. The argument about happiness in the first questions of Part I-II is philosophical, even though the conclusion is also a theological conviction that would stand without the appeal to reason. So when Aquinas concludes that human beings can-

1. *ST* I.II.2:1c. See the translations in Thomas Aquinas, *Summa Theologica,* trans. Fathers of the English Dominican Province, 5 vols. (Westminster, Md.: Christian Classics, 1948) and Thomas Aquinas, *Summa Theologiae,* ed. Thomas Gilby, 60 vols. (London: Blackfriars/Eyre & Spottiswoode, 1963ff) (which curiously uses "happiness" in the text and "beatitude" in some of the headings).

2. *BN* 90; *EN* 127/134.

3. The Prologue to Part II, for example, sets the whole question of the nature of the human being in a theological context: The human being "is made in God's image" (*factus ad imaginem Dei*), and Aquinas only treats of God's *image* here because he has already spent the 119 questions of Part I treating, broadly speaking, of *God himself.*

not be perfectly happy in this life the impasse he reaches is philosophical, just as Sartre's is. When Aquinas goes on to argue that we must be able to find happiness beyond this life in God, he is using the desire for happiness as an argument to lead one to God (even though he already believes in God). Aquinas does not use theology to plug a philosophical gap, he uses philosophy to open up a theological horizon. At this level, he and Sartre are doing the same kind of thinking.

The Ideal of Self-Coincidence

According to Sartre, there is a fundamental lack in human beings. We have examined this lack in earlier chapters. Self-consciousness brings with it a presence-to-self. At one and the same time we acknowledge our identity and perceive a distance from it. We try to resolve this constitutive tension by mapping out a meaningful future and projecting ourselves toward a particular goal. In this way we freely establish an identity in relation to this future through our actions.

The problem is that as soon as we reflect on this newly established identity, we dissociate ourselves from it and once again become caught in the same trap. Ideally, we would like two things *at the same time:* (i) a secure and stable identity, the satisfaction of our desires, a conclusion to our endless seeking; and (ii) the freedom and distance that come with self-consciousness, the ability to choose our goals, the responsibility for founding the identity that unfolds through our choices. In other words, we want to be being-in-itself and being-for-itself at the same time, we want to be *l'en-soi-pour-soi,* "in-itself-for-itself."[4] We seek a "failed synthesis of consciousness and being."[5] This is an impossible ideal since being-for-itself is by definition the surpassing of being-in-itself. We are always beyond what we are and we never quite reach what we could be—there is always another "horizon of possibilities."[6] The ideal totality is not just a factual impossibility but also a theoretical contradiction.

We are by nature restless, searching, inquisitive, unsettled, and yearning for more, and if we ever stopped wanting and wondering and looking further we would stop being human. Human being-for-itself is the up-

4. *BN* 194; *EN* 230/244.

5. *BN* 626; *EN* 674/720, *manquée* can mean both "failed" and "missing."

6. *BN* 101; *EN* 138/146.

surge of the negation of its being-in-itself. "What the for-itself lacks is the self—or itself as in-itself [*Ce que le pour-soi manque, c'est le soi—ou soi-même comme en-soi*]."[7] Sartre's anthropology flows out of his phenomenology. To be human is to exist *in-between* two poles as a "lived relation [*rapport vécu*]": these poles are the present facticity of being-in-itself and the future ideal of the in-itself-for-itself. "Human beings are neither the one nor the other of these beings, since there is no sense in which we *are*. We are what we are not and we are not what we are."[8] In other words, it is a constitutive part of our nature to consider and seek a perfection that we do not yet have ("we are what we are not"), and it is a constitutive part of our nature to be conscious of a lack of complete identification with who we are now ("we are not what we are").

Sartre writes about the ideal of self-coincidence in a number of ways.[9] It is "the impossible synthesis of the for-itself and the in-itself" which would "preserve within it the necessary translucency of consciousness along with the coincidence with itself of being-in-itself."[10] He identifies the ideal with value insofar as the values we seek are precisely things that do not exist, things that define the persons we wish to become. Value is the "beyond" that draws us out of ourselves toward a future self that does not exist.[11] Sartre writes about "value taken in its origin, or the supreme value,"[12] which bears a great similarity to the universal good in Aquinas. It is not the particular good sought but the good as good for us: the fact that a good allows us to surpass ourselves and constitute ourselves in relation to a perfection we have not yet achieved. The supreme value is the underlying fulfillment of the self that we seek *as* we seek particular values, "the absolute being of the self with its characteristics of identity, of purity, or permanence, etc., and as its own foundation."[13] Beauty represents for us this ideal state of fulfillment.[14] Yet even beauty is apprehended only as an absence that haunts the imperfection of the world. We can only realize the beautiful through our imagination, which grasps the ideal but simultaneously recognizes the unreality of what is imagined.

The ideal is "an unrealisable totality which haunts the for-itself and

7. *BN* 89; *EN* 125/132.
8. *BN* 575; *EN* 621/664.
9. See *BN* 101; *EN* 138/146.
10. *BN* 90; *EN* 126/133.
11. *BN* 92–95; *EN* 129–32/136–39. Cf. *BN* 194; *EN* 230/244.
12. *BN* 93; *EN* 130/137.
13. *BN* 93; *EN* 130/137.
14. *BN* 194–195; *EN* 230–31/244–45.

constitutes its very being as nothingness of being"; it is a "perpetually indicated but impossible fusion of essence and existence."[15] If it were ever realized the very structure of temporality would evaporate, and past, present, and future would collapse into each other. What we fail to appreciate is that the future we aim at is not just something we wish to make present. The future *as* future always remains beyond us; it is what allows us to go beyond ourselves, to think and act and exist as human beings. This future is never realized. "What is realised is a for-itself which is *designated* by the future and is constituted in connection with this future."[16] We know that the ideal is unrealizable, yet at the same time we have to live as if we were in the process of achieving it. It is not simply a regulative ideal that structures human behavior, it is a constitutive ideal that establishes human identity.

This begs the question of whether we can aim at an ideal even if we believe it can never be achieved. Aquinas, as we shall see later, believes that our orientation to this final goal proves that it must exist. If we are constituted by something else, even by an ideal that seems unreachable within the limitations of our present thinking, then it must (objectively) be possible, and we must (subjectively) act as if it were possible. Sartre, however, accepts a lack of integration in his philosophy. On the one hand, he insists that human beings continually have to live and act for a final goal beyond the reality of their present circumstances. On the other hand, he argues that this goal is a self-contradictory ideal. In other words, for Sartre, acting human beings have to live as if the goal were possible and direct their practical thoughts to it, but their more reflective thinking reveals that the goal is actually impossible.

Existential Denial and Human Relationships

There are many ways of trying to avoid these existential dilemmas, and they all involve some kind of bad faith or self-deception, "*la mauvaise foi.*"[17] We looked in chapter 1, for example, at the attempt to be "sincere," which occurs when people deny their freedom and lose themselves in some particular identity or role.[18] Ultimately these strategies all prove futile. Not even death can provide a resolution.[19] Death makes this synthesis impossible

15. *BN* 194; *EN* 230–31/244.
16. *BN* 128; *EN* 163/172.
17. *BN* 47–70; *EN* 81–106/85–110.
18. *BN* 58–67; *EN* 93–102/98–108.
19. *BN* 531–48; *EN* 576–92/615–33.

not simply because it is the end of consciousness and temporality—which would be a fairly banal truth. It is the unpredictability of death that thwarts us. This unpredictability makes it impossible for us to fix the significance of all that we are striving to achieve because anything at all might be reinterpreted or undermined by a new future. If the future gives meaning to all the past, and if our death cannot be chosen, then the ultimate meaning of our whole life is beyond our control and outside the scope of our freedom. The final term that would give meaning to all our waiting and striving is on principle never given, as it is the ideal in-itself-for-itself.

If death is not the free determination of our being, it can not *complete* [terminer] our life. One minute more or less may perhaps change everything, and if this minute is added to or removed from my account, then even admitting that I use it freely, the meaning of my life escapes me.[20]

In the play *In Camera* Garcin remarks, "I died too soon. I wasn't allowed time to carry out *my* acts." To which Inès replies, "One always dies too soon—or too late. And yet life is over with, finished; the deed is done and you must add it all up. You are nothing other than your life."[21]

Many aspects of the dilemma of ontological unhappiness are played out in human relationships.[22] "The look" *(le regard)* of "the other" *(autrui)* confers on our being a kind of objectivity and allows us to observe our freedom from the outside.[23] "*I* see *myself* because *somebody* sees me."[24] In the eyes of the other our projects and identities, which are so precarious, take on a certain stability and seem like essential features of our being. Our recognition of the subjectivity of the other gives us an unreflective experience of our own objectivity, and for a moment takes away the anguish of having to go beyond what we are. Objectification in itself is not necessarily negative, even though Sartre illustrates it by describing experiences of shame *(la honte)*.[25] Shame can be an authentic attitude because it allows us to apprehend our nature as an object.[26] "Pride" *(la fierté)*, however, is yet another form of bad faith. In pride we resign ourselves to being only what

20. *BN* 538–39; *EN* 583/623.

21. Jean-Paul Sartre, *Huis Clos and Other Plays* (London: Penguin Books, 2000), 221; original French text in Jean-Paul Sartre, *Huis Clos* (London: Routledge, 1987), 93.

22. See *BN* 252–302; *EN* 292–341/310–64.

23. *BN* 259–65; *EN* 298–304/316–23.

24. *BN* 260; *EN* 299/318.

25. See *BN* 221–23 and 259–61; *EN* 259–61/275–77 and 298–300/316–18.

26. *BN* 290; *EN* 330/351.

we are and take refuge from freedom in this objectified being.[27] An authentic response to shame is not pride but *l'orgueil,* which is perhaps best translated as "assertiveness" rather than "arrogance" (or again "pride"), since it means simply the reaffirmation of our freedom and the consequent objectification of the other's subjectivity.[28]

The two defining characteristics of human relationships emerge from these primary phenomenological experiences. In *Being and Nothingness* the words *"amour"* (love) and *"le désir"* (desire) are given technical meanings that should be distinguished from their everyday ones. Through *l'amour* we seek to become the object of the other's freedom, so our freedom becomes more and more alienated. This is why Sartre relates his concept of love to masochism, because it holds a passive face to the subjectivity of the other.[29] Through *le désir* we seek to turn the other into an object and to possess the other's freedom. This is why Sartre's concept of desire is related to sadism, because we use our own subjectivity to take hold of the other.[30] Love allows us to be appreciated for who we are—which limits our freedom; and desire allows us to appreciate who the other person is—which restores our own freedom, but restricts our ability to experience *being loved.* We oscillate between loving and desiring the other.

The failure to construct harmonious, stabilized relations, which is such a notable feature of Sartre's philosophy, is actually a guarantee that each person in the relationship is free. If we love others as persons then there is always the possibility that their freedom will take us by surprise. This creates conflict. We can appreciate whatever objective face they show in the present, but this is quite different from objectifying them and denying that they are free to change this face. The fact that others do not always fit with our expectations is a sign that we are relating to their freedom as well as to their identity. Conflict in a relationship is, for Sartre, a positive sign that two people have not turned themselves or each other into objects that can be possessed and manipulated.[31] Just as we can never find perfect happiness in a stabilized in-itself-for-itself, so we can never find perfect happiness with another. The lack of perfect harmony in any human relationship is, strangely, a sign that the relationship is still alive.[32]

27. *BN* 290; *EN* 330/351.
28. *BN* 290; *EN* 330/351.
29. *BN* 364–79; *EN* 404–19/432–47.
30. *BN* 379–412; *EN* 419–53/448–84.
31. See *BN* 361–415; *EN* 401–55/428–86.
32. It might be possible to construct an ethic of long-term commitment from the same

The Link between Ontology and Theology

Sartre puts the whole ontological dilemma in explicitly theological terms.[33] *Dieu,* "God," represents the ideal synthesis between being and consciousness that we can never achieve.

> Is not God a being who is what he is, in that he is all positivity and the foundation of the world, and at the same time a being who is not what he is and who is what he is not, in that he is self-consciousness and the necessary foundation of himself?[34]

God is for Sartre the ideal of *securely having* an identity and *freely founding* it at the same time. The fundamental project of human beings is to be God. "To be human means to reach toward being God; or, if you prefer, the human being fundamentally is the desire to be God."[35] We desire to be "consciousness become substance, substance become the cause of self, the Human-God [*la conscience devenue substance, la substance devenue cause de soi, l'Homme-Dieu*]."[36]

Sartre adopts, for his own phenomenological purposes, the religious vocabulary of the Judeo-Christian culture in which he stood. This tradition recognized the transcendent possibility of a being who can be both perfectly free and perfectly fulfilled, beyond himself and in possession of himself, ecstatic and recollected. At the same time Sartre insists that such a being, in the terms of his phenomenological ontology, by definition cannot exist. This is because consciousness and freedom are inextricably associated for Sartre with distance, negation, doubt, lack, and incompletion. Consciousness always involves an openness to what one is not, an aware-

---

principles: No matter how strongly we love others, if we love them solely for who they are now, this is an act of bad faith, since it restricts them to their present identity. If we love them as persons we will love them for who they could be and not just for who they are, which is to love a future self that could arise from the freedom of the one loved. Part of loving others in the present is the desire to love whoever they will become through their free choices. So long-term commitment to a relationship is not an additional factor we might give in the future but an essential element of loving a person now in the present.

33. There is an excellent assessment of the relationship between Sartre's theology and his phenomenology by Frederick J. Crosson, "Intentionality and Atheism: Sartre and Maritain," *The Modern Schoolman* 64 (1987). See also James McLachlan, "The Theological Character of Sartre's Atheology in 'Being and Nothingness,'" *Epoche* 5, nos. 1–2 (1997).

34. *BN* 90; *EN* 126/133.

35. *BN* 566; *EN* 612/654.

36. *BN* 575; *EN* 621/664.

ness of one's own insufficiency, a projection beyond the present. It is a lack of identity. If God were conscious, he would not be independent, self-sufficient, and complete. The idea of completion is inseparable for Sartre from the darkness and impenetrability of being-in-itself.

Sartre's conceptions of being-in-itself and being-for-itself are inextricably associated in his phenomenological scheme with time. His reluctance to engage in metaphysics meant that he could not allow himself to speculate about any alternative models of being that might make sense of an existence "outside" or "beyond" the limitations of time.[37] He couldn't postulate a scheme in which the freedom and distance of being-for-itself could somehow exist "simultaneously" with the identity and positivity of being-in-itself. So when he thought about a God whose existence might be one with his essence, and about a human being who might be perfectly free and perfectly happy, he rightly concluded that in the limited world of time that we experience these notions are self-contradictory.[38]

> Every human reality is a passion in that it projects losing itself so as to found being and by the same stroke to constitute the in-itself which escapes contingency by being its own foundation, the *Ens causa sui,* which religions call God. Thus the passion of the human being is the reverse of that of Christ, for we lose ourselves as human beings in order that God may be born. But the idea of God is contradictory and we lose ourselves in vain. The human being is a useless passion.[39]

If this seems like a rather depressing conclusion, we should remember that in the context of Sartre's phenomenology it is the only one that respects and preserves our distinctive "nature" as beings who go beyond themselves. Sartre almost delights in the paradox that to be ourselves is to wish we were not ourselves, that to be human is to be unsettled and un-

37. Note the brief foray into metaphysical speculation at *BN* 619–25; *EN* 667–73/713–20.

38. Frederick Crosson speculates about how Sartre's view of consciousness might allow for a conception of God in which he would know himself (and all things as they participate in his infinite being) through a completely actualized and timeless *self*-consciousness, without there being any duality or knowledge of himself *as object.* There could be some kind of self-coincidence and completion that would not destroy consciousness. In other words, the absence of self-identity and substantiality which Sartre knows to be a condition of temporal *human* consciousness may not be a condition of *all* consciousnesses. See Crosson, "Intentionality and Atheism: Sartre and Maritain," 156–60.

39. *BN* 615; *EN* 662/708.

happy. "Human reality is suffering in its being" because "it could not attain the in-itself without losing itself as for-itself." It is therefore "by nature an unhappy consciousness with no possibility of surpassing its unhappy state [*par nature conscience malheureuse, sans dépassement possible de l'état de malheur*]."[40] A "constant disappointment" accompanies every momentary achievement. We ask ourselves "Is it only this? [*n'est-ce que cela?*]" and another horizon of possibilities immediately opens out.[41] The disillusion, we should remember, is not connected with circumstances, it is an "ontological disappointment."[42]

Even a sympathetic critic like Frederick Olafson found these conclusions too pessimistic and wished that Sartre had recognized that some human lives seem more disappointing and disappointed than others.

> There is, after all, a distinction between lives that are crowned by achievement and those that issue in frustration and failure, and this is a distinction that is surely relevant to the business of making out—however difficult that may be—whether a man is happy or not.[43]

I think that Olafson misses the point of Sartre's argument. Sartre does not deny that human beings can find some satisfaction in their achievements, nor does he deny that some lives are full of success and some full of failure. He simply draws attention to the continual necessity of moving on. Any achievement becomes part of our facticity—we have to take a view on it, interpret it, and project ourselves beyond it toward a future goal. If we cling to it and define ourselves in terms of it, then it diminishes our freedom and becomes an aspect of bad faith. Yet if we see beyond the achievement (and admit that we are *not yet* fully happy), then the achievement becomes part of our unfolding identity and we preserve our freedom and openness to the future. Unhappiness, as a manifestation of our constant going beyond the present, is the guarantee that we are still conscious, desiring human beings.[44] There are less pessimistic ways of expressing the

40. *BN* 90; *EN* 126–27/134.
41. *BN* 101; *EN* 138/146.
42. *BN* 128; *EN* 163/173.
43. Frederick A. Olafson, *Principles and Persons: An Ethical Interpretation of Existentialism* (Baltimore, Md.: John Hopkins University Press, 1967), 137.
44. This could perhaps provide a starting point for an existentialist ethics: the recognition that human beings, as a fact of experience, *are* seeking a universally satisfying good. *If* we want to seek perfect happiness (which we do), *then* it is self-defeating to be satisfied with anything

same convictions. It sounds much less dispiriting to say "there is always *more* happiness awaiting us" or "we can always be *even happier than we are*" than to say "we are never fully happy." This is not just a rhetorical trick, as long as we are clear that the restlessness in consideration is caused by a lack of perfect happiness.

Failure and Hope

Existential failure is what saves us from the immobility and stagnation associated with success. *Qui perd gagne:* "Whoever loses wins." This does not mean that losing becomes another self-defeating form of success, it means that the perpetual failure to fix our identity is the very thing that reassures us of our freedom. This is a nonrecuperative ontology and Sartre persistently refuses to allow that we can reach some synthesis just beyond the contradictions of the human condition.[45] To be human is to seek this synthesis, it is not to reach it. By the same token, however, even our recurring failure to reach this synthesis is provisional. Each failure becomes a fact of experience that has to be surpassed. We have to seek further values and project ourselves into a newly constituted future. This is why it's inappropriate to think that Sartre's ontology is pessimistic. If it is impossible for human beings to find ultimate happiness in a perfect synthesis, it is equally impossible for us to meet irrevocable failure in our projects. We always have the chance, and indeed the necessity, of going beyond and building something new.

Sartre's critics broadly agree that human beings cannot find happiness in his ontological scheme and that the in-itself-for-itself is an ideal that can never be achieved. There is much more disagreement about whether or not Sartre recommends an alternative approach to the human project that could take us beyond this impasse. There are a few enigmatic references in *BN* to a mode of living that might resolve the intractable problems raised by Sartre's ontology. Authenticity might allow a "recovery of being" (*une*

---

less than complete happiness. There is no need to argue that human beings *should* seek certain goods, or *should* seek the good of others. Ethics simply needs to start with the nature of human desire and human freedom.

45. See Christina Howells, *Sartre: The Necessity of Freedom* (Cambridge: Cambridge University Press, 1988), 44–45 and 198–99; and Jean-Paul Sartre, *Cahiers Pour Une Morale* (Paris: Gallimard, 1983), 450–53, translated as Jean-Paul Sartre, *Notebooks for an Ethics,* trans. David Pellauer (Chicago and London: University of Chicago Press, 1992), 435–39.

reprise de l'être) that would take us beyond the categories of good and bad faith.[46] A radical conversion might lead to "an ethics of deliverance and salvation."[47] The activity of play releases us from the spirit of seriousness and allows us to appreciate our own subjectivity.[48] Through existential psychoanalysis our freedom might become more conscious of itself and might be able "to take itself as a value as the source of all value."[49]

There is no space here to dwell on these provocative suggestions,[50] nor to delve into the notebooks that represent Sartre's own attempts to take these issues forward and open up further avenues for exploration.[51] I want to make just one point here, which is that however much Sartre's thought develops in his later works, however much nuance he adds, he never puts in question the essential conclusions of phenomenological ontology made in *Being and Nothingness*.His enigmatic references to authenticity and conversion do not represent a repudiation of the basic ontology of freedom mapped out in *Being and Nothingness*.[52] He continues to hold in his later work that we are fundamentally incomplete beings. We have an identity (as "being-in-itself"); we are present to this identity and have to go beyond

46. *BN* 70, footnote 9; *EN* 106/110, footnote.

47. *BN* 412, footnote 14; *EN* 453/484, footnote. Cf. *BN* 627; *EN* 675/721.

48. *BN* 580–81; *EN* 626–27/669–70.

49. *BN* 627; *EN* 675/722.

50. For some helpful interpretations of what Sartre might have meant, see Francis Jeanson, *Sartre and the Problem of Morality*, trans. Robert V. Stone (Bloomington: Indiana University Press, 1980), esp. 208–19; Hazel E. Barnes, *An Existentialist Ethics* (New York: Alfred A. Knopf, 1967), esp. 55; Juliette Simont, "Sartrean Ethics," in *The Cambridge Companion to Sartre*, ed. Christina Howells (Cambridge: Cambridge University Press, 1992), esp. 180–84; Howells, *Sartre: The Necessity of Freedom*, esp. 24–25; David Detmer, *Freedom as a Value: A Critique of the Ethical Theory of Jean-Paul Sartre* (La Salle, Ill.: Open Court, 1988), esp. 107–23; Thomas W. Busch, "Sartre's Use of the Reduction: *Being and Nothingness* Reconsidered," in *Jean-Paul Sartre: Contemporary Approaches to His Philosophy*, ed. Hugh J. Silverman and Frederick A. Elliston (Pittsburgh, Pa.: Duquesne University Press, 1980); and Thomas W. Busch, *The Power of Consciousness and the Force of Circumstances in Sartre's Philosophy* (Bloomington: Indiana University Press, 1990), esp. 30–39.

51. Sartre, *Cahiers Pour Une Morale*, translated as *Notebooks for an Ethics*. See Thomas C. Anderson, *Sartre's Two Ethics: From Authenticity to Integral Humanity* (Chicago: Open Court, 1993).

52. Sartre himself famously referred to his work of 1943 as "une eidétique de la mauvaise foi," an *eidetic* or presentation of bad faith. He is not, however, rejecting the phenomenological picture of the human being proposed in *BN*. The context of the phrase makes it clear that he is comparing unfavourably his own *theoretical and abstract* phenomenology with Merleau-Ponty's more *empirical* studies of the concrete and often inhuman forces that actually shape history. With hindsight he is criticizing his own analysis of the human situation for being detached and insufficient, and not for being wrong. See Jean-Paul Sartre, *Situations IV* (Paris: Gallimard, 1964), 196 and footnote.

it (as "being-for-itself"); and we seek a freely chosen future identity (in "being-in-itself-for-itself").

Human beings cannot renounce this fundamental desire to be God, to attain completion, without renouncing ourselves. We avoid this necessity of going beyond ourselves and constituting ourselves in relation to an ideal future. There may be additional attitudes we can adopt within this quest, there may be further inferences we can draw from this quest, there may be the possibility of turning the exercise of freedom into a goal, or of accepting that the ultimate goal will never be reached—but Sartre never implies that we can abandon this quest altogether. The refusal to rest satisfied, the constant push beyond, over the horizon, is all that human beings can hope for—at least by their own resources. Consciousness is not only consciousness of not being what is present and having to be what is future (which is where Sartre began), it is also consciousness of never being able to be this future. This is the most profound sense of being human.

Chapter 8

THE POSSIBILITY OF HUMAN HAPPINESS IN AQUINAS

Different Kinds of Happiness

There are elements of Aquinas's understanding of the human being that could lead one to conclude that human fulfillment in this life is an achievable goal. The good is not *always* beyond us—sometimes it is present and possessed. Intellect and will, for example, are not always restless and unsatisfied in Aquinas's scheme. Although the reason does advance from one piece of understanding to the next, opening our soul up to further horizons of being, the work of the intellect is "simply to apprehend intelligible truth."[1] The movement of reason leads the intellect to rest *(quiescere)* in the possessing *(habere)* of what is true.[2] The will, likewise, is not just the faculty that takes us beyond who we are through desire, it is also the faculty that allows us to enjoy the good we have desired once we attain it. The will is directed to the end even when it is present, and not just when it is absent.[3] *Fruitio,* "enjoyment," is connected with "the delight [*delectationem*] which one has in realizing the longed-for term, which is the end."[4] The intellect perceives the good as agreeable *(perceptio convenientis),* and the will finds *complacentia* in it ("satisfaction" or "pleasure").[5]

1. *ST* I.79:8c.
2. *ST* I.79:8c.
3. *ST* I-II.3:4c.
4. *ST* I-II.11:1c.
5. *ST* I-II.11:1ad3.

This notion of rest and enjoyment may seem to undermine the central argument of this book. I have been suggesting that intellect and will function for Aquinas in a similar way to Sartre's consciousness and being-for-itself. We are by nature open to what we are not (through intellect) and striving to become what we are not (through will), and our identity as human beings consists in a perpetual going-beyond ourselves toward another identity that does not yet exist, toward our future perfection. Whenever we seek a particular good, we are seeking our own good, which is precisely our being insofar as it does not yet exist.[6] Even if the good we seek is simply the preservation of what we already have (like health or friendship), there is still a sense in which this preservation of our being in the future is something we do not yet have, which is the very reason why we are seeking it. Our being is necessarily fractured by the decentering that intellect and will bring about.

If in fact we can reach this perfection and actually be happy with it, if we can possess an identity without having any distance from it, if we can halt this constant movement beyond, then the picture I have presented of Aquinas's human being is false. For Sartre, to be human is to go beyond what we have and what we are. For Aquinas, it seems, we can at some point rest content with what we have and what we are; in Sartre's terms, we can reach a state of becoming pure being-in-itself. *Rest, possession, enjoyment, satisfaction:* these are concepts that would indicate to Sartre the dark night of identity and the dissolution of consciousness. With these questions in mind we can examine the extent to which Aquinas thinks that we can and cannot be happy in this life.

Happiness, *beatitudo,* as we saw in chapter 6, is the satisfaction we hope to find when we reach our final goal and attain the perfection we have longed for. We can want many different things at the same time, large and small, yet at any one moment there must be a deepest desire that motivates us, an overriding goal that functions as an organizing principle to our actions, one which we long for as our "perfect and fulfilling good [*bonum perfectum et completivum*]."[7] Happiness is the perfect good, "which satis-

6. This is true even when our attention is directed away from ourselves to the good of other people or other things, since our desire is still personal and part of what we wish our own life to be about. See the discussion of "the good" in chapter 2 above.

7. *ST* I-II.1:5c.

fies the appetite altogether, else it would not be the last end, if something yet remained to be desired."[8] If we find the ultimate good we are seeking and fulfill our desire, then we will be happy.

Aquinas makes three important distinctions as he writes about happiness.[9] The first, which we have already come across, is between the general meaning of the last end (the *ratio* of the last end, the last end as such) and the particular object we are seeking as our last end ("the thing in which the last end is found [*id in quo finis ultimi ratio invenitur*]").[10] We all seek our last end as such, we all want to be happy and to find fulfillment in our perfect good. Yet we don't all agree on *how* to be happy, on where we will find that fulfillment. The second distinction is between *beatitudo imperfecta* and *beatitudo perfecta.*[11] Imperfect or incomplete happiness is simply happiness to the extent that we can find it in this life: it is "that which is had in this life [*quae habetur in hac vita*]." Perfect or complete happiness "consists in the vision of God."[12] Only perfect happiness "attains to the true notion of happiness," while imperfect happiness "does not attain thereto, but partakes of some particular likeness of happiness [*participat quandam particularem beatitudinis similitudinem*]."[13] The third distinction is between possessing an end imperfectly, "only in intention," and possessing an end perfectly, "not only in intention but also in reality [*in re*]."[14] The

8. *ST* I-II.2:8c.

9. For the historical background to Aquinas's discussion of happiness and for an account of some of the influences on him, see Georg Wieland, "Happiness: The Perfection of Man," in *The Cambridge History of Later Medieval Philosophy,* ed. Norman Kretzmann, Anthony Kenny, and Jan Pinborg (Cambridge: Cambridge University Press, 1982).

10. *ST* I-II.1:7c. See the discussion of the indetermination of ends in chapter 6 above.

11. The theological distinction goes back to William of Auxerre, died 1231; see Wieland, "Happiness: The Perfection of Man," 679. Aquinas uses it to develop some unresolved themes in Aristotle's *Nicomachean Ethics,* where, for example, worldly happiness is subject to fortune, and contemplation, although the best activity of the human being, is also something beyond human attainment. See Aristotle, *Nicomachean Ethics,* trans. Terence Irwin (Indianapolis, Ind.: Hackett, 1985), 10:7, 1177b26 to 1178a6; and Anthony Kenny, "Aquinas on Aristotelian Happiness," in *Aquinas's Moral Theory: Essays in Honour of Norman Kretzmann,* ed. Scott MacDonald and Eleonore Stump (Ithaca, N.Y., and London: Cornell University Press, 1998), 24. Anthony Celano argues convincingly that in formalizing these distinctions Aquinas draws out the implications of Aristotle's ethics without betraying his thought; see Anthony J. Celano, "The Concept of Worldly Beatitude in the Writings of Thomas Aquinas," *Journal of the History of Philosophy* 25 (1987).

12. *ST* I-II.4:5c.

13. *ST* I-II.3:6c.

14. *ST* I-II.11:4c.

will can thus have a true but imperfect enjoyment of the last end even before it reaches it, through its active striving toward this goal.

Aquinas writes with great simplicity in *ST* I-II.5:3 that "perfect and true happiness cannot be had in this life [*perfecta autem et vera beatitudo non potest haberi in hac vita*]."[15] This statement alone should puzzle us. On the one hand, the whole point of human life is happiness. On the other hand, Aquinas now insists, we can never find true happiness in this life. Aquinas believes that human beings by their very nature cannot find perfect happiness in this life—the "rest" we can achieve is never total. As bodily creatures who exist in time and who have an infinite desire to understand and be fulfilled, we can never find the final rest we are searching for in this life. This is not because of some circumstantial difficulty or personal weakness, it is because of our nature as temporal creatures with intellect and will. Aquinas agrees with Sartre that the perfection human beings naturally desire, being-in-itself-for-itself, is a self-contradictory synthesis that cannot be attained in this life. Whether it is possible for us to attain another kind of life, beyond time, is a separate question to which we will return later.

The Impossibility of Perfect Happiness in This Life

We can now look more closely at the texts that support this interpretation. In *ST* I-II.5:3 Aquinas asks whether one can be happy in this life. Happiness is the perfect and sufficient good that "excludes every ill and fulfils every desire."[16] He concludes that "in this life every ill cannot be excluded" and "the desire for good in this life cannot be satisfied."[17] These are extraordinarily bold statements. Aquinas believes that human desire, in this life, never ends. As long as we are living we are unsatisfied with what we have. The desire for a good, as we saw in chapter 2, always reflects a desire to become what we are not, because in every good we seek we are always seeking our own good, that is, the being that we do not yet have.[18] So Aquinas is arguing that as long as we are living we are seeking to go beyond the present to a future perfection that we do not yet possess. It is an essential part of our nature as creatures in time to be incomplete and looking beyond. To be human is to lack the fullness of being that we could attain, which is to lack ourselves. Human be-

15. *ST* I-II.5:3c.
16. *ST* I-II.5:3c.
17. *ST* I-II.5:3c.
18. See *ST* I-II.18:1.

ings, as far as the life we know is concerned, are an essential insufficiency.

The examples given in *ST* I-II.5:3 may seem too weak to support these sweeping ontological conclusions. Aquinas writes that this present life is subject "to ignorance on the part of the intellect, to inordinate affection on the part of the appetite, and to many penalties on the part of the body."[19] One could argue that these ills might be removed in a utopian society, at least in theory. Yet for Aquinas they are identified with temporal, bodily life as such, and not just with the shortcomings of a particular culture or society. Ignorance, for example, is far more than the consequence of a bad education. Aquinas demonstrates in *ST* I-II.3:8 that the human intellect has a natural desire to know the causes of things. We wonder *(admirari)*. This desire cannot be fully satisfied until we know the first cause of all created things through union with God. Even without the reference to God, Aquinas is saying something quite radical about human desire. It is part of our nature as intellectual creatures to question things, and as long as we are alive we will be questioning things and seeking more fundamental explanations, therefore our desire for understanding (and so for happiness) can never be fully satisfied in this life. The intellect takes us beyond to what we do not yet know, and there is no end to what we can discover. One proof of the endlessness of human desire is thus our incessant curiosity.

Human longing concerns much more than the desire for understanding. *ST* I-II.2 deals with a range of human goods that appear to promise happiness, such as riches, honor, fame, power, etc. Hidden in one of the replies Aquinas makes a kind of phenomenological observation that points to a larger truth. In the desire for riches "and for whatsoever temporal goods," we find that "when we already possess them, we despise them, and seek others." This is because "we realise more their insufficiency when we possess them [*eorum insufficientia magis cognoscitur cum habentur*], and this very fact shows that they are imperfect, and the sovereign good does not consist therein."[20] Notice that this is not because some goods disappoint us with their inferior quality, it is because *all* temporal goods, *when possessed,* cause us to despise them and seek beyond them. We want to leave, as it were, as soon as we have arrived. Whichever goods we seek in time, the provisional happiness we might attain through them is always

19. *ST* I-II.5:3c, referring to Augustine's *De civitate dei,* 19:4.
20. *ST* I-II.2:1ad3.

accompanied by a deepening appreciation of their insufficiency. However great the good we achieve, however secure the happiness we find, it is always threatened by the possibility that we will move on and desire something else. We can never force ourselves to continue to want in the future what we want in the present. To do so would be to abandon our freedom—which is impossible as long as we are creatures of intellect and will living in time. Aquinas's point here is similar to Sartre's when he describes *anguish.* Our identity is never absolutely secure, and the most stable goals imaginable are always threatened, at least implicitly, by the possibility of appreciating their insufficiency and freely choosing something else.

The more our desire is fulfilled, the greater our desire becomes, since it inevitably carries us beyond the momentary fulfillment of the present toward a deeper fulfillment. In the final article of this question about the nature of the good that constitutes our happiness (*ST* I-II.2), Aquinas goes so far as to say that the good of which we are capable is *infinitum,* "infinite." The good that intrinsically and inherently belongs to us in virtue of our existence is of course created and finite, since we are only creatures. But the good to which we are open, "as an object" (of our intellect and will), is nevertheless infinite.[21] In other words, our understanding and desire are quite literally without limits, never ending, infinite.

In a later article about enjoyment Aquinas admits that we find a kind of temporary delight in reaching certain goals, but this is never perfect enjoyment. He cites Augustine: "We enjoy what we know, when the delighted will is at rest therein."[22] He then concludes that the will never rests completely *(simpliciter)* "save in the last end: for as long as something is waited for, the movement of the will remains in suspense, although it has reached something."[23] Aquinas thus believes that we must always be looking for something in this life. Sartre has written that self-coincidence is impossible for human beings, because we can never catch up with the self we want to become, there is always something else opening up ahead of us. Aquinas agrees here that the desire to find rest and perfection necessarily brings with it a movement beyond any fleeting rest we might find in the goods of this world. There is a pleasing coincidence of language here. For Aquinas

21. *ST* I-II.2:8ad3.
22. *ST* I-II.11:3c, referring to *De Trinitate,* 10:10.
23. *ST* I-II.11:3c.

the movement of the will "remains in suspense [*remanet in suspenso*]" despite the fact that it has found rest in a provisional object of delight.[24] We always desire *more* even though we have attained what we previously desired. For Sartre it is the meaning of one's past that is perpetually "in suspense [*en sursis*]," because one's future projects and desires may always put the goals that one has already achieved into a new perspective.[25] Being-for-itself, like the will, must always go beyond the achievements of the past and the present and reach toward a future goal.

Temporal goods are not only insufficient, they are also unstable. Aquinas writes in *ST* I-II.5:3:

Human beings naturally desire the good, which they have, to be permanent. Now the goods of the present life pass away, since life itself passes away, which we naturally desire, and would wish to endure unceasingly, for we naturally shrink from death. Wherefore it is impossible to have true happiness in this life.[26]

This is an uncontroversial but nevertheless shattering point. Everything we attain will pass. It is not just the fact that particular goods may be lost, it is the deeper principle that all goods will be lost, and all meaning and happiness will thus be undermined. We cannot hold on to anything. There is no point in trying to suggest that we are indifferent to this loss. The starting point of Aquinas's anthropology is that human beings are seeking their own fulfillment through the pursuit of particular goods. It is our nature to seek happiness. Now we find that we will ultimately be denied happiness by the transitory nature of life as a whole and of all the particular goods of life. Aquinas returns to this need for stability in the following article.

Now human beings naturally desire to hold onto the good that they have, and to gain the security of holding onto it, else they must of necessity be afflicted with the fear of losing it, or with the sorrow of being certain to lose it. Therefore it is necessary for true happiness that human beings have the opinion of never losing the good that they have.[27]

24. *ST* I-II.11:3c.
25. *BN* 501, see 501–4; *EN* 546/582, see 546–49/582–85.
26. *ST* I-II.5:3c.
27. *ST* I-II.5:4c.

This lack of stability, and the anxiety that follows with it, are a necessary part of temporal existence. Aquinas writes that vicissitudes such as these are "for such things as are subject to time and movement."[28]

Even if we could somehow reach an infinite good in this life, and possess it without fear of ever losing it, there is still a final reason why perfect happiness would be beyond us. Aquinas writes in *ST* I-II.3:2 that insofar as happiness is a created reality in us it must involve our own activity *(operatio).* Happiness, in other words, is not just something that happens *to* us. Part of our fulfillment is to be actively involved in that fulfillment.[29] It is not enough for us to be alive, we want to be actively living.[30] But in this present life human activity can never be unified or continual.[31] We have to act in time, in the present, moment by moment, and therefore our activity is necessarily fragmented. Although contemplation of the truth is an activity that has more unity than an active life occupied with many things, Aquinas is realistic about the fact that even this has to be interrupted by sleeping and doing other things. So we can never act *now* in a way that ensures that all our future activity will be part of (or even consistent with) this present act. We cannot collapse the future into the present and take possession of a total, everlasting happiness. This is another example of how our failure to be happy relates to our nature and not to certain unfortunate circumstances. We are beings who operate progressively in time, and we cannot unify this activity and bring it to completion in one integrated movement.

For the many reasons outlined in this section, Aquinas is convinced that human beings cannot find perfect happiness in this life. We should not lose sight of the force of this conclusion. Aquinas does not say that perfect happiness in this life is a difficult achievement, one that is too much for us in practice, and that we therefore need God's help to find it. Instead he says that perfect happiness in this life is in principle an impossible idea. It would contradict our very nature to find perfect happiness. Human life itself is fragmented and we have only a precarious hold on ourselves. We are temporal creatures whose nature is to look beyond the present to the

28. *ST* I-II.5:4c.

29. *ST* I-II.3:2c.

30. Life involves the being of the living thing *(esse viventis)* and also the activity of the living thing *(operatio viventis);* see *ST* I-II.3:2ad1.

31. *ST* I-II.3:2ad4.

future, to the good we do not yet possess, to the person we have not yet become. Human beings in time are always seeking a further good. Aquinas is absolutely insistent on this point. The temporal goods we seek are necessarily insufficient and necessarily unstable. We have an infinite and therefore insatiable desire to have more and to know more, and we know that everything we do lay hold of will eventually pass. Aquinas has no conception of what it might be like for human beings to achieve their perfection in this life. A perfectly happy human being could bear no resemblance to the human beings that we know. Temporal human perfection is self-contradictory because it would mean that we had finally become all that we could be, which would be a kind of not-being-human. Aquinas believes, for the same reasons as Sartre, that perfect human happiness is impossible in this life because it would mean the end and not the fulfillment of the human life that we know.

The Possibility of Perfect Happiness in God

Perfect happiness, according to Sartre and Aquinas, cannot be found in this life. Aquinas, as part of his broad theological project, gives *philosophical* reasons for this, as we have already noted. These reasons flow from a rationally argued account of human nature. By observing human life, by analyzing the nature of intellect and will, Aquinas arrives at the same philosophical impasse as Sartre. We want to be perfectly happy, *and* we realize that we can never be perfectly happy in this life, so our existence is played out in this uncertain space between desire and frustration, between possibility and failure, between hope and despair. In Sartre's language, we are caught between the necessity of being-for-itself and the impossibility of being-in-itself-for-itself. Sartre cannot see any further. Aquinas, however, does see further, and states that despite the fact that human beings cannot find perfect happiness in this life it must still be possible for them to find perfect happiness. This seems like a contradiction, and we now need to explore why for Aquinas it is not.

For Aquinas, as for Sartre, "happiness is the perfect good, which lulls the appetite altogether, else it would not be the last end, if something yet remained to be desired."[32] We are characterized by our ability to understand all that is true and to desire all that is good. We are capable of an *in-*

32. *ST* I-II.2:8c.

finite good.[33] The universal good, however, that alone can satisfy our will, is not just a theoretical synthesis for Aquinas, it must also be a real possibility, and he argues from the nature of our desire for the universal good to the possibility of our finding it. In Aquinas's understanding, it makes perfect sense to say that the existence of a desire or capacity is enough to establish that the desire or capacity could in principle be fulfilled (although it may in the circumstances not be fulfilled). Similarly, the existence of any potentiality is enough to establish that the potentiality could in principle be actualized (although it may in the circumstances not be actualized). Desire and potentiality are by definition aspects of a thing insofar as it relates to the fullness of being it could have. They signify a relationship with the perfection that is due to, appropriate to, and possible for this being.[34] This is the metaphysical background that allows Aquinas to state with great simplicity:

> Happiness is called the attainment of the perfect good. Whoever, therefore, is capable of the perfect good can attain happiness. Now, that human beings are capable of the perfect good, is proved both because their intellect can apprehend the universal and perfect good, and because their will can desire it. And therefore human beings can attain happiness.[35]

It is an Aristotelian philosophy of nature and not just a Judeo-Christian theology of creation that makes Aquinas think that happiness must be possible for the simple reason that we are creatures who want to be happy. To say that a desire cannot in principle be fulfilled is to say that it is not really a desire at all. Appetite (whether that of inanimate objects, plants, animals, or rational creatures) is an orientation to what can fulfill, it is a movement toward a good that perfects. There is a necessary correlation between the subject who desires and the desired state of fulfillment. Without this correlation it makes no sense to say that the subject is inclined to anything.

So there is no such thing as a natural desire that cannot in principle be fulfilled. This is why Aquinas can argue in *ST* I.12:1 that a created intellect must be able to see the divine essence, since otherwise "the natural desire [to know the first cause of things] would remain in vain [*remanebit*

33. *ST* I-II.2:8ad3.

34. Cf. *ST* I-II.18:1c, where some things are said to lack the fullness of being "due to them" *(eis debitam).*

35. *ST* I-II.5:1c.

inane]."[36] It is true that he first gives a *theological* reason for this, and states bluntly that it is "opposed to the faith" to suppose that the created intellect cannot find happiness in the vision of God, or can find it in something else.[37] Yet we should note that the argument from natural desire is explicitly given as an additional nontheological reason for thinking that the created intellect can see the essence of God.[38]

Aquinas makes a similar argument in the body of *ST* I-II.3:8, this time without the appeal to faith. He writes that our curious intellects, which wonder incessantly about causes, cannot be satisfied with knowing *that* God exists as First Cause, since we want to know what he is and reach "the very essence of the first cause."[39] Final and perfect happiness must therefore consist in nothing less than the vision of the Divine Essence.

Aquinas thus shows not only that we are capable of perfect happiness but that we can find this in God alone. Once again, I want to insist that there is a philosophical argument here that makes sense without the support of faith or religious revelation. Of course Aquinas never steps outside of the theological framework of the *Summa,* and he draws continually on biblical and theological resources. But he also recognizes that a philosophical investigation into the nature of human longing would necessarily lead one to the idea of God. God is the universal good and the First Cause of all things who must exist if our infinite desire for happiness and for understanding are not to be in vain. Human desire necessarily points to God. Right at the beginning of the *Summa* Aquinas writes that we can be brought to an initial, imprecise conception of God by reflecting on the nature of human desire:

> To know that God exists in a general and confused way is implanted in us by nature, inasmuch as God is the happiness of human beings. For we naturally desire happiness, and what is naturally desired by us must be naturally known to us. This, however, is not simply speaking to know that God exists [*non est simpliciter cognoscere Deum esse*], just as to know that someone is approaching is not the same as to know that Peter is approaching, even though it is Peter who is approaching; for many there are who imagine that our perfect good which is happiness, consists in riches, and others in pleasures, and others in something else.[40]

36. *ST* I.12:1c.
37. *ST* I.12:1c.
38. To argue otherwise "is also against reason."; *ST* I.12:1c.
39. *ST* I-II.3:8c.
40. *ST* I.2:1ad1.

God is the universal good, the possibility of perfect happiness, which we have to believe in somehow if we are seeking our own happiness. To deny this is to deny the nature of human willing, which always seeks beyond to a more complete, a more perfect goal. "Our last end is the uncreated good, namely, God, who alone by his infinite goodness can perfectly satisfy our will [*qui solus sua infinita bonitate potest voluntatem hominis perfecte implere*]."[41]

Sartre's Theological Pessimism

So for Aquinas *willing happiness* and *thinking (at least implicitly) that God exists (as the universal good)* are inseparable. Sartre accepts this, insofar as he accepts that being-for-itself has to seek completion in a God-like state of being-in-itself-for-itself.[42] He acknowledges that we cannot be free unless we act as if the possibility of perfect happiness lies ahead of us. "Value" is this future ideal that cannot be renounced in the practical sphere. Yet by insisting that this ideal is a self-contradiction Sartre resigned himself to a different kind of contradiction—a contradiction between what we might call practical thinking and philosophical thinking. He implies that in the very moment of acting we have to believe that we are actually seeking a final fulfillment that is achievable, yet in our phenomenological reflections we have to conclude that this fulfillment is impossible. We act on the basis of one thought that contradicts with another thought.[43]

41. *ST* I-II.3:1c.

42. It is important to recognize that Sartre has different ideas in mind when he refers to "God." There is God *as symbol of an impossible human fulfillment,* which concerns us here. See, for example, *BN* 90; *EN* 126/133 and the section "The Ideal of Self-Coincidence" in chapter 7 above. There is also God *as external lawgiver who imposes values on human beings and thus takes away their freedom.* See Jean-Paul Sartre, *L'Existentialisme Est Un Humanisme* (Paris: Gallimard, 1996), 73–78, translated as Jean-Paul Sartre, "Existentialism and Humanism," in *Jean-Paul Sartre: Basic Writings,* ed. Stephen Priest (London: Routledge, 2001), 44–46. Of this second idea, as present in *Existentialism and Humanism,* Terry Keefe writes: "One does not have to be religious to see how ill-founded is his implication that belief in the existence of God is incompatible with the belief that man is what he makes of himself. It is no surprise that Christian critics have sometimes argued that the God that Sartre rejects in *L'Existentialisme* bears little resemblance to the God of Christianity" (Terry Keefe, "Sartre's *L'Existentialisme Est Un Humanisme,*" in *Critical Essays on Jean-Paul Sartre,* ed. Robert Wilcocks [Boston: G. K. Hall & Co., 1988], 90).

43. This question obviously connects with broader post-Nietzschean attempts to keep a regulative ideal fixed in the space formerly occupied by God, while rejecting the need to hold onto the reality of such an ideal. A psychological or cultural symbol thus preserves its function without preserving its reality, like the grin that remains once Alice's Cheshire cat has all but

Gianfranco Basti is sympathetic to Sartre's contention that ultimate fulfillment is contradictory and impossible in this life. He argues that Sartre should have recognized, as Aquinas did, that freedom depends on postulating the existence of a final goal beyond the limitations and contradictions of this life.[44] This is true even if we are not sure what form that final goal will take or how such a final goal can be possible. Freedom is not possible if we really think that the ultimate goal (being-in-itself-for-itself) is by its very nature an impossible contradiction. It is not enough to argue that this final goal is merely a symbol or a regulative ideal, as if we could acknowledge its symbolic value and at the same time deny that its achievement could be a real possibility. A practical goal, by its very nature, is more than symbolic. It is only a goal, an end for our action, if we are actively seeking to achieve it; and we can only act for something if we believe that it can be achieved. A goal cannot regulate a human action as an ideal if the agent does not believe that it is a real possibility, and an agent would stop acting straight away if it were actually shown that the goal could not be achieved.

So if we are to be free we have to believe that there is some kind of transcendent goal beyond everything we can conceive, beyond even the contradictions our philosophy seems to have arrived at. This is not a move against reason—it is accepting the limits of reason in order to save the reasonableness of freedom. We have to believe that God exists as the ultimate, transcendent goal of all our seeking even though we have not worked out exactly what it means for God to exist or exactly how we can be fulfilled in God. We thus recognize, as Aquinas has said in the passage cited above, that God exists "in a general and confused way."[45] In other words "God" (our perfect good, our final end, as a real possibility) is an existential condition of the exercise of human freedom.

disappeared. The problem is not so much the contradiction; indeed, the postmodern instinct is to rejoice in such contradictions. The real problem is that this account does not do justice to the existential experience. Our actions betray our deepest understanding of what is real and what we understand to be actually possible. We act not just "as if" the ideal were achievable. We act, instead, *for* or *toward* an ideal; thoroughly committed to achieving it; orienting our minds, our bodies, our plans, our energies, our whole lives around this ideal. It is not enough to insist that we don't "really" believe in it when everything connected with our own reality is constituted by it.

44. Gianfranco Basti, *Filosofia Dell'uomo* (Bologna: Edizioni Studio Domenicano, 1995), 293–96.

45. *ST* I.2:1ad1.

Sartre admits that in order to be free we have to avoid "seriousness" and accept that we will never find ultimate meaning in this present life. Basti and Aquinas take this a step further and argue that in order to be free we have to think that we can somehow find ultimate meaning beyond this present life in God. God may be First Cause of our being, yet it is just as important to recognize that he is the ultimate goal or final cause of our existing. Sartre says that we have an existential goal that cannot actually exist. He could instead have said that we have an existential goal without understanding how it can exist. This would have resolved a contradiction in his thought without undermining his well-founded conviction that the idea of achieving perfect happiness in this life is self-contradictory.

Aquinas would accept Sartre's basic ontological scheme. In this scheme human beings are constitutively orientated to the beyond, to the future. We have an inexhaustible desire for good, an unquenchable longing for truth, an identity that is essentially open-ended. Knowing this, we have to accept that nothing in this life will make us completely happy. There are more positive ways of saying this, but they amount to the same thing: We have to accept that we could always be even happier. It is not a question of giving up the search for happiness, but of refusing ever to give up on the search for happiness, even when we are tempted to think we have found it.[46] However we phrase it, we have to accept the limitations of happiness in this life, and this means not choosing a final goal that is within this life. Anything else would trap us in a limited identity and be an act of bad faith—it would suggest that our life could be complete, and our freedom ended, if only this goal could be achieved.

Aquinas would then try and push Sartre to accept the consequences of this ontological scheme. He would argue that our continual openness to the future is a condition of freedom even at the moment of death, which means that when we are dying we have to act as if there is a point to our life beyond death. This is not about religious "faith," it is about the phenome-

46. This refusal might also provide a "reason" for changing projects, for conversion, which was so lacking in chapter 5 because of the incommensurability of alternative projects. If we recognize that our desire is *always* to go further than the present goal we have set ourselves, then this will give us a reason for choosing a new goal if it has more and richer possibilities. The only bad choice, the only "sin," is *not wanting to be happy enough,* or *not wanting enough to be happy.* It is resigning ourselves to a limited good, a limited vision of the self, when a greater good beckons.

nology of freedom. Human beings do seek meaning, we do make sense of our life by projecting ourselves beyond the present—whether we "believe" that there is something beyond or not. It is a necessary part of freedom that we orientate our lives to a life beyond the present, which means that at the moment of death we must orientate our lives to a life beyond death, even if we are skeptical about what this can possibly mean.

The human world only makes sense if there is something beyond the totality of the world, and we cannot avoid acting as if death is not the final end of human life. This kind of "faith" arises naturally from the structure of human freedom. The unavoidable search for human meaning and happiness requires us to believe in something beyond the boundaries of this life. This does not mean that reason depends on religion, or philosophy on theology—it means that an essential aspect of reason and philosophy is an openness to what is beyond comprehension, beyond the world, and beyond death. If we are free, which we are, we inevitably seek what is beyond, even when we are at the limits of our ability to conceive what that beyond might be. In one very specific sense of the word, we cannot be free unless we seek "God," unless we recognize that we are seeking a supreme good beyond the limitations of all the contingent and temporal goods that we can recognize at present. There is a necessary openness and incompletion to human life. It is a paradox that our desire is not free if it seeks to find perfect satisfaction in anything in this life. If we seek happiness, which we do, Aquinas argues that we have to seek God.

A Natural Desire That Cannot Be Fulfilled Naturally

The purpose of this book has been to explore the nature of human freedom. This exploration has brought us to the brink of a philosophical theology, as we realize that human beings seek a happiness that can in principle never be found within this life. Aquinas suggests that perfect happiness can, nevertheless, be found, and it can be found only in God. Without entering too deeply into these theological aspects of Aquinas's anthropology, I simply want to make it clear that he is not sidestepping the very difficulties he has established. Aquinas continues to believe that perfect happiness with God is impossible for us to achieve in this life and is impossible for us to achieve in our own natural state by our own natural powers. The fundamental philosophical dilemma about human happiness remains for Aquinas even when God is present. Aquinas writes that the vision of the Divine

Essence "surpasses the nature not only of human beings, but also of every creature" and "neither human beings, nor any creature, can attain final happiness by their natural powers."[47] "It is impossible that it be bestowed through the action of any creature: but by God's work alone is the human being made happy [*homo beatus fit solo Deo agente*], if we speak of perfect Happiness."[48]

Aquinas states two conclusions with absolute clarity, and he is able to reach these conclusions without appealing to revelation (even though at various points he *also* draws on revelation): (i) Human beings, *by their very nature* as creatures of intellect and will, desire a perfect happiness that cannot be found in this life. This perfect happiness can only be found in union with God, since there is no end to our seeking in this life, and God alone is the universal good that can entirely satisfy our will.[49] (ii) Union with God, the vision of God's essence, *surpasses the very nature* of every creature including the human being. All creaturely knowledge falls short of the vision of the Divine Essence, "which infinitely surpasses all created substance. Consequently neither human beings, nor any creatures, can attain final happiness by their natural powers."[50]

These two conclusions create a paradox. The perfect and crowning good, to which we naturally tend, cannot be reached naturally. The vision of the Divine Essence, which is absolutely necessary if we are to be happy, is beyond our natural powers. Put very simply: we have a natural desire for God that cannot be naturally fulfilled. This is no stranger than Sartre writing that the goal we all strive toward (being-in-itself-for-itself) is at the same time an impossible ideal, one that is by definition unachievable because it would involve the dissolution of consciousness and being-for-itself.

Denis Bradley gives a very helpful account of Aquinas's position in his book *Aquinas on the Twofold Human Good,* drawing on texts beyond the few we have been looking at in *ST* I-II. Bradley writes that the thrust of Aquinas's philosophical thinking about "the natural endlessness of human nature" leads to an *aporia.* As philosophy, it cannot rest satisfied with the idea that human nature can find some natural fulfillment in this life, yet *as*

47. *ST* I-II.5:5c, referring to *ST* I.12:4.

48. *ST* I-II.5:6c.

49. Cf. *ST* I-II.2:8 and I-II.3:8.

50. *ST* I-II.5:5c. Cf. I.12:4.

philosophy it cannot "go forward to a theological affirmation of man's supernatural end."[51] Bradley believes that in Aquinas's view reason, without the aid of faith and revelation, can come to two conclusions that seem to be at odds with each other: (A) that "human nature is forever unsatisfied unless man attains the vision of God" and (B) that the "attainment of this knowledge must be considered a supernatural achievement that is beyond any merely human activity."[52]

I will not go into all the questions generated by these paradoxical conclusions—they have been fiercely debated through the centuries.[53] I just want to point out how tempting it is to dissolve the paradox in one of two ways. (i) One could insist that if we have a natural desire for God, then it must be possible for it to be fulfilled naturally. This would be a purely natural theology and it would do away with the need for God's "supernatural" help.[54] (ii) Conversely, one could insist that if the fulfillment of our desire for God is beyond our natural powers, then we cannot naturally desire it. This second type of thinking could go in one of two directions. It could lead one to conclude that some human beings do not desire God (if they do not receive his supernatural help), or it could lead one to conclude that all human beings desire God (in which case this desire must be a "supernatural" gift laid on top of their human nature).

Aquinas does not give in to these temptations. He holds fast to the fact that we naturally desire what we cannot naturally attain. He does, however, go a step further, and ask whether there may be another way of finding the happiness that we cannot achieve by nature, a way that is natural to us but that does not depend on our nature for its fulfillment. He goes beyond the paradox without dissolving it:

51. Denis J. M. Bradley, *Aquinas on the Twofold Human Good: Reason and Human Happiness in Aquinas's Moral Science* (Washington, D.C.: The Catholic University of America Press, 1997), xiii.

52. Ibid., 514.

53. Recent debate was provoked by the publication of Henri De Lubac, *Surnaturel: Études Historiques* (Paris: Aubier, 1946). For an excellent discussion of some contemporary views, see Benedict M. Ashley, "What Is the End of the Human Person? The Vision of God and Integral Human Fulfillment," in *Moral Truth and Moral Tradition: Essays in Honour of Peter Geach and Elizabeth Anscombe,* ed. Luke Gormally (Blackrock, Co. Dublin: Four Courts Press, 1994).

54. In Scholastic philosophy and theology "supernatural" simply means what is above or beyond nature, what is beyond the unaided powers of any creature—it has nothing to do with spooks or spells (which, as created things, might be quite "natural").

Just as nature does not fail human beings [referring to *homo*] in things that are necessary, although it has not provided them with weapons and clothing, as it provided other animals, because it gave them reason and hands, with which they are able to get these things for themselves; so neither did it fail human beings in things that are necessary, although it did not give them the means by which they could attain happiness [*quamvis non daret sibi aliquod principium quo posset beatitudinem consequi*]: since this is impossible. But it did give them freedom, with which they can turn to God, so that he may make them happy [*Sed dedit ei liberum arbitrium, quo possit converti ad Deum, qui eum faceret beatum*]. "For what we are enabled to do by our friends, we ourselves, in a sense, are able to do," as it is said in *Ethics* 3.[55]

So it is our part of our nature not only to seek happiness but also to have the ability to ask for what we cannot find through our own efforts. It is part of our nature not only to be frustrated but to find a way out of our frustration. The fact that the achievement of happiness can only be a supernatural gift from God does not mean that our desire or request for it needs some supernatural cause. We can ask God to allow us to share in this way of life, and perhaps he will grant it to us.

55. *ST* I-II.5:5ad1, citing Aristotle's *Nicomachean Ethics* 3:3, 1112b27. For an English version, see Aristotle, *Nicomachean Ethics,* 63.

CONCLUSION

There are a number of ways of characterizing the shifts in human sensibility and self-understanding that have occurred in the West in the modern period. In his much-discussed book *Sources of the Self* Charles Taylor argues that in our late modern or postmodern era we are unable to justify the constitutive goods we seek because we have lost an ability to trust in the established moral orders that founded them in the first place.[1] The extended self of the premodern period (a self that is defined by its place in an external web of belonging and interdependence), which became the nuclear self of the modern period (a subject at the center of its own experiences, both rational and affective, without any constitutive relations to anything else), is now losing confidence in its own integrity and fragmenting into any number of changing and ill-defined identities: the decentered self of postmodernism. Cosmic metanarratives are viewed with suspicion. We are like Buzz Lightyear in the Pixar film *Toy Story,* who discovers that he is not a space ranger on an intergalactic mission to destroy the evil emperor Zurg, but is just a toy.[2] In fact we fare much worse than Buzz, since being a toy brings with it at least a sense of identity and purpose, and a place in an alternative order. We have forsaken the hope of ever finding such an order again.

Taylor believes that the modern period has engendered two predominant and seemingly incompatible approaches to moral reflection. One approach exalts the virtues of disengaged reason: it is the moral force behind the modern scientific quest; it

1. Charles Taylor, *Sources of the Self: The Making of the Modern Identity* (Cambridge: Cambridge University Press, 1989), esp. 495–521. See also Taylor's *The Ethics of Authenticity* (Cambridge, Mass.: Harvard University Press, 1991).

2. This is my analogy and not Taylor's.

gives rise to a utilitarian approach to ethics; it tends to depersonalize human choices and create abstract and universally applicable moral norms. The other approach grows out of the Romantic protest against this scientific worldview: it emphasizes the more subjective goods of self-expression and self-fulfillment; it pits the personal against the institutional and social; it risks reducing all questions of value to questions of personal feeling.

In Taylor's view there are two particular challenges facing us in our own times. One is to recognize that both these approaches involve a search for genuine goods that need to be understood on their own terms. There are ideals at work here that we should respect and value. The modern period is not simply one of moral decline; and the collapse of the old cosmic orders has brought some gains. The other challenge, however, is to rediscover some richer moral sources, without undermining the gains that modernity has brought to our sense of self. Taylor worries that we are living beyond our moral means. He longs to reestablish some connection between the personal and the cosmic, a connection that would provide some foundation for our high moral convictions. The modern self, whether scientific or romantic, is inward looking and largely incapable of placing itself within a set of obligations or purposes that might give it a meaning beyond that which it has determined for itself. Taylor is preoccupied with "the search for moral sources outside the subject through languages which resonate within him or her, the grasping of an order which is inseparably indexed to a personal vision."[3]

I mention this analysis not because Taylor is particularly interested in Aquinas or Sartre, but because his articulation of the impasse reached by modernity helps us to see that the Thomistic and Sartrean questions examined in this present work are not just of historical interest—they throw light on these contemporary questions. This relatively recent conflict between disengaged reason and Romantic self-expression connects us with more perennial philosophical questions. It is essentially about the relationship between objectivity and subjectivity; between the true and the good; between the world and the self; between knowledge and desire; between necessity and freedom; between the scientific and the aesthetic; between human conditioning and human independence; between our immersion in this world and our longing for a form of existence beyond the boundar-

3. Charles Taylor, *Sources of the Self,* 510.

ies of this world. These are some of the issues that Aquinas and Sartre are grappling with. They both argue, in answer to Charles Taylor, that it is possible to take one's place in a public moral order without self-alienation as long as there is a personal appropriation of that order; that a proper objectivity can be discovered only through a creative subjective commitment; that personal freedom requires a recognition and acceptance of the circumstances that condition one; that one's identity is both inherited and chosen, formed and fluid, open to fulfillment and haunted by the threat of disintegration.

The main aim of this study has been to show that despite their significant differences there are profound similarities in the way Aquinas and Sartre understand the questions of human freedom, personal identity, and the possibility of perfect happiness in this life—similarities that are unacknowledged or assumed to be nonexistent by most scholars. I hope I have achieved this aim to some degree, and established that there is a common approach to the way in which these questions are framed and answered. A secondary aim of this study, often more implicit than explicit, has been to show that there is much value in this common Thomistic-Sartrean approach, and that it sheds a great deal of light on some of the philosophical issues facing us today.

For just a moment I want to set aside their differences, and present a view of what it means to be a human being as if it came from a single Thomistic-Sartrean pen, a view that has emerged from the four parts of this study. This will act both as a conclusion to my study and as an invitation to consider the implications of this vision of the human being.

In part one, it became clear that human beings both have an identity and go beyond it. We identify with our thoughts and feelings and values, with our circumstances, with the totality of our experience. There is an immediacy about our presence to the world. We share in the being of other things. Yet at the same time we are conscious of this experience and are therefore distant from it. We are aware of our own incompletion. We have questions, dilemmas, and moments of existential and moral anguish. Nothing can completely determine for us the meaning of the world or the direction of our life.

There is a fundamental lack within the present that paralyzes our thought and action. We have to go beyond all that we are and conceive of a future that will make sense of the present. We have to act for an end that does not yet exist and orientate ourselves to this goal. In this way we make sense of the world and give meaning to our life. The human person is neither the present static identity nor the intangible future goal. We are constituted, rather, by this freely chosen relationship between identity and end. Personhood, therefore, necessarily involves both the facts that determine us and the movement beyond these facts to the one we seek to become. It involves essence and existence, self-possession and dispossession, introspection and ecstasy, present and future, the real and the ideal, the indicative and the conditional. It involves what *is* true and what *could be* good. We constitute ourselves by accepting who we are and moving beyond this.

In part two, it was shown that there is an objective and a subjective aspect to all human understanding. In one sense, our understanding is determined by the being of whatever object is understood. We need to be transparent and responsive to the reality of the world. Everything we encounter has an independence, a weight, and we cannot manipulate the facts of our experience. If we make unrealistic plans or propose false interpretations of the world, we are checked and even constrained by the resistance things show.

In another sense, however, our understanding depends completely on our personal involvement in the world. We can't understand anything unless we take an active interest in it. Everything is seen from a certain perspective and understood in terms of the language and categories of the one who understands. These categories are inseparable from the values of those who use them, since all understanding embodies the lived priorities of the individuals and groups who choose to understand. These categories also make possible certain kinds of desires, since we can only desire what we understand to be worthwhile. So desire, understanding, and purposeful activity interconnect and unavoidably influence each other. Nevertheless, the element of circularity diminishes neither the objectivity of truth nor the personal nature of desire. The truth is human, and objectivity is always grasped through the subject. Knowledge is impossible without human commitment, and this commitment is impossible without an understanding of what we are like and what the world is like.

In part three, it was concluded that at any one moment, if we take into account all the relevant facts at our disposal, there are always different ways of looking at any situation, different reasons for acting, different goals we can pursue. Any of them would make sense of the objective understanding we have of the world. We are free to act because we are free to think about things in different ways. Uncertainty is the starting point of deliberation, choice, and responsibility. We have to choose from the different possible goods before us and project ourselves into a single future. In this way we choose which person we will become. From the plethora of potentially significant motives, we make some motives real by acting for them. Within the constraints of our circumstances, we choose to live in one way rather than another.

Freedom thus depends on two things: on accepting the limits of one's situation, and on reinterpreting these limits in the light of a particular future. We have to accept our beginning and choose our end. Our actions are not determined by our being, since our being is open-ended and ambiguous. Our being, rather, is determined by our activity, as we project ourselves toward a future self that does not yet exist. We decide the meaning of our life and the priorities that will give it shape. For these reasons, the person we are aiming to become is more significant than the person we are. We constitute ourselves through our free choices, even though this very freedom is something we have not chosen and something we cannot disown.

In part four, it was shown that within each particular desire there is a deeper and more universal longing for completion and perfect fulfillment. Human beings do not just want to travel, we also want to arrive. We are frustrated that our understanding is limited, our possessions insufficient, and our identity insecure. In other words, we want to be happy. So we chase after an ideal moment in the future when desire as such will be fulfilled and when we will finally become the person we wish to be. This moment never comes because desire is infinite and self-coincidence impossible. Even though we create an identity through our free choices, and may find a certain stability and satisfaction in recommitting ourselves to that identity, we still have a distance from ourselves. We always see a future opening up before us. We have some transitory experiences of happiness, but perfect happiness eludes us and is in principle impossible to achieve in the life that we know.

So for both Aquinas and Sartre, we are fragmented persons, internally displaced, perpetually in exile from ourselves. This prospect both liberates and terrifies us. We can try to escape the dilemma by pretending that we are perfectly happy in the present, or by pretending that we will be perfectly happy in the future, or by pretending that we do not care about happiness at all. Yet the dilemma comes back to haunt us, since it is a constitutive part of our nature to seek a deeper happiness and to be aware that any happiness we do achieve in the future will soon slip through our fingers. The whole paradox can be expressed negatively ("human beings can never be perfectly happy in this life") or positively ("human beings can always seek a deeper happiness in this life"). Either way, it begs the question of whether there is another kind of life possible for human beings, one in which happiness could be found. Perhaps it is possible to attain to some God-like kind of life beyond all the contradictions of temporal existence. Perhaps it is possible to have all desire satisfied, and still to act; to understand everything, and still to wonder; to have one's life completed, and still to live; to arrive, and still to keep moving. Perhaps it is possible to be happy and to be free.

The question of freedom leads to the question of happiness, and the question of happiness leads to the question of God. One's thinking about the possibility of final human happiness is part of what will determine one's thinking about the existence of God. Despite the identity we continually create for ourselves, and the commitments we freely make, human life is necessarily insufficient. We are constituted by incompletion since it is our nature to go beyond ourselves and beyond the present. Our desire always goes beyond anything in this life to an ideal of perfection which Sartre and Aquinas associate with the divine. Both thinkers conclude that we cannot find happiness without God. Their understanding of human freedom, personal identity, and the meaning of ultimate happiness is almost identical. They disagree only about whether this happiness can ever be found.

BIBLIOGRAPHY

Works by Sartre

Sartre, Jean-Paul. *The Age of Reason* (London: Penguin Books, 2001).

———. *Being and Nothingness: An Essay on Phenomenological Ontology,* translated by Hazel Barnes (London: Routledge, 1958).

———. *Cahiers pour une Morale* (Paris: Gallimard, 1983).

———. "Cartesian Freedom." In *Literary and Philosophical Essays* (New York: Collier Books, 1962).

———. *Critique de la Raison Dialectique, Vol. 1: Théorie des ensembles pratiques, Bibliothèque des Idées* (Paris: Gallimard, 1960).

———. *L'être et le néant: Essai d'ontologie phénoménologique* (Paris: Gallimard, 1943).

———. *L'être et le néant: Essai d'ontologie phénoménologique,* édition corrigée avec index par Arlette Elkaïm-Sartre (Paris: Gallimard, 1996).

———. "Existentialism and Humanism." In *Jean-Paul Sartre: Basic Writings,* ed. Stephen Priest (London: Routledge, 2001).

———. *L'Existentialisme Est un Humanisme* (Paris: Gallimard, 1996).

———. *Huis Clos* (London: Routledge, 1987).

———. *Huis Clos and Other Plays* (London: Penguin Books, 2000).

———. *L'Imaginaire* (Paris: Gallimard, 1986).

———. "The Itinerary of a Thought." In *Between Existentialism and Marxism* (New York: Pantheon Books, 1974).

———. *Lettres au Castor,* vol. 1 (Paris: Gallimard, 1983).

———. "Materialism and Revolution." In *Literary and Philosophical Essays* (New York: Collier, 1962).

———. *Notebooks for an Ethics,* trans. David Pellauer (Chicago and London: University of Chicago Press, 1992).

———. *The Psychology of the Imagination* (London: Routledge, 1972).

———. *Situations I* (Paris: Gallimard, 1947).

———. *Situations III* (Paris: Gallimard, 1949).

———. *Situations IV* (Paris: Gallimard, 1964).

———. *Situations IX* (Paris: Gallimard, 1972).

———. *La transcendance de l'ego: Esquisse d'une description phénoménologique* (Paris: Librairie Philosophique J. Vrin, 1972).

———. *The Transcendence of the Ego: An Existentialist Theory of Con-*

sciousness, trans. Forrest Williams and Robert Kirkpatrick (New York: Hill & Wang, 1957).

———. *The Words,* trans. Bernard Frechtman (New York: Braziller, 1964).

Works by Aquinas

Aquinas, Thomas. *Commentum in quatuor libros Sententiarum Magistri Petri Lombardi,* in *Sancti Thomae Aquinatis Doctoris angelici ordinis predicatorum Opera omnia ad fidem optimarum editionum accurate recognita,* vols. 6–7 (Parma: *typis Petri Fiaccadori,* 1856–1858).

———. *De potentia.* In *Quaestiones disputatae,* vol. 2, ed. P. Pession (Turin/Rome: Marietti, 1953).

———. "De Unitate Intellectus Contra Averroistas." In *Sancti Thomae De Aquino Opera Omnia. Iussu Impensaqu Leonis XIII P. M. Edita,* vol. 43 (Rome: Editori di San Tommaso, 1976).

———. *The Disputed Questions on Truth,* trans. Robert W. Mulligan, James V. McGlynn, and Robert W. Schmidt, 3 vols. (Chicago: Henry Regnery Company, 1952).

———. *On Evil,* trans. Jean Oesterle (South Bend, Ind.: University of Notre Dame Press, 1995).

———. *On Evil,* trans. Richard Regan, ed. Brian Davies (New York: Oxford University Press, 2003).

———. *On Human Nature* (Indianapolis, Ind./Cambridge: Hackett, 1999).

———. *On the Unity of the Intellect against the Averroists,* trans. Beatrice H. Zedler (Milwaukee, Wis.: Marquette University Press, 1968).

———. *Sancti Thomae Aquinatis Doctoris Angelici Opera Omnia.* (Rome: 1882–). ["Leonine" edition].

———. *Selected Philosophical Writings,* trans. Timothy McDermott (Oxford: Oxford University Press, 1993).

———. *Summa Theologiae,* ed. Thomas Gilby, 60 vols. (London: Blackfriars/Eyre & Spottiswoode, 1963ff).

———. *Summa Theologica,* trans. Fathers of the English Dominican Province, 5 vols. (Westminster, Md.: Christian Classics, 1948).

———. *Summa Theologiae: A Concise Translation,* ed. Timothy McDermott (London: Methuen, 1989).

Works about Sartre

Anderson, Thomas C., ed., *American Catholic Philosophical Quarterly* 70, no. 4 (1996). Special issue: Jean-Paul Sartre.

———. "Editor's Introduction." *American Catholic Philosophical Quarterly* 70, no. 4 (1996). Special issue: Jean-Paul Sartre.

———. "Sartre and Human Nature," *American Catholic Philosophical Quarterly* 70, no. 4 (1996). Special issue: Jean-Paul Sartre.

———. *Sartre's Two Ethics: From Authenticity to Integral Humanity* (Chicago: Open Court, 1993).

Aronson, Ronald. *Jean-Paul Sartre: Philosophy in the World* (London: Verso, 1980).

———. "Sartre's Return to Ontology." *Journal of the History of Ideas* 48 (1987).

Aronson, Ronald, and Adrian Van den Hoven. *Sartre Alive* (Detroit, Mich.: Wayne State University Press, 1991).

Atwell, John E. "Sartre and Action Theory." In *Jean Paul Sartre: Contemporary Approaches to His Philosophy,* ed. Hugh J. Silverman and Frederick A. Elliston (Pittsburgh, Pa.: Duquesne University Press, 1980).

Ayer, A. J. "Novelist-Philosophers: V. Jean-Paul Sartre," *Horizon* 12 (1945).

Barnes, Hazel E. *An Existentialist Ethics* (New York: Alfred A. Knopf, 1967).

———. "Sartre's Ontology: The Revealing and Making of Being." In *The Cambridge Companion to Sartre,* ed. Christina Howells (Cambridge: Cambridge University Press, 1992).

Beauvoir, Simone de. "Merleau-Ponty et le Pseudo-Sartrisme." *Les Temps Modernes* 10, nos. 114–15 (1955).

Busch, Thomas W. *The Power of Consciousness and the Force of Circumstances in Sartre's Philosophy* (Bloomington: Indiana University Press, 1990).

———. "Sartre's Use of the Reduction: *Being and Nothingness* Reconsidered." In *Jean-Paul Sartre: Contemporary Approaches to His Philosophy,* ed. Hugh J. Silverman and Frederick A. Elliston (Pittsburgh, Pa.: Duquesne University Press, 1980).

Catalano, Joseph S. *A Commentary on Jean-Paul Sartre's "Being and Nothingness"* (New York: Harper & Row, 1974).

Cavaciuti, Santino. *L'ontologia di Jean-Paul Sartre* (Milan: Marzorati, 1969).

Caws, Peter. *Sartre: The Arguments of the Philosophers* (London, Boston, and Henley, U.K.: Routledge & Kegan Paul, 1979).

Cohen-Solal, Annie. *Sartre: A Life* (London: Heinemann, 1987).

Contat, Michel, and Michel Rybalka, eds. *Les Écrits de Sartre: Chronologie, Bibliographie Commentée* (Paris: Gallimard, 1970).

Crosson, Frederick J. "Intentionality and Atheism: Sartre and Maritain." *The Modern Schoolman* 64 (1987).

Davison, Ray. "Sartre Resartus: The Circuit of 'Ipséité' from London to Clermont Ferrand. 'L'être et le néant' at 50." *Journal of European Studies* 24 (1994).

Detmer, David. *Freedom as a Value: A Critique of the Ethical Theory of Jean-Paul Sartre* (La Salle, Ill.: Open Court, 1988).

Dilman, Ilham. "Sartre and Our Identity as Individuals." In *Human Beings: Royal Institute of Philosophy Supplement: 29,* ed. David Cockburn (Cambridge: Cambridge University Press, 1991).

Dreyfus, Hubert L., and Piotr Hoffman. "Sartre's Changed Conception of Consciousness: From Lucidity to Opacity." In *The Philosophy of Jean Paul Sartre,* ed. Paul A. Schilpp (La Salle, Ill.: Open Court, 1981).

Dupont, Christian. "Receptions of Phenomenology in French Philosophy and Religious Thought, 1889–1939." Ph.D. dissertation, University of Notre Dame, 1997.

Edie, James M. "The Question of the Transcendental Ego: Sartre's Critique of Husserl." *Journal of the British Society for Phenomenology* 24 (1993).

———. "The Roots of the Existentialist Theory of Freedom in 'Ideas I.'" *Husserl Studies* 1 (1984).

Ellis, Fiona. "Sartre on Mind and World." *Sartre Studies International* 6 (2000).

Fell, Joseph P. "Battle of the Giants over Being." In *The Philosophy of Jean Paul Sartre,* ed. Paul A. Schilpp (La Salle, Ill.: Open Court, 1981).

———. *Heidegger and Sartre: An Essay on Being and Place* (New York: Columbia University Press, 1979).

Flynn, Thomas R. "Phenomenology and Faith: From Description to Explanation and Back." *Proceedings of the American Catholic Philosophical Association* 64 (1990).

———. *Sartre and Marxist Existentialism: The Test Case of Collective Responsibility* (Chicago and London: University of Chicago Press, 1984).

Fourny, Jean-François, and Charles D. Minahen. *Situating Sartre in Twentieth-Century Thought and Culture* (Basingstoke, U.K.: Macmillan, 1997).

Fretz, Leo. "Individuality in Sartre's Philosophy." In *The Cambridge Companion to Sartre,* ed. Christina Howells (Cambridge: Cambridge University Press, 1992).

Fry, Christopher M. *Sartre and Hegel: The Variations of an Enigma in L'être et le néant, Neuzeit Und Gegenwart: 4* (Bonn: Bouvier, 1988).

Gardner, Sebastian. "Splitting the Subject: An Overview of Sartre, Lacan and Derrida." *Auslegung* 10 (1983).

Gennaro, Rocco J. "Jean-Paul Sartre and the Hot Theory of Consciousness." *Canadian Journal of Philosophy* 32, no. 3 (2002).

Goldthorpe, Rhiannon. "Sartre and the Self: Discontinuity or Continuity?" *American Catholic Philosophical Quarterly* 70, no. 4 (1996). Special issue: Jean-Paul Sartre.

Gutting, Gary. *French Philosophy in the Twentieth Century* (Cambridge: Cambridge University Press, 2001).

Haar, Michel. "Sartre and Heidegger." In *Jean Paul Sartre: Contemporary Approaches to His Philosophy,* ed. Hugh J. Silverman and Frederick A. Elliston (Pittsburgh, Pa.: Duquesne University Press, 1980).

Hammond, Michael, Jane Howarth, and Russell Keat. *Understanding Phenomenology* (Oxford: Basil Blackwell, 1991).

Hartmann, Klaus. *Sartre's Ontology: A Study of Being and Nothingness in the Light of Hegel's Logic* (Evanston, Ill.: Northwestern University Press, 1966).

Hayman, Ronald. *Writing Against: A Biography of Sartre* (London: Weidenfeld & Nicolson, 1986).

Howells, Christina, ed. *The Cambridge Companion to Sartre* (Cambridge: Cambridge University Press, 1992).

———. "Conclusion: Sartre and the Deconstruction of the Subject." In *The Cambridge Companion to Sartre,* ed. Christina Howells (Cambridge: Cambridge University Press, 1992).

———. *Sartre: The Necessity of Freedom* (Cambridge: Cambridge University Press, 1988).

Jager, Bernd. "Sartre's Anthropology: A Philosophical Reflection on *La Nausee.*" In *The Philosophy of Jean-Paul Sartre,* ed. Paul A. Schilpp, The Library of Living Philosophers Vol. XVI (La Salle, Ill.: Open Court, 1981).

Jeanson, Francis. *Sartre and the Problem of Morality,* trans. Robert V. Stone (Bloomington: Indiana University Press, 1980).

Jopling, David A. "Sartre's Moral Psychology." In *The Cambridge Companion to Sartre,* ed. Christina Howells (Cambridge: Cambridge University Press, 1992).

Keefe, Terry. "Sartre's *L'Existentialisme Est un Humanisme.*" In *Critical Essays on Jean-Paul Sartre,* ed. Robert Wilcocks (Boston: G. K. Hall & Co., 1988).
LaCapra, Dominick. *A Preface to Sartre* (London: Methuen, 1979).
Laing, R. D., and D. G. Cooper. *Reason and Violence: A Decade of Sartre's Philosophy, 1950–1960* (London: Tavistock, 1964).
Langer, Monika. "Sartre and Merleau-Ponty: A Reappraisal." In *The Philosophy of Jean Paul Sartre,* ed. Paul A. Schilpp (La Salle, Ill.: Open Court, 1981).
Leland, Dorothy. "The Sartrean *Cogito:* A Journey between Versions." *Research in Phenomenology* 5 (1975).
Marcel, Gabriel. "Being and Nothingness." In *Homo Viator,* ed. Gabriel Marcel (New York: Harper & Row, 1951).
Marcuse, Herbert. "Existentialism: Remarks on Jean-Paul Sartre's 'L'être et le néant.'" *Philosophy and Phenomenological Research* 8 (1948).
Maritain, Jacques. *Existence and the Existent,* trans. Lewis Galantiere and Gerald B. Phelan (Garden City, N.Y.: Doubleday & Company, 1956).
McBride, William Leon. *Existentialist Ontology and Human Consciousness* (New York and London: Garland, 1997).
McCulloch, Gregory. *Using Sartre: An Analytical Introduction to Early Sartrean Themes* (London: Routledge, 1994).
McLachlan, James. "The Theological Character of Sartre's Atheology in 'Being and Nothingness.'" *Epoche* 5, nos. 1–2 (1997).
Mirvish, Adrian. "Sartre and the Gestaltists." *Journal of the British Society for Phenomenology* 11 (1980).
———. "Sartre on Perception and the World." *Journal of the British Society for Phenomenology* 14 (1983).
Morris, Phyllis Sutton. *Sartre's Concept of a Person: An Analytic Approach* (Amherst: University of Massachusetts Press, 1976).
———. "Self-Creating Selves: Sartre and Foucault." *American Catholic Philosophical Quarterly* 70, no. 4 (1996). Special issue: Jean-Paul Sartre.
Natanson, Maurice. *A Critique of Jean-Paul Sartre's Ontology.* Reprint. ed. (The Hague, The Netherlands: Martinus Nijhoff, 1973).
Olafson, Frederick A. *Principles and Persons: An Ethical Interpretation of Existentialism* (Baltimore, Md.: Johns Hopkins University Press, 1967).
Plantinga, Alvin. "An Existentialist's Ethics." *Review of Metaphysics* 12 (1958).
Qizilbash, M. "Aristotle and Sartre on the Human Condition: Lack, Responsibility and the Desire to Be God." *Angelaki* 3, no. 1 (1998).
Rybalka, Michel, Oreste F. Pucciani, and Susan Gruenheck. "An Interview with Jean-Paul Sartre." In *The Philosophy of Jean-Paul Sartre,* ed. Paul A. Schilpp, The Library of Living Philosophers Vol. XVI (La Salle, Ill.: Open Court, 1981).
Schilpp, Paul Arthur, ed. *The Philosophy of Jean-Paul Sartre,* The Library of Living Philosophers, Vol. XVI (La Salle, Ill.: Open Court, 1981).
Silverman, Hugh J., and Frederick A. Elliston. *Jean-Paul Sartre: Contemporary Approaches to His Philosophy* (Pittsburgh, Pa.: Duquesne University Press, 1980).
Simont, Juliette. "Sartrean Ethics." In *The Cambridge Companion to Sartre,* ed. Christina Howells (Cambridge: Cambridge University Press, 1992).

Spiegelberg, Herbert. *The Context of the Phenomenological Movement* (The Hague, The Netherlands: Martinus Nijhoff, 1981).

———. *The Phenomenological Movement.* 3rd ed. (The Hague, The Netherlands: Martinus Nijhoff, 1982).

Thompson, Kenneth, and Margaret Thompson. *Sartre: Life and Works* (New York; Bicester: Facts on File Publications, 1984).

Verstraeten, Pierre. "'I Am No Longer a Realist': An Interview with Jean-Paul Sartre." In *Sartre Alive,* ed. Ronald Aronson and Adrian Van den Hoven (Detroit, Mich.: Wayne State University Press, 1991).

Warnock, Mary. "Imagination in Sartre." *British Journal of Aesthetics* 10 (1970).

Wider, Kathleen. *The Bodily Nature of Consciousness: Sartre and Contemporary Philosophy of Mind* (Ithaca, N.Y., and London: Cornell University Press, 1997).

———. "The Failure of Self-Consciousness in Sartre's *Being and Nothingness.*" *Dialogue: Canadian Philosophical Review* 32 (1993).

———. "A Nothing about Which Something Can Be Said: Sartre and Wittgenstein on the Self." In *Sartre Alive,* ed. Ronald Aronson and Adrian Van den Hoven (Detroit, Mich.: Wayne State University Press, 1991).

Wilcocks, Robert, ed. *Critical Essays on Jean-Paul Sartre* (Boston: G. K. Hall, 1988).

———. *Jean-Paul Sartre: A Bibliography of International Criticism* (Edmonton: University of Alberta Press, 1975).

Wood, Philip R. "A Revisionary Account of the Apotheosis and Demise of the Philosophy of the Subject: Hegel, Sartre, Heidegger, Structuralism, and Poststructuralism." In *Situating Sartre in Twentieth-Century Thought and Culture,* ed. Jean-François Fourny and Charles D. Minahen (Basingstoke, U.K., and London: Macmillan Press, 1997).

Works about Aquinas

Aertsen, Jan A. "Aquinas's Philosophy in Its Historical Setting." In *The Cambridge Companion to Aquinas,* ed. Norman Kretzmann and Eleonore Stump (Cambridge: Cambridge University Press, 1993).

Ashley, Benedict M. "What Is the End of the Human Person? The Vision of God and Integral Human Fulfillment." In *Moral Truth and Moral Tradition: Essays in Honour of Peter Geach and Elizabeth Anscombe,* ed. Luke Gormally (Blackrock, Co. Dublin: Four Courts Press, 1994).

Basti, Gianfranco. *Filosofia dell'uomo* (Bologna: Edizioni Studio Domenicano, 1995).

Bowlin, John. *Contingency and Fortune in Aquinas's Ethics* (Cambridge: Cambridge University Press, 1999).

Boyle, Leonard E. "The Setting of the *Summa Theologiae* of St. Thomas—Revisited." In *The Ethics of Aquinas,* ed. Stephen J. Pope (Washington, D.C.: Georgetown University Press, 2002).

Bradley, Denis J. M. *Aquinas on the Twofold Human Good: Reason and Human Happiness in Aquinas's Moral Science* (Washington, D.C.: The Catholic University of America Press, 1997).

Brock, Stephen. *Action and Conduct: Thomas Aquinas and the Theory of Action* (Edinburgh: T & T Clark, 1998).

Burrell, David B. *Aquinas: God and Action* (South Bend, Ind.: University of Notre Dame Press, 1979).

Caputo, John D. *Heidegger and Aquinas: An Essay in Overcoming Metaphysics* (New York: Fordham University Press, 1982).

Celano, Anthony J. "The Concept of Worldly Beatitude in the Writings of Thomas Aquinas." *Journal of the History of Philosophy* 25 (1987).

Cessario, Romanus. *Moral Virtues and Theological Ethics* (South Bend, Ind.: University of Notre Dame Press, 1991).

Chenu, Marie-Dominique. *Toward Understanding Saint Thomas* (Chicago: Regnery Press, 1964).

Deferrari, Roy J., and Sister M. Inviolata Barry. *A Lexicon of St. Thomas Aquinas* (Washington, D.C.: The Catholic University of America Press, 1948).

Donagan, Alan. "Thomas Aquinas on Human Action." In *The Cambridge History of Later Medieval Philosophy,* ed. Norman Kretzmann, Anthony Kenny and Jan Pinborg (Cambridge: Cambridge University Press, 1982).

Eardley, P. S. "Thomas Aquinas and Giles of Rome on the Will." *Review of Metaphysics* 56 (2003).

Eschmann, Ignatius Theodore. *The Ethics of Saint Thomas Aquinas: Two Courses* (Toronto: Pontifical Institute of Mediaeval Studies, 1997).

Finnis, John. *Aquinas: Moral, Political, and Legal Theory* (Oxford: Oxford University Press, 1998).

———. "Object and Intention in Moral Judgements According to Aquinas." *The Thomist* 55 (1991).

Flannery, Kevin L. *Acts Amid Precepts* (Edinburgh: T & T Clark, 2001).

Gallagher, David M. "Aquinas on Goodness and Moral Goodness." In *Thomas Aquinas and His Legacy,* ed. David M. Gallagher, Studies in Philosophy and the History of Philosophy (Washington, D.C.: The Catholic University of America Press, 1994).

———. "Desire for Beatitude and Love for Friendship in Thomas Aquinas." *Mediaeval Studies* 58 (1996).

———. "Free Choice and Free Judgement in Thomas Aquinas." *Archiv für Geschichte der Philosophie* 76 (1994).

———. "Thomas Aquinas on Will as Rational Appetite." *Journal of the History of Philosophy* 29 (1991).

———. "The Will and Its Acts (Ia Iiae, Qq. 6–17)." In *The Ethics of Aquinas,* ed. Stephen J. Pope (Washington, D.C.: Georgetown University Press, 2002).

Gilson, Etienne. *The Spirit of Mediaeval Philosophy,* trans. A. H. C. Downes (London: Sheed & Ward, 1936).

Haldane, John. "Mind-World Identity Theory and the Anti-Realist Challenge." In *Reality, Representation, and Projection,* ed. John Haldane and Crispin Wright (Oxford: Oxford University Press, 1993).

Hayden, R. Mary. "Natural Inclinations and Moral Absolutes: A Mediated Correspondance for Aquinas." *Proceedings of the American Catholic Philosophical Association* 64 (1990).

Hause, Jeffrey. "Thomas Aquinas and the Voluntarists." *Medieval Philosophy and Theology* 6 (1997).

Hittinger, F. Russell. "When Is It More Excellent to Love Than to Know?" *Proceedings of the American Catholic Philosophical Association* 57 (1983).

Irwin, T. H. "The Scope of Deliberation: A Conflict in Aquinas." *Review of Metaphysics* 44 (1990).

Kenny, Anthony. "Aquinas on Aristotelian Happiness." In *Aquinas's Moral Theory: Essays in Honour of Norman Kretzmann,* ed. Scott MacDonald and Eleonore Stump (Ithaca, N.Y., and London: Cornell University Press, 1998).

Kerr, Fergus. *After Aquinas: Versions of Thomism* (Oxford: Blackwell, 2002).

Knasas, John F. X. "The Postmodern Notion of Freedom and Aquinas's *Ratio Entis.*" In *The Failure of Modernism,* ed. Brendan Sweetman (Mishawaka, Ind.: American Maritain Association, 1999).

Korolec, J. B. "Free Will and Free Choice." In *The Cambridge History of Later Medieval Philosophy,* ed. Norman Kretzmann, Anthony Kenny, and Jan Pinborg (Cambridge: Cambridge University Press, 1982).

Kretzmann, Norman. "Philosophy of Mind." In *The Cambridge Companion to Aquinas,* ed. Norman Kretzmann and Eleonore Stump (Cambridge: Cambridge University Press, 1993).

Kretzmann, Norman, and Eleonore Stump, eds. *The Cambridge Companion to Aquinas* (Cambridge: Cambridge University Press, 1993).

Lisska, Anthony J. *Aquinas's Theory of Natural Law: An Analytic Reconstruction* (Oxford: Clarendon Press, 1996).

Loughran, Thomas J. "Aquinas, Compatibilist." In *Human and Divine Agency: Anglican, Catholic, and Lutheran Perspectives,* ed. Michael F. McLain and Mark W. Richardson (Lanham, Md.: University Press of America, 1999).

MacDonald, Scott. "Aquinas's Libertarian Account of Free Choice." *Revue Internationale de Philosophie* 2 (1998).

———. "Practical Reasoning and Reasons-Explanations: Aquinas's Account of Reason's Role in Action." In *Aquinas's Moral Theory: Essays in Honour of Norman Kretzmann,* ed. Scott MacDonald and Eleonore Stump (Ithaca, N.Y., and London: Cornell University Press, 1998).

Mahoney, Edward P. "Aquinas's Critique of Averroes' Doctrine of the Unity of the Intellect." In *Thomas Aquinas and His Legacy,* ed. David M. Gallagher, Studies in Philosophy and the History of Philosophy (Washington, D.C.: The Catholic University of America Press, 1994).

Maritain, Jacques. "The Thomist Idea of Freedom." In *Scholasticism and Politics* (London: Geoffrey Bles/The Centenary Press, 1945).

McCabe, Herbert. "The Immortality of the Soul." In *Aquinas: A Collection of Critical Essays,* ed. Anthony Kenny (London and South Bend, Ind.: University of Notre Dame Press, 1976).

McCool, Gerald A. "Is Thomas' Way of Philosophizing Still Viable Today?" *Proceedings of the American Catholic Philosophical Association* 64 (1990).

O'Conner, William R. "The Natural Desire for Happiness." *The Modern Schoolman* 26 (1949).

O'Meara, Thomas F. *Thomas Aquinas Theologian* (South Bend, Ind., and London: University of Notre Dame Press, 1997).

Pasnau, Robert. *Thomas Aquinas on Human Nature* (Cambridge: Cambridge University Press, 2002).

Pinckaers, Servais. *The Sources of Christian Ethics,* trans. Sr. Mary Thomas Noble (Edinburgh: T & T Clark, 1995).

Pinckaers, Servais-Théodore. "The Sources of the Ethics of St. Thomas Aquinas." In *The Ethics of Aquinas,* ed. Stephen J. Pope (Washington, D.C.: Georgetown University Press, 2002).

Pope, Stephen J., ed. *The Ethics of Aquinas* (Washington, D.C.: Georgetown University Press, 2002).

———. "Overview of the Ethics of Thomas Aquinas." In *The Ethics of Aquinas,* ed. Stephen J. Pope (Washington, D.C.: Georgetown University Press, 2002).

Porter, Jean. *The Recovery of Virtue* (London: SPCK, 1990).

Reichberg, Gregory Martin. "Aquinas on Moral Responsibility in the Pursuit of Knowledge." In *Thomas Aquinas and His Legacy,* ed. David M. Gallagher, Studies in Philosophy and the History of Philosophy (Washington, D.C.: The Catholic University of America Press, 1994).

Rhonheimer, Martin. *Natural Law and Practical Reason: A Thomist View of Moral Autonomy* (New York: Fordham University Press, 2000).

Romano, Joseph J. "Between Being and Nothingness: The Relevancy of Thomistic Habit." *The Thomist* 44 (1980).

Schroeder, William Ralph. *Sartre and His Predecessors: The Self and the Other* (London: Routledge & Kegan Paul, 1984).

Stump, Eleonore. *Aquinas* (Abingdon, U.K.: Routledge, 2003).

Stump, Eleonore, and Norman Kretzmann. "Absolute Simplicity." *Faith and Philosophy* 2, no. 4 (1985).

Sullivan, Robert P. "Natural Necessitation of the Human Will." *The Thomist* 14 (1951).

Torrell, Jean-Pierre, *Saint Thomas Aquinas, Vol. 1: The Person and His Work* (Washington, D.C.: The Catholic University of America Press, 1996).

Tugwell, Simon. "Thomas Aquinas: Introduction." In *Albert and Thomas: Selected Writings,* ed. Simon Tugwell (Mahwah, N.J.: Paulist Press, 1988).

Weisheipl, James A. *Friar Thomas D'aquino: His Life, Thought, and Works* (Washington, D.C.: The Catholic University of America Press, 1983).

Westberg, Daniel. "Did Aquinas Change His Mind about the Will?" *The Thomist* 58 (1994).

———. *Right Practical Reason: Aristotle, Action, and Prudence in Aquinas* (Oxford: Clarendon Press, 1994).

Wieland, Georg. "Happiness (Ia Iiae, Qq. 1–5)." In *The Ethics of Aquinas,* ed. Stephen J. Pope (Washington, D.C.: Georgetown University Press, 2002).

———. "Happiness: The Perfection of Man." In *The Cambridge History of Later Medieval Philosophy,* ed. Norman Kretzmann, Anthony Kenny, and Jan Pinborg (Cambridge: Cambridge University Press, 1982).

Other Works

Ackrill, J. L., ed. *A New Aristotle Reader* (Oxford: Clarendon Press, 1987).

Anscombe, G. E. M. *Intention.* 2nd ed. (Cambridge, Mass.: Harvard University Press, 2000).

Aristotle. *De Motu Animalium,* trans. Martha Craven Nussbaum (Princeton, N.J.: Princeton University Press, 1978).

———. *The Metaphysics: Books I–IX,* ed. G. P. Goold, trans. Hugh Tredennick, The Loeb Classical Library (Cambridge, Mass.: Harvard University Press, 1933).

———. *Nicomachean Ethics,* trans. Terence Irwin (Indianapolis, Ind.: Hackett, 1985).

Balthasar, Hans Urs von. "On the Tasks of Catholic Philosophy in Our Time." *Communio* 20 (1993).

Bauman, Zygmunt. *Intimations of Postmodernity* (London: Routledge, 1992).

Bell, David. *Husserl* (London and New York: Routledge, 1990).

Bourke, Vernon J., *Will in Western Thought: An Historico-Critical Study* (New York: Sheed & Ward, 1964).

Boyle, Joseph M., Germain Grisez, and Olaf Tollefsen. *Free Choice: A Self-Referential Argument* (South Bend, Ind., and London: University of Notre Dame Press, 1976).

Caputo, John D. "The End of Ethics." In *The Blackwell Guide to Ethical Theory,* ed. Hugh LaFollette (Malden, Mass., and Oxford: Blackwell, 2000).

Crisp, Roger, and Michael Slote, eds. *Virtue Ethics* (Oxford: Oxford University Press, 1997).

De Lubac, Henri. *Surnaturel: Études Historiques* (Paris: Aubier, 1946).

Donagan, Alan. *Choice: The Essential Element in Human Action* (London: Routledge & Kegan Paul, 1987).

Finnis, John. *Fundamentals of Ethics* (Oxford: Clarendon Press, 1983).

———. *Natural Law and Natural Rights* (Oxford: Clarendon Press, 1980).

Gaita, Raimond. *A Common Humanity: Thinking about Love and Truth and Justice.* 2nd ed. (London and New York: Routledge, 2002).

Harris, André, and Marcel Ophüls. *Le Chagrin et la Pitié* [Documentary film], directed by Marcel Ophüls (1969).

Harvey, David. *The Condition of Postmodernity* (Oxford: Basil Blackwell, 1989).

Heidegger, Martin. *Basic Writings* (San Francisco: HarperSanFrancisco, 1993).

———. *Being and Time,* trans. John Macquarrie and Edward Robinson (Oxford: Blackwell, 1962).

Husserl, Edmund. *Cartesian Meditations: An Introduction to Phenomenology,* trans. Dorion Cairns (The Hague, The Netherlands: Martinus Nijhoff, 1960).

———. *Ideas Pertaining to a Pure Phenomenology and to a Phenomenological Philosophy. Book 1: General Introduction to a Pure Phenomenology,* trans. F. Kersten (The Hague, The Netherlands: Martinus Nijhoff, 1982).

Kahn, Charles H. "Discovering the Will: From Aristotle to Augustine." In *The Question of "Eclecticism": Studies in Later Greek Philosophy,* ed. John M. Dillon and A. A. Long (Berkeley and Los Angeles: University of California Press, 1988).

Kerr, Fergus. *Immortal Longings* (London: SPCK, 1997).

Köhler, Wolfgang. *Gestalt Psychology: An Introduction to New Concepts in Modern Psychology* (New York: Liveright, 1947).

Kotva, Joseph J. *The Case for Christian Virtue Ethics* (Washington, D.C.: Georgetown University Press, 1996).

Lacan, Jacques. *Écrits: A Selection,* trans. Alan Sheridan (London: Tavistock, 1977).

Lear, Jonathan. *Happiness, Death, and the Remainder of Life* (Cambridge, Mass., and London: Harvard University Press, 2000).

Levinas, Emmanuel. "Martin Buber and the Theory of Knowledge." In *The Levinas Reader,* ed. Seán Hand (Oxford and Cambridge, Mass.: Blackwell, 1989).

Lottin, Odon. "Libre arbitre et liberté depuis saint Anselme jusqu'à la fin du XIIIe siècle." In *Psychologie et morale aux XIIe et XIIIe siècles,* Vol. 1, 2nd ed. (Gembloux, France: J. Duculot, 1957).

MacDonald, Paul S., ed. *The Existentialist Reader: An Anthology of Key Texts* (Edinburgh: Edinburgh University Press, 2000).

MacIntyre, Alasdair. *After Virtue.* 2nd ed. (London: Duckworth, 1985).

McCabe, Herbert. *Law, Love and Language* (London and Sydney, Australia: Sheed & Ward, 1968).

McDowell, J. "Virtue and Reason." *The Monist* 62 (1976).

McInerney, Ralph. *The Very Rich Hours of Jacques Maritain: A Spiritual Life* (South Bend, Ind.: University of Notre Dame Press, 2003).

Merleau-Ponty, M. *Phenomenology of Perception,* trans. Colin Smith (London: Routledge & Kegan Paul, 1962).

Midgley, Mary. *Beast and Man: The Roots of Human Nature* (London: Methuen, 1979).

———. "The Objection to Systematic Humbug." *Philosophy* 53 (1978).

Mihalich, Joseph C. *Existentialism and Thomism* (New York: Philosophical Library, 1960).

Murdoch, Iris. *The Sovereignty of Good* (London: Routledge, 2001).

Norris, Christopher. *The Truth about Postmodernism* (Oxford and Cambridge, Mass.: Blackwell, 1993).

Popper, Karl R. "Epistemology without a Knowing Subject." In *Objective Knowledge, an Evolutionary Approach* (Oxford: Clarendon Press, 1979).

Simon, Yves R. *Freedom of Choice* (New York: Fordham University Press, 1969).

Sokolowski, Robert. *The Formation of Husserl's Concept of Constitution* (The Hague, The Netherlands: Martinus Nijhoff, 1964).

Stoker, Michael. "The Schizophrenia of Modern Ethical Theories." In *Virtue Ethics,* ed. Roger Crisp and Michael Slote (Oxford: Oxford University Press, 1997).

Taylor, Charles. *The Ethics of Authenticity* (Cambridge, Mass.: Harvard University Press, 1991).

———. "Explanation and Practical Reason." In *Philosophical Arguments* (Cambridge, Mass., and London: Harvard University Press, 1995).

———. *Sources of the Self: The Making of the Modern Identity* (Cambridge: Cambridge University Press, 1989).

Wippel, John F. "The Condemnations of 1270 and 1277 at Paris." *Journal of Medieval and Renaissance Studies* 7 (1977).

Wittgenstein, Ludwig. *Notebooks, 1914–1916,* trans. G. E. M. Anscombe, 2nd ed. (Oxford: Basil Blackwell, 1979).

Wolf, Susan, "Moral Saints." In *Virtue Ethics,* ed. Roger Crisp and Michael Slote (Oxford: Oxford University Press, 1997).

INDEX

Aquinas & Sartre on Freedom, Personal Identity, and the Possibility of Happiness was designed and typeset in Minion by Kachergis Book Design of Pittsboro, North Carolina. It was printed on 60-pound House Natural Smooth and bound by Sheridan Books of Ann Arbor, Michigan.